EMPRESS MARIA THERESA

EMPRESS
MARIA THERESA

THE EARLIER YEARS,

1717-1757

by

Robert Pick

HARPER & ROW, PUBLISHERS
NEW YORK

To my wife,
PRISCILLA

Contents

Illustrations

MAP

Author's Note

I have put into my narrative whatever I considered essential for delineating the job that "the most human of the Hapsburgs" (G. P. Gooch) was called upon to perform. In general, I touch on its various aspects as they enter her own purview.

For all that, it may not be supererogatory to point out one particular part of the Habsburg affairs notorious for bedeviling the general reader.

The landed possessions of the House of Habsburg ("The Monarchy" in the parlance of its court, or, in wider but also looser usage, "Austria") were at no time identical with the Holy Roman Empire of the German Nation (the *Reich*). Some of the Habsburg dominions lay outside the Empire. The larger part of *its* territory was not Habsburg land. Still, from 1438 on, the *Reich's* Electors regularly had chosen the Habsburg ruler as its anointed head.

The actual power of his imperial office had always been at variance, to a larger or smaller degree, with the glamour of the emperor's dignity, or the mystique of the ancient crown. The religious wars, intertwined with the Habsburgs' dynastic aspirations, served to whittle down that power still more. The treaty that ended the Thirty Years War in 1648 handed the Empire's individual sovereigns and its Free Cities—some three hundred of them in all—full control over their subjects, and, for all practical purposes, also the right to enter foreign alliances; their own obligations toward the elected emperor were not spelled out in that treaty, which carried, besides Sweden's, the formidable guarantee of France.

Nevertheless, certain rights remained to the Holy Roman Emperor; and some of these have been dealt with, in brief, in the following pages. So has, by implication, the fact that the position of the Habsburg monarch in his own dominions was not decisively influenced by the decay of imperial power.

In an attempt to keep the singular situation of the Habsburg ruler before the reader's eyes, I have spelled "emperor" lower case, and capitalized "Empire."

EMPRESS MARIA THERESA

I

In the Aftermath of a World War

H OW TIMES HAVE CHANGED!" Maria Theresa's most devoted confidant wrote to a friend on her twenty-fourth birthday. "To think that we on our glorious campaign . . . paid not the slightest attention to her birth."[1]*

The imperial army driving the Turks before it in May, 1717, had in fact little reason to give thought to the happy event in Vienna's Hofburg. True, the baby's father held, as his ancestors had for three hundred years, the elective office of the Holy Roman Empire's head; but the Empire's ancient charter barred women from its purple. True again, Charles VI was the head of the house of Habsburg; but no woman had ever ruled its dominions; and female succession to these, while occupying the lawyers of the court, was a notion still as strange to army men as it was to the generality of the Habsburg subjects.

Yet the Viennese—in a manner of speaking, the sovereign's next-door neighbors—were not insensitive to the nativity of the archduchess, or for that matter, to the elaborate celebrations that followed her christening. Lacing their vicarious pleasure, there was some talk about the ill-omened date of the birth, the thirteenth of the month. And some people also pitied the emperor. Charles VI was the only male Habsburg alive. A son, the first issue of a nine-year marriage, had recently died as an infant.

He himself did not appear to be disheartened. Thirty-three years of age, he had mastered the art of *disimular* that his great forebear Charles V used to impress on his son as a royal virtue. Charles VI's daughter was never to master it.

* Superior numbers refer to Notes and References, page 305.

Charles had been a lad of sixteen when the scramble over the Spanish succession erupted in war. Two different partition treaties had been
outrun while Spain's childless monarch, the last of her Habsburg rulers,
was still alive. Succumbing to papal intrigues, the feeble-minded ruler
had on his deathbed willed all of his far-flung possessions to Philip of
Anjou, a grandson of Louis XIV. The resulting danger of Bourbon
supremacy on the Continent was as a nightmare to the English even
before the French king provoked them by recognizing the Stuart Pretender as their rightful master. Louis XIV, alert to the imminence of
armed conflict, proceeded to seize a number of Dutch places. His assurance that his grandson—who meanwhile had been welcomed by the
Spanish assembly—would never become King of France now sounded
hollow indeed.

Charles's father, Emperor Leopold, had been desperate from the
moment of the death of his Spanish cousin. He had not originally aimed
at the whole of the gigantic inheritance. But Bourbon rule in Naples,
Sicily, and above all, Milan—an imperial fief dangerously close to his
dominions—could not leave him indifferent. His renowned captain, Prince
Eugene of Savoy, broke into Milanese territory.

Marlborough, who had been ordered to open parleys with the representatives of the French king and his grandson, was confident that "the
French will be reasonable."[2] When Louis XIV, however, prompted Philip
to grant the French crown the right of importing African slaves into the
American appendages of his realm, William III was stung into action.
England and the Dutch republic revived the coalition of an earlier war
with the Habsburg court and the Empire. Partition of the Spanish
heritage was, at least tacitly, the aim of that Grand Alliance. A year and
a half after the common declaration of war Leopold arrived at a different
interpretation. Encouraged by Portugal, England's new ally, he proclaimed his younger son, Charles, King of Spain.

His own court was on the brink of bankruptcy. Its troops were insufficient in number and their training was notoriously inadequate. A
French army from the south was overrunning the Tyrol, whose northern
part was in the hands of the Bavarian Elector, who considered himself
tricked out of his Spanish claims, and indeed was set to invade Upper
Austria in a movement concerted with France. Hungarian rebels were
raiding Lower Austria, Styria, and even Moravia.* It was not, then, a

---

* For Hungary, see p. 80.

The "Hereditary Lands" consisted of Low Austria (Lower and Upper Austria),
Interior Austria (Styria, Carinthia, Carniola) and Anterior Austria (the Tyrol and
the possessions in southern Germany). By this time the Bohemian dominions
(Bohemia, Moravia and Silesia) were likewise referred to as part of the Hereditary
Lands.

high-spirited court from which Charles departed to take possession of his Iberian kingdom. "If the people who run this court are not traitors," Eugene, back in Vienna, had written some months previously to his second-in-command, "they assuredly are the biggest asses I have ever seen in my life." The emperor "promises everything, issues peremptory orders . . . but nothing happens."[3]

Stopping over in England, the Archduke (as he was called, realistically, in the court of Queen Anne) was received by Marlborough and escorted to Windsor. "He had a gravity beyond his age, tempered with modesty. His behavior was in all points so exact that there was not a circumstance in his whole deportment that was liable to censure. . . . He had the art of seeming well pleased with every thing without so much as smiling once. He spoke but little, and all he said was judicious and obliging."[4]

Early in 1704 Charles sailed from Portsmouth to Portugal with a sizable squadron. He set foot in his kingdom at Barcelona, after great hardships, to take command of the army financed by the Maritime Powers.

While, from Blenheim on, Marlborough and Eugene outwitted and trounced the French marshals nearly everywhere they joined battle with them—in Italy and on the banks of the Rhine, in Flanders and in the Danube valley—the war in Spain remained inconclusive. Twice Charles entered Madrid, only to be thrown back. His determination "rather to be buried under Barcelona's ruins than to yield"[5] filled his Catalan followers with admiration. As the war dragged on they came to appreciate Charles's "wonderful spirit which formed a striking contrast to his natural phlegm."[6] At the same time, his ceremoniousness exasperated the Englishmen in his shadowy court. Once the queen's envoy made bold to tell him that William of Orange had "entered London in a coach with a cloak bag behind it, and was made king not many weeks after."[7] England's "special institutions,"[8] as they would his daughter, ofttimes baffled Charles.

His father had died in 1705, embroiled in large-scale operations against the rebellious Hungarians. It was left to Charles's brother Joseph I to fight to a standstill the insurgents, whose dreaded hordes at one time had threatened Vienna itself. No sooner had Joseph, exercising some wisdom as well as a great deal of vigor, made peace with the defeated insurgents in January, 1711, than the smallpox killed him.

Conflicts over strategy and manpower had weakened the court's bond with its allies. Yet the ministers in Vienna—or Charles in Spain, for that matter—failed to gauge the effect of Joseph's death on the coalition. As he was survived by two daughters only, Charles fell heir to all Habsburg lands; and the danger of *their* union with the Spanish crown strengthened the hands of the new cabinet in London, who wished to take the nation out of the costly war. In fact, they had opened clandestine negotiations with the French even before Joseph's demise.

With French men-of-war blockading Barcelona, Charles did not at once have to make up his mind whether to depart from the foothold he held in Spain—whose actual master, Philip V, was safely ensconced in Madrid—and heed the pleas of the ministers in Vienna and his mother to take up his duties in the Hofburg. Meantime Eugene canvassed the electors to secure the imperial crown.* When a British convoy enabled Charles to start out on his voyage, he made his young wife regent and captain general of the army, leaving her behind in Barcelona.

Queen Anne's new first minister signed preliminaries with France even as Charles was on his journey from Genoa to Frankfurt to stand in the imperial election. At the same time, however, Charles's ambassador in London was assured of the queen's continued support of his master's aspirations on the peninsula. His Spanish titles were written into the coronation instrument in Frankfurt.

Before proceeding to Vienna, Charles, ignorant of the depth of Marlborough's fall, dispatched Eugene to London to enlist the help of the old comrade-in-arms. The deaths of the French heir apparent and his son, which left but a sickly child—the future Louis XV—between the crown of France and Philip V, should have revived the British fears of Bourbon supremacy. But Louis XIV, old, ailing, and yearning for peace, allayed these misgivings by extracting from Philip a solemn renunciation, on his own and his heirs' part, of the French succession. The monopoly of the American slave trade, which was granted the British, did the rest. Eugene's visit, if marked by public ovations, was to end in humiliating failure. Its record did not endear him to his young master.

On a raw January day of 1712 Charles VI disembarked, some miles west of Vienna, from the craft that had carried him down the Danube. He was markedly different from his predecessor, a high-spirited prince most winsome in appearance. Charles was of medium height and somewhat broad of hip. There was nothing martial in his bearing. His pointed chin and drooping lip, the Habsburg lip of common parlance, all but disfigured the swarthy face. Measured in movement and slow in address, he seemed distant, punctilious, haughty. So forbidding, in fact, was his demeanor in this first hour that the kindly, if guarded, expression of his eyes startled men who waited on him in the following days.

Scores of his Spanish and Catalan followers had come with him to Vienna. Neither its privileged classes nor its lower orders were strangers

---

* At that time the electoral college consisted of the archbishops of Mainz, Treves, and Cologne, the King of Bohemia, the King in Prussia, the Duke of Bavaria, the Count Palatine, and the sovereigns of Saxony and of Hanover.

to their kind. Still, they formed an instantaneous dislike to the new arrivals. Leeches on the emperor's purse, they also turned out to have his ear. His declared favorite was John Althan, a most handsome Moravian count who had been with him in Barcelona; and people did not tire of commenting on the pleasure that Charles took in the company of that nobleman and his beautiful wife, a lady of Spanish-Italian descent. She was spoken of as the emperor's mistress. This couple, passionately supporting his pursuit of the Spanish will-o'-the-wisp, set about undermining the influence of Eugene, who more than doubted his master's chance of wresting the Spanish crown from Philip. But he shared Charles's determination to strike a decisive blow at the French, who for two centuries had been the arch enemies of the Habsburgs.

Not until Marlborough's successor in the field deserted Eugene on the very eve of battle did Charles's hopes for crushing the French begin fading. England's betrayal was to leave a deep imprint on the court of Vienna. These feelings were still to echo in much of what the princess, born five years after that black day, was to say and to do. In those years, still distant, *her* arch enemy sometimes would speak, with a smirk, of the "Austrian miracles" that seemed to turn the tide in her favor. No miracle came the way of Charles VI once Great Britain had made peace with Louis XIV and Philip V in the spring of 1713 at Utrecht.

Still, Charles VI was far from having lost out altogether by the time of Theresa's birth. Out of the Spanish heritage he had garnered rich bounty—the duchy of Milan, the kingdom of Naples, the Sardinian island kingdom, and the southern Netherlands, that gem of the Spanish crown.* He had made peace with France without recognizing the Bourbon ruler in Madrid, who irritated him no end by arrogating the grandmastership of the Order of the Golden Fleece, an ancient Habsburg prerogative. In August, 1717, a Spanish squadron seized Sardinia.

In the same month—a hundred days after Theresa's birth—Eugene captured the fortress of Belgrade, capping the triumph of his Turkish campaigns. A mere generation before, the Turks had besieged Vienna, bombarded the town, all but escaladed the ramparts of the Hofburg, and nearly starved the garrison into surrender. Now the emperor basked in Eugene's reflected glory. The Viennese, who had been totally indifferent to Charles's tribulations in Spain, grew proud of the emperor. They had begun to like him, since, contrary to royal custom, he stayed in the town despite the outbreak of an epidemic in the summer of 1713.

Later in 1713 his empress joined him. Although his arms had been

---

* For convenience's sake, the southern Netherlands will be referred to as "Belgium" in this study (though the boundary somewhat differed from today's kingdom's) and the duchy of Milan as "Lombardy."

successful during her solitary stay in Barcelona, those belated victories had proved to be sterile by the time of her return to Vienna. Another large group of self-exiled Spaniards had come with her and reinforced what had become known in Vienna as the emperor's camarilla. The empress herself "takes a hand in affairs of state" while giving "the impression that she did not intend to do so."[9]

On her journey from her native Brunswick to Spain in 1708 she had come to Vienna to be married by proxy in front of a miracle-working picture of the Virgin. "The universal *applauso* this incomparable princess has attracted here through her beauty and kindly demeanor is altogether beyond description,"[10] wrote the then empress, Joseph I's spouse, to a friend. In Brescia and Milan people waxed lyrical, trying to do justice to her perfection. The admiration aroused by Elizabeth Christina had been a triumph for Charles's matchmaking mother.

Born into the ducal house of Brunswick-Wolfenbüttel, the princess had been raised in the Reformed Church. She was fifteen years old when the marriage was arranged. Unlike the run of German nobility, she refused steadfastly to forswear her faith for the sake of elevating her station. Only amid sighs and tears did she bring herself to listen to the Jesuit dispatched from Vienna for her instruction in the catechism. It needed the persuasion of the illustrious Leibniz to break her resistance, though he too could not dry her tears. From Bamberg, where the bishop received her in the Habsburgs' faith, she wrote to her grandfather: "I have been comforted by the assurance that I will be allowed to receive communion in both kinds."[11] This privilege, which sometimes had been granted to royal converts in earlier times, apparently was withdrawn from Elizabeth in Barcelona. Yet tales about heretical practices on her part persisted. As late as 1747 a foreign envoy in Vienna related a rumor of her "secretly reading Protestants books."[12]

Perhaps gossip of this sort preceded her to Vienna in 1713. It would seem that something had gone out of the high-spirited princess with her conversion. She still was a strikingly beautiful woman, endowed with a fine physique, rich ash-blond hair, and violet-colored, if small, eyes. Although an insect bite suffered in Barcelona had left a scar on her face, whoever saw her could not but appreciate the nickname "White Liz" that Charles had coined on meeting his bride, of such fine texture and delicate tints was her complexion. Lady Mary Wortley Montagu, who saw her in 1716—shortly after her baby son's death—was "perfectly charmed with [her]. . . . When she smiles, 'tis with a beauty and sweetness that forces adoration."[13]

However, there was an aura of coldness about her. Her lagging fertility had caused experienced courtiers to wonder about the passion she might kindle in Charles. However weighty his motives for leaving the empress behind in Barcelona, the decision had raised eyebrows. To put it bluntly, the sole prince of the "Arch House" had no business removing himself from the bedchamber of his childless consort.

Nor, speaking with the bluntness of farsighted men in the spring of 1717, had Elizabeth's baby any business being a girl. To be sure, even the emperor's father had opened the succession to females; and Charles himself, in 1713—after five years of waiting in vain for offspring —had promulgated a "House Law" which not only confirmed the indivisibility of the Habsburg possessions but also appeared to secure their future as a whole. In default of male heirs, they must pass, by primogeniture, on to Charles's female issue, and in default of any descendancy of his own, to his late brother's daughters and their children. This act of succession still lacked the ratifications by the individual estates of the lands. It also was inconsistent with Leopold's settlement, which, in default of male progeny, had given precedence to Joseph's daughters over any daughters of Charles; and Charles, on the eve of his departure for Spain, had sworn to abide by his father's "House Law."

That painful personal matter did not trouble the estates. Within three years after Theresa's birth all of them had ratified the instrument, which was henceforth referred to by the archaic term of Pragmatic Sanction. Europe was to hear a great deal about it in the following thirty years.

Only the Hungarian estates were recalcitrant. They contended that an extinction of the Habsburgs' male line would revive their ancient right of electing a king. Even though they proposed to declare Theresa heir apparent, her father did not for nearly five years accept the offer. When he did accept it four years had passed since his wife had been brought to bed with another child—another girl.

Elizabeth was pregnant again a few months after Charles's compromise with the Hungarians; and he was praying with fervor for a son, whose existence, along with other blessings, would set things aright again in the matter of the troublesome Hungarian kingdom's succession.

Nothing indicates more clearly the strength of his hopes, even after a third daughter was born to him, than the paucity of information on Theresa's early childhood. No doubt Charles VI persuaded himself that she was destined to yield the heir's place to a brother sooner or later and go down in the family chronicle as but another of the countless archduchesses who over the centuries had been married to foreign princes, or cousins, with varying profit for the Arch House and its unflagging zest for aggrandizement.

There exists a portrait of the six-year-old. It shows her wearing, as was the fashion, a miniature copy of a lady's gown with low neckline and train. Holding in one hand a nosegay, and its ribbon in the other, she is caught in an artificial posture. About her chubby face there is nothing artificial—or for that matter, any of the timidity of Habsburg children, as the Spanish masters have portrayed them. Theresa's unsmiling mien expresses premature determination. Only the very large light-blue eyes, beneath the high forehead, make the child's face engaging.

Marriage plans were considered even at that time. The King of Portugal* offered his crown prince. The Duke of Lorraine proposed his firstborn. The Lorraine match attracted Charles: Duke Leopold was a first cousin of his and a childhood friend; he was the son of the storied soldier who had driven the Turks from the gates of Vienna; and the Lorraine dynasty, while anything but powerful or wealthy, was second to none in lineage.

No sooner, however, had Charles voiced some interest in Prince Clement, an apparently gifted boy, than word of his death came to Vienna. The bereaved father, a hearty man, promptly put forth the elder of his two surviving boys, Francis Stephen. Charles informed the ducal court in Lunéville that he was favorably inclined. The fact that the candidate's mother was a French princess did not disturb him, much as he disliked the French court. She was reputed to have some of the charm of her brother, the Duke of Orléans, much of his brains, and nothing of his profligacy.

Regent of France since the death of the Sun King, Orléans had reacted with speed to Spain's evident intention to overturn the peace settlement of Utrecht. Philip V, an oversexed man, besides being half a fool, had fallen under the spell of his second wife, Elizabeth Farnese. She was an extraordinary woman even in an age that soon was to see others. Guided by Cardinal Alberoni, an unscrupulous fellow Italian, she put both her native energy and her erotic inventiveness into the service of her single-minded ambition. As Philip had heirs by his first wife, Elizabeth set out to win principalities of their own to Don Carlos and Don Philip, the sons she had given the king. Farnese claims were at hand in Italy. The dismemberment of Spain's empire had dealt a heavy blow to the pride of its nobility and put the Italian sinecures out of their reach. Queen Elizabeth found this large class to be natural partisans of her aspirations.

After the occupation of Sardinia the Spaniards proceeded to land troops on Sicily, which the Duke of Savoy had been able to get title to

---

* His queen was the emperor's sister, and the Pragmatic Sanction made her and her issue heir to the Habsburg dominions should his line, as well as his brother's, ever become extinct.

at Utrecht. In August, 1718, France, exhausted though she was, joined Great Britain, Holland,* and Charles VI in what became known as the Quadruple Alliance.

Spain's forces were no match for that coalition, though the Dutch remained aloof from operations. An Austrian force was put ashore in Sicily early in 1719, and some coastal places on the Spanish mainland fell into the hands of French and British detachments. The court of Madrid, after Alberoni's dismissal, was forced to make peace in 1720. It had to abandon the protests lodged at Utrecht and confirm the cession of Belgium to Charles VI, who was also confirmed as Sicily's ruler. (Sardinia went to the Savoy duke, together with the ancient royal style due the master of that island.) In return, Charles promised Don Carlos the succession in the imperial fiefs of Parma, Piacenza, and Tuscany— whose dynasties were facing extinction—and at long last recognized Philip V as Spain's rightful king.

Not since Charles V in 1556 had split his worldwide possessions in two had any Habsburg held more land in Europe than did Charles VI at this juncture. As head of the Arch House, Theresa's father could consider himself the greatest monarch in Christendom.

Did he? He was not unaware of the economic backwardness of his Hereditary Lands, of the political obstacles thwarting Hungary's reconstruction after a century and a half of Turkish rule, or of the manifold problems posed by the transition from Spanish to Austrian government in his Italian and Belgian provinces. He hoped that their wealth would fill his coffers. His Spanish sojourn had imbued Charles with a love of the sea and taught him to realize the benefits its lanes might bring to its masters. Even before 1719 he had decided to offset the restrictions on Belgium's maritime trade imposed at Utrecht. To the dismay of London's merchants, he engaged the services of a Jacobite adventurer and founded the East India Company of Ostend. Overriding Venetian protests, he gave a free-port charter to his Trieste. His ships, although lacking the protection of a navy, began trading as far as China.

Charles VI was not without education. Nor, his pigheadedness notwithstanding, was he wholly devoid of common sense. But an insensate delight in flattery crippled what gifts he had. It was to estrange him from Eugene, the architect of the dynasty's victories on the battlefields and at the conference tables.

The fruits of Eugene's statesmanship gave impetus to the Balkan trade. "It is a pleasure," wrote a Salzburg cleric from Vienna, "to see

---

* The name of the Dutch republic was The United Provinces. It will nevertheless be convenient to refer to the republic, anachronistically, as "Holland."

in the streets Hungarians, Croats, Greeks, Armenians, Persians, and Moors. Merchants from these nations have storehouses here, and so have Protestants."[14] The old town, though not lacking in artisan skills, no longer could boast an indigenous merchant class of importance. As the nobility had bought up more and more property of burghers over the past generation, their share of real estate had declined greatly;[15] and many of them had slid down on the social ladder. Still, a flurry of prosperity was coming to Vienna in these years.

Vienna was not the capital of the Holy Roman Empire. Nor was it a Free Imperial City. Its administration was not much more than a façade for the powers that the Lower Austrian estates had delegated to its citizenry in a succession of more or less restrictive, vague arrangements. Its entire life lay in the long shadow cast by the court, whose ubiquity had stunted the civic pride and enterprise of an earlier day. Now and then some courageous men deplored this state of affairs, only to be told, as in one instance they were by one of Leopold's ministers, that, "deprived of the imperial household, trade, such as it is, would disappear, artificers would decamp, foreigners leave, the wine remain unsold in the cellars . . ."[16]

The Renaissance had virtually bypassed this fortified town, which up to 1683 was situated less than two hundred miles from the Turkish border. Baroque art had come late to Vienna. Some of the aristocracy had erected Italianate mansions outside the walls as early as the 1660's. But within them only the court and the Church had done any large-scale building prior to the defeat of the Turks. From that year on a veritable mania for intramural architecture seized the magnates from the Hereditary Lands. One of them, with a foresight matched only by the self-assurance of their class, told the Viennese that their town, "built badly and without any taste," would be "so adorned . . . as to be second to none in the whole Empire."[17]

Actually the fascination with building on the part of those great lords had not, by the 1720's, given a new face to Vienna itself. Its narrow streets, lined by four- and five-story tenements—sometimes cheek by jowl with a new palazzo or a house of worship—were without sidewalks, ill-paved, and dirty. Medieval structures and towers encumbered the access to thoroughfares or turned lanes into blind alleys. Not one public garden existed. The booths of vendors and public performers crammed the public squares, of which there were few to begin with. The court took these conditions as much for granted as the foul odors that penetrated the precincts of the Hofburg.

A thirteenth-century Bohemian king, fated to be driven out soon by Rudolph, the first of the Habsburgs to wear a crown, had chosen the site protected by the southern section of the city's ramparts. The Hofburg of Charles (or, rather, his father's) was still within its wall. Its main buildings, dating from different periods, fronted an unpaved quadrangle. A moat surrounded the most ancient of them, and its turrets reminded the beholder of the defense needs of the 1450's. Facing the "accountancy office," erected about a century later,* there stood the sprawling "Leopoldian Wing," in which the sovereign and his family had their living quarters. It had been put up at a right angle to the late-sixteenth-century "New Burg," a construction disfigured by a large cube-shaped clockhouse, which, topped by a small cupola, surmounted the steep roof.

To us the most attractive structure of the Hofburg is the Renaissance archway that leads from the great courtyard to another one of very modest proportions. The medieval Court Chapel fronts it. Surely that antiquated archway was not to the taste of Charles VI. He could not help contrasting the Hofburg's congeries with the great nobles' modern palazzos, the soaring exuberance of their façades, the statuary on their rooftops—in short, the sense of wealth and representation about those mansions.

Nothing even suggesting their ostentatious interiors, or the sculptures that flanked the staircases and stood on landings, could be found in the Hofburg. According to a gossip writer, the emperor's own apartments, the Retirada, were "of mean appearance, the walls thick and ponderous, the rooms low-ceilinged and narrow."[18] The wartime establishment at Barcelona had not spoiled Charles, and surely the tastes of Elizabeth's Brunswick family had not bred in the princess a taste for beautiful furnishings or modern comforts. One of the first things her daughter would do as a queen was to have some of the furniture and panelings of the summer palace brought to the Hofburg.

No prince of Charles's race had ever devoted greater attention than he did to ceremonial. Yet he could free himself of its chains, as well as its panoply, in his personal habits without feeling that he was play-acting in public. Habsburg tradition favored him. While points of etiquette probably kept no fewer courtiers busy in Vienna than in Versailles. the ritual staged about the French sovereign's person throughout his waking hours had no counterpart in the Habsburg court. Charles VI would dine in state on the prescribed occasions, wearing the clumsy "Spanish mantle garment," the heavy plumed hat atop the long wig, calculating his every movement, sparse of talk, and unsmiling. On the other hand, he would allow his Spanish pensioners to keep him company, would listen to their petty, and not so petty, political schemes or discuss with them "those Spanish ideas that kept cropping up all the

---

* This three-story building was remodeled grandiosely in Charles' own day to house the Empire's chancery.

time."[19] Rumors, frequently exaggerated, of these comparatively informal meetings met with popular criticism. They were, however, offset by the stories common people retailed about his *gemütlich* family life.

Hunting and music-making were the poles of his schedule. There was no closed season in his preserves; and, weather permitting, he would roam three or four times a week in the forests to the southeast or the west of Vienna to stalk deer or boar, have hare driven to him, or go hawking on horseback. Like most princes of his race, Charles was insatiable in bagging game. His musical mentor, J. J. Fux,* was at his beck and call at every hour. Performances of "musical dramas" Charles attended with abandon, and the concerts arranged at the palace theater found him an avid listener.

But neither these two time-consuming hobbies nor his manifold duties prevented Charles from seeing his children daily, with the empress present. At an unchanging hour, Theresa, Maria Anne, and Amalia† were taken down a gloomy staircase, past bare walls, and along chilly hallways, to the Retirada; two halberdiers stood at its door, ready to cup the tip of their halberds with the left hand in the salute due the blood of Habsburg, at the approach of the little archduchesses and throw open the door to the parental apartments.

Judging by Charles's letters from a later period, he was a pleasant father. He appears to have used the baby talk of the period without patronizing. Theresa he called "Mutz," adopting an upper-class abbreviation for "Maria." No one at court or in the nursery ever called her "Resi," as common folk would their own young Theresas, and contended the emperor did, too. The Viennese may not have been equally mistaken when they imagined the monarch not being averse to joking with his children or making them gape at tales he would tell them about the wonders of the lands he had seen. Charles VI was not without a sense of humor. Life, to be sure, was to warp it.

Viennese stories of the girl's free behavior were, on the whole, fantasy. (Most of them, incidentally, as they have entered legend, bear the stamp of the bourgeois sentimentality of a much later period.) One of these stories has the three- or four-year-old Theresa, startled by the first sight of her father walking in his imperial robes in procession, call down from a window: "O, turn round, daddy, to let me have another look at you!" The grown-up Theresa was never once to allude to such conduct tolerated even in early childhood. An Italian dancing master began to instruct her in comportment, besides dancing, when she entered her fifth year. If she should ever have spent some truly frolicsome time in the

---

* Fux was the author of *Gradus ad Parnassum,* a counterpoint manual widely used even long after his day.

† Amalia was to die in her fifth year.

Retirada, she never once was to reminisce about it. Nor do the instructions she wrote out for her own children tempt us to presume that
youthful lack of inhibition, to her mind, was proper for Habsburg
youngsters.

The childhood relation to her beautiful mother left a total blank in
her memory. Surely the princesses did not without deep-seated motives
call their *ayah** "Mami"—a habit that the empress, not without cause,
came to resent. The most candid of Maria Theresa's counselors must
have known she would not take it amiss as, many years later, he reminded her that her mother "hardly was much beloved."[20]

By the time Theresa met her first tutors, Jesuits both, there were
marvels to gaze at about the Hofburg. The building craze of the period
had taken hold of Charles VI. Defying the chronic shortage of funds,
he embarked on a number of ambitious projects, conscious also—the
first of the dynasty to be so—of what we should call city planning.
Huge scaffoldings had gone up off the southwestern front of the Hofburg compound, on a recently leveled site, for work on the library
building. Facing it, a spacious riding hall was under construction, where
the court's grooms were to train, as they had for close to two hundred
years, its Lipizza horses in the Spanish manner. We know that the
children were permitted to watch the men who worked on these buildings. Neither is it far-fetched to assume that they were driven, beyond
the city wall, to the site of their father's most original architectural undertaking, the church he had vowed during the plague of 1713 to his
patron saint, St. Carlo Borromeo. It is more doubtful that they were, in
these years, ever taken to the nearby summer palace of Eugene and its
gardens, an establishment that surpassed in grandeur by far any of the
magnates' mansions and any of the dwellings Charles VI called his own
or planned for.

Eugene had come to Vienna at the time of its siege as a penniless
apprentice in warfare. Imperial bounty had made him a very rich man.
As this was a road by no means untrodden by others, it was less his
wealth than his singular rise to fame and power that had earned him
enemies among the great clans. Worse to their minds, Eugene was a
man of intellectual interests, open to the New Thought that had arisen
in western countries. Had Charles VI been of a different kidney than
he was, he might have welcomed the counterweight Eugene's power provided to the great landowners of the Hereditary Lands, who by fair means
and foul were eating away at the crown's puissance. But his misfortunes
in Spain and the English betrayal had turned him mistrustful. Like
many heirs, he was jealous of the lofty reputation the much older man

* This title for governesses had come, via Portugal, from India to the court of
Vienna. The governors of its young princes had the title of *ayo*.

had garnered under his own predecessors, and resented the domineering position that Eugene had gained in his council.

Some time around 1720 a group of influential men began plotting a drastic curtailment of his power. While these schemers were close to the camarilla and Althan, Charles does not seem to have been privy to the cabal. He certainly knew nothing of the plan of discrediting Eugene altogether. And this was what Eugene denounced his enemies for to his master. At the same time, he virtually refused to discharge his duties as president of the defense committee (Hofkriegsrat) and as the guide of the foreign policy of both the monarchy and the Holy Empire. Thus bringing all business virtually to a standstill, Eugene compelled the sovereign to initiate a formal investigation, which in fact uncovered both a conspiracy and its ineptness. In the teeth of violent objections on the part of Althan and his attractive wife, Charles, who had no choice, punished two members of the clique with conspicuous severity.

Up to 1724 Eugene for all practical purposes stayed away from the court. The rift was healed in that year, and from then on Charles went out of his way to beg the aging man take care of his health and to impress upon him his indispensability for the realm. Still, Charles was never to forget the humiliation. It deepened his suspicion of men of genius.

Maria Theresa was to seek them. Yet an English diplomat visiting Vienna at the time of the ascendancy of the most extraordinary of her ministers, considered it pertinent to report that "she is not afraid of his parts [i.e., talents]."[21]

II

"Sweet Little Cavalier"

A LTHOUGH Charles VI was far less dependent than had been his
father upon his confessor, he was aware at every hour that he
ruled by the grace of God. Points of theology, such as occupied many
of his fellow princes, were alien to his cast of mind. In days still remote
Theresa's husband would pride himself on his "charcoal burner's faith";
Charles's own was not very different from it.

Religious observances loomed large in his life. Early on he and his
empress took the children along on some of the court's pilgrimages to
shrines, local or suburban, preferably those of the Virgin, the *magna
mater Austriae*, as she was spoken of in a singular blend of reverence
and familial claim. As the imperial couple covered at least the last leg
of such processions on foot, they afforded Theresa a glimpse of her
father's commoner subjects, who would line the streets or cluster on the
glacis, which had to be crossed to reach certain monastic shrines. This,
then, was the *publicum* of which Theresa would overhear some talk in
the nursery and the corridors of the palace. The hosts of its servants
did not form part of the *publicum*; except for masters in the crafts,
lawyers, auditors, doctors, and salaried musicians, townspeople considered liveried servants, in both the court and the establishments of the
great, superior to themselves on the social ladder. The impressions
Theresa gained of these flunkies, whose order of precedence equaled the
nobility's in rigidity, were still vivid when she had small children herself.

For her First Communion Theresa was taken to Maria Zell, an
ancient cathedral in the somber mountains of Styria. The miracle-
working Madonna of that fane wore a replica of the dynasty's crown.
A life-size effigy of the lamented son of Charles VI, wrought of solid

gold, reposed at the feet of that statue. Presumably the melancholy artifact was pointed out to little Theresa. She was to see it many times. But, for all we know, she never once spoke of the infant whose untimely death determined the course of her life.

Religion held a place of honor in Theresa's schooling as a matter of course. She was alert and attentive during the long hours spent with her tutors. These men followed their order's *Ratio Studiorum* of 1599, a revolutionary teaching manual in its day. The history course started with such examination questions as "Which of the ten patriarchs lived before the Flood, which ones after it?" Next, the "four world monarchies"— the "Assyrian-Babylonian empire," Persia, Greece, and Rome— were discussed in this text. "Where do we find an account of how Dido built Carthage?" the princess would be asked. "In prose, in Justin,* in verse, in Virgil,"[1] she was required to answer, only to be queried about the pertinent passages in these authorities. From Roman history the lectures proceeded to the history of Byzantium, which was fashioned to lead up to the Holy Roman Empire's chronicle.

Its author wasted little space on Charlemagne or on the subsequent predecessors of Theresa's own family on his throne. As taught her, the history of the Habsburgs could not but convince the princess of their uniqueness as a race set apart by the Almighty from all other royal houses, as well as the common run of mortals. Though growing up in a court bare of men save her father, she does not seem to have wondered what monarch was to assume the imperial office which his line had held since what to a child must have seemed time immemorial. When precisely Theresa realized the role that God's will appeared to be reserving to her in the succession to the dominions of the Arch House, when, in other words, she was told of the Pragmatic Sanction—this must remain conjecture.

Nothing was taught her about the lands of her father's that lay outside the Empire's borders. Historical references are rare in Maria Theresa's letters or the accounts of her talks. Even the history of her own house, prior to her grandfather's rule, is touched upon with a prudence that betokens spotty information. As an aging woman Maria Theresa admonished her married daughters to study historical books; she herself was never to read such works.

Languages came easy to her. She spoke French with fluency, Italian fairly well, and had a smattering of Spanish. She also was tutored in Latin, in which the Hungarians transacted business. Her mother tongue was paid small attention to. To her dying day, whatever she wrote in German remained archaic in style and syntax, and lacking even consistency in its semiphonetical spelling. Stories that make much of her

* A Roman historian of wide scope and short grasp, popular in the Middle Ages.

propensity toward adopting the slurring pronunciation of Vienna's lower orders must be taken with a grain of salt. Empress Elizabeth spoke the precise German of her native Brunswick, and the widowed Countess Fuchs, who became the girls' *ayah* when Theresa entered her tenth year, hailed from the Rhineland.

Great care was devoted to Theresa's musical talent. Her teachers, Wagenseil and Hasse, cultivated in her the Italian taste of Charles VI, who, besides being an accomplished *viola da gamba* player, was (as his father and grandfather had been) something of a composer himself.* She matured to be a *clavecin* player of some distinction, if limited repertoire. Her singing voice proved good schooling. She was in her eighth year when she performed for the first time in a "musical drama." The Venetian ambassador, who was in the audience, gave an enthusiastic account of the graceful appearance of the archduchess and her lack of self-consciousness. It was his countryman Apostolo Zeno who implanted the love of Italian poetry in the child. She was to adore the "divine Metastasio," who came to Vienna in 1730. The naïve imagery of his poems and libretti, and the latters' simplicity of action, enraptured high society. Maria Theresa was never to share the more sophisticated tastes of a later period.

The masterworks of French writing had made but little headway even among well-read aristocrats in the Habsburg dominions. Perhaps Theresa was encouraged, as were other highborn youngsters, to read Racine's *Athalie* or some of the work of Jean Baptiste Rousseau, a minor poet who, an exile from France, enjoyed Eugene's patronage in Vienna.

'In brief, Theresa's education could neither refine her taste nor imbue her with intellectual curiosity. Nevertheless, the "notoriously dry-as-dust and tedious methods of the instructors,"[2] which the grown-up woman was to recall only too well, did not stifle her spirit. Unlike her sister who developed into a "princess of meek temper,"[3] Theresa remained lively and energetic and possessed of the happy gift of resilience.

In the warm months the family resided less than a mile south of the city, in the New Favorita. Its mansions, simple in the adornment of their facades, were well ventilated and airy, and their windows admitted a flood of light. Acres of gardens surrounded the buildings, in whose vicinity a large pond had been laid out. Lawns and meadows extended east to the orchards and vineyards and fields of a rich nunnery. No doubt the girls engaged in some outdoor play on these lovely grounds under the eyes of their *ayah*. They were allowed to try their hand at target shooting, a fad their mother had brought to Vienna and which, next to

---

* While Wagenseil introduced some of Vienna's music-minded nobles to the harpsichord suites of Bach and Handel, he did not make the archduchess listen to any of the music of these heretic composers.

gambling, was her favored pastime. As ladies were not supposed to mount a horse, the archduchesses received no riding instruction.

The sojourn at the New Favorita did not interfere with their father's love of baroque spectacles and music; and we know that his children were among the spectators of the outdoor performances of ballets, operas, or "naval battles."* Often they were present when the emperor was conducting his own orchestra or auditioning a singer from Italy who was to join his own troupe.

Outside the children's theatricals and the rehearsals for them, the girls were given no opportunity of mixing with coevals, however high-born. Maria Theresa, loyal to old friends to a fault, was never to mention any childhood playmates. Francis Stephen of Lorraine, who came to Vienna on Christmas Eve of 1723, was nine years her elder.

She had met him, in August, in Prague at her father's belated coronation as King of Bohemia. Duke Leopold had prevailed on Charles to invite the young man. Surely the prince made little impression on Theresa amid all the strange sights she was exposed to.

The easygoing ways of Lunéville had not prepared Francis for Habsburg protocol. Dr. Pfütschner, his tutor from childhood days, who traveled with the fifteen-year-old, frequently had to restrain his high spirits; and the Prince of Craon, who headed his suite, had to impress on the youngster that he must not talk to His Majesty unless talked to first. Yet Charles VI, this stickler for etiquette, found himself attracted by the comely son of his cousin—by his sparkling blue eyes, his ready smile, and indeed his garrulousness. The sudden death of Althan, that cherished companion whose feelings Charles had been compelled to hurt in the crisis of Eugene's making, had thrown the monarch in a deep dejection. The visitor from Lunéville was dispelling those humors. "Find Prince Lorraine handsome, well-built, well-mannered. Speaks German," the emperor noted in his diary. The next day: "Prince Lorraine jolly . . . Good shot." And then on August 14: "Much talk about Prince Lorraine also with chancellor. Marriage daughter, yes, *in tempore* . . ." Francis

---

* In 1716 Lady Mary Wortley Montagu "so far wandered from the discipline of the Church of England to have been last Sunday at the opera . . . in the garden of the Favorita. . . . Nothing of that kind was more magnificent; and I can easily believe what I am told that the decorations and habits cost the emperor thirty thousand pounds sterling. The stage was built over a very large canal, and at the beginning of the second act, divided into two parts, discovering the water on which there immediately came from different parts two fleets of little gilded vessels that gave the representation of a naval fight. . . . No house could hold such large decorations. But the ladies, all sitting in the open air, expose themselves to great inconveniences, for there is but one canopy—for the imperial family. . . . A shower of rain happening, the opera was broken off, and the [spectators] crowded away in such confusion that I was almost squeezed to death." (Ed., Lord Wharncliffe, I, 210.)

was given the Golden Fleece the following day. "Sweet little cavalier,"[4] the emperor jotted down.

"My very dear cousin," he wrote to Leopold from Prague, "we are such close friends, offspring of one and the same House, as it were, and brought up together. Also, I hold Your Highness in such esteem, and am so greatly devoted to you, I feel I can open my heart in trust to you, even though time does not seem ripe yet. . . . Assuredly, a still closer union would be the best means of consolidating our friendship, and make it last. This has been my intention for a long time, and will remain so." And with that the monarch went on to inform the duke that it was his intention to "merge our dynasties further."[5]

Leopold lost no time. For one thing, he did his best to pin down Charles: he thanked him for "accepting my unworthy son as a son-in-law."[6] Then he ordered Craon to keep Francis in Prague after the court's departure, and at the same time suggested to His Majesty that the prince be invited to take up residence in Vienna. The emperor, taken aback, flatly demurred. When Leopold grew insistent, Charles told him, truthfully enough, that there was not a single person in Vienna capable of educating the prince. Leopold, nothing daunted, emphatically mentioned the Empire's interests: would it not be unfortunate to let Lorraine's future ruler grow up under the influence of his French mother? This argument may have carried some weight with Charles. Of greater weight was his missing the company of the young fellow huntsman. The invitation was extended.

Francis was given the apartment that the emperor's mother used to occupy in the Hofburg. And Donato, the Venetian ambassador, reported promptly that "this young prince draws the eyes of the whole Empire upon himself."[7] While this no doubt was exaggeration, the emperor's own grandees certainly watched the Lorrainer. They admired his skill at fencing, dancing, tennis, and hunting and spoke with admiration about his uncanny proficiency in shooting fowl on the wing. They also told one another, and their ladies, of the extraordinary pleasure the emperor derived from Francis' sportsmanship on their stag and boar hunts in the hilly woods around Laxenburg Lodge, or during the hawking rides which took them, before sunrise, to the marshy banks of the Danube, preceded by the Lord Falconer, buglers blowing their horns. However, stories of a very different kind became current within the year.

The trouble with Francis was his disinclination to apply himself to studies. He could not bring himself to peruse the books his tutors pressed upon him. He was likely to falter when reading aloud. His penmanship was abominable. The most elemental rules of spelling kept eluding him both in his mother's tongue and in German. History bored him, as did jurisprudence, a field of learning Charles VI set great store by. Leopold sent one set of instructions after another to Pfütschner. In due time the emperor appointed a fairly well-read noble—a graduate of Leyden—to the grand-mastership of Francis' establishment and directed him to supervise his studies. He also attached to his suite a worldly-wise army man, Count William Neipperg, whose reputation rested on a *coup de main* performed during the brief Sicilian campaign and on some semidiplomatic and quasi-administrative assignments that Eugene had entrusted to him. Little progress was made. While the grand master's obsequious praise of Francis did not fool Charles—or Leopold, for that matter—their correspondence did not reflect the regrettable state of affairs. The emperor kept alluding to his unaltered hope for a "closer union." The phrase, repeated over and over again, slowly was losing its persuasiveness. It sounded downright ambiguous by mid-1725.

The Spanish queen had grown impatient of the halfhearted moves of the signatories of the settlement of 1720 to implement the gains it had given the kingdom. As she started playing with the thought of bilateral parleys with Charles VI, her attention was caught by one Ripperdá, a Dutch politician and businessman who had entered her service after embracing the Roman faith, a person as glib of speech as sanguine of imagination. This man, then, turned up in Vienna in the autumn of 1724. Whatever his authority, his credentials satisfied the emperor, who, egged on by the camarilla and riding roughshod over Eugene's warnings, began to listen to what were represented to him as offers from the rival of old in Madrid. English efforts to suppress his Ostend Company had been vexing him for some time; and Spain's offer, as put forth by Ripperdá, to open her ports to the company's vessels sounded sweet to Charles's ears. Greater allurements were to come after the French had mortally wounded the pride of the court of Madrid.* A desire to wreck the Quadruple Alliance and isolate France had been growing before in Philip's court. Now it rose to a pitch.

Eugene's warnings became passionate. Although he had been the immediate victim of the English desertion, he consistently advocated good relations with the Maritime Powers. Not only had he, ahead of other men in Vienna, realized the new element that had entered the Empire's affairs with the accession of the Hanoverians to the throne of Great Britain. He also was one of the few to appreciate her ever-growing wealth under the leadership of Walpole. Her recovery from the ravages of the South Sea Bubble impressed Eugene, who, if extravagant in indulging his artistic tastes, yet had a sound respect for money.

---

* Anxious to marry off Louis XV so he might father an heir, they had sent home the Spanish princess, who—a child of nine at that time—had been living at the French court as the fiancée of the young king. Subsequently Louis was married to Maria Leszczynska, the daughter of the deposed King of Poland.

Ripperdá's presence in Vienna threw Europe's chancelleries into turmoil. He was said to be laying the groundwork for Austro-Spanish support of Russia's aspirations in the Baltic, or to have given the Ostend Company the monopoly on the Spanish Main trade, or to have promised the emperor bullion from the New World, or to have secured his assistance in the recovery of Gibraltar and Minorca.* These and some other ideas did find their way, in one vague form or some other, into the agreement Charles VI affixed his sign manual to in April, 1725. He precipitated a crisis which resulted in a defensive alliance between Britain, France, and the upstart kingdom of Prussia, Hanover's neighbor.

Francis of Lorraine, even had he known of the emperor's dealings with Ripperdá and grasped their risks, would not have been concerned in the least. He would have given no thought to the monarch's promise to support, more actively than foreseen five years before, Don Carlos' admission to the Italian duchies. It was just as well that Francis knew nothing of the wish of Charles VI, as expressed in a letter to the Spanish queen, to marry two of his daughters to her sons.

As Charles still had three daughters, this promise did not necessarily include the hand of Theresa. The queen in Madrid thought that it did, however; and Leopold in Lunéville, had he been privy to her correspondence with his imperial cousin, might well have asked a blunt question. Even as it was, he could not but realize that Theresa was becoming a bargaining counter of Vienna's policies, despite the commitment he had chosen to read into his cousin's letter from Prague. Her value increased with every month Heaven refused to heed Charles's supplication for a son.

He showered churches and monasteries with donations such as he could ill afford. He made many pilgrimages to Maria Zell. He tried to please the Almighty by interfering with Protestant services in the few places in his realm guaranteed freedom of worship. In foreign courts it was bruited about that, to excite the imagination of the empress and thereby stimulate her fertility, he had her bedroom decorated with erotic paintings of manly vigor. He besought his physicians to help him. They prescribed a fattening diet and heavy cordials. All they achieved was to destroy Elizabeth's beauty.

When Charles VI approved the blueprints for the transformation of Klosterneuburg Abbey, some miles upstream from Vienna, into what he envisaged as his own Escorial, rivaling Philip's, he ordered the architects to top the cupola with a gigantic stone replica of the Holy Roman Empire's crown—as though to defy any doubts about the long line of future Habsburg princes who would wear it. At the same time, he did not lose sight of the dreaded possibility that his prayers might remain

* Both had been seized by the English early in the War of the Spanish Succession.

futile. The recognition of his act of succession by the Empire's princes and the foreign powers had occupied Charles's thinking even while he was busy adding to the girth of his territory. From the mid-twenties on, those recognitions grew to constitute the lodestar of his actions.

There was a price to be offered wherever his ambassadors negotiated for a recognition, or more boldly, a guarantee of the Pragmatic Sanction. And not many statesmen abroad doubted but that Theresa might become part of that price in some instance. People in Charles's own court were not squeamish about such ideas either. At one time there was some speculation about the son of Frederick William, the gruff, military-minded King in Prussia; indeed, his crown prince, an amiable youngster and lover of music, might be brought back to the fold. And then, there were the sons of the Farnese woman. . . . To believe a story current at one time, Theresa, having got wind of one of these projects, flew into a tantrum and refused to take food for a day or two. Nine, or ten, or eleven years of age, she was aware of the purpose of Francis' presence in Vienna. Assuredly, he had charmed her.

She was twelve when the sudden death of Francis' father called him back to Lorraine. Neipperg, who accompanied Francis, had nothing but good to report. The serious-mindedness of the young duke was astounding the court of Lunéville; he was turning a deaf ear to the blandishments of certain attractive ladies; and, most surprising, he was taking a hand in Lorraine's financial affairs.

Francis was still in Lunéville at the time Charles VI got word of a face-about of the Spanish queen. Exasperated by his vacillations, she had sacked Ripperdá, the architect of the amateurish agreements with the court of Vienna*; and Philip V had, at Seville, concluded a treaty with Britain and France, the anti-Habsburg animus of which could not be questioned. Some men in Vienna felt uncomfortable about Francis' residing so close to the frontier of the French, who, in their notorious designs on Lorraine, might try to get hold of his person. The duke had no such fears. He journeyed straight to Versailles to be invested as Duke of Bar, a fief his dynasty held from the French crown. His meeting with Louis XV, who was two years his junior, was formal and brief. Cardinal Fleury, the young king's famous mentor, who after Orléans' death had risen to political power, had a long talk with the visitor.

The emperor was not at all eager to let him come back to Vienna. The Lorraine ambassador, Jaquemin, kept Francis abreast of goings-on

* Ripperdá escaped to Holland and became a Protestant again, only to take himself to Morocco and turn Muslim some few years later. After he led the sultan's army into disaster, he was exiled to Tetuan, and left to mourn the dukedom that Philip V had bestowed on him, together with the premiership, upon his short-lived triumph at Vienna.

without reporting on the crisis the Treaty of Seville had engendered. He made much of his efforts to keep Theresa aware of Francis' wish to see her again very soon. The duke could not, in propriety, write to the archduchess. But Jaquemin managed to get into the good graces of her *ayah* and prevail upon her to convey Francis' compliments to the princess. Sometimes Mme. Fuchs allowed her to peruse one of the missives Francis addressed to the empress. For by that time Theresa's mother— perhaps not insensitive herself to his charm, perhaps jealous of the *ayah's* role as the girl's confidante—had joined the little intrigue.

On the day before Christmas Eve, 1730, the emperor handed a miniature likeness of the duke to Mme. Fuchs, asking her to appraise him of his daughter's reaction. Jaquemin, writing to his distant master, pretended to know that the archduchess had "contemplated the painting for a long time, her face changing colors." Her father may have been told likewise by the *ayah*. He gave orders that the picture "must not be listed in the official record of the Christmas presents."[8] At the chancellery, however, all papers relating to Francis had been filed for some time under the label of *"la grande affaire de Lorraine."*[9]

Jaquemin was not more romantic than the chancery clerks. Once, mentioning rumors that had the empress with child, he hastened to add that there was no truth in the story. "There is little news, as far as I am concerned," Charles wrote at about that time to Francis, "except that I am missing my dearest hunting and spring companion everywhere, and especially in Laxenburg." On the affairs of the world, the emperor hardly touched. "I do not wish to detain Your Highness by unnecessary news. All I am asking you is not to forget Vienna, and the old and verily true friend who loves a certain young cavalier, will never cease doing so, and will prove it."[10] Nice words, these, and probably sincere too. But Francis could not possibly be blind to their inconsistency with his virtual banishment from Vienna. Besides, life in Lunéville bored him. He requested the emperor's permission to install the dowager duchess as regent and take himself on a tour of Belgium and Holland.

Permission was granted. Both the Belgian administration and the embassy at The Hague were instructed to do neither too much nor too little in arranging for Francis' reception and his sojourn. While the emperor's oldest sister, who held the governor's office in Brussels, does not seem to have done "too much" by any means, high society in The Hague was as generous to the duke as it was impressed by the affability of his manners. The British ambassador introduced him to the Freemasons' recently established Amsterdam lodge. He also hinted at the pleasure that His Royal Highness would give his nation by visiting the island.*

* As collateral descendants of Balduin (1058-1118), the first Christian king of Jerusalem, all Lorraine princes boasted royal rank.

Neipperg related the proposal to Vienna. Charles pondered it for many weeks. Eugene pressed acceptance. The Seville treaty had threatened war with Spain—a danger that was depleting Charles's coffers still further—and at one time Britain also had exerted military pressure on him. The dissolution of the treaty in January, 1731, had come as a relief to Charles. Two months later he rose to the bait held out by Walpole—a guarantee, if still qualified, of the Pragmatic Sanction—and concluded a new agreement with Great Britain. It opened the Parmese duchies to a Spanish garrison, made Tuscany's Leghorn a free port, and passed over in silence Hanoverian aspirations in the *Reich*. But Walpole also forced Charles to dissolve his Ostend Company. The emperor was mourning this pet of his with a depth of feeling second only to the melancholy thought of the throne of Madrid.

Having at long last decided that Francis should voyage to England, he informed him on the hazards of the Channel, to which he himself was not, after all, a stranger, and also admonished the duke to "take special care of your health . . . what with the drastic change of the climate, and amid all those outlandish customs. . . . Don't spoil your stomach."[11]

The young fellow educated under the tutelage of Charles VI was not expected with great warmth in London, where Walpole's solution of the Continental crisis had not silenced his hostile critics. A few short years before, the memories of Charles's "gravity . . . [and] exactness"[12] on his visit to Queen Anne had been revived by the publication of *Gulliver's Travels*. The pompous six-inch king of the Lilliputians obviously owed some of his makeup to the "Archduke" the English had seen in 1703 and who now, as Walpole maintained, was the mainstay of his policy of keeping France in diplomatic isolation. When Francis turned out not to have been infected by the emperor's love of punctilio and his slowness of temper—and, in fact, revealed himself as a convivial gentleman and a competent horseman and excellent shot to boot—the English took a fancy to him. Count Philip Kinsky, Vienna's ambassador (and, as Theresa was to find out, not a person given to flattery), described in glowing terms the impression Francis had made on the king, as well as his queen. Walpole entertained him at his splendid new country home, where the London Freemasons' lodge assembled to extend a rousing welcome to "Brother Lorraine."

The great kindness shown him in Walpole's circles was not merely due to the visitor's social talents. Presumably Walpole saw the emperor's letters to the duke ahead of their reaching the addressee, and he must have been struck by their warmth. The recent treaty had made Britain's guarantee of Charles's act of succession contingent upon Theresa's not marrying a prince who in his own right was of consequence to the equilibrium of Europe. The Lorrainer would fill the bill.

His enjoyment of English hospitality was overcast by news received from Jaquemin shortly before the embarkment for the island. Some governorship was being planned in Vienna for Francis to keep him out of Theresa's sight. "I must not conceal [Jaquemin wrote] that during the past two months the powers hostile to you and their hangers-on have been exceedingly ouspoken about the dim view they would take of the emperor's choice of Your Highness as a son-in-law."[13] Francis, while still in Vienna, had not been worrying overly about those "hostile powers." He did not know that the emperor, at one point in his search for a Spanish settlement, had said that, "if driven to extremities, he could effect a conciliation . . . by giving his daughter to Don Carlos; and the queen would purchase that object on any condition."[14]

In a portrait of that time Theresa's face is no longer chubby. The underslung chin seems to bespeak weakness. The large eyes, not very deep-set—in fact, slightly protruding—show nervous anxiety rather than maidenly wonderment. There is not a whiff of high spirits or determination about the countenance of the slender princess, and not the slightest trace of coquetry.

It was His Majesty's will, wrote Eugene to Neipperg, that "the duke call on the courts of some of the other of the Empire's princes* (Bavaria and Saxony must not be among these) and then travel to Berlin. . . . Inasmuch as the Prussian king takes an interest in the duke, the latter will not fail to win him over."[15] In fact, Frederick William was looking forward to having Francis attend the betrothal of his firstborn, Frederick, to a Brunswick niece of the empress.† No sooner had Francis set foot in Berlin than Count Lewis Seckendorf, the emperor's representative at the Prussian court, apprised him of the delicate situation engendered by Frederick's attitude toward his father's choice of the Brunswick girl in lieu of Amalia, the object, as it would seem—or as the crown prince pretended—of a romantic attachment. Charles VI, "even though he was in favor of the match, wished to avoid recommending to the crown prince a step which might not be consonant with his desires."[16] (Francis must have noted with bitterness such consideration for a young man's personal feelings.) As Seckendorf went on to inform the visitor, his host expected him to prejudice Frederick in favor of the marriage. Although Francis politely said no, Frederick William, for all his native rudeness,

* As Elector of Hanover, George II was of course himself a prince of the Empire.
† An old project of marrying Princess Amalia of England to the crown prince, her cousin—and his eldest sister, Wilhelmina, to the eldest son of the Prince of Wales —had foundered on the tergiversations of the Prussian king, who, with relations to England as complex as they were, would agree to a Hanoverian marriage of his daughter, but not of his son.

swallowed his pride. He "cannot marvel enough at the intelligence and great experience with which the duke talks about all matters. . . ." Seckendorf reported.[17]

"You must have seen many soldiers, a lot of grenadiers' play, and a court altogether different from all others," Charles VI suggested in one of his letters to Francis.[18] The oversized guardsmen and their drill— half admired, half laughed at, by foreigners—did not, for all we know, engage Francis' interest. He was having a good deal of fun, not excluding some horseplay, in the company of the groom-to-be, whose harrowing experiences at the hands of his bullying, cane-swinging father seemed to have left no scars on his spirit.* Under strict supervision he did duty in a small garrison, read books smuggled to him, composed bad French verse, and played the flute.

The betrothal took place on March 10, 1732. Incensed about the new humiliation, Frederick yet was not in despair. He was determined not to let the mate foisted on him encroach on his way of life, which had less and less room for women. While he had run up debts and played at being the rake, he thirsted for the friendship of men of learning and wit. Francis surely was neither. Judging by a letter that Frederick wrote to Wilhelmina (now married to the heir of the Margrave of Bayreuth) on the day of the duke's departure, his courtly deportment, vivacity, and sense of humor had established a bond of friendship between the two princes.

On his road to Vienna Francis learned of his appointment as governor of Hungary. "Duke Lorraine here," Charles jotted down in his diary on April 16. "Good. Strong. Clever, too. Nice." For the following day the entry reads: "Duke here. Still talking little. Shall see about Hungary."[19] Francis' sulky silence did not last. He pleaded total ignorance of Hungarian affairs. In all deference, he also touched on his concern about his own future. His social success in London and Berlin had given him a measure of self-assurance.

If Francis had changed in the three years of his travels, so had the emperor. Considering himself the victim of his own rashness, he now

---

* That conflict had been the talk of a scandalized Europe less than two years before. Frederick, smarting under the king's brutish disciplinarianism, had tried unsuccessfully to escape to England. Holding an army commission, he was technically an apprehended deserter. Frederick William, after attempting to run his sword through the culprit, had him thrown into prison. He forced Frederick to watch the beheading of the officer who had abetted the plan (or, as a less shocking version has it, to watch him being marched off to the scaffold). Then the king, in the teeth of his top generals' passionate pleas and objections, demanded that the court-martial he had convoked pass sentence on his "criminal" heir. He relented in the end— probably before a letter from the emperor's own hand reached him—and, after keeping Frederick for about a year in confinement, restored him to freedom and rank.

dreaded any decision he would have to face and in every instance clung to divers reasons for postponing settlements. The death of the youngest of his daughters might allow the Spanish queen to claim Theresa as one of the "two archduchesses" promised her sons. The French court would not take kindly to Theresa's marriage to the duke regnant of Lorraine and in fact had hinted at the desirability of his abdication in his brother's favor. And Theresa was but fifteen years old—and Charles's physicians had told him that his wife's unsatisfactory performance as a bearer of children might well have been caused by her early marriage.

Whatever the way Charles rationalized his disinclination to have *la grande affaire de Lorraine* consummated, he left no doubt as to his firmness of will. Except for an intercession on the part of his empress, he would have given Francis the governorship of some such faraway land as Silesia or the Tyrol. One of the few consolations that Francis could derive from his actual appointment was the fact that Pressburg, the pro-tem capital of the Hungarian kingdom, was no more than a half day's ride from Vienna. The duke was asked to spend the snipe-shooting season with the imperial family at Laxenburg Lodge. The celebration of Theresa's birthday, in which he took part, was a stiff affair. On May 27 he was on his way to Pressburg.

Francis' office was not in accord with the constitution of the kingdom. But as he showed no intention of interfering with its business, the magnates did not mind the presence of the *"locumtenens."* Letters from Jacquemin relieved the tedium. They persuaded the duke that his removal from Vienna had not impinged on his importance in the world. "I cannot possibly do justice to the assurances of friendship for Your Royal Highness on the part of the king," he wrote from Prague, where Charles, traveling to the waters of Carlsbad, had met Frederick William. "As he told me, he is at a loss to express the strength of his desire to see Your Royal Highness once more in his life. He commends his crown prince to your good graces, and regards your intention to correspond with him as a unique favor. . . . Mr. Robinson, the ambassador of the king of England, arrived yesterday from Hanover, and asked me to convey the assurance of his master's great friendship to Your Royal Highness." As a token of these sentiments, the king had sent a "small rectangular box filled with sundry gems. . . . I am certain they will give pleasure to Your Royal Highness."[20]

But all the jewels from London could not soothe Francis' restlessness. He realized that his objections to the Hungarian post had annoyed the emperor. Not until late in August did he receive a sign of forgiveness. Charles invited Francis to Linz, where he had traveled from Prague to receive the Upper Austrian estates' homage and do some chamois shooting in the nearby mountains. As the two archduchesses were staying in the Hofburg, Francis, to comply with protocol, journeyed to Linz without setting foot in Vienna. He found himself treated with marked kindness. Perhaps the project of an extended trip through Hungary which he had submitted made Charles wonder whether he had not dealt too harshly with a prince who seemed to take his duties seriously enough to hazard the discomforts of such an undertaking. Unless one wished to discredit the young governor's courage, his plan had to be approved.

Francis began to travel from one manor to the next with his suite, and his guilelessness won him some friends among the proud lords of the kingdom, who did not fail to show the splendors of their establishment. *Battues* were arranged for the governor (and he in turn indebted two of the most powerful magnates by presenting each with a pack of blooded hounds imported from England). He also visited the battlefields where Eugene had won immortal glory.

Jaquemin was tireless. "The emperor told me that he had received word from Buda [he wrote] and was most eager to embrace Your Royal Highness upon your return. I also saw the empress. I said that Your Royal Highness had instructed me to deliver a letter to her, and that I had also been given a missive for the archduchess. The empress took both letters . . . and asked me to suggest that you so arrange your journey as to be in Vienna on St. Charles's Day. . . . She said that she accepted the responsibility, and that you were above soliciting permission for a trip to Vienna. You should keep [the plan] a secret, and thus give the emperor the pleasure of a surprise. In Linz, I learned from a good source that the court will start working on the *grande affaire*. . . ." Two weeks later Jaquemin was "utterly wretched as Your Royal Highness did not instruct me what to do on St. Theresa's Day, which is today. . . . I decided to notify the archduchess of your arrival in Belgrade [and] convey Your Royal Highness's good wishes. . . . The archduchess said that whatever came from Your Royal Highness was most pleasing to her. But she neither could, nor wished to, conceal from me the fact that her satisfaction would have been immeasurably greater, if she had received congratulations from Your Highness in person. She asked several times whether you would be here for St. Charles's."[21]

One scarcely could have blamed Francis for keeping Theresa in suspense or for expressing by a show of coolness how greatly he resented being kept at arm's length. However, he was not the man to devise such stratagems. Promptly on the emperor's name day he arrived in Vienna. Attending an opera performance, he sat in one of the boxes with Theresa's sister, while she herself was seated on a special dais with her parents.

He made another trip to Vienna in January to join a masked ball of the court. Jaquemin, briefed by Mme. Fuchs, informed Francis that His Majesty had "strong motives, or reasons, for not wanting Your Royal Highness to escort either of the archduchesses." At the same time, he "does not wish you to escort some other [lady] as the resulting confusion would be great."[22] Some weeks after the patient suitor went through the trials of that *bal masqué*, the confusion in Charles's court was far greater indeed than any that Francis' leading his daughter in one of the counter-dances might have engendered.

III

A Pot of Mushrooms

Fleury, that vigorous octogenarian, had been searching the horizon for a chance of pulling his country out of its isolation. His chance came with the death of Augustus II of Saxony, king of the elective monarchy of Poland, and the recall, by a large group of her nobles, of the exiled king, Stanislas Leszczynski, the father-in-law of Louis XV.

The czarina, Anne, wanted Augustus' son and namesake to be elected; and as the Russian court had committed itself in 1726 to upholding the Pragmatic Sanction, she expected Charles VI to support her nominee. Little persuasion was needed in Vienna. Young Augustus, married to the elder of the daughters of Joseph I, had not acknowledged the emperor's act of succession. Hence Charles was eager to indebt the Saxon dynasty to his own. He did not foresee the conflagration he was kindling.

Actually it was Fleury who ignited the fire. Smuggling Leszczynski into Poland ahead of the election, he declared its freedom to be a matter of grave concern to the court of Versailles. And even before war was declared on the Empire, the Habsburg court, or Russia, a French army occupied Lorraine, and Louis XV, adding insult to injury, summoned its duke, Francis, to take up residence in his French fief of Bar.

The sovereignty of the house of Lorraine had been a precarious one for a long time. Legally part of the Empire, the duchy had been at the mercy of Louis XIV. Francis' grandfather had had to flee before French aggression. He spent the rest of his life on Habsburg territory, was given a widowed Habsburg princess in marriage, and commanded imperial armies. Leopold, Francis' father, born in exile—in Innsbruck, to be exact—could return to the duchy only after granting France the permanent right of passage. His marriage to the Orléans princess had not blunted French designs on Lorraine.

Its invasion was only the first move of Fleury's strategy. He lured the king of Sardinia away from obligations to the emperor and drew Spain into the alliance. Villars, the eighty-year-old veteran, crossed the Alps to attack Lombardy, the weakest spot in the Habsburg defenses, and the Duke of Berwick, a coeval of his, advanced toward the upper Rhine.

Eugene was ten years younger than either of the French marshals. But he was old beyond his years. He had failed to train a new generation of senior officers, or for that matter, the troops. A sense of sterility pervaded the Hofkriegsrat. Charles VI had no choice but to entrust Eugene with the command of the forces on the Empire's western frontier. They were vastly outnumbered by Berwick's. Some German princes had delivered token auxiliaries. Frederick William was among them with ten thousand troops; accompanied by his curiosity-ridden crown prince, he stayed some weeks at headquarters, where Eugene had arrived in May, 1734. The Prussian would have come with a far greater force had Charles VI accepted him as an ally, as foreseen in an earlier treaty, instead of an imperial liegeman only. But Charles had declined Frederick William's offer.

Eugene did not conceal the low ebb of his hopes even as the fighting spirit of the French began lagging in the course of the summer. From Vienna, where he spent the winter, only to realize that the Hofkriegsrat could not provide his troops with even the necessaries, he implored George II to live up to the terms of his treaty with Vienna and bring assistance. In that respect, too, Eugene was a man of the past. He was unable to gauge Walpole's power to overcome his king's scruples and to keep the nation aloof from the war. No help could be expected from the Dutch republic, which Fleury had bound by a pact of neutrality.

While Charles's role—or mission—as the Empire's defender was in jeopardy on the Rhine, his own dynasty's Italian possessions were in mortal danger despite a victory won at Parma in June. Don Carlos, egged on by his mother, set out to conquer the Two Sicilies.* Eugene, in pitiable health, was horrified at Charles VI's adamant refusal to cut his Italian losses and listen to the French overtures, word of which he himself had brought to Vienna. Charles still entertained hopes for British intervention; moreover, he had secured a Russian auxiliary corps, which would be on its march to the Rhineland shortly.

Meanwhile, Don Carlos was progressing on his road to what his mother called the "most beautiful crown in Italy."[1] Over the past

* The kingdoms of Naples and Sicily. (Don Carlos, to protect his "reversionary" rights, had been in Tuscany with a strong garrison.)

twenty-odd years a succession of viceroys from Vienna had bled the Neapolitans white to meet its treasury's needs. Even though the memories of the former Spanish rule were not sweet either, the population was willing to welcome Don Carlos. Attempts on the part of the incumbent viceroy to conscript its sons ran afoul of open resistance. The emperor's troops were wholly inadequate to stop Don Carlos. No reinforcements were available, and no naval craft to keep Spanish reinforcements from approaching the shore.

The camarilla in Vienna trembled for their pensions, which year after year had been paid out of the remittances from Naples. Regaining Charles's ear in step with his waxing dissatisfaction with Eugene, they urged the emperor to detach Spain from France through an unequivocal offer of Theresa's hand to Don Carlos. Charles VI, despairing of all counsel, turned to God alone. On the first day of the year he recorded the prayers by which he asked Him for the firmness still lacking in his wish to give his Theresa to Francis.

His demand for a resounding victory on the Rhine, once Eugene had returned to the field, grew pressing when Don Carlos' victory no longer could be doubted, and Spanish, French, and Sardinian troops stood deep in Lombardy. Eugene, who had not the heart to describe the decayed state of his army, responded with evasions. But his fear that the Russians' approach might be interfered with by the Bavarian elector instilled the hero of old, for the last time, with the courage needed to stand up to Charles VI.

Bavaria occupied the key position in Eugene's plan of pacification. Elector Charles Albert had been educated in Vienna, where he and his brother had been held as prisoners after the conquest of their father's land during the War of the Spanish Succession. Released when the treaties restored Bavaria to their dynasty, Charles Albert, young as he was, led the Bavarian contingent in Eugene's triumphal march on Belgrade. He later married the younger of the orphaned daughters of Joseph I. Although Charles VI had extorted from him an acknowledgment of the Pragmatic Sanction, the actual wording of that instrument made it valueless in practice. Eugene's memory may have been deteriorating, but he had not forgotten the age-old rivalry of the Bavarian house. Mindful of its sympathies for the Bourbons, and the menace it posed to the Arch House, he submitted to Charles VI a project which, in effect, would revoke his act of succession.

Although Eugene had tried to bias Charles against the Lorraine match upon meeting Francis, he had not in the eleven years since objected to his position at court. But neither had he ever been close to Francis. At the time of the duke's visit to England Jacquemin suggested a letter from his own hand to Eugene, which might be of help in making the emperor end Francis' peregrinations; the Lorrainer, for once wiser than Jaquemin, had thought such a letter useless. Nothing shows that Eugene ever talked to Francis, when he came to Vienna from Pressburg, about what the whole world knew was uppermost in his mind. Or to Theresa. Nevertheless, it must have been with a heavy heart that the old prince penned his plan and sent it off to Vienna.

Charles Albert had a son. Although only eight years of age, he should be betrothed to Theresa and declared co-heir to all Habsburg possessions. As soon as he was married to the archduchess, the Bavarian prince should be elected as King of the Romans—an act that in practice guaranteed the succession to the Empire's crown. His election, of this Eugene was certain, would find the wholehearted support of the French court, whose close connections with some of the electors were of no smaller import than the moneys it could distribute to them all.*

This, to us, is the moment when Theresa emerges from the mists of legend and conjecture that cloud the story of her adolescence. "She is a princess of the highest spirit," the British ambassador, Thomas Robinson, reported on July 5, 1735. "Her father's losses are her own. She reasons already. . . . She admires his virtues, but condemns his mismanagement; and is of a temper so formed for rule and ambition as to look at him as little more than her administrator. Notwithstanding this lofty humor by day, she sighs and pines all night for her duke of Lorraine. If she sleeps, it is only to dream of him; if she wakes, it is but to talk of him to the lady in waiting; so that there is no more probability of her forgetting the very individual government, and the very individual husband, which she thinks herself born to than [of] her forgiving the authors of [the danger of] her losing either."[2]

Charles VI had been talked to before about the imperial succession. Shortly after Francis' visit in England George II had touched on the matter and even offered his largesse to procure the Roman kingship to the Lorrainer upon his marriage to Theresa. In 1732 the emperor had still been of two minds about the union. He no longer was so in 1735. Yet he remained deaf to renewed hints from London.

An heir male, should one be born, would take precedence over Theresa within the Habsburg dominions; but the existence of a King of the Romans, duly elected before the birth of a Habsburg prince, would bar him from the Empire's crown. It was true that Charles no longer could hope for a son from his empress. She was past forty. Having grown fond of her regimen, she had put on so much weight, she barely could walk. Her health was miserable. But did not its very wretchedness send

* While a majority vote sufficed in the imperial election, the King of the Romans could be elected only unanimously.

Charles dreaming again of male issue? He had no reason to doubt that he could sire another brood of children, should Heaven end Elizabeth's life and make him decide on a second marriage. His father had married three times.

Eugene's revolutionary ideas were outdated as the summer of 1735 turned into autumn. The French had become suspicious of the intents of their Sardinian ally, and although the Russians had arrived on the Rhine, the emperor realized he could fight no longer. Peace preliminaries were signed in October. Don Carlos was to be recognized as King of the Two Sicilies and to relinquish the Parmese duchies, which he had been able to claim as his on the recent death of the last Parmese duke. The Polish crown, actually worn by Augustus for two years (after a Russian army cowed the Diet into compliance), was to remain on his head. His rival, Stanislas, once again in exile, would be compensated by Lorraine, and Bar incorporated into the French kingdom—as would Lorraine itself upon his demise. Francis was expected to forswear all rights to the duchy for himself and his heirs. He would be indemnified by the grand-ducal coronet of Tuscany on the death of Gian Gastone, the last of the Medici. A French guarantee of the Pragmatic Sanction was to follow the ratification of the treaty and its implementation.

The demand for Lorraine's cession was only one humiliation among many to Charles VI. To Francis it came as a fearful blow, even though he had not been blind to its approach. To stave it off, he had made several trips to Vienna from Pressburg. Walpole in his memoirs quotes a dispatch from Robinson's purple pen as follows: "In an audience which I demanded of him to announce the marriage of the Prince of Wales with the Princess of Saxe-Gotha, he interrupted me in the midst of compliments to pour out his joy at the marriage and his respect and veneration for the king, which he first expressed aloud. But, lest any of the attendants in the next room might overhear, he retreated to the window of an adjoining apartment, and said with the greatest emotion, 'Good God, where are you? where are the Maritime Powers? As for my part,' he continued, 'I rely upon the king singly, and not upon treaties; not upon formal promises, but upon what his majesty has told me over and over by word of mouth.'" It seems that George II had engaged in some brave talk with Francis in Walpole's absence. "If [the duke's] words expressed the highest agony and distress," Robinson went on, "his gestures and actions expressed no less: he threw himself in a reclining posture, and in an inconsolable manner, upon the arms and end of the adjoining table and chair. Such also is the extreme agitation of his mind that his health is affected by it. . . ."[3]

Even as a hailstorm of warnings descended on Francis from his mother's retreat at Commerçy, the emperor had resolved that Theresa's husband-to-be must bear what he himself could not avert. Moreover, he had begun to nurse the hope of recouping some of his losses at the expense of Turkey, which had been caught in a conflict with Russia. His treaty with the czarina obligated him to come to her assistance. It was high time to make peace with the French, the allies of old of the Porte, who were indeed doing mischief in Constantinople. Charles VI ordered the secretary to the Privy Conference,* Baron Bartenstein, to obtain Francis' renunciations of all sovereign rights in Lorraine.

John Christopher Bartenstein was at this time approaching the apex of a remarkable career. The son of a Protestant university teacher at Strasbourg, he had come to Vienna as the tutor to the children of a nobleman. Having attracted attention, and turned Catholic, he was hired by the Lower Austrian estates. His industry and knowledgeableness soon made him a person to watch. When the incumbent secretary to the Privy Conference started ailing in 1730, the chancellor put Bartenstein into that office. Its influence was bound to grow with the lagging spirit of the conference and Eugene's estrangement from the routine of its business.

Charles VI had not ceased cultivating his Spaniards, even after their counsel had got him in trouble. But he harbored few illusions about their worth as advisers. As for his ministers, he had reason aplenty to mistrust the integrity of most of them, along with their competence. His own vacillation, which sometimes turned him disingenuous, had long withered the independence of judgment in them all. His fascination with punctilio had always encumbered his day-to-day contacts with the conference. As, from the late twenties onward, he took to transacting much of his business with it in writing, he came to see reams of memorials and minutes from Bartenstein's hand. Their good, if long-winded, style appealed to Charles. He admitted the secretary to his presence and proceeded to receive him alone.

Advisers of humble birth were no novelty to Habsburg monarchs. The dynasty's peculiar relationship to the great landowning families made such educated commoners (as a rule immigrants from the Empire's non-Habsburg territory) valuable in the conduct of domestic affairs. Bartenstein's role was of a different nature. His legal training came in handy to Charles's growing pleasure in "perplexing his ministers."[4] He had a knack for gathering information, however trifling. He was incorruptible and discreet. His manners, when he stood before Charles, were dictated by flattery and obsequiousness. Unlike the conference members or the

* Originally the Privy Conference had been the executive committee of the Privy Council, a body comprising up to four scores of members. Under Charles' father the conference had grown to be the council of ministers—the cabinet, in a manner of speaking.

generals, he was without any class allegiance or regional roots. His arguments showed familiarity, however superficial or biased, with modern thought; and Charles, this embodiment of Habsburg tradition, was yet not insensitive to the lure of change and curious about its working in foreign parts. When he started to correspond with his envoys abroad over the heads of his ministers, he called upon Bartenstein to draft those communications. By 1735 the ubiquitous upstart, now a baron, had the unconditional trust of his master.

Deferential as Bartenstein was in the emperor's closet, even when enlarging on his views in the face of a master still to be won over to them, negotiators from abroad and cabinet ministers alike were wary of the self-righteousness of the powerful man. As one English diplomat related, Bartenstein "talked for near an hour without my being able to get in one word, though I endeavored several times to interrupt him."[5] Francis could not but dread the encounter with the baron. In fact, neither his charm nor his melancholy situation made the slightest impact on him. The brutal words with which Bartenstein cut him short were soon repeated in every court of Europe. "Your Highness," he was quoted as saying, "no cession—no archduchess."[6] And Francis, anything but tongue-tied by nature, was reported to have kept his counsel.

Theresa knew of his ordeal. "Only much later did I learn," she was to reminisce, "that Bartenstein singlehandedly foiled the Spanish marriage."[7] But in 1735 Bartenstein was evil incarnate to Theresa, and she showed her feelings. "She displays a marked awareness of her future station," wrote the Venetian ambassador, "and leaves people in no doubt that, once she has gained it, the men on whose advice she might call will not influence her decisions."[8]

Her formal education (if this is the word for the hours spent with her tutors) ended on the eighteenth birthday of the princess. The history lectures closed with a long chapter on her father, a "sovereign as majestic through his virtues and talents as any monarch can possibly be."[9] At the time the archduchess was made to listen to that sort of instruction, the church of St. Carlo Borromeo was as good as completed. She had been in swaddling clothes when its foundations were laid. But the "program" drawn up by a group of savants to go with the venturesome blueprints of J. B. Fischer von Erlach, the celebrated Styrian-born pupil of the aged Bernini, had been a pet topic of society talk while she was a child. That program had envisaged the twin columns flanking the church as an allusion to the Pillars of Hercules, "an apposite symbol for the true successor of Charles V, the Spanish Hercules,"[10] while the "drum" of the great cupola was to suggest the basic circlet of the Holy Empire's crown. If Theresa still recalled the "program"—Leibniz was said to have been one of its authors—she hardly could be insensitive to the ironical light her father's misfortunes had cast on those grand ideas. To be sure, her personal happiness left little room for somber thoughts.

On January 31, 1736, Duke Francis with great ceremony asked, first the emperor and then the empress, for the hand of their firstborn daughter.* "His Imperial Majesty answered the suit of the Duke in person, whereupon the latter directed his speech toward his fiancée, who, after looking at her mother and being given a nod, received from His Royal Highness a [miniature] portrait of his person, adorned with diamonds."[11] The next morning the Privy Council assembled, and Theresa solemnly swore that she would forego any right of succession should a son be born to Charles VI.

The wedding day having been set, Francis retreated to Pressburg again. Before leaving Vienna he signed and sealed a pledge not to advance any claims on his wife's patrimony, should she predecease him without issue.

Five letters that Theresa wrote him in the ten days during which protocol forbade him to appear at court have been preserved in Vienna. Her schooling has, in its own way, borne fruit: she uses three languages with evident ease, cavalier about spelling and syntax in each.†[12] As for the contents of these missives, allowance must be made for the baby talk, customary then as today, among young people on the threshold of marriage. The names of endearment Theresa uses prove that she and Francis—probably favored by Mme. Fuchs—could exchange some words out of their elders' earshot during the duke's visits.

The naïveté of her billets is surprising. Close to nineteen, Theresa was, as we have heard, a rather strong-willed young lady. Stressing her "submissive devotion" as she was, did not this "most faithful fiancée" try to gloss over the fact that her future dignities would set limits to wifely obedience? Francis' letters are far less informal than hers. The first of them referred stiffly to the "permission that His Majesty granted me to write to Your Highness."[13] The smooth style and correct spelling reveal the help he received from Dr. Pfütschner, who no doubt was in seventh heaven, with twelve years' vicissitudes overcome.

---

* To take a letter from Charles to Eugene at face value, Eugene, after the rejection of his Bavarian project, had advised the monarch "no longer to postpone my daughter's wedding." (A. R. von Arneth, *Prinz Eugen von Savoyen*, III, 610.)

† No translation could hope to do justice to these letters. This is the original text of one of them:

"caro viso, je vous suis infiniment obliges pour votre attention de m'ecrire de vos nouvelles, car j'etais en peine comme une pauvre chienne; aimez moi un peu et me pardonnez si je ne vous repons pas assez, mais c'est 10 heure et herbeville [the courier?] attende pour ma letter. adieu mäusl, je vous embrasse de tout mon coeur, menagez vous bien, adieu caro viso

je suis la votre
sponsia dilectissima.

Francis himself could not question the ardor of Theresa's feelings. In his twenty-ninth year, he must have been certain of his good looks and his attraction for women.* His mother had relented in one respect. Having originally enjoined her younger son, Charles, from going to Vienna for his brother's wedding—Bartenstein surely was planning to "cut the throat"[14] of Charles, as well as of Francis!—she now, giving way to the latter's entreaties, had dropped her objections. She equipped Charles with an extensive memorandum which not only forbade him to sign away his own claims to the Lorraine succession but also contained a last minute appeal to the emperor. Prince Charles, upon his arrival in Vienna, had some success. The monarch, impressed by the firmness of the young prince, directed Bartenstein to interrupt the negotiations about Lorraine's cession until after the wedding. Theresa's heart went out to her fiery brother-in-law.

The nuptials were celebrated on February 12, a Sunday. At six o'clock in the evening the cortege assembled in the Hofburg's spacious Knights' Hall, to advance down the new wide staircase and along the corridor that connected the Hofburg compound with the church of the Barefoot Augustinians. Imperial chamberlains in their scarlet garb and some Lorraine chamberlains led the procession. The privy counselors and the conference members followed, and behind them, the knights of the Golden Fleece in their medieval long robes.

The most illustrious of them was absent. He had come home in October, broken in spirit, senile in appearance, his speech impeded by a torturing cough, and barely able to stand on his feet. Did Charles VI, in this hour, recall the Prince Eugenio of an earlier day? Did he recall his warnings against all those dearly bought parchments that bore so many guarantees, or recognitions, or acknowledgments, of the Pragmatic Sanction? Did he remember Eugene's futile insistence on raising more troops and collecting higher taxes? We may surmise that the absence of the old servant failed to stir Charles's emotions. This curious man, who was to think of protocol even on his deathbed, surely was fully absorbed watching the solemn procession, with an eagle's eye checking its compliance with the hallowed ceremonial of the Arch House.

* Next to nothing is known about the private life of the bachelor. If he should have engaged in some dalliance in London, Neipperg made no mention of it. In Pressburg Dr. Pfütschner would not have stood for any nonsense. One anecdote, current in Vienna some months before the wedding, was more farcical than scandalous. Francis was supposed to have made amorous advances to one of three "odalisques" a Prince Trautson had brought to Vienna from the Balkans and was keeping in his summer palace; but, to believe gossip, the most unlikely of all lovers, the emperor's court dwarf, had displaced the duke in the favors of the exotic beauty. Some people wanted to know that Francis' involvement, however abortive, had hastened the monarch's decision to go ahead with the preparation for Theresa's engagement.

Preceded by four torch-bearing pages and accompanied only by the captain of halberdiers, he must have felt some satisfaction as his glance came to rest on the lord chamberlain of Lorraine, to the left of the bridegroom; whatever the duchy's ultimate fate, Francis' styles and titles would not be touched.

Although he had grown somewhat stout in Pressburg, the groom cut a fine figure, clad in cloth of silver, wearing a white hat with white plumes, and the heavy collar of the Golden Fleece. The bride, flanked by her obese mother and her aunt, Joseph I's widow, wore a gown of silver-thread fabric studded with diamonds and pearls. Mme. Fuchs, now mistress of the robes, carried the train. Theresa's sister followed at a distance. Some people pretended to know that the groom's brother—he was occupying a modest place in the wedding procession—did not displease the young archduchess. Neither Francis' mother nor his two sisters had come to Vienna.

The ancient church had been lit with thousands of candles, and the most splendid of the Flemish tapestries of the court had been hung to cover the sparsely adorned walls. As the cortege entered the church the bass viols and oboes of Charles's own orchestra struck up a tune composed by the famous Caldara. In the Loretto Chapel the papal nuncio was waiting to read out the breve that permitted him to officiate standing up. The pontiff's original wish to have his envoy remain seated in the emperor's presence had provoked violent protests on his part.

An ornate canopy had been put up for him and his empress facing the high altar. Before Theresa pronounced her *"volo,"* she turned toward the parents, who with a measured motion of the head expressed their consent. Bride and groom exchanged rings, and the nuncio blessed their hands joined beneath his stole. After celebrating the nuptial mass he himself intoned the *Te Deum.* But the horns and kettledrums drowned the chant, along with all of the city's bells, which were tolling, and the guns that on the bastions were firing the salute. The town militia, defying the bitter cold in the street, discharged three salvos. Their uneven performance elicited much hilarity in the crowd.

At the banquet, with the imperial family dining in state, Charles of Lorraine shocked the empress by bantering with one of the ladies waiting on her. It was bruited about that the incident had amused Theresa. The following day a performance of Metastasio's *Achille in Sciro,* complete with ballet and new stage machinery, was marveled at copiously. The production reminded older people of all the glamour of such affairs during the 1690's. Because Lent was approaching, the consummation of *la grande affaire de Lorraine* was celebrated for two days only. On the third day the ducal couple set out on a pilgrimage to Maria Zell to deposit two life-sized golden hearts at the feet of the Virgin.

They were given an apartment in the Leopoldian Wing, as good as next door to the Retirada. An allowance of twenty thousand florins had been pledged to their household. The first payment could be made only after the Vienna City Bank had granted the emperor a loan without security. By that time his agents had for two years been traveling the length and the breadth of Europe in search of short-term money. Whatever collateral might be acceptable to potential lenders was exhausted.

The wedding had not interrupted the frantic attempts of Francis' mother to dissuade him from renouncing his ancestral duchy. His brother was stiffening the duke's backbone and trying to impress the cause of his dynasty on Charles VI. The emperor did not remain unmoved. He had his chancellery inquire of the French whether his son-in-law could not be spared the indignity of a formal cession until after the death of the Tuscan ruler. Fleury treated the suggestion with scorn and even threatened to resume hostilities on the Rhine. Charles directed Bartenstein to take up his assignment again and carry it through with dispatch. To sweeten the bitter pill, he had prevailed on the court of Madrid to withdraw its rump garrison from Florence.

Francis did not do justice to Charles's determination. In the glow of his honeymoon, he flattered himself that as His Majesty's son-in-law he could deal with a respectful Bartenstein and might succeed where he had failed as the archduchess' cornered suitor. He was in for a sorry surprise. There was no end to the widespread talk, some of it gleeful, about his tempestuous interview with the implacable secretary. According to one account Bartenstein three times pressed the quill on Francis, who three times flung it down before signing the instrument of surrender.

To salve the hurt pride of the landless prince—and also to lighten the court's financial burden—the emperor, in a secret message, promised the Belgian governorship to Francis. Less unequivocal was Charles's promise "not to dispose of my . . . daughter, Maria Anne" contrary to the idea of making "so to speak, one family of my Arch House and the House of Lorraine."[15]

The conference were afraid that Francis' residence in Brussels, comparatively close to the ceded duchy, might provoke the French to advance new demands in the dragged-out peace negotiations; and Bartenstein managed to postpone the duke's appointment from one month to the next. It would seem that the young couple were not themselves impatient to go to Belgium. And in July, 1737, Gian Gastone suddenly died in Florence. Some weeks afterwards Maria Theresa, Grand Duchess of Tuscany, was delivered of her first child. It was a girl.

Word of both events came to Francis on the Turkish frontier. During the Rhine campaign there had been more than a few whispers about his presumed disinclination to join Eugene's army. Whether or not that criticism prompted him to volunteer for the Turkish war, Francis had done so; and he and his brother departed from Vienna on June 10 with the proper retinue and a huge train of baggage, which included arm-chairs of the kind due their royal rank.

Eugene had died on April 21 of the foregoing year, freeing Charles VI of the last shadow of a warning finger. Returning from the state funeral, he jotted down in his journal: "Now, see, everything will be better organized."[16] The emperor could have done his duty by the czarina with the dispatch of an auxiliary corps. He chose to fight a cam-paign of his own. He stood in need of new glory and also was appre-hensive lest a Russian victory thwart his intentions in the Balkans. The freshly assembled army was not badly equipped. Thanks to some new loans the court had succeeded in raising, the troops had been paid part of the arrears, and their morale, as seen from Vienna, was good.

To lead them, Charles picked Seckendorf, whose long service in Ber-lin had kept him aloof from the dissensions rending the generals' corps. In a minor engagement on the Rhine Seckendorf also had vindicated the repute earned in the field a lifetime earlier. Apparently Bartenstein did not give voice to his feelings about the appointee, whose diplomatic activities at the Prussian court had been a source of annoyance to him. Charles VI, however, could not possibly ignore the misgivings with which his new generalissimo, a Lutheran, was looked upon in Vienna, down to its common people.

He had acquired a sound respect for military preparedness at Fred-erick William's court. In one of his first reports from the field he de-scribed the deplorable state of the fortifications, the corruption in ord-nance, and the poor care devoted to the rank and file. These "melancholy circumstances . . . portend the loss of these fine kingdoms with the same rapidity as the states of Italy."[17] By the time the two Lorraine princes arrived and began shooting bear in the frontier forests, a thrust into enemy territory had bogged down. Francis tried to mediate between the quarreling generals. Having failed, he asked for permission to return to Vienna.

Charles proposed that his son-in-law take himself to Florence to look into his grand duchy's affairs. Francis demurred. Tuscany's business was in the hands of Craon, that old confidant of the house of Lorraine.* Theresa's husband did not intend to miss his chance in the service of

---

* "Duke Leopold, walking abroad in the meadows one day, saw a buxom girl in a field driving turkeys. . . . In a week the thoroughly washed and decked beauty was lolling from one of the windows of the ducal palace. . . . This lady was after-wards married to M. de Beauvou, and for their respective services they became [through an act of the emperor] Prince and Princess de Craon." (Dr. Doran, " 'Mann' and Manners at the Court of Florence, 1740–86," I, 12.)

her dynasty. There lay his future, and there he must anchor his hope for the Roman kingship. The emperor kept avoiding that subject. But he did, late in the year, swear Francis to the Privy Conference and even gave him its chair should he himself be prevented from presiding. The empress was said to have had a hand in that advancement of the grand duke, who was brooding over his abortive venture in the war. He never had had any military training. But military talent, and certainly stamina, were taken for granted in princes.

Seckendorf, blamed for negligence, accused of peculation in certain quarters and of treachery in some others, had been relieved of command and was held in confinement in his mansion in Vienna. The man put in charge of operations was Count Lothar Königsegg, president of the Hof-kriegsrat since Eugene's death, and as such a conference member also. Eugene had had a weak spot for the imposing-looking, high-living man, the repute of whose gifts as a commander, originating in young Charles's army in Spain, had survived a crushing defeat suffered in the course of the recent Italian campaign. Charles VI must have thought highly of him, for, simultaneously with the appointment, he made Francis general-issimo of the army in the field.

It took the offensive on July 4. Sanguine accounts quick to reach Vienna prompted Francis' Lorrainers to talk about him as a second Prince Eugenio. In fact, his personal bravery was attested to even by generals prone to look down upon him. In their discussions at head-quarters, to be sure, he was as a babe in the woods, and just as confused as they were by the ever-changing instructions issued by the Hofkriegsrat. Finding his health affected, the grand duke withdrew as far as Ofen to recuperate.

With ammunition lacking, and the army ridden by dysentery, it could not withstand the counteroffensive launched by the Turks. The bewilderment rife in Königsegg's councils emboldened the enemy. The growing élan of the Turks turned the retreat into a rout. Francis, back from his rest cure, wrote, after a mere five days, to his father-in-law: "I have no alternative to reporting that I am full of sorrow at my being unable to accomplish that which one may have believed in and hoped for. . . . I implore Your Majesty to consider what kind of figure I am cutting. I am at a loss to describe how deeply I feel Your Majesty's situation. . . ."[18] The grand duchess "knows full well what is going on,"[19] wrote the Sardinian ambassador.

Francis returned to Vienna, as thoroughly beaten a general as the publicum cared to remember. As they chose to see it, he above all men was to blame for the debacle. His fair-minded efforts to shield Königsegg from a court-martial made him doubly the culprit. Even the year before, the favored treatment accorded the most inept of Seckendorf's sub-

commanders, one of the *Reich's* princelings by name of Saxe-Hildburghausen, had been laid on the doorstep of the emperor's son-in-law.

Stories about Francis' breaches of etiquette had, in their time, amused
common people. His long courtship, and what became known of its
tribulations, had made for an enjoyable love tale. The Viennese had
shown some affection for him at the time of the wedding. They had
been willing to forget that the beloved of the archduchess, even though
worsted himself by the French, was something of a Frenchie. Public
opinion had begun changing, however, shortly after he moved in at the
Hofburg. Contrary to expectations, he had not dismissed his Lorraine
entourage. More and more of such hangers-on, men out of bread in the
ceded duchy, were coming to Vienna; and while the special talents of
some of them became the butt of scorn on the part of easygoing civil
servants, the frivolity of most grew to be a topic of disapproving talk
among townsfolk. Now they spread it about that the disaster on the
Turkish frontier had lowered the grand duke's prestige in the Hofburg
immensely. The emperor was rumored to consider betrothing Theresa's
sister to the Bavarian boy prince and altering the succession. Such was
the temper of the public that a contingent of Bavarian auxiliaries marching through Vienna was hailed with cheers for their sovereign, Charles
Albert.

Francis had never lacked hostile critics high up, even outside the
camarilla. Jaquemin had been too much in appearance all along. His
insistence on Francis' royal title had annoyed many a great lord even
long before the duchy's cession made twice a mockery of that style.
Francis' own informality rubbed courtiers the wrong way. He talked too
much and too often showed his emotions. He gesticulated and tended
to grimace. Unlike other men of exalted lineage and spotty education, he
did not put up pretenses and thereby invited gibes at his "illiteracy."
After he came into the Tuscan heritage men in the know wondered
why he continued to draw on the court's bounty instead of living on the
revenue of his own grand duchy.* Such and similar talk had, via clerks
and footmen and grooms, seeped down to the lower classes. Their whis-
pering campaign had gained momentum at the time Theresa went into
her second confinement.

The newborn was a girl, and a weak thing, at that. So openly did
the Viennese accuse Francis of failing in the conjugal bed, as well as
on the field of battle, that Charles VI, a ruler rarely impressed by the
publicum's mood, decided to humor it. During the open-air performance

---

* In fact, the Tuscans, who knew only too well of the flood of money siphoned
to Vienna from Naples, had not hesitated to vent their fears on that score. The grand
duke had assured them that he did not expect his new subjects to support his
establishment in Vienna.

of a farce, such as was customary upon a nativity in the Hofburg, he had a hundred doves released, each carrying a ribbon with a rhymed message that predicted the arrival of boys in his daughter's home. Her fertility, the doggerel implied, left nothing to desire. The prophecy did Francis no good. At best he was derided among common people, who, at worst, called him a fortune hunter who with his French wiles had wormed his way into the Arch House. His situation became so uncomfortable, Charles up and bundled him off, together with Theresa, on a midwinter trip to Florence barely six weeks after her *accouchement*. The baby archduchess and her sister were left in their grandparents' care as the party, which included Francis' brother, set out, taking the fine southern highway which Charles had built in the days of his dreams of world commerce.

Christmas was spent on the road. The estates of the lands through which the couple journeyed made little fuss about them. An unpleasant surprise awaited the travelers at the border of Venice: out of thoughtlessness—or, as Theresa presumed, through spite on Bartenstein's part—the chancellery had not obtained exemption from the quarantine regulations of the republic. The emperor's daughter and her consort had to spend a fortnight in an ill-heated villa near Verona cordoned off by a picket of mounted soldiers. Not until January 20 did Grand Duke Francis III and his wife enter Florence.

He was handed its keys at a triumphal arch whose stonework was still surrounded by scaffolds, such short notice had been given of his journey. The archbishop received the couple in front of the cathedral. The *Te Deum* over, they were escorted to the Palazzo Pitti by the high magistrates of the city and a delegation of the Tuscan nobles.

Directly after the demise of Gian Gastone, his sister, the widowed Electress Palatine, had been offered Tuscany's regency by Francis. Next, after the lady had declined the honor, he had informed his subjects that the grand duchy was not part of the Habsburg possessions, and hence, the succession not regulated by the Pragmatic Sanction. It was the emperor's pleasure that Francis' second son, unborn as yet (as was the first) should establish a dynasty of his own.

The public festivities following the entry of the grand duke, from an illumination of the town to a *calcio* match on the Piazza Sta. Croce some days later, amused the grand duke, as such affairs always would. Having escaped a hostile Vienna, he and Theresa did not at first sense the discontent beneath the colorful welcoming program.

Judging by the emperor's letters to his son-in-law (which have survived), the grand duke, in his own (which have not), mentioned none of the problems that Craon step by step brought to his notice. It appears to have been an exclusively personal and even chummy correspondence. There is Charles reporting on "the two little angels who, Heaven be praised, are well,"[20] and expressing the hope that Francis will "bring us a third one inside the mother, to be unwrapped here"; or, with the worldliness of the traveled man, delighting in the imagined amazement of "our Viennese at the sight of the sea . . . [which] my Mutz, too, must have seen by now,"[21] or speaking of his "greatest solace," namely, his conviction that "my daughter is in such good hands."[22] She obviously was in the hands of a very amorous husband. "I wish no greater misfortune should ever befall you. . . ." wrote Charles upon learning that the young couple's bed had collapsed one night. "God willing, this break-down contributed toward creating something whole and new, for a few pleasant *casus* must have preceded it. . . . Only *moderato*. . . . No overdoing. Bide your time."[23] Not once did the emperor touch on Francis' misfortunes on the Turkish frontier or the opprobrium they had brought him, however unfairly.

The idea of proving statesmanship in Florence attracted Francis. Gian Gastone, though literally confining himself to his bedroom and the unsavory capers enacted in it with his low-class minions, had not been the idiot foreign courts had thought him to be. A streak of Medici shrewdness had enabled him to pay off some of his debts even while he lowered taxes, or to protect the Greek, Armenian, and Jewish merchants of Leghorn after its enforced free-port status confronted them with new issues. Still, the population by and large lived in great poverty, and it was on Francis' instance that the public pawnbroker's shop was compelled to reduce its interest rate. Trying to win over the patricians, he established a boarding school for their boys on the model of an old Lorraine institution. But that sense of activity did not last. It never would in Francis.

One would love to know how Theresa felt among the sophisticated, lascivious society of Florence or how she bore the company of Mme. Craon, whose *faux-pas* afforded the nobility unending pleasure. Alas, the records fail our curiosity. "Italy . . . at first amused me a little,"[24] wrote Maria Theresa a great many years later. We know that she attended some dances and concerts and at one of these parties sang a duet with the famous *castrato*, Senosio. Perhaps her evident innocence disarmed the superciliousness of her hosts. Her way of dressing or her coiffure can hardly have matched the modishness of their wives. Such jewelry as the empress may have lent Theresa for the Tuscan sojourn must have seemed mediocre to the Florentine ladies.*

The antiquated town made no impression on her. When the em-

---

* On the morrow of their entry, she and Francis called on the electress Palatine, who showed them the Medici jewels, including a 139-carat diamond, the storied "Florentine." "That was kind of her," remarked Charles in a letter to Francis, adding, in a surprisingly coarse vein: "All the more commendable was your *moderation* in that you refrained from asking her to hand over the family gems." (F. Hennings, *Und sitzet ihr zur linken Hand; Franz Stephan von Lothringen*, 198.)

peror wrote about "those many beautiful paintings" in the Pitti palace, he recommended them to the attention not of his daughter but of her husband, "for Your Highness are a connoisseur."[25] Bustling Leghorn aroused Theresa's interest as little as did the olive groves and cypresses of the countryside. More than a decade afterward she said that she "would have been glad to be just the grand duchess of Tuscany, if I had thought that God so willed it."[26] It was a remark designed to discredit her reputation as a power-hungry ruler rather than a nostalgic remembrance. The authoritarian queen regnant did not cherish the memory of her tacit exclusion from affairs in Florence. However, this kind of jealousy lay still far in the future in the spring of 1739. And farther still lay the sad knowledge that *"le fol amour se dissipe bientôt."*[27] She was very much in love with her handsome Francis.

Prince Charles was unhappy in Florence. He did not give a hoot for the Tuscan succession guaranteed him should Francis die without having fathered "a second son." He had greater fish to fry. The rumors that linked Maria Anne's name to the Bavarian heir seemed to have some substance. Not only did the prince pine to be back in Vienna and remind the emperor of what the Lorraine brothers regarded as a commitment (Charles, in fact, seems to have departed from Florence some time ahead of the grand-ducal couple), he also wanted Theresa to talk, on the spot, to her father; and the grand duchess, convinced that her sister would find happiness by the side of her brother-in-law, was herself anxious to further his cause. She too grew impatient. And early in March the court in Florence got word of another Turkish campaign being mapped in Vienna and of new generals about to be appointed as its leaders.

Charles VI had been careful to prevent the sojourn in Florence from being branded exile; he had left its duration to the grand duke's pleasure. Yet, replying to his offer to take the field again, the emperor proposed that his son-in-law spend the summer in the grand duchy and devote himself to its business. Moreover, an epidemic had broken out on the Turkish frontier, and why "tempt the Almighty . . . [with] bravour" which surely could "not fight malignant fevers"?[28]

Francis, nothing daunted, apprised the emperor of his impending departure. On April 27 he took his leave from the electress Palatine. Theresa, who was pregnant, now disliked returning to Vienna. "I was in tears," she wrote more than forty years later to one of her daughters traveling in those parts. "To be sure, we were setting out to fight the Turks, the plague, and [a] famine."*[29] But though having her Francis exposed to that threefold peril frightened Theresa, as no doubt did the

* Crops had been poor in 1738 throughout central Europe.

danger of his failing again as a soldier, she did not object to his brave decision. She still was a docile wife.

Travel arrangements foresaw her going to Milan without Francis. He wished to voyage by ship to Genoa, journey from there to Turin for a visit with his sister, the Queen of Sardinia, and rejoin Theresa in Milan. As the Sardinian king had not recognized the Pragmatic Sanction, Charles VI deemed it not suitable for his heiress to call upon him. Thus Francis bid Theresa goodbye at the triumphal arch and was off to Leghorn. But the sight of the choppy sea deterred him from carrying out his resolve. Having changed the itinerary, he overtook Theresa on the highway to Milan. From there he journeyed to Turin, while she was waiting for his return.

In Innsbruck, where the travelers arrived on May 15, she met her mother-in-law. The dowager duchess and her daughter had come all the way to the Tyrol from Commerçy.* Even though the duchess was far from reconciled to the cession—the Polish usurper was holding court in Nancy with a glitter such as the true Lorraine dynasty had never displayed—she spent an apparently pleasant week with Francis and his wife in Innsbruck. Theresa "treated her with the greatest reverence."[30]

A somewhat rickety craft brought the couple down the Inn and Danube rivers. There was little ceremony at their disembarkation, and they were driven to Laxenburg Lodge without entering the city. Charles VI and his empress welcomed them at the lodge with the "two little angels."

Francis lost no time pressing his desire for the command of the army. The emperor declined. According to Robinson, he had granted "an interview . . . to the Elector of Bavaria"[31] even before the return of Francis, who soon was exposed to hearsay about the part that that cousin by marriage of Theresa's was expected to play in the campaign. While that story mortified Francis, the subsequent actual choice of a commander amounted to a slap in the face. For not only had the appointee, Count Oliver Wallis, engaged him in heated discussions during the past year's campaign, it also was not least Wallis' talk that had blackened Francis' name in the officers' corps.

Had he been a gleeful man he might have felt some satisfaction reading Wallis' reports from the field, which appeared to give the lie to his reputation as an experienced soldier. Their gloom was unmitigated. Premature news of Belgrade's encirclement, reaching Vienna in the first days of August, bore out Wallis' forebodings. The Hofkriegsrat was close to panic, and the conference ministers blamed one another for

---

* Louis XV had given her seigniorial rights in that patch of land. At the same time, he had settled seigniorial annuities on her son Charles and Princess Charlotte.

having failed to dissuade the sovereign from starting the war to begin with.

As Wallis became known to consider Belgrade's surrender, Charles VI curtailed his powers. He recalled Baron Samuel Schmettau from the retirement into which he had forced him, along with some others of Königsegg's subcommanders, and ordered him to "use the utmost diligence to ... assume the defense of Belgrade, and save it, if not too late, from falling into the hands of the enemy."[32] But no sooner had Schmettau taken up his duties, stiffened Wallis' backbone, and begun raising the morale of the ranks by bringing up reinforcements than Neipperg arrived from Vienna, empowered to examine the chance of preliminaries.

Afterwards the extent of his authority became a matter of passionate controversy. On the eve of his departure from Vienna a large crowd had assembled in front of his mansion, shouting out their alarm. There was cholera in the town, the cost of living kept rising, and the populace in their imagination saw the dreaded Turks already at the gates of their city. Perhaps the incident had unnerved Neipperg.

Overriding Schmettau's objections—and probably also deluding him—Neipperg walked into the Turks' camp without having required hostages, only to be received with contempt by the grand vizier, spat upon, and put under guard. The French plenipotentiary to the Turkish commander rescued him from further indignities and dangers, and Neipperg rushed into signing the preliminaries that were presented to him. They had been drawn up by the Frenchman. By their terms all the Habsburg holdings in Bosnia, Serbia, and Wallachia were lost, besides Belgrade; and as if to force the emperor's hand, Neipperg defied Schmettau's vehement protests, ordering the troops to withdraw from the southern sector of the fortress. Instructions from Vienna warning Neipperg against any commitments had failed to reach him in time. Or so he said after having signed away the proudest of Eugene's conquests.

When the news came to Vienna the populace rose in a fury. Turkey had been their enemy for two centuries. To them Eugene's fame rested on his having banished the Turkish menace. An army song celebrating his grand assault on Belgrade had become something like an anthem. Oblivious to their own clamor for peace, the Viennese were maddened by its price and by accounts of the confusion amid which it had been paid. Moreover, a premature frost had destroyed the harvest in Lower Austria, and famine seemed imminent. A mob assaulted Bartenstein's house, and Aloysius Wöber, the virtual master of the Hofkriegsrat, barely escaped being lynched. Dragoons were called out to quell the tumults.

Looking for bigger scapegoats, the *publicum* turned their wrath on Francis again. As Neipperg had been close to him since his adolescence, even sober-minded men accused him of complicity in the alleged treachery of the general. It was said that the grand duke and his wife had sent secret instructions to Neipperg in Belgrade, countermanding in advance whatever new orders he might receive from the emperor. "The only event we can pin our hope on is the birth of a prince," one of Francis' gentlemen wrote to a fellow Lorrainer in Florence. "The situation might change once people have such an object to fasten their loyalty on."[33] On January 12 the grand duchess gave birth to another princess.

By that time Charles's ambassador to the Porte had signed the treaty of peace on the terms of the preliminaries. Wallis and Neipperg had each been confined to a fortress. The emperor, writing to a general who had tried to save Belgrade by a diversion—and who had the further distinction of ancient lineage—no longer used the art of *disimular*. "Not only my dignity, prestige, and loving and trust [in Wallis and Neipperg] have been dealt such a heavy blow, but, what is the worst, my honor and conscience, as well."[34] The Russian court considered itself the victim of desertion. Its generals claimed that their attempts at concerting operations had been frustrated by the ineptness of Charles's commanders; and Neipperg's surrender of Belgrade seemed to have robbed the Russians of the fruits of victories in their own theater of war. Robinson reported that the emperor, in an audience granted the ambassador of the czarina, "appeared under the pressure of the deepest affliction."[35] Abrogating the preliminaries had been out of the question, Charles woefully wrote to the czarina herself. Bartenstein, in an attempt to stem the precipitous decline of his court's prestige, sent a circular note to the envoys abroad— "a jumble of jarring facts."[36]

The French, who had maneuvered themselves into the role of mediator with Turkey, chose this moment to sign at long last the treaty of peace. Their guarantee of the Pragmatic Sanction was Charles's only gain. Fleury flaunted his triumph in Vienna. On his orders, his envoy complained that Grand Duke Francis was hatching with Robinson some intrigue against France.

It was true that the British statesmen, with their nation at war again with the Spanish crown, looked with grave misgivings at the French ascendancy in Vienna. But if Robinson really thought that Francis could be of any help, he was mistaken. Conference meetings had become rare; and, next to Königsegg, the grand duke, much against his nature, was the least loquacious of the members present. Charles, still the "loyal old father, the daddy"[37] he had called himself in one of his missives to Florence, treated him still with great affability. Discuss affairs, he did not. Small wonder Robinson vented his frustration in angry reports. In a note to Walpole he declared that "everything in this court is running into the last confusion and ruin, where there are as visible signs of folly and madness as ever were inflicted upon a people whom Heaven is determined to destroy, no less by domestic divisions than by the more public calamities of repeated defeats, defenselessness, poverty, and plague."[38]

"It never pleased my father's Majesty," Maria Theresa was to recall with a bitterness barely tempered by filial love, "to have me present when he transacted business, domestic or foreign. Neither did he ever tell me what had been transacted."[39] Considering the queen regnant's fascination with work and her tirelessness, one is at a loss to picture her daily life in those years. The day-to-day problems in the nursery can scarcely have taken much of her time. She may have listened more patiently than she would later to her husband. Sometimes she accompanied him on the hunt, following the party in a carriage, or turned up at some of the target-shooting parties that her mother, for all her physical complaints, was still partial to. Wagenseil came to practice music with her. She had a game of faro at night with her ladies-in-waiting, although the stakes must have been modest. Religious observances were of course time-consuming. She did not read any books. There were few people she could have corresponded with. A Countess Edling, who had been in the service of the empress for sixteen years—Maria Theresa still addressed her as "my dearest, best, and oldest friend."[40] in a letter of 1766—had moved to Italy in 1739; she may well have been the recipient of some billets from the grand duchess.

Her isolation grew. The great nobles all but paraded their indifference toward the heiress, on top of the low opinion they held of her consort. Their wives shunned her. "As long as the emperor was alive," she recalled as late as 1762, "no one so much as looked at me. . . ."[41] In March, 1740, her firstborn daughter was carried away by the smallpox. Her death affected the emperor beyond ordinary grief.

No one will ever know how clearly he realized the low estate to which his reputation in Europe had sunk or whether he blamed himself for its decay. During the first Turkish campaign he had been heard to exclaim: "Has then our lucky star completely disappeared with the death of Eugene?"[42] There was a trace of the old jealousy in that groan, along with a fatalism unimaginable in the stubborn young king in Barcelona, or even in Ripperdá's dupe. A profound melancholy had seized Charles VI since the disaster of Belgrade.* It cast upon him the shadows of the "dark Habsburgs," those brooding princes marked by the heritage from the insane Spanish mother of Charles V. For all practical purposes the

---

* "In Charles' very last years some amorous involvement of his appears to have existed. It is referred to only in code in his diary." (Oswald Redlich, "Die Tagebücher Kaiser Karl VI," in *Gestamtdeutsche Vergangenheit*, Festgabe für Heinrich Ritter von Srbik, Munich, 1938. 141–51.)

Maria Theresa at six or seven years of age

The fifteen-year-old Archduchess

The fianceé

The Queen of Hungary dressed for a
masked ball

The Queen of Hungary & Script.

1742.   Indiana Sc.

government was in Bartenstein's hands. "The most secret orders . . ." Robinson wrote to Lord Harrington, "[issue] out of the imperial cabinet through the hands of Bartenstein, Wöber, and, it is said, one Carl Dier, formerly a common halberdier and doorkeeper, and now a kind of private pursekeeper. . . ."*43

Bartenstein, in his aversion to the Maritime Powers, made no attempt to revive the connection with Britain. Yet Britain alone might have reined the French diplomacy in the *Reich*, even though Hanover's lingering dispute with Prussia had thwarted the hope of uniting the Protestant princes against those sinister encroachments. The death, in April, 1740, of the Prussian king generated some optimism in Vienna.

His son Frederick II was thought well of in the Hofburg. Veterans of the Rhine campaign remembered him as a courteous and high-spirited, if somewhat volatile, young man. Charles had it from Eugene that "a great deal depends on winning the prince, who one day can make more friends in the world than his father has. . . ."44 To be sure, Seckendorf had not been equally certain of the prince's talent for winning true friends himself; but Seckendorf, demoted and disgraced, was the last man whose views Charles would have put stock in. According to the latest accounts of Charles's resident at Berlin, Frederick had been discharging his officer's duties to the satisfaction of his ailing father. He had still been versifying. He had struck up a friendship with Voltaire and written a philosophical treatise said to be ready for publication in Holland. While neglecting his wife, if treating her with civility, he did not seem devoid of the qualities of a cavalier. His fellow musician Charles VI did not look down upon his modish hobbies and may even have felt some admiration for Frederick's learnedness. He was convinced that his own intercession with Frederick William a decade earlier had not fallen in oblivion with the son. Moreover, the Prussian heir had been the recipient of a generous allowance from Charles behind the back of the miserly king. The emperor also knew of the friendly letters Francis had been exchanging with Frederick during the Hungarian governorship.

He was pleased to learn that the new ruler was disbanding the giants' battalion of his father. He was less pleased by reports on the unceremonious manner of Frederick's assuming power and his refusal to have himself anointed. The style of "King of the Prussians" Frederick adopted without even informing him beforehand was another unpleasant sur-

---

* Upon Dier's death, in 1756, Maria Theresa's lord marshal noted in his diary: "This man occupied, as it were, the position of a *petit favorit* [sic] with the late master. . . . On his deathbed [Charles VI] not only recommended him with great warmth to the present sovereigns, but also ordered that he must not be asked to render accounts, and set up for him a legacy of fl. 100,000. . . . Dier's estate is estimated to amount to fl. 500,000." (Khevenhüller, December 19, 1756.)

prise for Charles.* When the young king, to force the settlement of an old dispute with a neighboring prince bishop, sent half a regiment into his territory, the emperor was shocked and demanded that those troops be withdrawn forthwith. Frederick, his aggression having accomplished its purpose, did not reply to the imperial "*dehortatorium.*" The Empire's chancellery was not alone in wondering about the course he might chart for himself.

In London his father had had the worst possible reputation. The size of Frederick William's military establishment had been loathsome to all informed men, his disgraceful clash with the crown prince had branded him a monster, and his rejection of the marriage proposals had kept rankling. Frederick, on the other hand, had been considered a prince "adorned with every virtue";[45] thus at least he had been dubbed in a widely read book printed in 1738. Some months after his accession the British ambassador reported that Frederick very much wished to see Anglo-Prussian relations improved. He "would proceed entirely on a new bottom,"[46] that diplomat quoted him as saying six weeks later. The men in Whitehall did not think these words were necessarily reassuring. Once again, George II drew Charles's attention to the imperial succession and again offered to predispose the electoral college in favor of Francis' election as King of the Romans.

Nothing could be less welcome to Charles than the reopening of that question. Theresa was pregnant again. Should she give birth to a boy, the act of succession would make this prince heir to the Habsburg dominions—and in due course, the electors' natural choice for the Roman kingship. Time was not pressing. Even though Charles was prone to speak of "those many years that one year took out of me,"[47] his lowness of spirit did not appear to be harming his health. He was as nimble a huntsman as ever and as little likely to tire in the saddle as he had been while campaigning in Spain.

His fifty-fifth birthday was celebrated on October 1 in the illuminated park of the New Favorita. For the first time since Theresa's homecoming she and her sister had taken parts in a musical drama. Their father seemed to enjoy it with some of his old abandon. There were fireworks late at night, and these too gave some pleasure to the monarch. But common people, so decidedly given as a rule to a vicarious participation in the court's amusements, even in times of stress, did not trouble to hide their ill humor. Irreverent talk was overheard at public fountains running wine, and the imprisoned generals were discussed with pointed

---

* His grandfather, Elector Margrave of Brandenburg, had been given the title "King *in* Prussia" by Leopold in 1701 in return for his delivery of ten thousand auxiliaries during the War of the Spanish Succession. (The dynasty's East Prussia was separated from the margraviate by Polish-owned West Prussia.) In Eugene's opinion the emperor "should have hanged the person who advised him to sanction Prussia's claim to become a kingdom." (N. Henderson, *Prince Eugen of Savoy*, 271.)

pity. Wild tales about conflicts in the court had been making the rounds of taverns and coffeehouses for several months, acquiring urgency in the process. They had played into the hands of Bavarian agents, who abounded both in Vienna and in the countryside of Upper Austria, Bavaria's neighbor.

Five days after the birthday party Charles had an attack of the "flying gout."[48] Yet he would not hear of postponing his customary shooting sojourn at Halbthurn, a lodge just across the Hungarian border. The empress, defying her ills, went with him, and so did both daughters. Francis, that "dearest hunting companion," remained in Vienna.

While stalking a deer before nightfall of October 9 the emperor caught a cold. Returning to the lodge, he asked for a favorite dish of his, mushrooms stewed in Catalan oil. He took three helpings. In the small hours he started vomiting. It was decided to transport him to Vienna. He suffered several fainting spells in the traveling coach. Having been brought to a manor whose lord was absent, Charles asked to see Theresa. At the sight of his distorted face the grand duchess nearly fainted herself and was barely able to reach for one of the chairs in the ill-lit room. As her husband was to relate, the emperor gave her his blessing and then waved her away.

On reaching Vienna he demanded to be taken to the New Favorita. The effect of the news on nobility and townsfolk was such that the Venetian ambassador signaled to his senate: "It can be foreseen only too clearly that this mighty Monarchy will face dissolution."[49] But Charles rallied.

On the morning of the fourteenth he started retching again and vomiting bile. Visibly wracked by pains, he nevertheless showed a keenness of mind that amazed all those who had been so many witnesses to his lethargy throughout the past months. His composure surprised no one; the last of the Habsburg princes had always been a fearless man and a believer bowing to God's will even as He denied him the most passionate of his wishes.

His surgeons bled Charles many times and purged him profusely. His physicians were helpless. "Stop squabbling about what the trouble might be," he told them in a flash of the dry humor that had sometimes baffled his entourage in less grievous hours. "You will open my body soon, and find out. But then one of you had better make haste to catch up with me in the hereafter to tell me."[50] He also asked to be shown the receptacle in which his heart would be encased.* The small size of the silver vessel astounded the monarch.

* The encased heart of every Habsburg prince was deposited at the Loretto Chapel of the Augustinian church. His silver-encapsuled entrails were turned over to St. Stephen's.

The empress scarcely budged from his bedside, and he was heard calling her "my White Liz." Maria Anne came to receive his blessing. On the doctors' advice, Theresa was not admitted to the sickroom. With Francis the emperor remained closeted for two hours. When the grand duke's brother was allowed in he could not hold back his tears. The moribund man did not confirm him, in so many words, as Maria Anne's betrothed. "Do not lament," he said, ambiguous to the last, "even though, it is true, you are about to lose a loyal friend."[51]

Bartenstein, carrying an armful of papers, was received several times. It would appear that Charles did not summon any of his Spanish exiles; but as they fell into disgrace after his death, the records may have been tampered with. To his old treasury secretary the emperor dictated a document that should ensure an independent income to his widow. And then, in a last will and testament, he once more confirmed the validity of the Pragmatic Sanction. Was the breach of his father's act of succession haunting the moribund Charles?

On the eighteenth he bid adieu to the conference ministers one by one, talking clearly even as his powers were sinking. When his dwarf was called in the following day to kiss hands—he had been with him since the journey to the court of Queen Anne—the power of speech seemed to have left Charles forever. But as the priest, coming shortly before midnight of the nineteenth, approached his bed to administer the last rites, Charles distinctly bade him wait until two more candles were lit. Only two were burning, and four of them were an emperor's due. He expired before dawn. The last word his lips formed was "Barcelona."

A treasury clerk from London had an opportunity to talk with "Mr. Leibsetter [actually, Lebzelter]" the "most confidential physician" of the deceased monarch some time later. This doctor opined that the "haughty behavior of France . . . and the internal combats he underwent by a servile compliance he had reduced himself to preyed on his mind, and was the proximate cause of that ill habit of body which at last put a period to his life."[52] Obviously Charles VI had brought a coronary thrombosis upon himself by partaking so richly of that indigestible Catalan dish while his system was weakened by a fever. As the consequences of his death became manifest, Voltaire's quip about the "pot of mushrooms that changed the history of Europe" was repeated over and over again in the drawing rooms of Paris.

Maria Theresa, five months gone with child, was twenty-three years old. She was wholly ignorant of the affairs of the dominions to which she had fallen heir.

IV

Enters Frederick

The privy conference was summoned a mere twelve hours after Charles VI had breathed his last. The new sovereign received them in the Knights' Chamber, a hall on the second floor of the ancient building next door to the chapel. As Maria Theresa stood under the canopy on the dais she could see the sun setting over the roof of the "New Burg," and farther off, the wooded hills stripped of their foliage.

Francis stood to the left of his wife—in front of an armchair the size of her own, to be sure—and it was she alone who addressed the men before her. Clad in mourning, a veil over her hair, she was standing erect, her hands clutching a fan. Her eyes did not flinch or her voice tremble as she spoke of her trust in the Almighty, referred to the esteem in which the emperor's Majesty had held his ministers, and bade them carry on. She was fighting tears as she concluded the brief oration.

The chancellor, Count Philip Sinzendorf, read the note to be dispatched to the foreign courts. It styled her Queen of Hungary, Queen of Bohemia, Archduchess of Austria. Unlike Bohemia and the Austrian duchies, the Hungarian kingdom owed no fealty to the Holy Roman Empire; and as its crown was not certain to come to the grand duke, the precedence of the Hungarian title had been chosen with foresight— and with no regard to the ironical fact that Maria Theresa was presented to Europe, *primo loco*, as the queen of her least pliable subjects.

Among the ministers there was only one man she trusted, Count Gundacker Starhemberg. This rarest of birds, a selfless magnate, had served the court since the turn of the century. Whatever financial reforms were attempted had been on his instance. He had been the "scourge of army contractors and profiteers."[1] "Despising the arts of

(57)

flattery . . . [and] always delivering his opinion with frankness,"[2] he was considered overbearing and cold by his peers. Jealous of Eugene, he yet had joined him in beseeching Charles to "make as complete as feasible a *totum* of Your Majesty's far-flung beautiful Monarchy."[3] As he grew older, and Charles less willing to listen to reports from the treasury, Starhemberg's influence had been waning. He was in his seventy-eighth year.

Sinzendorf was sixty-nine. "He was a great statesman, but confide in him I did not."[4] Having at one time been ambassador to Louis XIV, he prided himself on his knowledge of the world. "Flattering the chimerical schemes" of Charles and "affecting an entire deference to his will," he had gained the ascendancy over Eugene. He had urged Ripperdá's project on the monarch. Abroad it was said that much of the Spanish largesse in Vienna had gone to the chancellor, the "magnificence of whose establishment . . . far exceeded his income."[5] Nor had this been the only time he had yielded to the "lure of foreign gold."[6] When Francis' father negotiated with the emperor the sale of one of the appendages of Lorraine, he had paid no less than one hundred thousand florins to the chancellor to get a good price. Sinzendorf's "dilatory and procrastinating spirit"[7] had grown to be the despair of foreign diplomats. His "fondness of the pleasures . . . of society, and his attachment to play," including a dabbling in theology, had long made him "unable to attend to the multiplicity of business."[8] But, as Maria Theresa was to say in her famous memoir, "the inborn clemency of the House of Austria has always prevented the dismissal of any man who had not become wholly unworthy of his office."[9]

This clemency had also profited Count Aloysius Harrach. No man ever was sent on a more momentous mission than had been his in Madrid during the long illness of the last Spanish Habsburg. Saint-Simon has left a secondhand description of the look of triumph on Harrach's face as the king's will was being unsealed—and of Harrach's being laughed at an hour later by those present. Nor had he distinguished himself in the forty years since that day. A "candid man with pleasant manners,"[10] he had, as viceroy of Naples, succeeded neither in winning over the natives nor in thwarting Spanish intrigues. As likely as not Charles VI spoke tongue in cheek when, on Count Aloysius' request for recall he said that he had "no second Harrach"[11] to replace him.

Aloysius' younger brother, Count Joseph, held his seat in the conference as president of the Hofkriegsrat, an office he had been elevated to when Königsegg was appointed to the field. Charles had not pretended to think the world of Joseph Harrach's gifts; "there were not many to choose from,"[12] he had written to his son-in-law in Florence. But dilatory as Harrach was, he had, single-handed, objected to the army reduction after the Peace of Belgrade. He was sixty-nine years of age.

The sixty-seven-year-old Königsegg, who had retained his conference membership even under the threat of court-martial, had in those months grown "so cautious, one never can grasp his views . . . he never commits himself."[13] He had not supported Joseph Harrach's warnings against weakening the armed forces.

Their bulk had remained stationed in Hungary and Croatia after the war. Of the mounted regiments, only six were garrisoned outside those kingdoms. Artillery had dwindled to two score of cannon. "And who would believe that no regulations whatsoever existed for my troops? Each [regiment] had its own way of marching and maneuvering. . . . Some men fired fast, some others at long intervals, and commands were expressed by different words in each unit. . . . In short, the conditions I discovered were beyond description."[14] Both officers and enlisted men had gone without pay for several months by the time of Maria Theresa's accession. Desertion was rampant.

This state of affairs could not be blamed on Charles VI alone. The very organization of the Habsburg dominions had undermined finances for at least two generations. The congeries of kingdoms, duchies, margraviates, principalities, and territories did not, in effect, constitute a country. They differed in law and custom and often in language. Each of those entities was governed by its estates under the overlordship of the sovereign; and these assemblies were dominated by the great landowning families—the same clans that also held sway in the central government, such as it was.

Its offices operated side by side, and not seldom at loggerheads, with the magistracy of the provincial estates. Besides the Hofkriegsrat, the monarch's government had only one agency to supervise the affairs of his dominions—the Hofkammer (*camera*), or aulic exchequer. A number of organizational changes, dictated by need for money, had narrowed the Hofkammer's authority, brought confusion to its business, and bred conflict with the new agencies set up to counteract the financial misery their own way.

It was the estates that levied the land tax; and the government in Vienna every year had to haggle over their individual contribution toward common defense.* "Whenever [the sovereign] was negotiating with the Hereditary Lands about the necessary *subsidia* . . . he found himself compelled to give way to personal demands on the part of his

---

* The expenditures of the court proper and the salaries of ministers and clerks were, in theory, covered by the revenues of the dynasty's private domains, the mines and the mint, the excise taxes, and certain tolls.

cabinet ministers who alone," through their family connections in the various assemblies, "could furnish him with what he asked for." At the same time, "many of these [great nobles] received sizable gratifications from the Estates"[15] of the land in which their properties lay.*

As were the prelates, the aristocracy were exempt from paying taxes. While the peasants lived in serfdom only in some of the dominions, they nearly everywhere held their patches of land in fee from the manor lord and everywhere owed him labor services. Rural folk looked upon him, rather than the distant sovereign, as their supreme master.

As long as the monarch's dynasty was certain of the succession to the imperial crown, its mystique and vestigial rights had somewhat strengthened his hold over what, in practice, was a loose federation of feudal families. The catastrophes of the 1730's, however, had weakened that hold. So had the nonexistence of a male heir and the insecurity of the imperial succession. Those haughty magnates, unchecked in the mastery of their *latifundia*, no longer cared who would take Charles's place as their liege lord in the Habsburg lands or who would attain to the crown of the *Reich*. The preservation of their estates was the sole concern of the great.

They had short memories. It was the sovereign's good graces that had lifted many of those families from obscurity little more than a century earlier. About four out of five of the Bohemian grandees were the descendants of foreign soldiers in the Habsburgs' service who had been given, or had purchased for a song, the sequestered vast holdings of Protestants of the original Bohemian peerage and gentry—rebels who had suffered disgrace or even decapitation early in the Thirty Years' War.

As funds in Vienna were dwindling, some of those "new" aristocrats, as certain monasteries, had granted loans to the court against surety. By 1740 the income of the mines had been pawned for many years without hope to redeem the collateral. The royal domains were mortgaged. Gone were the days when a loan could be floated in London. The mismanagement of the revenue in Naples had estranged Italian bankers. The hazards of loans to the Habsburg court no longer attracted Amster-

---

* An audit in 1747 of the records of the duchy of Carinthia, whose annual contribution had never surpassed two hundred thousand florins, revealed debts of about four million. From 1645 to 1745 the estates had spent close to one and a half million on "unlawful *largationes* and *donationes*," with more than seventy thousand florins going to men in the central government.

Sometimes the estates chose even a more unorthodox way to have their will prevail. "When once, under Emperor Charles VI, the discrepancy between the demands of Vienna . . . and the offer of the Carinthian Estates was particularly great, the latter solved the problem by remitting a sizable part of what the *camera* had requested directly to the privy purse of the emperor. In other words, they bribed the emperor at the expense of the State." Charles, this account suggests, "surely did not recognize the remittance for what it was." ("*Kaiserin Maria Theresias politisches Testament*," *Einleitung*, 14.)

dam financiers, who were offered investment in London. The credit abroad of the handful of bankers in Vienna had dried up. The court's inability to pay interest on the domestic loan Starhemberg managed to place had destroyed the small money market in the monarchy proper.

Thus Maria Theresa, in her own words, found herself "all at once without money, without troops, and without advice."[16] She also found herself deprived of any sympathy on the part of the *publicum* in Vienna. Even while she addressed the conference for the first time, crude placards had been posted in several places reading: "Hurrah, the Emperor is dead./ Now we'll get full-sized bread./ We're not on the Lorrainer's side./ The Bavarian is just right."[17] Theresa, "in the unhappy last ten years of my father's reign, had heard of the *lamenti* of the *publicum*, just as any private person would, without knowing whence they came, and what their causes were."[18] She would have been surprised to learn that people by and large did not think of her as the new sovereign. Even though Charles's act of succession had been a matter of common knowledge for a good many years, the lower classes wondered whether Habsburg rule everywhere had not ended with the emperor's death. They could neither imagine an occupant of the Hofburg owing allegiance to an emperor not a Habsburg nor a woman ruling in the Habsburg dominions. And Maria Theresa, besides being a woman, was a woman in love. The same people who but a few years previous had savored the royal romance now stressed its hazardous implications. What authority could an enamored wife have over her husband? Should the archduchess succeed in establishing her rule, the despised "Frenchie" would be the ruler.

The actual ruler at this hour, Bartenstein, did not share this misconception. The grand duke, who had turned to him for succor on his return from the war, had ever since been gracious to him. But as Bartenstein did not think Maria Theresa susceptible to Francis' advice and had no illusions about her own feelings, he tendered his resignation even before Charles VI was laid to rest in the family crypt of the Capuchin monastery in Vienna. The young queen told Bartenstein that this was not the time for a change; he should try to do his best, and she would know how to prevent his doing harm.

Neither was this the only sign of determination on her part. There was her speedy action in thwarting an outbreak of lawlessness in the rural suburbs of Vienna, where the vintners, in pent-up indignation at the damage done by deer and wild boar for many years, had set about destroying the game in the preserves of the court; she ordered court rangers to kill off the beasts. Or there was the audit of the count's household, an investigation which bared regular disbursements for such items as the nightcap of the emperor's aged mother (twelve carafes of wine *per diem*), the vintage Tokay added to the food of his parrots, or the kitchen supply of parsley (four thousand florins per year). The revelation of such minor abuses—they were redressed with a speed unwonted in the palace—gave rise to some amusement among common people. Their indifference toward the new mistress began to be tempered by a benevolent condescension toward her naïveté. Indeed, so profound was her inexperience, it seemed to keep her unaware of her own courage. One of the stories spread in those days concerned the spokesman of the Lower Austrian estates and his futile attempts to modify their oath of allegiance. It seems that, stepping out of the audience chamber, this prelate had been pelted with reproaches by his peers. "Why don't you go in yourselves," he was quoted as rejoining, "and find out if you can say no to her."[19]

She did not know the first thing about public finances. Had she been told that the revenue had scarcely covered half of the expenditures in 1739—or that the court's debt had risen from sixty to ninety million florins in the course of her father's reign—the figures would only have puzzled her untrained mind. Starhemberg took it upon himself to inform her that less than one hundred thousand florins were on hand. Mme. Fuchs found her weeping after the old man left her. "I do not think anyone would deny that history hardly knows of a crowned head who started his rule under circumstances more grievous than those attending my accession,"[20] she was to write a decade later.

"God has given this woman the gift of winning people, and bending them to her will, by a kindly demeanor. . . ."[21] No objections were raised, in the conference or in the provincial estates, when Maria Theresa, "considering my sex and the heavy burdens of government," made Francis her co-regent in the Austrian and Bohemian lands—a dignity "for which his high birth, his glorious qualities, and our own happy union, recommend him."[22] Office and title were without precedent. They were not in accord with either the letter or the spirit of the Pragmatic Sanction, even though Bartenstein's text made it clear that the co-regency "does not in any way whatever encroach on [Maria Theresa's] possessions and rights."[23] Among the motives for the action was her expectation that the new status would increase Francis' chances in the imperial election. The elector of Saxony, one of the two Hereditary Vicars of the Empire during the interregnum, was quick to grasp the intention and lodged a protest against the co-regency with the Empire's Diet in Ratisbon.*

Francis, this least resentful of men, went out of his way to woo the

---

* Comprising, besides the nine electors, some three hundred princes, sovereign prelates, and the Free Cities, this assembly had retained little more than a nuisance value.

very courtiers who had shunned and maligned him. They, in turn, met him halfway. His unpopularity with the Viennese was a different matter. His wife was reluctant to probe their feelings. The co-regent was absent from the traditional procession that preceded the homage of the estates of Lower Austria. The archducal coronet, which had been brought to the Hofburg from Klosterneuburg Abbey the day before, "rode" ahead of the archduchess regnant to St. Stephen's. Intent on offering the public a good view of their pregnant mistress, she had herself carried in a sedan chair, followed by the empty gilded carriage and six. The magnificent cortege was gazed at by the crowds and cheered. But scarcely had Maria Theresa returned to the palace than riots broke out in several parts of the city. One particularly embittered mob made for Wöber's house, stoned its windows, and manhandled the municipal police. The prices of victuals had been rising from day to day. There was talk of war. And the Bavarian agents were busy telling people that only an emperor could count on assistance from the Empire's princes.

Even while the emperor was alive, Charles Albert of Bavaria had given notice of his intention to contest the Pragmatic Sanction. He did not base his claim to the Habsburg heritage upon the rights of his wife, but asked the Vienna court to take heed of the will of Ferdinand I (d. 1564), which supposedly made his own house heir to all the possessions of the Habsburgs upon the extinction of their male line. Charles VI had left the demand unanswered. Now Charles Albert, pressing the claim, notified all the courts of Europe. Sinzendorf summoned their ambassadors to the Hofburg, and the yellowed parchment bearing Ferdinand's last will was put before them. The proviso adduced by Charles Albert turned out to refer to legitimate, not to male, Habsburg issue. It was said that Maria Theresa herself had set the stage for the public humiliation of the claimant, who meanwhile had also announced his candidacy for the imperial throne. And behind Charles Albert there stood France.

The court of Versailles had acknowledged receipt of Sinzendorf's note, adding that the foreign ministry was still searching the archives for the style due the daughter of Charles VI. Their client sovereign in the Empire, the Elector Archbishop of Cologne, sent a letter, by the ordinary mails, addressed to the "Archduchess Maria Theresa." Her ambassador to the Court of St. James's, Count Ostein, who heard George II declare from the throne that he would "adhere to the engagements I am under,"[24] had also noticed the lack of a reference to the Pragmatic Sanction; and the Duke of Newcastle (one of the two secretaries of state) had told the Lords that "the only attachment we have to the court of Vienna is on account of preserving the balance of power in Europe. We are on this account to shew ourselves friends to the House of

Austria . . . but we are not to be slaves of that house. . . . The preservation of the balance of power and liberties of Europe does not so much depend upon preserving entire the dominions of the House of Austria as in taking care that none of these dominions shall devolve to any potentate in Europe whose power by that accession may become dangerous to the public liberty."[25]

But there was good news too. The provinces of the Dutch republic had each passed a resolution to stand by their treaty with the court of Vienna. The Russian court, Venice, the Holy See, and even Augustus of Saxony-Poland seemed willing to honor the promises made to Maria Theresa's father. By the time Fleury decided to address her as "Your Majesty" Bartenstein had gained some confidence in the immediate future. What above all raised his spirit was a letter from King Frederick to the grand duke, his fellow Freemason and pleasant guest at his own betrothal.

The emperor's death had drawn the eyes of Europe's chancelleries to Berlin. The territories of the Hohenzollern dynasty were sorely disconnected, and Frederick's father had not been the first of its princes to dream of increasing the unity of the realm. But inventive, as well as ruthless, as he was in domestic affairs, Frederick William "remained in what was deemed . . . pusillanimous inaction"[26] in the power politics of his day. Notwithstanding his delight in parade-ground drill, this martinet was a peaceful king. His very prudence, however, had handed his son an alluring instrument for military adventure. Even the Great Elector (1640–1688) had destroyed the power of the provincial estates. Frederick William had taught the bureaucracy to consider themselves inferior to the military. Heavy excise duties kept filling his coffers. The royal domains were managed with model efficiency. His army, partly recruited by conscription, had grown to be second to none in discipline.

"The great loss that Your Royal Highness have suffered through the demise of the emperor arouses my deepest sympathy," Frederick wrote to Francis. "This event will bring the affairs of the whole of Europe into flux, and its consequences will be all the more terrible as it had not been expected anywhere. You know the great esteem in which I hold you, and the great friendship I have felt for you always. Following these sentiments, I beg Your Royal Highness to look upon me as your good and tender cousin."[27] And, answering Maria Theresa's request for support of her husband's candidacy, the young king expressed his desire to be of service. "The court resounded with joy,"[28] and the "sweet words . . . confused even the ministers."[29]

The joy, if not the confusion, was short-lived. The court's resident in Berlin reported on long talks the king was having with his field marshals. "There are rumors of menacing designs on a slice of the duchy of Silesia. . . . But it is to be hoped that Divine Providence will guide the hearts of the foreign princes toward justice."[30] Meantime the British government had instructed their ambassador to ask Frederick bluntly whether he intended to stand by his father's pledge concerning the Pragmatic Sanction. His answer was evasive. He did not mention what he considered unfinished business between his dynasty and the Habsburgs. For, as it happened, that business was of some concern to Hanover also.

It was connected with the most formidable of the rights left to Empire's anointed head—the disposal of escheated *Reich* fiefs. The foremost goal of Frederick William's foreign policies had been the succession to the duchies of Jülich and Berg on the lower Rhine. After much procrastination Charles VI, in return for the king's guarantee of the Pragmatic Sanction, bestowed on him the reversion in Berg upon the decease of its childless ruler. Under British and Dutch, as well as French, pressure, Charles went back on his word within the year. Not so Frederick William. At heart he was an imperialist. But, to believe his crown prince, as he was talking to Eugene one day during the Rhine campaign, the Prussian king kept his heir ignorant of the commitment to Charles. When Eugene touched upon it Frederick said that he would of course abide by the Pragmatic Sanction upon his accession—only to add, in the next breath, that, fearful of his irascible father, he must ask Eugene not to bring up the matter in his reports to Vienna.

Apparently Charles VI, in the throes of compounding disaster, paid no attention to this curious story. Neither, in 1739, had the chancellery intelligence to the effect that the Prussian ambassador at Versailles had been discussing the issue of the Rhenish duchies. Fleury had guaranteed some of the Jülich-Berg inheritance to Prussia.

Frederick, then, along with his father's old grievance against Charles VI, had inherited the seeds of a friendship with the arch enemy of the emperor's house. Although the ministers in Vienna, "in particular Sinzendorf . . . could not bring themselves, and did not wish, to believe in an impending hostile move"[31] on the part of the new king, Maria Theresa wrote as early as November 14 to Ostein: "You had better realize that no one is to be trusted less than the Prussian."[32] The peremptory phrasing of this note must have surprised the ambassador, who surely had never before speculated on what manner of woman Charles's daughter might be.

News from Prussia began disconcerting the conference only toward the end of the month. A general-turned-diplomat, Marchese Botta d'Adorno, who sometime during the thirties had held a job at the Berlin legation, was dispatched as envoy extraordinary to Frederick. In an audience granted him, the king again expressed his feelings of friendship for the Queen of Hungary and her consort. But were not these very sentiments bound to turn her enemies against *him?* Therefore, he went on without troubling to disguise the non sequitur; he was compelled to occupy Silesia and assert the ancient claims of his house in that duchy. Botta, who on his journey had found the highways bristling with Prussian soldiers, pointed out that the adversaries of the queen, if such existed, were not planning to attack her lands, let alone turn against the king. Frederick could not be deflected. He kept talking, engaged in some bantering, and in the course of a second audience told Botta that Count Gotter was on his way as his own special envoy.

Gotter was no stranger to Vienna. He had lived there in the mid-1720's, provided with ample means by his father, a commoner. Some people of quality liked his good looks, and he soon was presented at court. His brashness at the gaming table amused the empress, a lady seldom amused. A title of nobility was his reward. Some years later Frederick William attached Gotter to the Prussian embassy in Vienna. He was absent from Berlin during the great family crisis, and having after his return aroused the interest of the crown prince, divided his time between his native Gotha, where he enjoyed a wealthy bachelor's life, and Frederick's delightful retreat at Rheinsberg. He had risen to a cabinet post upon Frederick's accession. Libertinage had not dulled his mind, nor success slackened his vigor. In his late forties, Gotter was still very handsome, still a great hand with the ladies. He expected the young queen to receive him forthwith.

He was received, instead, by her co-regent.

"I am come," Gotter said, "with safety for the House of Austria in one hand, and the imperial crown for Your Royal Highness in the other." His master's troops and money were "at the service of the queen . . . who is in want of both." As this alliance would expose his master to great danger, he hoped that the queen "will not offer him less than the whole duchy of Silesia as an indemnification." If the king were "not secured by the immediate cession of that province, his troops and money will be offered to the Electors of Saxony and Bavaria."

Francis, who had been informed of the demand, though not of its extent, by Botta, as indeed by Von Borcke, the king's ambassador in Vienna, replied that the queen had "not the power to alienate the smallest portion of the Habsburg dominions." This reference to their indivisibility, as laid down in the Pragmatic Sanction, might have drawn a response from a man more knowledgeable than Gotter: had not Charles VI himself "alienated" Naples and parts of Serbia and Bosnia after the Pragmatic Sanction became the law of the land? The envoy did not take up the argument. When the grand duke proceeded to "expatiate on the wide scene of confusion which was opening by the impatience of

CENTRAL EUROPE, 1740

St. Petersburg

SWEDEN

RUSSIA

NORTH
SEA

BALTIC SEA

DENMARK

EAST
PRUSSIA

UNITED
PROVINCES
(HOLLAND)

HANOVER

BRANDENBURG
Berlin

POLAND

Dnieper

SAXONY
Dresden

SILESIA

Vistula

AUSTRIAN
NETHERLANDS
(BELGIUM)

Rhine

Frankfurt

Elbe

Prague

MORAVIA

BOHEMIA

AUSTRIA

LORRAINE

Danube

BAVARIA
Munich

Linz

Vienna

Pressburg

FRANCE

STYRIA

HUNGARY

TYROL

TRANSYLVANIA

SWITZERLAND

CARINTHIA

BLACK
SEA

SAVOY

VENICE

CARNIOLA

CROATIA

MILAN
(LOMBARDY)

Venice

Genoa

Parma

MODENA

Belgrade

Danube

GENOESE
REP.

Florence

OTTOMAN

TUSCANY

Constantinople

CORSICA
(to Genoa)

PAPAL
STATES
Rome

SEA

SARDINIA
(to Savoy)

Naples

TWO

EMPIRE

TYRRHENIAN
SEA

SICILIES

AEGEAN
SEA

MEDITERRANEAN SEA

+ + + + Habsburg Possessions and Tuscany

/// Prussian Possessions

——— Boundary of Holy Roman Empire

L M

H S

the king of Prussia, which might be equally destructive to himself and others," Gotter only stiffened and finally said that he had "no further business here."

"Are your troops in Silesia?" Francis asked, though he cannot but have known they had crossed the frontier a week before the audience. Being answered in the affirmative, he said with dignity: "Return to your master, and tell him that, while he has one man in Silesia, we will rather perish than enter into any discussion. But if he will return, we will treat with him . . . [and he] may be gratified without presuming to extort what is not in our power to grant."[33]

Maria Theresa refused to see Gotter. To give credence to Frederick's recollection, his envoy was told "by her courtiers . . . that it ill became his master, whose duty, in quality of [elector of Brandenburg and] Arch-Chamberlain of the Empire, had been to present the ewer and basin to the late emperor, to give laws to his daughter."[34] Her entourage tended to gloss over the transition from an imperial to a royal-archducal court. Some men addressed Charles's daughter as Imperial Highness, or even Your Imperial Majesty, and thus helped her dismiss from her mind the dreaded possibility of the emergence of an emperor other than Francis.

While Gotter withdrew to a suburb of Vienna, waiting for instructions, his king's army kept advancing. It met with scant resistance. Maria Theresa's commanding general in Silesia, Count Maximilian Ulysses Browne, urged the "dispatch of the considerable forces which we need here in order to comfort the frightened, and allay the suspicions of the simple-minded. I make bold to report . . . that by this means we may silence the talk that stems from the belief that we have arranged to cede Silesia to the Prussians. . . ."[35]

Frederick's claim to four Silesian counties, going back to the sixteenth century, was based on trumped-up revisionary interpretations. His claim to the entire duchy could not even be supported by such constructions. A man as close to him as the old Prince of Anhalt-Dessau, one of the petty sovereigns doing service in the Prussian army—and one of its principal reformers—spoke of outright perfidy. However, its prize was enormous to the young king: ruling over two and a half million people, he set out to conquer a duchy of one and a half million inhabitants.

On the Rhine he had seen with his own eyes the decay of the Habsburg army. He knew it to be scattered from Ostend to Transylvania, from Silesia to Lombardy and Francis' Tuscan grand duchy. The virtual bankruptcy of the Vienna court was manifest, its helplessness against its selfish nobles the derisive talk of Europe. He was all but convinced that neither the British nor Holland would block his aggression. And Russia, whose czarina had died in October, was governed by venal regents. For all that, Frederick was not insensitive to the unpleasant surprise his undertaking caused in London, or even at Versailles, for that matter. Not that he stayed the progress of his army. But he modified his proposals. Or rather Gotter did, somewhat archly, and without committing his king. His second talk with the grand duke took place in the late afternoon of New Year's Day, 1741.

No sooner had Gotter entered the room than Francis burst out in indignant complaints. Thirty thousand Prussian soldiers in Silesia! The duchy's nobility suborned, its authorities pressed into obedience, its towns bled white by contributions, the countryside foraged! And all that with a brazen pretense of legality, which bewildered all and sundry.

When the envoy at last succeeded in putting in a word, he suggested that the queen borrow two million thalers from the king, with a sizable portion of Silesia as collateral. Of course, she must pledge herself never to redeem this "mortgage." A feasible transaction—did not His Royal Highness think so? At any rate, it would prevent a "public breach of the Pragmatic Sanction."[36]

Francis insisted on Silesia's evacuation prior to any parleys.

Gotter made no pertinent reply and went on to belittle the loss that the queen would suffer in the bargain. When the grand duke, not very felicitously, compared Silesia to one of the sleeves of his coat, Gotter submitted that the duchy could be likened, at best, to the sleeve's row of buttons. And changing his tactics, he abruptly produced a communication from his master, which closed with these words: "If the Duke of Lorraine should insist on destroying himself, let him act as he sees fit."

Francis faltered immediately. The king must not blame *him*. If only the king had not entered Silesia. "The *facti* [sic] are bad. They are terrible. They are not to be swallowed!"

Gotter tried to calm the grand duke.

"Yes, one must always discuss such matters calmly," Francis agreed, and as quickly mollified as he had grown excited, declared that whatever course the matter might take, it would never diminish his respect and friendship for the king, who considered him worthy of the imperial crown. "But I have no desire to advance my good fortune at the expense of the queen."

The envoy professed to appreciate the personal dilemma. With which of the ministers, then, might he discuss the proposal further?

"With any of them."

Gotter exclaimed that His Royal Highness' answer was a "sign that things are not beyond hope."

"It will not be easy. Still I do not mean to say that the situation is hopeless."[37]

At this moment there was a knock on the door, which had been ajar throughout the audience, and Maria Theresa, who did not enter the room, was heard reminding her husband of the late hour, eight o'clock. King Frederick must have been amused as he was told of the incident. Some weeks earlier Von Borcke had had a similar experience. Things seemed to have come to a pretty pass in the punctilious court of Vienna if the queen made it her business to eavesdrop on the co-regent!

The co-regency had not got off to a happy start. Instead of acting as the spokesman of her resolve never to compromise with the aggressor, Francis had allowed Gotter to turn him into a mediator between her total denial of Prussian rights in any part of Silesia and Frederick's brazen claim to its whole.

The duchy, an adjunct of the Bohemian crown, was rich in pasture and arable land, in timber and mineral deposits. The industriousness of its peasants and linen weavers, as the comparatively enlightened stance of the landed nobility, had made the province flourish beyond all others. The contribution of its estates formed one of the pillars of the Vienna treasury. Maria Theresa did not know yet how accurate was the phrase she adopted in referring to Silesia as the "crown's most precious jewel," or how great its importance for the place of her house within the Empire. Her determination to hold fast to what was hers in the teeth of black-mail was nurtured only by an outraged sense of justice.

She cannot but have known that the court looked askance at the size of Silesia's Lutheran communities, and their freedom of worship. It had been guaranteed them in the settlement of the Thirty Years' War but ridden roughshod over until Charles XII of Sweden forced the emperor under humiliating conditions to respect the agreement.* The welcome that the Silesian Protestants were reported to extend to the Prussian invaders incensed Maria Theresa and added an element of religious fervor to her defiance. The *chargé d'affaires* at Versailles was warning against the deceitfulness of Fleury; recruitments were being intensified in Bavaria; and an agent in Madrid wrote about sinister plans afoot there. But all of her thoughts centered on the King of Prussia.

The Hofkriegsrat appealed to Count Lewis Khevenhüller, a general who had emerged from the campaigns of the past decade, his reputation comparatively untainted. Though close to sixty, he had been entrusted with the defenses of Vienna. To take the field against the Prussians, he asked for an army such as could not be mustered and moneys such as could not be raised, even though two Bohemian magnates had come forth with substantial loans and the "Austrian prelates had remitted fl. 500,000 which, to bolster the credit," were turned over "to some of the bankers. . . ."[38] The generals in disgrace had been released upon

* This took place during the Great Northern War, which was contemporaneous to the War of the Spanish Succession, and partly influenced its course.

the emperor's death. But Seckendorf and Schmettau had decamped—the former to offer his services to Bavaria, the latter to throw in his lot with Frederick—and Wallis was ailing. The grand duke suggested the appointment of Neipperg.

But, more passionately, he suggested negotiations with Prussia. Both Joseph Harrach and the Bohemian chancellor, Count Philip Kinsky, "thought it best to come to terms"[39] with the aggressor; and so did Sinzendorf, about whose appeasing mood there was "something not entirely clean."[40]

No such ulterior motive seemed to color Kinsky's advice. Thirty-nine years old, he combined the natural energy of his years with the moroseness of an aged man. As ambassador in London, he had adopted the outspokenness of the English. "He would throw me into such restlessness and confusion," an older Maria Theresa recalled, "I could find no peace of mind . . . in my chagrin."[41] "What crotchety behavior!" she wrote him after one of their talks, "and why all those grimaces, pray? Why do you discourage the poor queen, instead of offering advice and help?"[42]

Starhemberg, as head of the exchequer, might well have been tempted by Gotter's two-million offer. He gave it no thought. He shared Bartenstein's view that "the cession of even a part of Silesia . . . would be prejudicial to the Pragmatic Sanction, and release the powers of their guarantees, as the agreement with Prussia would be regarded as voiding the [act of] succession."[43]

Frederick's proposal was rejected on January 5. Bartenstein's acrimonious note ridiculed the Prussian offer of protection, where the only protection needed was against the self-styled protector. It concluded with the announcement that the queen did not intend to start her reign by dismembering her patrimony. Bartenstein's strong stand, while not leading her out of the "labyrinth and darkness,"[44] went a long way toward restoring him to her good graces.

But the "inherited system" being what it was, "each minister was, as it were, lord and master in his department . . . and carried out only those agreed-on measures that were agreeable to him and compatible with his preconceived notions."[45] All of them dissuaded her from asking the provincial estates for extraordinary deliveries of money and recruits, warning her that "such demands . . . would only arouse passionate hatred"[46] for her person. It had not yet dawned on her that the ministers "were protecting themselves"[47] and their cousinage. Kinsky went beyond such self-protection. Asserting that "the Austrians had always kept the Bohemians at arm's length in the Monarchy," and supporting his request with "numerous old documents and many arguments," he prevailed on Maria Theresa to give him, "against everybody's advice," a seat in the Privy Conference. And "no sooner had I done so than his violent temper could no longer be bridled." As the Hofkriegsrat bestirred themselves at last and began mapping a campaign, Kinsky objected to "having the Bohemian lands flooded by so many soldiers." One "would manage anyway to overmaster the Prusians."[48] Had not Eugene himself six years before reported that their "senior officers . . . lack experience, many of them having never taken part in a campaign"?[49] To use the contemptuous expression of the period, most of those Prussians had "not seen the wolf" for a whole generation!

Unlike Khevenhüller, Neipperg did not insist on a large body of troops before accepting command. Nor did he hasten to leave Vienna while his forces—veterans of the Turkish campaigns, Croat irregulars, and raw Bohemian recruits—were assembled on the southern slopes of the Sudeten mountains. "I can see very well that everything is done much too slowly . . ." the queen on February 4 wrote to the commander of Neisse (the key fortress that was in vain expecting reinforcements). "Sluggishness will be our undoing."[50] It is debatable whether it was up to her to correspond with a mere colonel over the head of the commander. But she did not precisely know what her business was.

As an astute English diplomat some years later summed up the paradox inherent in the succession, "The emperor took all pains imaginable to procure her the . . . great kingdoms and provinces, and at the same time did all that in him lay to render her incapable to govern them."[51] Yet she was capable of facing her own shortcomings. She decided "not to conceal her ignorance, listen to each [of the ministers], and gather information."[52] The resolve, brave and humble at once, was not easy to carry out. She did not know how to organize her day, and the volubility of her husband frustrated all attempts to establish a schedule of work. What experience her ladies-in-waiting had acquired in the grand-ducal household scarcely enabled them to assist the queen regnant; and, odd to say, she had made no changes in her female entourage, which still was ruled over by her childhood *ayah*. It was she who drew Maria Theresa's attention to Count Sylva-Tarouca, a man outside the cliques of magnates, and second to none in lineage.

Emanuel Sylva was one of the younger sons of Count (or Duke) Tarouca, a Portuguese. As a page at the court of Lisbon, he became a close friend of the king's brother, and one day the two of them secretly boarded an English man-of-war bound for Amsterdam. In Utrecht, where the powers were carving up the Spanish heritage, the runaways plunged into the social whirl. One of its gossipy chroniclers called Sylva an "accomplished young cavalier who has more wit than can be imagined."[53] Leaving Utrecht, the two Portuguese went to Vienna to join the imperial army in the fight against the Turks—the thing to do for young bloods. While the prince turned out to be something of a nuisance for Eugene, his companion (who had added the name of Tarouca to his own) endeared himself to the great captain. He seems to have cut quite a figure in Vienna the following winter, when Lady Mary met him. In the summer of 1717 Tarouca distinguished himself before Belgrade, and on the conclusion of the campaign Eugene recommended him for a post in the administration. As it happened, Tarouca's father, who had been helpful in one of the court's financial transactions abroad, had meanwhile become his country's ambassador at Vienna. Young Tarouca, employed in the Netherlands (Belgian) Council amid its Spanish idlers and schemers, did not treat his office entirely as a sinecure. He developed into a keen, though not profound, observer of the civil service and its perpetual ills. Writing in mid-December, 1740, to Frederic Harrach, Count Aloysius' son, in Brussels, Tarouca minced no words in castigating the "slowness and irresolution" of the governmental machine. "To think that our ministers simply refuse to believe that the Prussians could start marching!" In the same letter he also showed a sympathy for Maria Theresa rare among nobles. "For all that [he concluded his account of woe] our young mistress and the grand duke remain brave and courageous. . . . They treat the ministers with affability, as though their services were efficient and gave no cause for lament."[54] By that time Tarouca had been appointed to the presidency of the Netherlands Council. Although he was not wealthy and had recently married a lady half his age, he had suggested a forty-percent cut in the salary that went with the office.

This, then, was the man Maria Theresa entrusted with a task as delicate as it was unique. She asked him to watch her conduct in matters large and small, offer his comments, and point out to her all mistakes "just as if I were an ordinary person."[55] He must come daily to see her. Even though Tarouca had lived well over twenty years in Vienna, his German was very poor. Nor was his French flawless. But there was, from the first, an affinity between the young queen and the middle-aged man that was not in need of well-turned phrases.

"Madame [he wrote after having watched her for about three months], you must be smiling about the 'little pedagogue' who, himself sleeping by day and writing by night, takes it upon himself to regulate the schedule of his sovereign. But since your clemency is even greater than his temerity, these are his suggestions.

"I assume that Your Majesty will rise shortly after eight o'clock. You will be occupied till nine with your prayers, attending Mass . . . while the coffee is getting cold! Spoiled coffee may upset the stomach.

"Knowing how little time is devoted to Your Majesty's toilet, I put down only half an hour for it. After which, as a good mother, you should inquire about the royal family.

"From 9.30 to 11 Your Majesty should use the time in reading, or listening to, the reports of the ministers, granting one audience a week to some of them, two to some others. . . . My suggestion aims at keeping the ministers from importuning Your Majesty, as well as saving them time. Also, their reports will be shorter that way. Extraordinary and pressing matters do not come up every day; they will not on the whole interfere with that arrangement.

"Now I come back to the morning hours. At 11.30 the private secretary must be ready in the antechamber to be handed the papers disposed of and the orders written out. I wish Your Majesty would be free from serious business from that hour to the time of sitting down at table.

"You should be punctual for your meal and never allow it to become stale and cold. That will be profitable to both Your Majesty's enjoyment and your health, and also will make it easier for you to stick to the afternoon schedule. Should someone turn up unexpectedly, making him wait for an hour will not harm Your Majesty's affairs. Should he come to say just one word, he could be allowed to approach your chair and talk to you from behind it. Your Majesty then will know what it all is about, and may either ask him to come back, or dismiss him altogether.

"I assume that Your Majesty will sit down at table at 12.15 and rise at 1.15. Even if . . . after that you should be inclined to listen to a person who has been asked to return, you nevertheless ought to be able to take a cup of coffee at 1.30 and then rest in your rooms till 2.30 without devoting your attention to anything more serious than listening to the Most Serene Archduchess [Marianne, born 1738]. After 2.30 Your Majesty have another hour to go and see the [Dowager] Empress. . . . In these two hours, then, Your Majesty should discharge family duties, giving them as much of your time as body and soul require on a particular day; human nature refuses to be the same all the time.

"At 3.30 Your Majesty should return to the reports of the ministers. . . . Then, until 6, you might receive some of the chamberlains or Privy Councilors After 6 o'clock, with the secretary dismissed, you still have two and a half hours until supper time, my opinion being that Your Majesty under all circumstances must have supper at 8.30. The first half of those two and a half hours will be for Vespers or the Rosary, the second for listening to someone who has been asked, and also for praying, or amusing yourself. But after supper nothing likely to encroach on the night's rest ought to be done, even if Your Majesty put in a good hour's time before retiring."

The detailed schedule for the individual days of the week were discussed in another three pages. Sunday, Tarouca suggested, was the appropriate day for audiences to "needy supplicants." He went on to advise the queen on how to shorten the interviews with foreign ambassadors and how to preside over the conference meetings. Finally, he submitted that she and her consort should be able to help each other "*à merveille*" in their tasks and find time for playing as well as working, "the former in fact being a prerequisite for the latter."[56]

By the time Maria Theresa read this memorial, she had given birth to a boy. Time had played the whore with Charles VI. The male heir he had hoped for in vain for twenty-three years was born five months after his death. Destined to grow up to be one of the century's most active rulers, the infant, christened Joseph, presently did something for his house: his birth restored the popularity of his parents.

Some days before the happy event, Neipperg had arrived at headquarters. Of the hardships confronting his small, ill-organized army, the *publicum* knew nothing. The Viennese gave the baby archduke a rousing welcome, complete with an impromptu illumination of the town. A more elaborate celebration took place on April 23. Vienna's only newspaper, the government-controlled *Wienerisches Diarum*, has immortalized, in a quarto volume of 320 pages, the inscriptions of all the streamers strung across the streets or put up on the façades of the buildings. The "boy-maker" Francis was the focus of an outburst of affection and loyalty. The boy himself was greeted as the guarantor of the imperial dignity of the Habsburgs. Scornful warnings directed at Frederick abounded among the poetic productions on display; one of these read: "The enemy has lost his chance/For Austria now wears pants!"

But even while Maria Theresa was riding to St. Stephen's with her son amidst the din of acclamations in the traditional *Hervorgang*, one of her magnates (and one of the court's biggest creditors), Prince Wenceslas Liechtenstein, was receiving an eyewitness of the battle that Neipperg had lost near the village of Mollwitz. An acquaintance of Liechtenstein's from the days of his recent embassage in France, the famous mathematician Maupertuis, riding into battle with the king, had been taken prisoner by a picket of Austrian hussars. "M. de Maupertuis gives the most melancholy account of the whole duchy of Silesia," Robinson reported, "and says that, after having studied very closely the character of the king of Prussia, that prince's great misfortune is to have heard that there had been a Charles XII of Sweden in the world."[57]

The defeat in the Silesian lowlands came as a great disappointment to the grand duke, who had been glorying in the future accomplishments of his friend. Fighting mud and inclement weather, Neipperg had taken his army across the mountains. Relieving Neisse, he seemed to have frustrated the Prussians. As he advanced toward the invested stronghold of Brieg he had not been able to find the enemy. He had seen him, however, from the encampment of Mollwitz at daybreak on April 10.

Although the rapid and regular fire of the Prussian musketry threw Neipperg's foot in panic, a charge of his cavalry, if premature, overran the Prussians. The young king lost his head, and galloping off, put twenty miles between the battlefield and himself. Only the following morning did a messenger from Count Schwerin, his field marshal, catch up with Frederick to give him word of the victory. Maupertuis described the inglorious episode; and Liechtenstein, talking to Robinson soon afterward, jested about it with great good humor. At any rate, the story dispelled some of the gloom at court.

Schwerin's infantry had outnumbered Neipperg's by two to one. "But for the headless zeal" of the cavalry, wrote Maria Theresa to Neipperg, "its success might have been of greater consequence." She was "by no means blaming" him for the outcome of the engagement. "The measures you took were diligent, prudent, and reasonable."[58] The Hofkriegsrat was pleased that Neisse remained in Austrian hands.

Frederick, at his headquarters, chose I Timothy, 2, 11–12, as the text for the thanksgiving service: "Let the woman learn in silence with all subjection. But I suffer not a woman to teach, nor to usurp authority over the man, but to be in silence."

V

Queen of Hungary

SOME WEEKS BEFORE THE BATTLE of Mollwitz the Berlin newspapers had accused the court of Vienna of having hired bravos to do away with the king. His Silesian camp was "honeycombed with assassins"; and one of them had confessed and told how "Grand Duke Francis swore him in before the assembled Hofkriegsrat."[1] When it became known that Frederick had barely escaped capture on his gallop from the battlefield, the sordid story assumed some importance. "The House of Habsburg has never employed killers," the chancellor wrote to all foreign courts. "The tale of the swearing-in of one of those *banditti* is of such poor invention it cannot possibly find credence. To anyone conversant with the customs of the Court of Vienna, the fraudulent nature of this alleged confession is evident."[2] It was on this occasion that Maria Theresa for the first time called Frederick "*le méchant homme*—the wicked man."

Having made much of the story, he now dissociated himself from it, talking airily of misinformed underlings. The victor of Mollwitz could afford to do without that kind of appeal for friendship. April was not over yet when Belle-Isle, marshal of France, arrived at the king's headquarters.

The grandson of an intendant who had risen to immense wealth and power, only to be stripped of both by young Louis XIV, Charles Fouquet de Belle-Isle was a man of boundless ambition. He had won some renown in three wars and recouped some of his family's losses. In his late fifties, he had lost none of his native energy. Though living in great splendor, he had kept himself free from vices. In the past two years he had emerged as the spokesman of the military nobility, their itch for new glory, and their time-honored hostility toward the Habsburgs. He had

(77)

prevailed on Fleury to notify the court of Vienna that his king deemed himself no longer bound by his guarantee of the Pragmatic Sanction. Any bilateral agreement that violated the rights of a third party—the Bavarian claimant, in the present instance—was to be considered invalid.*

Maria Theresa did not of course see the redrawn map of Europe that Belle-Isle had shown to Louis XV. But she knew that Belle-Isle was journeying through the empire with a glittering retinue, canvassing for the election of Charles Albert. When Sinzendorf acknowledged the receipt of Fleury's congratulations on the birth of the archduke, she added with her own hand: "May this event turn the Most Christian King more willing to hearken to my wishes."[3] The proud allusion to the male heir, coupled with an appeal to the consideration due a woman risen from childbed, made no impact on the French court. Fleury, yielding to Belle-Isle's pressure, shelved the plans for a maritime war with Britain.

The Privy Conference assumed rightly that Frederick's attack had alarmed George II and some of his ministers. But Bartenstein alone gauged public opinion in the island correctly. Opposition to the pursuit of Hanoverian interests and some sympathy for the Silesian Protestants made action against Prussia unlikely. To be sure, Parliament had voted a three-hundred-thousand-pound subsidy to the Queen of Hungary, to be paid in case of a French attack; and the promise of an army of German mercenaries for that contingency was in the air. At the same time, however, Robinson kept urging "accommodation" in Vienna and even said that the king of Prussia did "not question the validity of the Pragmatic Sanction"; he merely had "advanced some old claims."[4]

Thomas Robinson, the youngest son of a landed Yorkshireman, was not a polished courtier. A French diplomat meeting him some years later thought him "possessed of all the gruffness we usually impute to Englishmen; he is a hard drinker. . . ."[5] Having watched the mismanagement of Charles VI for ten years and the helplessness of the grand duke for five, he assumed a tutorial tone toward Maria Theresa. He was contemptuous of her ministers and impatient of Bartenstein's verbosity, which rivaled his own. Pleased to find himself close to the center of big events, he negotiated "in a wordy, high-droning way, as if he were speaking in Parliament,"[6] pitting what he thought to be prescience against the inexperience of the young queen. But, persistent to the point of boorishness as he was in her presence, out of it he spoke with warmth about her. Frederick said, with a smirk, that "the fool"[7] was in love with Maria Theresa.

Early in May the British government sent a special envoy to the king in Silesia. It was the first appointment of the Earl of Hyndford, a "rather course-grained Scotsman [who was] basically very decent and utterly dis-

---

* The French guarantee of the Pragmatic Sanction contained an article referring to "a third party."

creet."[8] "Burning with zeal to be the instrument of a reconciliation beween the king and Maria Theresa,"[9] he was not sufficiently well prepared for the task. In fact, he amused Frederick by broaching the hoary matter of the Berg-Jülich succession—which, as imperial business, no longer was within the power of the Vienna court to resolve. As the king refused to state his own terms, Hyndford, on instructions from London, offered three Silesian counties to him. "At the beginning of the war I might have been contented with these proposals," Frederick replied, "but after the expense incurred, and the success, the offer . . . is too small." And when Hyndford appealed to his magnanimity, Frederick interrupted. "Do not, my lord, talk to me about magnanimity! A prince ought first to consult his own interests."[10] Well, then, he might be satisfied with Lower Silesia, including Breslau, and was prepared to indemnify the queen to the tune of three million thalers.

In Vienna the conference hesitated to reject the proposal out of hand. Bartenstein was alone in his protests. The cession would be the first step on the road to disaster, he said, and hoping to alter the king's ultimate goal, the annexation of the whole duchy, was tantamount to expecting a blackamoor to turn white. Robinson received Maria Theresa's decision in writing: she would be grateful to His Britannic Majesty if she were shown a way of reaching an accord with Prussia without infringing on the Pragmatic Sanction. Hyndford accused her of "obstinacy, procrastination [and] perverseness."[11] Older men in his country might have reminded him that she was the daughter of a prince who for many years had refused to acknowledge the loss of a kingdom.

Her stubbornness had been fortified by an event whose impact was overlooked in foreign courts. A Turkish legation had brought the ratification of the Treaty of Belgrade to Vienna. The entry of the *agha*—a dazzling spectacle, complete with dark-skinned guards and a band and camels laden with costly presents—made for a holiday week among townsfolk. From both town and court it also lifted the fear of a renewal of Turkish hostilities, an assault on Hungary—which was all but denuded of troops—and a march on Vienna. A pamphlet published in London some months later inserted a measure of melodrama into the pacific mood of the Porte: "[The queen] laid her case before the Grand Signior without reserve, and conjured him in the most earnest and pathetic manner not to take advantage and complete her ruin. . . . The Turk manifested a compassion for a princess on all sides surrounded with calamities, declared himself incapable of preying on the miserable . . . and set such an example of humanity, moderation, and disinterestedness, as his Christian brethren might have been proud to imitate."[12] (The Porte, to be sure, was having troubles on the Persian frontier, and Constantinople was in the throes of a famine.)

Barely had the *agha* departed from Vienna than a delegation of the

Hungarian Diet called on the Hofburg, invited Maria Theresa to come and have herself crowned. For "the Hungarians do not recognize any-one as their king . . . until the crown of St. Stephen's has been put on his head with the traditional ceremony."[13]

Hungary's first Habsburg sovereign, whose claims were based on the rights of his wife, had been crowned in 1527. But this king, Charles V's brother and his successor to the imperial purple, never could take posses-sion of the whole kingdom. Its central part was in effect a Turkish prov-ince. He held sway only in a narrow strip of Hungary's northwestern territory. Like the princes of Transylvania, the easternmost region Hun-gary laid claim to, the Habsburg king had to pay tribute to the Porte. Only in 1606 could one of his successors free his house from that in-dignity against payment of a lump sum.

Most of the Hungarian magnates had moved to "Habsburg Hungary," abandoning large parts of their holdings and also their mansions in the capital city, Buda. Not all of these clans remained consistently loyal to the Habsburgs, whose repressive policies were not made to woo them. During the Thirty Years' War the dynasty's varying fortunes invited resistance to the policies of the Hungarian Chancellery in Vienna, its bureaucrats, and its Jesuits. A conspiracy of some magnates brought their leaders to the scaffold in 1670. As late as 1678 a rump Diet declared one of their own nobles Hungary's "king"; and his guerrilla fighters, supported by French money, took part lustily in the Turkish assault on Vienna. After its relief in 1683 the Empire's army advanced to drive the Turks from Hungarian soil. But liberation everywhere was followed by ruthless sup-pression of the "liberties" which the Hungarians, spared the rigors of the Counter Reformation under Turkish dominion, had succeeded in pre-serving. A zealous bishop of Emperor Leopold's choice became the country's virtual ruler and made short shrift of freedom of worship, as indeed of the constitution. When Leopold declared the Hungarian crown hereditary in his house in 1687, the nobles were ripe for revolt. But not until the hated king in Vienna was engaged fully in the war over the Spanish succession did the insurgents break out to lead their hosts deep into Austrian lands. Only Joseph I had managed to put down the bloody insurrection.

Charles VI had dealt deftly with the kingdom. He issued a far-reaching amnesty, granted religious freedom to the numerous Protestants, and confirmed Hungary's constitution and her laws. Economic recovery, started even in his father's day, was fostered by some ingenious innova-tions—not all of them welcome, to be sure, to all Hungarians. A standing army was set up under the authority of the Diet. From the late 1720's on, Charles succeeded in strengthening royal prestige and—by various means—kept enlarging royal prerogative. While the fugitive leaders of the late rebellion tried to foment unrest from across the Turkish border, Hungarian soldiers fought bravely in the foreign wars of their Habsburg king. Still, no Hungarian held high command in the Habsburg army or high office in Vienna.

Maria Theresa had not met many Hungarians. The few friends her husband made during his governorship had not gone out of their way to wait on the grand-ducal couple in Vienna. She had, however, made friends even as a child with Count John Pálffy, Hungary's Lord Chief Justice, one of the architects of the compromise that had ensured her succession. An ailing septuagenarian, he had hastened to Vienna upon the emperor's death. Maria Theresa appointed him commander-in-chief in Hungary. But his plea to convoke the Diet was not heeded for two months. Preempting its right, Pálffy had called on a number of counties, to levy irregulars; and the conference, whose members could not help recalling the great rebellion, looked with misgivings upon these horsemen and on the promise of rich booty that Pálffy gave them.

By the time the Diet's delegation came to Vienna the court had been buzzing for some time with disquieting news from Pressburg. The requests which the queen, as had her predecessors, would be faced with ahead of the coronation had been drafted with an eye to restoring some rights passed in desuetude long before. Nor had the Diet any intention to fulfill her most ardent wish and accept the grand duke as co-regent.

The impending journey should have frightened her. Yet the record of these weeks affords us the first glimpse of the young queen in high spirits. As coronation protocol required Hungary's ruler to make an appearance on horseback, she had started taking riding lessons as soon as she emerged from her lying-in. She rode astraddle, wearing a long skirt over breeches of chamois leather and boots—a fashion adopted by the half score or so of ladies picked to join in the training. Even though the riding hall of a secluded château had been chosen for the practice, stories of the good times the amazons were having reached the *publicum* and raised eyebrows. But that gossip did not do full justice to the doings of the queen in these weeks. She was "gathering information" on Hungary's laws, which, "in view of possible consequences, it would be unwise to tamper with."[14] As it happened, the suitor of one of her *Kammerfräuleins*, an army officer, belonged to an Austrian family that owned some land in Hungary; and Maria Theresa, consulting no one, dispatched this man into a number of the garrisons of the kingdom to study their temper. She was no longer wholly ignorant of Hungarian affairs when, on June 19, she boarded the flagship of the flotilla that was to take the court down the Danube.

The mountain of debts had not prevented the court from putting on a great show. Sailing under Hungary's flag, the vessels were decked out with streamers in Hungary's colors, and a magnificent tent had been put up in the bow of the flagship. Even the crews had been clothed in Hungarian garb. At sundown the ships docked on this side of the border, and the queen accepted the hospitality of a nearby manor. The following morning, after Mass, a committee of the Diet, led by a prelate, came to escort her across the border.

Two pavilions had been pitched on the field cleared for the occasion. A deputation of both chambers had assembled in the larger tent, while Maria Theresa, after leaving her carriage, took herself to the smaller tent to don a gold-embroidered dress cut in the Hungarian fashion. In the Diet's pavilion, seated on its only armchair—the grand duke was standing behind it, bareheaded—she heard herself addressed, for the first time, as *domina et rex noster*—our mistress and king." She answered the primate's Latin speech in Latin.

The ministers and Bartenstein had remained aboard ship and gone quietly ashore in Pressburg. They were not in attendance when the queen and her husband entered the city at dusk. Bells were tolling, a salute was fired, and holiday crowds were lining the road up to the castle.

The huge Renaissance structure, overlooking the medieval town, enclosed some buildings more ancient than any part of the Hofburg. The belfry dated back to the eleventh century. Down in the vault two magnates kept watch over the royal insignia. The fabled crown of St. Stephen, abducted by Emperor Leopold and taken to Vienna, had been restored to the nation by Charles VI. But he had insisted on placing fifty Austrian men-at-arms, along with fifty Hungarians, under the command of the native crown guardians.

Charles had never visited Pressburg after his coronation and never again convoked the Diet. The castle, run down before, had barely been habitable when he resolved to send Francis to Hungary; and though a large sum was expended on repairs ahead of his arrival, it had been a gloomy place for Francis. As on this spring day he was approaching the castle, he must have recalled the wintry morning of his departure five years before to pluck at long last the great, the unique prize in Vienna. Unique it still was. How great was it still? In an interview with Von Borcke during the illness of Charles VI, Francis had said: "There is nobody but his Prussian majesty and the king of England I can rely upon [for the candidacy in the imperial election]."[15] Now, His Prussian Majesty was at war with Francis' wife, and the King of England's envoy, much as he talked, had ceased speaking of the Empire's crown.

The grand duke found himself excluded from all proceedings in Pressburg. He remained in his apartment while the members of the Diet the following morning presented themselves to Maria Theresa in

the great hall, whose newly damask-covered walls were hung with tapestries brought from Vienna. But his exclusion at least spared Francis the
hostility shown his wife's ministers even before the royal draft of the
coronation oath was handed the Hungarians. The magnates, still in
mourning for Charles, their king, did not cheer his daughter as she said
that she wanted to be the "Hungarians' mother, as well as their mistress"; and the members of the lower house, who wore the national garb,
were sullenly silent.

Yet she had made an important concession. Discarding the precedent
set by her father, she had agreed to the election of a native viceroy, the
Palatine. Nor did she wince when she saw the names of two Protestants
on the nominees' list besides those of Pálffy and another Catholic
grandee.

Pálffy's smooth election did not betoken a sense of submission.
The Diet asked for a confirmation of their right to fill the office again
by election after his, or any of his successors', death. The queen's refusal
was instantaneous. (The Venetian ambassador interpreted it shrewdly:
confronted with the Hungarians' unwillingness to accept Francis as co-
regent, and increasingly doubtful about his chances in the imperial election, Maria Theresa may have been nursing the project of returning him
to the Hungarian governorship upon Pálffy's demise.) She also advised
the Diet that she had no mind to "bargain over my *propositiones*"; she
"owned the [Hungarian] realm like an entail, and must pass royal power
on to her heir, precisely as it had come down to herself."[16]

If the man who put these words into her mouth had wished to provoke the Diet, he could not have succeeded more fully. It was the lower
house that became the center of the tempest. Its constitution reflected
the autonomous county government which the lesser nobility, having
preserved it under Turkish occupation, also had salvaged in the settlement with Joseph I. Elected to juridical and administrative offices by
their peers in the counties, the litigious half-educated squires were
bitterly jealous of Hungary's "liberties," as well as their own. Tax
exempt, as were prelates and magnates, this gentry resented such dynastic
feelings as had grown up among the great lords. Still, they were themselves divided in factions.* In their deliberations they "take the floor
without being recognized . . . tumult and confusion reign."[17] As it happened, the speaker of this assembly—no petty landowner he—was from the
first attracted to Maria Theresa.

Baron Andrew Grassalkovich was a commoner by birth and of south
Slav, rather than Magyar, descent. With not a penny to his name,
he had managed to receive a good education as a "mendicant student."

* The representatives of the thinly populated towns, mostly men of German
stock, carried little weight.

He acquired some land and was elected to the lower house, where he rose to prominence soon. He was a man of imposing appearance and insinuating manners and endowed with a remarkable aptitude for business. After the death of his wife he married the daughter of a magnate and put her dowry to good use. Army contracts brought him wealth, which he invested in land. His love of splendor had not alienated him from the lesser nobility, who in turn did not begrudge Grassalkovich his career. Indubitably the role of the knightly champion of a princess in distress appealed to the upstart. But he also realized that a drastic curtailment of royal power might lead to domestic trouble, indeed to social changes such as could only be loathsome to a man who himself had succeeded in changing his fortunes.

As he began steering the young queen through the crisis his common sense struck a kindred chord in Maria Theresa. When, to the dismay of her ministers, she received Grassalkovich—he had come with the new Lord Chief Justice (and Speaker of the upper house)—she patiently listened to his comments on the *gravamina*, as the requests of the Diet were called. But she did not yield any ground. Some magnates asked the grand duke to intercede. He obliged, only to find himself brushed aside by the ministers. June 25 was the day set for the coronation, and only after sundown of June 24 could Grassalkovich persuade her to accept an interim solution: some minor royal concessions were written into the oath, and she solemnly promised to continue negotiations. A few hours later the high clergy of the kingdom gathered at St. Martin's, where they were joined by the papal nuncio, the archbishop of Vienna, and the Palatine, Pálffy, who had been unable to ride up to the castle on horseback with the lords and nobles.

As this cavalcade trotted into the courtyard, they found the German lords from Vienna proudly arrayed there; and only the efforts of some level-headed men prevented a last-minute altercation about precedence. In the sunshine of the summer Sunday, the aigrette-topped headgear of the magnates, their sable-lined short capes, and jeweled scimitars vied with the scarlet robes, golden collars, and plumed hats of the knights of the Golden Fleece. Not even the imperial coronation of Charles VI, the Venetian envoy noted, or any of the ceremonies he witnessed at Versailles, had offered a more splendid sight than did this assemblage. Yet, as Maria Theresa stepped out of the portal all by herself to enter the gilded carriage, "a cloud of sorrow overcast her lovely features." But as the cheers of the people on both sides of the flower-strewn road fell on her ear, "some color returned to her face."[18] Hosts of peasants had come to the city, and their colorful costumes, as their exuberant mood, seemed to belie stories about the drudgery of their bondage.

As St. Martin's the primate opened the ceremonies by admonishing

Maria Theresia

oman: Imperatrix, Hungariæ et Bohemiæ &c: Regina
Archidux Austriæ &c: &c:

de Martens pinx.

Fr. L. Schmitner Sc Viens.

The young Empress

Francis I,
Holy Roman Empe

Maria Theresa to be a good ruler to the country. She went down on her knees to kiss the cross offered to her. Still kneeling, hand on the Gospel, she swore to uphold the laws of the land and "let justice reign."[19] The aged bishop bent down to anoint her and lay around her shoulders the mantle that Hungary's first king, St. Stephen, was said to have worn at his coronation in A.D. 1001. Then the primate put the crown on her head and handed her the orb and scepter.

The crown on her head, the queen rode in her carriage and six to the church of the Brethren of Charity. There, standing on a dais put up in front of the simple building, she took the oath which was read to her by the primate. The firmness of her voice surprised no one. Saddened as the Hungarian notables had found her during the past three days, they had not ever found her wavering in her speech.

With flags and gunfalons overhead, the procession inched its way through the narrow streets and moved toward the Royal Hill, an artificial mound, about twenty feet high, that had been erected in a public square. At the foot of this elevation Maria Theresa left the carriage to mount a black stallion, with the lord equerry of the kingdom holding the stirrup. Still wearing crown and mantle, she cantered up the hill, reined the horse, and drew the sword to brandish it toward the four quarters of the globe. It was an exacting job. But Maria Theresa herself had advised the Diet that nothing must be omitted from or altered in the ceremonial such as always had been observed at the coronation of a king.

Apparently precedent was not explicit about the place of the ruler's family at the coronation. The grand duke and his five-year-old eldest daughter, who had been in Pressburg since June 19 with the *ayah*, left the castle before the arrival of the grand cortege. They rode to St. Martin's, in whose churchyard the two smaller princesses, brought from Vienna during the night, had been kept waiting. A roofed wooden platform had been built in front of one of the tall windows of the choir; and from that lofty place, which was reached by a steep flight of stairs, the grand duke and his children had a view of the throne through the opened window. The three archduchesses were sent away with their *ayahs* after the long ceremonial. Only one noble, an acquaintance from his gubernatorial days, accompanied Francis as, threading his way through the multitudes, he walked to the vicinity of the Royal Hill, to enter the private mansion from one of whose windows he watched his wife canter up to the summit.

He was not placed next to his wife at the coronation banquet in the castle's courtyard. "An air of delicacy, occasioned by her recent confinement, increased the personal attraction of the beautiful princess . . . when she sat down to dine in public. . . ."[20] The day had grown very warm and her rich garments were weighing her down. Her health was drunk over and over again to the sounds of trumpets. Following a sudden impulse, she took off the crown and put it on the table before her. But "she appeared still more engaging while her hair flowed in ringlets over her shoulders and bosom."[21] "The Queen was all charm,"[22] related Robinson, who had come to Pressburg in one of the craft of the royal flotilla. No doubt he felt compassion for her. King Frederick had signed an agreement with Belle-Isle.

The assurance that Robinson's government had given Ostein in January that "His Majesty will fulfill his engagements in support of the Pragmatic Sanction"[23] had lost much of its worth with Walpole's triumph over both the Opposition and his king in February. Not only did Walpole detest the thought of military entanglements on the Continent, he also felt that Maria Theresa's conflict with Frederick threatened her dynasty's mission—or *raison d'être*—as an instrument for checking French power. Walpole meant to put a stop to that nuisance by a speedy reconciliation of the two rulers. And, save George II, whose sympathy for his nephew had turned into fierce dislike, there were few politicians in London who, in so many words or tacitly, did not share Walpole's desire.

Robinson's orders were to wrest from the queen concessions likely to pacify Frederick, take her proposals to his headquarters in Silesia, and thwart the ratification of his French treaty. He had an audience of her a short week after the coronation. Maria Theresa "listened to the communication with profound silence, and in reply . . . broke out in exclamations and sudden starts of passion." Yes, she might be induced to part with the Silesian county of Glogau, she said, taking up one of Robinson's suggestions. "If only I could be secure of peace on all sides. But no sooner is one enemy satisfied than another starts up. Another, and still another, must be contented, and all at my expense."[24]

The account of France's alignment with Prussia had also awakened her to a menace her counselors had thought remote. Spain's designs on her Italian dominions had been manifest since the turn of the year. (At that time Philip V's *chargé d'affaires* lodged a protest against Francis' assuming the grandmastership of the Golden Fleece and departed from Vienna without asking for passports.) The fantastic legal construction with which the king announced his claim to all Habsburg possessions had not alarmed the Hofkriegsrat: Britain, at war with Spain, would block Spanish transports to Italy. Now, however, France might give passage to Spanish troops. And Sardinia, fickle at best and greedy as a rule, was not likely to come to Maria Theresa's assistance.

"I am convinced of your good will," she said to Robinson, "but I pity you. Your mission in Silesia will be as fruitless as was that of Count

Gotter. Remember my words." And as the ambassador submitted that it was in her power to make his mission successful, she exclaimed: "What would I not give except in Silesia!" and went on to offer a small Habsburg enclave. And if the king could "not be gained by that sacrifice," she continued, "means might be found" to gain the elector of Bavaria. He "may be more flexible."[25] The indivisibility of her inheritance was not mentioned in this talk.

Nor, in her talks with the Diet's spokesmen, did the queen any longer liken Hungary to an entail. The grandees, who had bent the knee before her at St. Martin's, and at the coronation banquet had carved the roast, poured the wine, and offered her basin and ewer, were even more passionate than before in pressing the *gravamina*. They had, to be sure, abandoned the least acceptable of them—a demand to restore the law that entitled the Diet to depose their king should he infringe on the "liberties" of the nation. But the new king, Maria Theresa, must confirm these "liberties" and on her part abandon her desire to have the grand duke installed as co-regent.

Each day brought new proof of the growing lack of respect in the lower house. Grassalkovich's motion to give her the customary coronation gift of one hundred thousand florins was shouted down with scorn. In mid-July both chambers began to communicate with the queen in writing. One of their notes accused Charles VI of having set aside laws he had sworn to uphold. Grassalkovich, calling on Maria Theresa, found her in tears over this injury dealt the good name of her father. And as the Diet continued to harp on their request in regard to the Palatine's office, she complained bitterly about their mistrust. Her final answer to the *gravamina*, read to both houses, threw them into turmoil. "Enough of this long-winded stuff!" one noble called out. "Why not tell us, *Sic volo sic jubeo* [the notorious maxim of despotism]? Let's go home!"[26] The storm clouds gathering abroad only served to encourage the cockiness of the gentry. The ministers spoke of blackmail.

Meantime Robinson had received grave news. A "Grand Confederacy"[27] had been concluded between France, Spain, and Bavaria; and Lord Harrington directed the ambassador to bring pressure on the queen through her husband. Francis received Robinson on July 24. But barely had the envoy started talking than Maria Theresa swept into the room and engaged in invectives against Frederick as the architect of all her tribulations. After she had calmed down she again spoke of the sacrifices she was willing to make. Robinson expressed doubts about the conditions that she attached to her offer. "I wish he [would] reject it!"[28] she called out.

"The project of cession was drawn up. . . ." Robinson informed Harrington. "The queen, after much struggle forced to approve [the terms] changed them with her own hand. . . . What with despair, what with reluctance, what with irresolution, [she] spoiled the whole paper, and sent it back to the chancellor so mangled. Then she sent for it again."[29] To Kinsky she wrote: "I have deemed it necessary to deceive my ministers. As you are the only one I trust, I want you to know my real intentions. Robinson will be handed our terms today. He went so far as to threaten us, and therefore the door must be kept open. I am firmly resolved never to sign away any part of Silesia. . . . However, I have, through the chancellor, intimated to Robinson that I might be bargained with a little if Prussia used her whole power against our enemies, and helped us to the imperial crown. . . . God protect me from actually wishing [for such a deal]. No! I only want to deceive the ministers, so that they mention [the proposal] everywhere, and Robinson is put off until I get a reply from Bavaria." Some days earlier she had asked Emperor Joseph's widow, her aunt and the mother-in-law of Charles Albert, to divorce him from France by offering an Italian duchy. "You are the only person to know anything about this idea of mine," she went on in her letter to Kinsky. "You are free to discuss it with Bartenstein, and you may discuss it with me tonight. I shall be alone."[30] Evidently her husband was not privy to the plan.

She knew that he thought procrastination to be useless. But she also knew that he would not speak his mind. He had "hardly opened his mouth"[31] during Robinson's audience. When the Englishman gave an account of it to Starhemberg, the old man said angrily: "And to think that we made him co-regent!"[32] Yet Francis was not self-effacing by nature. Did the stiffened attitude of his wife toward both her British ally and her Hungarian subjects overawe the grand duke? Or did the growth of her strength increase her attraction for him? When all was said, he had not married Theresa for love. But he loved her just the same. Loving her, he feared a disagreement which might leave a scar on their conjugal happiness.

Three days after Robinson had presented himself to Frederick, his troops occupied Breslau. "Breslau is lost, and our propositions have been turned down," the queen wrote Kinsky. "This is the end. I am deeply dejected. But, pray, don't let on anything in front of *mon vieux*."[33] Let on what, one wonders. That she was dejected? Or that she felt this was the end? Besides some consideration, there was in either case some condescension in the admonishment.

"Beggarly offers," the king called the proposals. And, as Robinson spoke of a guarantee, Frederick said: "Who observes guarantees in these times? Has not France guaranteed the Pragmatic Sanction? Has not England guaranteed it? . . . Why do you not all fly to the queen's succor? . . . I am at the head of an invincible army, already master of a country which I must have and which I will have. . . . My ancestors would rise out of their tombs to reproach me, should I abandon the rights they have transmitted to me." The king too had a penchant for drama. "Reiterating his demand for the whole of Lower Silesia, he said to Robinson: 'Return with this answer. They who want peace will give me what I want. I am sick of ultimatums. I will have no more of them. My part is taken. This is my final answer. I will give no other.' He then interrupted all further representations, and, taking off his hat, precipitately retired, with looks of high indignation, behind the interior curtain of his tent."[34]

As Robinson, before leaving Pressburg, had advised the ministers of his government's disinclination to lend the queen military assistance, she instructed Ostein to plead her cause with redoubled urgency. At the same time, she attempted again to buy off Bavaria. Even as French troops were massing for an invasion of imperial territory, she asked Fleury to intercede with Charles Albert, indeed, offer him Belgium, "in order to deprive malevolent men of any pretext to sow discord between us and France."[35] Bartenstein's stubborn trust in Fleury had swayed the conference.

To Maria Theresa, any accord with France and Bavaria was preferable to an accommodation with Prussia. The former understanding, moreover, would remove the specter of Charles Albert's emperorship. Fleury did not answer her letter. So she up and journeyed to Vienna to talk to her aunt. All by herself, she called on the old lady at her residence in the convent of the Salesian Sisters. We have Maria Theresa's own account of the conversation—a crescendo of offers on her part, a monotone of refusal on the part of the dowager empress. Surely Joseph's widow did not mind watching the chickens come home to roost: had not Charles VI, overriding the earlier act of succession, excluded her daughters from the Habsburg inheritance and compelled them to swear an "oath of renunciation" before they got married?

On July 31 an army under the Duke of Broglie crossed the Rhine, the troops wearing Bavarian cockades. At the head of the vanguard rode Maurice de Saxe, a natural son of Augustus II of Saxony. Having served under Prince Eugene as a tyro, De Saxe had defeated him twenty years later on the Rhine. Belle-Isle was in actual command of the army, and Maria Theresa's hatred of him was second only to her hatred of Frederick. But she still refused to believe in the reality of the "great confederacy" arrayed against her and bent on denying the Empire's crown to her Francis. Her aunt tried to convince her of the futility of the offers to Charles Albert: allied to the French, he could not antagonize them by accepting Belgium, and as an ally of the court of Madrid, could not encroach on its Italian aspirations. The cession of Upper Austria might be a more tempting proposal for her son-in-law, the old lady ventured to say. Maria Theresa countered this mortifying suggestion by offering some tracts of Tyrolian territory, besides the royal title her husband upon his election might bestow upon Charles Albert. So seriously did she herself take that last idea, she directed the ambassador at Versailles to inform Fleury of the grand duke's intention. The cardinal, a man not given to jesting, assured the envoy that "we do not intend to despoil the queen, and merely wish to pluck one feather from her plumage."[36] "I am burning with impatience," Frederick wrote to Belle-Isle, "to meet you at the gates of Vienna and embrace you at the head of your victorious troops, even as I did, at the head of my victorious army," in the Silesian camp.[37]

In Pressburg the Diet was complaining about the inaccessibility of their queen. They openly inveighed against her ministers. Nasty pamphlets were being distributed. One of these denounced her for having come to Hungary in a disguise to worm her way into the nation's favor; now her countenance could be seen, stripped of the maternal traits she had feigned. Pálffy had the pamphlets publicly burned by the hangman. But he too had begun to wonder about the queen's ultimate intentions.

In the first days of September Charles Albert's army began streaming into Upper Austria. Augustus III of Saxony was on the eve of joining in the assault on Maria Theresa. Now she allowed herself to be talked into new concessions to Prussia, and Robinson journeyed again to Silesia. The king did not grant him an audience. "It is no longer time to defend the queen of Hungary," he wrote to Hyndford. "She must learn to support all the rigor of her destiny."[38]

Returning to Pressburg, Robinson found the ministers eager to make common cause with him. Even Bartenstein, horrified by the French aggression, urged Maria Theresa to give in and drafted a note to Hyndford. The queen was ready to cede Lower Silesia, as understood by the king, together with Breslau and the Upper Silesian counties he had designated, provided he turned against the Franco-Bavarian armies. "*Placet,*" she wrote in the margin of Bartenstein's draft, "as there is no other way, but with profound grief."[39] When the note was about to be dispatched she suggested changes once more. But as Sinzendorf would not hear of another delay, she said: "If it has to be, then, let it be. The whole matter has been settled against my will. Let it so take its course, also."[40] We are going to hear this mixture of resignation and reproof many a time.

On the very day of Robinson's return from his hapless mission, Maria Theresa had embarked on an undertaking entirely out of tune with resignation. The Bavarians were approaching Linz, Upper Austria's capital, and their junction with the French army appeared to be imminent. There were no forces to check the advance of either. Vienna itself was endangered.

Of all the Habsburg dominions, Hungary alone had a tradition of large-scale levies. In the teeth of the ministers' mistrust of the Hungarians and the hostility of the Diet, she determined to throw herself on its mercy. She summoned the most influential magnates and nobles up to the castle on September 7. After describing the state of her affairs, she told them point-blank that the safety of the kingdom, as well as her other lands, depended on the valor of its nation. The men realized that the queen, asking for help, was about to break the deadlock between herself and the Diet and meet its demands halfway. Moreover, being told that they alone could save her house from destruction restored to them some of the pride which the Habsburgs had hurt for generations. Self-asserting and selfish as they were, Hungarian noblemen were not cynics; their very backwardness had preserved among them some of the chivalry of an earlier age. Maria Theresa's female charm was not wasted on them. The men pledged themselves to her service and on the spot decided on a levy of forty thousand troops and twenty-five thousand horses. They also implored her not to expose herself to the dangers of enemy action and to take refuge with her son in the fortress of Győr. "Her Majesty seems to tend to accept the offer," the Venetian Capello closed his account from Pressburg, "but she considers it premature. . . . Only if the enemies should show the intention to lay siege to Vienna, would the queen take up residence in Hungary . . . Divine Providence has endowed this princess with all the virtues necessary to endure her misfortune."[41]

Two days later, on a short trip to Vienna, she dissuaded her mother from leaving the town, presided over a meeting that sped up preparations for defense, and took part in the thanksgiving procession commemorating Vienna's delivery from the Turks. "The *publicum* must not be told about the imminent peril," she wrote to Lewis Khevenhüller before she departed. "And, pray, keep in mind that the Viennese will do everything, if talked to kindly and shown affection."[42] Apparently the paroxysm of love shown on the archduke's birth had dispelled the memory of the injustice they had for so long done her Francis.

During her absence from Pressburg Pálffy had entertained his fellow magnates at a sumptuous dinner. He spoke to them of the queen's great confidence in the nation and blamed her German advisers for her unbendingness throughout the summer. Indeed, the young princess had been no better than a prisoner of those men! Supported by her Hungarians, she would henceforth be free to follow her own sentiments. The speech was loudly acclaimed. Hungarian wine is heady. When both chambers assembled in common session on September 11, they were, to the last man, aware that a new chapter was about to be written into the history of the kingdom's relations to the dynasty.

The queen entered the great hall, the crown on her head, but clad in mourning. "After an awful silence of a few minutes,"[43] the Hungarian chancellor detailed the project of the levy and expressed the sovereign's hope that the Diet, "without hazardous delay, would erect a dam to hold the unjust aspirations of her enemies."[44] Then she herself read her Latin address.

As it has come down to us, this *allocutio* is an awkward instrument. The vagueness of its promises marks it as Bartenstein's brainchild. It was more its delivery than its text that carried the day. "The disastrous state of our affairs [she said] has moved us to lay before our dear and faithful Estates of Hungary the recent invasion of Austria, the danger now impending over this kingdom, and a proposal for the consideration of a remedy. The very existence of the kingdom of Hungary, of our own person, of our children, and our crown, is now at stake. Forsaken by all, we place our sole resource in the fidelity, arms, and long-tried valor of the Hungarians, exhorting you . . . to deliberate . . . in this extreme danger the most effectual measures for the security of our person, of our children, and our crown, and to carry them out into immediate execution. In regard to ourself, the faithful Estates and Orders of Hungary shall experience our hearty co-operation in all things which may promote the pristine happiness of the ancient kingdom and the honor of the people."[45] As she mentioned her children tears trickled down her face, and as she ended the oration the voice of the queen, "who had hitherto preserved a calm and dignified deportment,"[46] was choked with emotion.

To the reply of the primate she listened "with an expression befitting innocence hurt. . . . Compassion with the grief of the queen as well as the magic emanating from her appearance, instilled those present with enthusiasm for her cause."[47] They may, as one chronicler has it, have "drawn their sabers half out of the scabbard and thrown them back as far as the hilt,"[48] or may have exclaimed, as another account insists, "We will give our lives for the king!"[49] Legends started growing up about this hour. It invited embroidery.

There was another side to the story. Even as the hall resounded with acclamations, some of the lesser nobles, who had noticed skeptic smiles on the ministers' faces, broke out in cursing, and, but for some moderate men, would have given these "Germans" a beating in front of the queen. The altercations grew wilder after her withdrawal. One squire swore he had heard one minister say that Her Majesty would have done better entrusting her safety to Satan than the Hungarians. Shouts of

"To the gallows with the Germans!"[50] rose from among the gentry, and the "Germans" in turn derided the display of gallantry on the part of the Diet. Where had that spirit of militant loyalty been all these weeks and months, they called out as they pursued some cursing squires down the great staircase.

On September 14 the Franco-Bavarian troops walked into Linz. The estates lost no time swearing fealty to Charles Albert, who had styled himself Archduke of Austria. Few of Upper Austria's prelates and nobles, and fewer still of its great lords, abstained from bending the knee before him. Compared to those turncoats, the Hungarians could not but appear as knights in shining armor to Maria Theresa.

They rebuffed, with scorn, the claim to St. Stephen's crown Charles Albert advanced from Linz. Irregulars were called up in some of the counties, and some of the magnates came forward with liberal loans. The queen on her part confirmed the tax privileges of the nobility, promised to designate Hungarians to the Privy Conference, guaranteed self-rule in domestic affairs, and held out the prospect of an abolishment of Austrian transit tariffs on Hungarian cattle. Grassalkovich kept beseeching the Diet to fulfill Maria Theresa's fondest wish and grant the co-regent's title to the grand duke. A bargain was struck after many days: the queen conceded the Diet the right of electing a Palatine within a year after any incumbent's death, and both chambers, not without many restrictive clauses, made Francis co-regent in the kingdom.

The baby archduke had been brought to Pressburg on September 20. He was not at all a strong child. "The six-months-old, in the arms of his nurse, peeped at the crowds, much like a squirrel,"[51] a Hungarian diarist noted. The following morning the Diet administered the oath to Francis in the queen's presence. The assembly was in a subdued mood. But when Maria Theresa had the infant brought in, the sight revived the spirits of the men, and their exclamations drowned the whimperings of the child. Popular stories love to combine this scene with Maria Theresa's speech from the throne ten days before. Scores of paintings show her, girded with St. Stephen's sword and the crown on her head, holding the heir high up for everybody to behold. Although nothing of the kind took place on September 21, she did steal the show on that morning. This was supposed to be the grand duke's belated hour of glory; she turned it into an hour of renewed ovations for herself.

The performance of the Diet did not live up to the raptures of love shown on both occasions. Whittling down their own promise, they finally voted the queen a levy of 21,622 foot and 14,407 mounted troops. In mid-October, while the Franco-Bavarian force stood a mere thirty miles from Vienna, they were still deliberating some of the *gravamina*. They also took up again a demand that the queen had rejected all along

—the "reunion" of Transylvania with the kingdom.* Maria Theresa used bluff language in turning them down. She had given the Hungarians enough, she said.

They too had given her much besides soldiers and horses. The pressure they brought to bear on her, talking to the sovereign in accents beyond her imagination a year before, served to free her of the eggshells of her grand duchess' life in the Hofburg. Robinson's persistence had merely challenged her endurance, that most precious of Habsburg heirlooms. It was the Hungarians' resistance that hardened the willpower of Maria Theresa. She had disarmed the opposition of the magnates. She had not weakened in the clash with the representative body of the squirarchy. At this nadir of her fortunes she had, as the first of her race to do so, got the Hungarians to make Habsburg business their own. Overruling the jaded men in her council, who trembled at the thought of hosts of armed Hungarians under Hungarian leaders, she had felt a novel kind of strength accruing to her. The days of Pressburg provided her, overnight, as it were, with a European reputation. Their memory was to keep her affection for the Hungarians alive to her dying day, surviving grave conflicts. As late as 1771 she wrote to one of her daughters-in-law: "I feel so greatly indebted to the Hungarian nation that I cannot but recommend it to you. . . ."[52]

She can hardly have been aware of the greatest boon of all coming to her in Pressburg. Under strain and pressure she had dealt with matters whose complexities were way beyond her intellectual grasp. A feminine instinct had done service for reasoned judgment, as, facing strange men, she had played it by ear.

---

* St. Stephen himself had incorporated Transylvania in his kingdom. Hungarian administration, however, remained shadowy for centuries in the highlands and cities of the principality. From 1526 on it was under Turkish vassalage, if but nominally over long periods. Its princes and estates played no mean role in the wars and the treaty politics of the following century and a half. It was a descendant of Transylvanian princes who led the great rebellion, even though Habsburg suzerainty had been accepted after the Turkish debacle, and a Transylvanian chancellery set up in Vienna in 1694.

The estates ratified Charles VI's act of succession, with no strings attached, some years ahead of the Hungarians. Widely Protestant, Transylvania was inhabited, next to Magyars, by Szeklers (an ethnic group akin to them), Rumanians, and "Saxons" (descendants of fourteenth-century immigrants from the Rhineland). It was a far more civilized place than Hungary proper.

VI

The "Mock Emperor"

ON OCTOBER 23 the Franco-Bavarian army broke camp to abandon the march on Vienna. Perhaps Belle-Isle did not wish to see Charles Albert ensconced in the Hofburg before the Habsburg dominions were carved up in accord with his own blueprint; or perhaps the Bavarian, who in Linz had proclaimed himself King of Bohemia, mistrusted his brother-in-law, the Saxon elector, and *his* designs on the kingdom, and prevailed on Belle-Isle to advance toward Prague. The sudden about-face, whatever its reasons, puzzled the court as much as did Frederick's intention, known in Pressburg since mid-September, to break faith with his allies.

The French thrust into the heart of Europe had alarmed him. He had no desire to "let Polyphemus gobble him up as the last of his victims."[1] Moreover, he still wondered whether Mollwitz had not been a mere stroke of good luck. Why not, then, let Neipperg tackle Belle-Isle's invading battalions, and give a rest to his own Prussians, whose cavalry had still not recovered from the shock experienced in battle?

The negotiations Frederick was seeking were entrusted to Neipperg. "I wish," Maria Theresa wrote him, "you could get the king's signature without signing anything yourself."[2] Hyndford was present when the general met the king in a château situated halfway between the fortresses of Neisse and Brieg and evacuated for secrecy's sake. Frederick's terms were bizarre. If Neipperg surrendered Neisse after a two-week siege, his army would not be molested on its withdrawal to Moravia and before the year's end the king would sign a treaty, which of course must leave him in possession of the fortress and Lower Silesia. Should the present understanding become known, however, the king would disavow

it and act as he saw fit. He allowed Hyndford to keep minutes but refused to initial them. "It is all a snare, a delusion," was the queen's
comment in a letter to Neipperg. And, on second thought, she would
prefer him to "bid [the king] goodbye without agreeing to anything.
Show regret that you just could not do it."[3] This communication came
to the general's hands only after he had accepted the king's conditions.
Recalling Charles VI's dispatch to Neipperg in Belgrade, one may wonder about his talent for receiving cautionary instructions too late.

Early in November the grand duke was appointed commander-in-
chief of the army in Bohemia. "Next to God," Maria Theresa was "pinning all my hopes on you."[4] The Franco-Bavarian approach had thrown
the Hofkriegsrat into utter confusion. Its orders were of no help to the
leadership in the field. Prince Christian Lobkowitz, encamped at Pilsen,
expected Neipperg to block the enemy; and when Charles Albert appeared before Prague on November 23 and summoned its commander
to surrender, this officer laughed off the threat, so certain was he of relief by Neipperg, whose advance patrols had in fact been sighted from
the towers of the city. In the small hours of the twenty-sixth, Maurice
de Saxe with a handpicked assault force scaled the wall of the fortress
and opened its gates to Belle-Isle's main force and the auxiliary corps
that Augustus of Saxony had sent into the kingdom without much ado.

"Now, Kinsky, is the moment to show courage and fortitude," the
queen wrote to the Bohemian chancellor, who had joined the grand
duke in the field. "My mind is made up. Everything has to be risked to
rescue Bohemia. Rather than cede any part of it, I would see all my
armies wiped out, not excluding the Hungarian regiments. Stay by the
side of my poor husband, who worries as much about his troops as
about Bohemia. Their condition arouses his pity. [The army] must take
whatever is not delivered. You will accuse me of cruelty. . . . But I
know that I will be able to make up for all hardships in the countryside. Yes, I will. . . . For the time being, I have banished compassion
from my heart."[5] This letter was, in effect, an appeal to the landed
nobility in regions not controlled by enemy troops. It was of no avail.
The estates paid homage to Charles Albert in Prague on December 7,
and a week later the archbishop crowned him, at St. Vitus's cathedral,
amid a press of lords and nobles. "My ministers completely lost heart,"
Maria Theresa was to recall. "Instead of trying to raise my spirits, they
openly intimated that everything was lost. And some of them . . . had
the impudence of soliciting my permission to write to the Elector and
swear fealty to him [as liegemen] of their Bohemian estates."[6]

She had returned to Vienna on December 5, welcomed by exuberant
acclamations on her ride, in an open carriage, through the snow-swept
streets. Her homecoming laid to rest the lingering fear of a siege. The

capture of Prague did not exercise the Viennese, and they were ignorant —as was the court—of the renewed Prussian peril. Not until Prussian troops had occupied a number of Bohemian places did the queen realize that the unsigned accord had indeed been a sham. Frederick repudiated it on December 16. The queen, he declared, had not kept the secret. Certainly a good many people—her aunt among them—had known of the arrangement. There also had been bickerings about it all along. In particular, Maria Theresa asserted that the king had pledged his electoral vote to the grand duke, whereas Frederick denied the arrangement. The "perjured king" she called him. But her sense of outraged morality could not buffet the consternation at the advance of his troops. Olmütz, the great Moravian fortress a bare eighty miles from the Hofburg, had fallen under the onslaught of Schwerin, the hero of Mollwitz.

Neipperg's failure to give battle was mauling his prestige in the officers' corps. The ruthlessness of the Hungarian irregulars was giving him a bad name in the countryside, as was the savagery of the Croat pandours. Their colonel, Francis von der Trenck, was a soldier of fortune famous since the mid-1730's. Having attained a free-corps patent through the good services of Prince Charles, Trenck had gathered a thousand-odd horsemen and waived pay for them, as well as for himself, at a time recruits were as hard to come by as was money. Although Neipperg denounced him in Vienna, Maria Theresa did not rebuke Trenck. She had not forgotten the sight of his regiment brought to Vienna on the eve of her journey to Pressburg and the tide of hope that had swept her as those wildly garbed warriors galloped past her on the parade ground, brandishing their sabers, and huzzaing at the top of their lungs. That sentimental remembrance, however, was not the sole cause for her indifference to the pandours' atrocities. Trenck's men, as did the Hungarians, brought to the field guerrilla tactics which were said to drive the Prussians out of their wits.

As early as December 13 Maria Theresa hinted at her wish to have Francis come back to Vienna. "I am *raisonable* enough not to request your return, though. . . ."[7] But only four days later she scrawled on a note sent him by the Hofkriegsrat: "The matter is so important that not a moment's time must be lost. I hope to see you here day after tomorrow, the 19th, in the afternoon. This will be a great comfort to me. . . . I shall not write again. I am looking forward to your return with indescribable impatience."[8] As Christmas came and went, and Francis was still with Neipperg, she did write again, telling the grand duke that he was "so-to-speak indispensable"[9] in Vienna. But the memories of returns from other miscarried campaigns were still with Francis. And his virtual isolation in Pressburg—there had scarcely been any hunting—made him appreciate a sense of belonging at headquarters.

"The return trip has to be sped up as much as possible,"[10] wrote the queen on December 29.

She most ardently wished to detach Francis' name from Neipperg's. But there also *was* a "matter . . . so important" it could not, in good conscience, be decided upon in the co-regent's absence. The plan had been conceived in Pressburg; and if the queen was not its author, she yet had adopted it with an alacrity that took by surprise the man picked for its execution, Lewis Khevenhüller. The enemy's scattered forces in Upper Austria must be dislodged, Linz retaken, and the war carried into Bavaria. The Vienna garrison, reinforced by eleven thousand troops from the Italian army and by Hungarian irregulars, could accomplish the task, according to Khevenhüller. The conference wondered. Did they not see, the queen asked, that he had done wonders, in the past months, preparing Vienna for siege? Did the Hofkriegsrat not recognize in him the sense of enterprise so sorely lacking in the run of her generals? The ministers requested a "categorical decision" on her part. "I am hard put to it to form a resolve," she replied. "But I just feel that we should go ahead, and leave dispositions for the offensive, and what is needed, to him."[11] "Funds for Khevenhüller must be raised," she wrote to Charles von Doblhoff, one of the councilors at the treasury (and a brother-in-law of Bartenstein's). "If the whole sum cannot be raised, at least something has to, something to count on besides the English subsidies. . . . Everybody is asleep! If I did not urge activity, nothing at all would be done."[12]

Looking at the changing structure of authority a decade later, Maria Theresa thanked the Almighty for having written finis to the lives of the aged conference ministers, "for otherwise I never would have been able to remedy anything."[13] Did not the chronic indecision of those men also give rope to her own authoritarian nature? Thirty years afterward her lord marshal spoke of the "light from above that filled her in her youth."[14] Wherever the light may have originated, impatience with inactivity was within its spectrum. It spurred her on, endowed her with a measure of self-confidence, and blinded her to evident hopelessness.

None but a foolhardy amateur strategist would have insisted on Khevenhüller's offensive despite the Prussian menace in his rear. It was not altogether an amateur diplomat who wrote him, as she did: "I never thought that you ought to postpone, much less interrupt, your operations because of the Prussian advance in Moravia. I do by no means misjudge the hazardous situation, and I am anything but averse to tolerable conditions of peace. But precisely to get these, operations must be pursued. . . . As only the surrender of Prague caused [the king] to break with us, so a fortunate outcome of your undertaking will, if not alter his intentions, prevent him from continuing his support of [our] other enemies. At the same time such an outcome would raise the chances of the Maritime Powers' siding with the right cause, and succor it with money and troops."[15]

By mid-January Khevenhüller had put the occupation forces in Upper Austria out of action and was closing in on Linz. Francis, home at long last, was anxious to throw in his lot with the field marshal and partake of his success; and after some hesitation the queen once again appointed him commander-in-chief. Meantime Neipperg had been replaced by Prince Charles in Bohemia.

The Prince was in his thirtieth year. Well-proportioned and robust, taller than his brother and more measured in movement, he looked the part of a royal soldier. "His florid face is engaging despite the ravages wrought by the smallpox. He has a high forehead, and beautifully shaped lively eyes."[16] A strong jaw seemed to betoken determination. While given to good living and gallant banter, he had kept his name unsullied in the five years of his bachelor life in Vienna. His steadfast refusal to renounce any future Lorraine claims on his part had impressed even the detractors of the Lorraine clique in Vienna. The queen's sister Maria Anne was —or believed she was—in love with Charles, and Maria Theresa still favored the match. Her mother did not. Should the prince gain distinction in the field, or even rise to fame, the old lady's objections might well be overcome. Nor was Charles without qualifications for generalship: he had devoted some time to military studies, had proved composure and fearlessness under enemy fire, and was reputed to command loyalty with little effort. Besides, Theresa had grown very fond of him.

Grand Duke Francis lost no time "taking over command" from Khevenhüller. He brought him a miniature painting as a gift from the queen, along with a letter, which read, in part: "Here, my dear and faithful Khevenhüller, you have before your eyes a queen and her son who have been deserted by the whole world. What do you think will become of this child? To you as a loyal servant . . . your most gracious sovereign entrusts herself, her possessions, her power. Act, O my hero, my liegeman, as in boldness you can take it upon yourself before the Almighty and the world. Take justice as your shield. Close your eyes sitting in judgment over the perjurers [of Linz]. Emulate your late lamented master, Eugene. Rest assured that you and your family will always enjoy my own and my successors' good graces. Fame, the world will bestow upon you. God-speed, and fight well."[17] She may not herself have drafted the baroque epistle. The terse notes sent to Khevenhüller during the past weeks had been all her own, however. The seasoned commander must have rubbed his eyes as the young woman was plying him with advice, down to the logistics of the campaign. Yet his voice was choked with emotion while, in Francis' presence, he was reading her letter to the assembled generals in the encampment before Linz.

Its French garrison surrendered on January 23. On January 24 Charles Albert was elected emperor at St. Bartholomew's at Frankfurt. There was not a single dissenter. Even George II, having been guaranteed Hanover's neutrality by the French, cast his vote for the Bavarian. As the Empire's charter disfranchised women, Maria Theresa had originally delegated the vote attached to the Bohemian kingdom to her co-regent. After Charles Albert's coronation in Prague the electoral college suspended the Bohemian suffrage, overriding her protests. Her envoy's demand in Frankfurt to be given the lodgings by tradition due to "Bohemia" was openly ridiculed. So low had the stock of the Vienna court sunk that the Empire's chancellor, the elector-archbishop of Mainz, did not dare to propose the queen's health at a banquet. Belle-Isle, having rushed to Frankfurt from Prague, entered the town with great pomp. French promises, bribes, and threats had rigged the election.

Crown, scepter, and orb were taken to Frankfurt from Nuremberg, the Free City that was their guardian. And on February 12 the Bavarian was crowned as Charles VII. The story that became current about the "colic which caused him great trouble and embarrassment during the ceremony"[18] or the description of his rotund spouse did not amuse her outraged cousin in Vienna. She summoned the Lower Austrian estates to the New Favorita, along with the papal nuncio, and there, the family crown on her head,* denounced the election as null and void, branding the "mock emperor" a French puppet.

Given the practical bent of her mind, she could not but realize the damage done her dynasty's business. No matter how ramshackle the Empire may have been, what was left of the rights of its crown had been of service to its bearer in Vienna. These rights had provided him with assistance in campaigns fought for the defense, or aggrandizement, of his own possessions, as well as in wars that he carried on for the protection of the Reich in discharge of imperial duty. The investiture of sovereign princes, secular or ecclesiastic, had been a means to further the interests of his house. The Aulic Council, located in Vienna under the Empire's vice-chancellor (as a rule an Austrian noble) had been useful in the pursuit of Habsburg policies both in foreign courts and the Reich. The Empire's archives were housed in Vienna. Charles VII, if not the healthiest of men, was but forty-four years of age. Having a son, he would strive to keep his dynasty's hold on the Empire's crown. Its return

---

* This crown, made during the reign of Emperor Rudolph II (1576–1612), a learned eccentric, had regularly been worn by his successors on the ride to the coronation act in Frankfurt.

to the court of Vienna, if to be hoped for at all, was tormentingly remote.

For all we know, Francis kept silent about the shattering blow. Speaking bluntly—as, incidentally, was his mother—he had been twice the loser. One of the countless pamphlets published in London put it as follows: "To see all the hopes of her husband, who sacrificed his own hereditary dominions to a dream of greatness, complimented away was such a sudden reverse as needed all the patience of a martyr to endure."[19] Did Maria Theresa ever see it that way? She could, after all, tell herself that Francis had ceded his duchy to gain his beloved. After six years of marriage she had no reason to question the constancy of his feeling.

There were two rays of light to pierce these glum days in the Hofburg: neither Charles Albert's Bohemian nor his archducal title had been written into the instrument at Frankfurt; and Khevenhüller, sweeping into the usurper's own Bavaria, had occupied its capital, Munich, on the very day of the coronation.

His offensive was meeting with criticism. Prince Charles submitted that "before carrying the torch of war into enemy country, we should try to extinguish it in our own."[20] The Hofkriegsrat had voiced the same thought before, and in fact ordered Khevenhüller to break off his advance and join the prince in his operations. "Granted the Prussian affair is unpleasant," the field marshal replied. "But surely the king will do nothing drastic with winter upon him. One must not always expect the worst."[21] Francis was enjoying the nominal command of the forward-marching army; and as for Frederick, he had put it into his head that the king could be made peace with and won as an ally into the bargain.

"My sweetheart," the queen wrote, "I implore you not to delay your return trip. . . . If you feel like it, go ahead and write him. I do not think it would be worth the effort, though. He only will take advantage of it. At any event, do not demean yourself. Use our conquests as a pretext."[22] And Francis' ideas did not keep her from adopting the plan of the Hofkriegsrat: Prince Charles must take the offensive against the French, and Khevenhüller attack them in the rear. At least a part of the latter's army must be marched into Bohemia, snowstorms or none, Maria Theresa ordered, closing the communication with a passionate plea. Khevenhüller demurred.

By the time the grand duke was back in Vienna his emissary to Frederick, Baron Pfütschner (as he now was) had returned from the king's headquarters in Olmütz. What an audience he had had of the Prussian! An alliance with the queen of Hungary? No. Certainly not. He, the king, did not scorn peace. But the queen had better realize that she was not welcome to him as a neighbor. She must "swallow the bitter pill,"[23] recognize Charles Albert's Bohemian kingship, and cede certain parts of Moravia and Upper Silesia to her cousin by marriage, Augustus. He himself would be content with the county of Glatz, to round off his Silesian dominion.

It scarcely needed such language to convince Maria Theresa that peace must be won in battle. But Prince Charles had not budged from his winter quarters and kept pressing for reinforcements. Another letter went off to Khevenhüller. "You need not be told [it closed] that success . . . depends largely on your co-operation with His Highness."[24] At last the field marshal complied and detached twelve thousand men to Bohemia. In February Frederick's hussars began penetrating Lower Austria, pillaging the countryside and "spreading terror to the gates of Vienna."[25] The town, having been spared the French siege in October, was buzzing with rumors of an impending Prussian assault. At court only Bartenstein fortified the resolve of the queen not to abandon the struggle—"and this gave him his great credit with me."[26] Appealing to Pálffy, she impressed on him the necessity for speeding up recruitments. Light troops were needed desperately to intercept the king's raids.

Early in March she had muskets distributed among Moravian peasants, giving them title to all booty they would make as guerrillas. Not for a hundred years had such armed bands been seen in European warfare. The innovation was Khevenhüller's. He had organized partisan groups of Tyrolians in the rear of the Bavarian army, and their raids had been of no mean value. But these mountaineers had been freeholders since time immemorial; and that distinction, well-nigh unique in the Hereditary Lands, was not lost on the queen. To the horror of her ministers, she promised the Moravian peasants—in guarded words, to be sure—a betterment of their lot.

In her father's, as her grandfather's day, attempts had been made to reduce the crushing labor services of the Slav peasantry. The aristocracy would not hear of any such change. "The peasantry is like pasture land," they would say, "the more you cut it, the better it serves."[27] But in the winter of 1741–42 the queen felt small sympathy for the great lords. She was determined to chasten the traitors of Prague and Linz. As soon as Upper Austria was cleared of the enemy, she had given notice of her intention to dissolve its estates. She belittled the repercussions Bartenstein thought the unprecedented measure would have in the other lands. And as he warned her of the administrative chaos bound to result in Upper Austria itself, she retorted: "I am certain that enough loyal and honest men can be found to fill the positions vacated by a purge. Many Silesians are out of bread because of their faithfulness, and are cooling their heels. Don't tell me that there are no able men among them."[28] There were.

As winter turned into spring Prince Charles's vacillations began to exasperate his sister-in-law. Indeed, indeed, so she wrote him on March 10, the French might endanger the movements of his army while it was dealing with the Prussians and Saxons (as the Hofkriegsrat had ordered), but would he not, conversely, invite *their* attack if he turned (as he himself was inclined to do) to take on the French? "I leave the decision to you. But strike you must—in one direction or the other. Nothing could be more pernicious than to prolong the inactivity which has lasted far too long already. . . ."[29] Orders—or, accurately speaking, directives—emanating from the Hofkriegsrat had always been subject to the decision of the field commander. He in turn would discuss them with his generals, and as a rule a vote was taken. Dissimilarities of temperaments and mutual jealousies often poisoned these meetings. On one occasion Browne, having run afoul of his superior, was reminded by Vienna that "while it is true that generals are in duty bound to tender their opinions . . . without reservation, there can be no justification for passing the bounds of propriety."[30] Even within those bounds the dissensions of his generals worsened Charles's dilemma.

His brother found no fault with what he called circumspection. His heart was still set on peace. He had dissuaded the queen from breaking off the talks with the "perjured king." A Moravian monsignor was dispatched to Frederick, only to have the door shut in his face. Shortly after this hapless mission to Olmütz the king abandoned the fortress. Irregulars and partisans were undermining the morale of his men. His Saxon allies had been halfhearted from the start, their generals muddle-headed and vainglorious. Belle-Isle had fallen ill, and Broglie was disinclined to accommodate himself to the strategy of the young king. Contrary to a pledge of the French court, its second army, poised on the Hanoverian border, had not marched on Bohemia. Charles VII, pressing for Bavaria's reconquest, was becoming a nuisance to Frederick. And great events in the world at large added to his discomfort. In Russia a palace revolt had brought Anne's sister, Elizabeth, to the throne after deposing the Prussophile regents. And in February Walpole had been driven from office.

"The Queen of Hungary!" had been a fashionable toast among his opponents even before her gallant performance caught the imagination of the public. Now the *Daily Advertiser* published an appeal to succor Maria Theresa by raising a purse, and Marlborough's widow put herself at the head of a ladies' committee.* An ode to the valorous Habsburg princess ("Thou wondrous woman! matchless queen! . . .")[31] found many readers.

* Some weeks afterward Maria Theresa appears to have inquired after the results of the money drive; Wasner's reply, relating its failure, has survived (Arneth, *op cit.*, II, 480).

Upon Ostein's resignation Ignatius Wasner had been appointed *chargé d'affaires* in London. This humbly born man, who had come to Prince Liechtenstein's notice at the Paris embassy, proved to be "very different from the run of Vienna's envoys abroad . . . who excel by their surly, sanguine, and overbearing demeanor."[32] He seemed to be the very person the queen needed in London to cope with the disparate velleities of its politicians. Lord Carteret, who for all practical purposes directed the new cabinet, had called himself "a good Englishman, and therefore an ardent Austrian,"[33] in a talk with Wasner shortly before Walpole's downfall. Once in office, he seemed insensitive to Wasner's proposal that the king declare war on Louis XV. George II was torn between his wrath at the lawbreaker. Frederick, and the concern for Hanover's safety. And for all of Wasner's exertions, public opinion, exposed to the propaganda of Frederick, the "defender of Protestantism," was still wavering and divided.

Frederick did not like what he heard from London. Surveying his situation, he had no doubt but that Silesia was firmly in his hands. His administration, well established by now in the duchy, was furnishing him with a splendid revenue. On the other hand, fodder and forage were hard to come by in Bohemia; fresh Hungarian troops were arriving; and judging by the low ratio of desertion from Prince Charles's army, its morale was improving.

Actually that army was better by far than its leadership. Charles had twice thrown away an opportunity to cut off the Prussian forces retreating to Bohemia from Olmütz, and even Khevenhüller's enterprise seemed to be flagging. Junior commanders who, often with great pluck, engaged enemy detachments regularly failed to exploit success. The stream of directives from Vienna had not succeeded in uniting operations in the field. A new French corps had crossed the Rhine, obviously bent on marching toward Bohemia. There were schemes afoot to embroil the Empire in Charles Albert's struggle against Maria Theresa; and though armed intervention on the part of its princes was not the most frightening of dangers, the thought of being branded the Empire's rebellious vassal was unbearable to the daughter of Charles VI.

She informed Frederick that she might cede the county of Glatz and evacuate Bavaria in return for his and his allies' withdrawal from Upper Silesia and Bohemia. Although the king procrastinated and continued to concentrate his forces in eastern Bohemia, he invited Lord Hyndford to Breslau. By mid-April Maria Theresa was ready to meet Frederick's territorial demands in Silesia. Of course, he would have to guarantee the integrity of her remaining possessions in the *Reich* and join her in clearing its soil of the French defilers. "An intolerable piece of presumption," Frederick called this condition. Why, he said to Hyndford, he was "about to faint." [34] He decided to attack—as, by this time, had Prince Charles—and in a spirited note to Fleury stressed the indissoluble bond between France and Prussia.

The battle was joined on May 17, near the towns of Chotusitz and Czaslau, on the south bank of the upper Elbe. As the king himself said afterwards, Charles was not defeated through lack of valor on the part of his troops. What won the day for Frederick was the superiority of his guns, both in kind and in numbers, the recent training of his cuirassiers, and his disregard for losses, whose speedy replacement in the lines stunned the Austrian soldiers. Charles did not lose his head and retreated only when encirclement left him no choice. Carrying away twelve Prussian flags, he yielded none to the enemy. He was eager to give him battle again and take revenge for the "engagement that did not entirely go the way we had wished for." [35] The grand duke, asked by the Hofkriegsrat to dissuade his brother, suggested that he take on the French instead. Maria Theresa did not herself write to the prince. Four days before he had lost the battle she had been brought to bed with a girl. Named Maria Christina, she was to grow up to become her favorite child.

No sooner had the queen left confinement than Robinson asked to be received. He pretended not to know that the king's victory had stiffened his peace terms. Bartenstein, however, had learned that he now was coveting a certain Bohemian county. As Robinson shrugged off what he contended was an unfounded rumor, Maria Theresa, her temper rising, told him that she would never give up so much as a square foot of Bohemian land, "even if Hell itself threatened to swallow me, and even if your king and master, together with Parliament, decided on my destruction." [36] The ambassador made bold to remind her of the magnanimity of his nation. She gave no pertinent answer and also abstained from reminding him of the pressure that his government had brought to bear on her in Italian affairs. This was not a story to endear his government to the court of Vienna.

To discourage Spanish encroachments it had put forward early in 1741 a plan of a confederation of all Italian states north of the Neapolitan border. After the project came to nothing Count Otto von Traun, in command of the queen's small army on the peninsula, was instructed to secure the king of Sardinia-Piedmont, duke of Savoy, as an ally.

For centuries the duchy of Savoy had enjoyed a consequence way out of proportion to its size and resources. Astride the slopes of the Alps, it commanded their passes, and in a narrow area touched on the Tyrrhenian Sea. During the War of the Spanish Succession its crafty ruler, jockeying between the belligerents, had muscled in on the spoils. His son

Charles Emmanuel tried to emulate the feat of skill during the war over the throne of Poland. Failure had only redoubled his greed.

Otto von Traun, of north-German birth, was a veteran of many battlefields. A glorious episode in the Neapolitan campaign of 1734 had attached renown to his name. But in his sixty-fourth year he hardly was a match for Charles Emmanuel and his first minister, D'Ormea. Moreover, the offers that Traun was entitled to make were paltry; and arriving in Turin, he learned that the court of Madrid had entered the bidding. The Spanish negotiator, seconded by France, offered to Charles Emmanuel nearly the whole of Lombardy as the price of cooperation. Bartenstein argued that the Spanish queen herself was known to have an eye on Lombardy for her younger son (who had married Louis XV's eldest daughter) and that D'Ormea was using the offer from Madrid only as a bargaining counter. It fell to Robinson's lot to tell Maria Theresa that Britain could not afford to put Bartenstein's theory to the test and risk a strengthening of the Bourbons' camp. Charles Emmanuel must be bought off.

His territorial wishes included the margraviate of Finale, a stretch of coastal land which Charles VI, in one of his desperate money transactions, had sold to the Republic of Genoa. The conference, who were above all eager to strike a good bargain in Lombardy, had no qualms about helping the little king to the margraviate. Not so Maria Theresa. The Venetian ambassador heard her say that she would "rather lose her crown . . . than secure her position at the expense of innocent people, no matter how small the injustice done them."[37] Robinson submitted that if Genoa owed Finale, as she maintained it did, ceding title to the margraviate would mean nothing. This sophistry seemed only to heighten her vexation. At the same time, she welcomed the opportunity the Finale question offered of postponing altogether an accommodation with the court of Turin. She was still resisting Robinson's persuasion when an event that in itself was a European sensation forced her hand.

On November 11 (1741) a Spanish flotilla landed eight thousand troops on the Tuscan coast, after sailing through waters the British were assumed to control. This expedition, followed in January by a second transport, created a dire threat to Habsburg territory, as well as Charles Emmanuel's; and the common danger compelled the two courts to arrive at an understanding. It was declared "provisional" by both, and, in particular, left the king free to rescind it should Maria Theresa fail to honor his Lombard demands. As for Finale, she virtually transferred her "claim" to Sardinia. It was high time to consolidate defense. Impressed by the Spanish coup, the duke of Modena allied himself with the Bourbons (and was promptly chased from his duchy by Traun). The Spanish army, led by Count de Gages, a Walloon, began operating on papal territory. And King Carlos of Naples, who in 1740 had pledged his neutrality, gave way to the proddings of his mother in Madrid and sent twelve thousand troops toward a junction with De Gages.

This move turned Maria Theresa's concern about defense into the desire to drive Carlos from his kingdoms, which had been her father's only five years before. "Naples and Sicily, whence several millions of cash used to come to Vienna . . . every year,"[38] must be recovered. Silesia would be lost, would it not? A *"dédommagement"* was in order, then, was it not? And England and Sardinia, she wrote to Wasner, must both assist her in the recovery of Naples. And "in order to give me at least some compensation for the wrong I have sustained . . . my beloved husband ought to be helped to the dignity of the Roman kingship. In that case—and if, furthermore, Bavaria severs all ties with France—I might be inclined to recognize the validity of [Charles VII's] election as emperor."[39]

Two days before she wrote this letter Hyndford had signed preliminaries in Breslau. They left her less than a fifth of Silesia and despoiled her of Glatz, a county of strategic importance. To her lasting regret, she had given wide powers to the Scotsman. As it was, he might have arranged for better terms, for an unexpected and successful maneuver of Prince Charles's had caused Frederick to hasten the negotiations. His impatience spared Maria Theresa the crowning indignity. To repay the Habsburgs in their own coin, he had tried to force her to assume the style of "Duchess *in* Silesia" as sovereign of the counties conceded to her. The final treaty was drafted and sealed in July at Berlin. Bartenstein called it "Volume Two of the Treaty of Belgrade." Maria Theresa herself would burst into tears at the mere sight of a Silesian.

VII

Carrousel in Vienna

AFTER AUGUSTUS OF SAXONY had made peace with Maria Theresa—
it brought him no gain—she wrote to his wife, her cousin, a con-
ciliatory letter. She was prepared to make up with the emperor, "indeed
let bygones be bygones, if only I could have security. He knows very
well how this can be achieved. All he has to do is put the Empire's welfare above his fatal connection with France."[1]

Left to her own devices by Frederick, France on her part was more
than willing to cut her losses. Fleury directed Belle-Isle to seek a meeting
with Königsegg, Prince Charles's foremost adviser at headquarters. Richelieu, in his memoirs, relates that the queen, receiving the news, flared up:
"I will receive no proposition from the cardinal. I am astonished that
[Belle-Isle] should make any advances—he who by money and promises
excited almost all the princes to crush me."[2] If these were not her actual
words, they yet fit her state of mind. The Tuscan minister at Versailles,
who had reported on overtures, received a note bristling with scorn. Had
not the cardinal only some months before declared that "the House
of Austria has ceased to exist"?[3] Her Majesty had "irrefutable evidence
of downright un-Christian plans for her doom. Now all hopes of their
success have vanished. . . . But her lands have been ravaged, the Empire's
foundations turned upside-down, the German liberties suppressed . . . and
all that with a brazen disregard for treaties solemnly sworn to. The
French boasted they would lay down the law from the ramparts of
Vienna. They aimed at no less than bringing the whole of Germany, yea,
of Europe, under their yoke. Thus, the Queen's cause has become the
cause of all powers that cherish their independence and love peace, as
well as of those princes who love their fatherland truly."[4] Copies of this

note were dispatched to London, The Hague, St. Petersburg, and Turin.

Now Fleury himself wrote to Königsegg, protesting that he had not been the originator of the Bavarian alliance. He could not foresee that Maria Theresa, taking a leaf out of Frederick's book, would make public the groveling communication. First printed in Utrecht, it made the nonagenarian the laughingstock of Europe. The hardening attitude toward France in London conjured up, to her mind, the image of a Bourbon confederacy humbled and helpless; and her yearning for *dédommagement*, ranging far afield now, sustained her defiance.

The Hofkriegsrat expected great things from the army that stood before Prague. They closed their eyes to the notorious incompetence of Austrian siege operations. The approach of Mallebois's army, which the French court, reanimated by Vienna's unbendingness, had ordered into Bohemia, did not disconcert the desk generals. Königsegg, however, in the teeth of his instructions, allowed himself to be "amused by the fulsome speeches and insidious confidences of Belle-Isle."[5] The grand duke, who was in his brother's camp, appears to have condoned the old field marshal's interview with the Frenchman. His wife's idea of the Roman kingship had caught Francis' imagination, and he was not averse to ingratiating himself with the court of Versailles which might support his candidacy. He was in for a rude awakening. Maria Theresa, so Robinson reported, declared that "she would not suffer a council in the army and a council in Vienna; she disclaimed, disallowed, and disavowed all such pernicious and unsanctioned proceedings, let the blame fall as it would."[6]

"*Mon cher Alter,*" she wrote Francis on August 24, "I am afraid this letter will not please you. But it will prove that I am opening my heart. You may correct my views. Everything depends on it [?] and, in particular my peace of mind and my happiness. As the matter concerns you, too, I gave it continuous thought last night and early this morning, and jotted down some of my thoughts." And with that she plunged into an analysis of the "three different ways" open to Francis' choice as a strategist. "I would prefer the first, but fear that it is too late for it. In my opinion, only the second plan can be executed, if we do not want to waste time. The third one goes against my grain. . . . In this life, and especially in war, risks cannot be avoided." And, then, once more: "It is up to you. You may do what you want. It is impossible anyway to lay down the law from here."[7]

While the Lorraine princes and their generals had been floundering in Bohemia—Francis was said to "pay more attention to the country's richly stocked preserves than to the troops and their operations"[8]—encouraging news had trickled in from Italy. At length Traun had started marching. And the Neapolitan barons, the prop of the regime in the days of the Austrian viceroys, were fomenting unrest in the kingdom. An emissary of theirs had arrived in Vienna, and the queen listened avidly to his account of an impending rebellion against King Carlos. When Maria Theresa penned her ill-humored missive to her *cher Alter*, she did not know yet of the collapse of her scheme for Naples' reconquest.

A light earthquake on August 17 had prejudiced the superstitious populace of Naples against any plot to unseat established authority. The following day a British squadron appeared off Baia, anchored in full view of the city, and "by threats of an immediate bombardment compelled the king . . . to withdraw his troops from the Spanish army [of De Gages] and to engage for the maintenance of strict neutrality."[9] This turn of events weakened the striking force of Maria Theresa's enemies on the peninsula. At the same time, it deprived her of a pretext for dethroning the Bourbon usurper in Naples.

In Bohemia the objective was to put Mallebois's army out of combat, take Prague, and capture its garrison and Belle-Isle.

The operations of September and October fell short of these goals. True, Mallebois's junction with Broglie was thwarted. But neither did Charles (whose army included Khevenhüller's corps) join battle with Mallebois, nor was the latter interfered with on his retreat. By the end of November, however, the Austrians were in control, such as it was, of the kingdom's countryside. Lobkowitz, who had strict orders from the queen not to arrange for any capitulation of Prague except for the occupiers' surrender as prisoners of war, was tightening the blockade of the city. With its provisions and fuel getting scarce, and the population shedding their initial docility, the French seemed to be doomed. Lobkowitz, having laid waste the country around the town, pitched tents at fifteen miles' distance beyond the river. He left only a detachment of hussars before the walls, as he thought the French "incapable of forcing a march . . . through country covered with snow, broken by almost impassable mountains, abounding in defiles, and infested with irregulars."[10] On the night of December 16 Belle-Isle "deceived the inhabitants of the town, and forming 11,000 foot and 3,000 horse in a single column, walked them out of Prague, leaving the sick and wounded with a guard in the citadel."[11]

His march across the wintry wastes inflicted on his troops "dreadful sufferings such as no European army had ever experienced."[12] But he brought their ragged remnants to safety in the fortress of Eger, close to the Bavarian border. "Not the smallest trophy" was left behind "to grace the triumph of the enemy."[13] There was no triumph in the heart of the queen in Vienna. Mallebois had rescued the flower of the French army; Belle-Isle had made fools of her commanders; and on Christmas

Day Lobkowitz granted the honors of war to the rump garrison of Prague, some five thousand men. His action, compounding the scandalous failure, soured Maria Theresa's gratification at the delivery of Prague. Yet she dissimulated in public what Robinson described as the "extreme agony of her mind."[14] Of the ordeal of Mallebois's men, she would speak often, pity them loudly, and denounce its author, Belle-Isle.

A *Te Deum* was sung at St. Stephen's on December 30. And three days afterward the count defied custom, which frowned on festivities between Christmas and Epiphany, and celebrated the capture of Prague by a magnificent spectacle—the carrousel for which preparations had been going on in the Spanish Riding Academy since September. Francis, writing to his brother on his return from the field in November, had observed that people in Vienna talked about nothing but the forthcoming tournament.

Only women had been permitted to enter the lists. The contestants formed four teams, two of them on horseback, the other two driving low-slung four-wheeled chariots. Maria Theresa, with child again and riding "as women do,"[15] wore a habit of crimson velvet and a tricorne studded with precious stones. Her mount's gear and saddle were ornamented with gold in the Turkish manner. Contemporary accounts agree that she acquitted herself very well in controlling the horse and leading it through the movements of the quadrille. Brandishing her dainty sword, she chopped off as many of the wooden "Turks' Heads" as any of her competitors and did better than most in target shooting with the pistol.*

Jean-Etienne Liotard, the Genevese artist, painted a likeness of her the following year. Presenting her in a low-cut bodice, it shows an ample-bosomed young matron. The eyes appear deeper set than in earlier portraits. Their sidewise glance is calm and assertive. A premature fold encroaches on the corners of her mouth. The chin has grown a bit plump. Liotard did not prettify her. But the candor of his art, which shocked Mme. Fuchs, has preserved the youthful freshness which tempers the strength of the features. Equally free from severity and conceit, this face exerts considerable attraction even in the repose of a portrait. The liveliness of Maria Theresa's eyes in converse, and a smile which bared faultless teeth, no doubt lent beauty to the countenance of the twenty-six-year-old.

On the white charger she rode in the carrousel she must have offered

---

* A canvas depicting the famous affair, done by the Swedish-born Martin van Meytens and some of his pupils, can still be seen in Schönbrunn. What strikes the eye, more forcefully than the amazons, grooms and blooded horses, is the beauty of the hall, its two tiers of pillared galleries, its vaulted ceiling, and the high windows. The original plans for the building and its interior had been drawn by Fischer von Erlach.

an exquisite sight. When the competitions had ended, the dowager empress, ensconced beneath the marble replica of the imperial crown, distributed the prizes. Then the four teams, following an impulsive decision of the queen, trotted out of the building, past St. Michael's, and into the courtyard of the Hofburg. Never had Charles VI shown himself in the streets save in solemnly slow-moving processions. His daughter's riding past *hoi polloi* at the head of the cavalcade of ladies—this was a spectacle about which townsfolk were to talk for a long time.

They would recall this winter for many years. All of a young person's natural longing for amusement burst out in Theresa. She plunged into the carnival season with a delight amounting to abandon. She came to love masked balls. "Never was she pleased more than when she went unrecognized in her disguise. However, she succeeded only seldom. Her beautiful carriage and the brisk gait gave her away."[16] Once Tarouca warned her of "overheating the bloodstream."[17] "Proceed," she told him, "even though I don't seem to be listening. Later [in Lent?] I shall recall what you said."[18] She "has no consideration for her health, and does not hearken to well-meaning counsel,"[19] the lord marshal noted.

Masquerades were no novelty in the court of Vienna. Even Charles VI had appeared with his empress at its weekly "innkeepers' parties" in rustic disguise during carnival. Foreigners thought these affairs were of deadly dullness. There was nothing particularly dull about the Tuesdays' masked balls that took place this winter either in two of the drafty halls of the Hofburg or in the overheated small theater, the old tennis hall that had been redecorated two years before. Outright merrymaking came into its own when the queen and her consort, with a small suite, went to the *Mehlgrube*, Vienna's most popular place for dances. Although these were "for nobility only" on certain nights, fancy dresses, masks, and perukes made a mockery of the restriction, and almost anybody, paying five florins, could enter the place even when the royal couple was expected. Francis adored these dances.

On Shrove Tuesday, 1743, he and his wife joined Prince Charles and some of his friends for the noonday collation at his suburban château, where the company danced the whole afternoon, returned to the Hofburg for dinner, dressed up as rustics, repaired to the *bal masqué* at the former tennis hall, after midnight donned Venetian dominoes, and rushed to the *Mehlgrube* to take part in several counterdances amid a far from select crowd. Back at the tennis-hall party, the queen did not stop dancing until eight A.M. We have it on the authority of the lord marshal that she was present at the Ash Wednesday service in the palace chapel at nine, and both in the forenoon and after luncheon attended to business. It may be too much to imagine her reading on that Ash Wednesday one of the notes with which her new ambassador to Turin bombarded the chancellery. We do know, however, that she became an assiduous reader of his reports in these very weeks.

Count Wenceslas Kaunitz-Rietberg came from a family of the original Bohemian peerage, whose fortunes the upheavals of the past century had not touched. The youngest of twenty children, and of delicate health, he had been destined for the cloth, and a canonship was attached to his name when he was a boy of thirteen. After several of his brothers died within a brief span of time, his father decided to have Wenceslas educated for the service of the court. His mother, a woman of Frisian origin, appears to have been interested in learning. But she so fretted about Wenceslas' health—as did the flock of his sisters—that he developed into a hypochondriac even during his student years at Leipzig and Leyden. On his return from the grand tour he married a Countess Starhemberg. Charles VI sent him to Ratisbon. In 1738 the chancellor dispatched him on an extended journey to the Italian courts to counteract the crumbling prestige of the house of Habsburg. It was Kaunitz who in 1741 notified the Holy See of the birth of the archduke. Notwithstanding Rome's coolness toward the new sovereign in Vienna, he discharged his duty with a dignity that attracted notice. He was just past thirty in 1742. Tall and slim, he was of striking appearance. His longish pale face was lit up by azure eyes whose sparkle belied the calm mien, if not the sensuous mouth. Of unabashed haughtiness, he tended to flaunt self-assurance. As he lacked the funds to cut a dazzling figure in the court of Turin, he had hesitated to accept the post. As soon as he was installed there he showed a methodical diligence at variance with his foppish pose and the languor that he affected.

The lucidity of his long memorials impressed Bartenstein from the start. The conditions the Vienna court had attached to its understanding with Sardinia had kept her king's suspicions alive. Even the Spanish advance had failed to secure the full cooperation of his generals with Traun. Kaunitz' diplomacy worked wonders within a few weeks.

When the Spaniards attacked the combined force on February 8 they were repelled after a long day's bitter fighting at Campo Santo. Traun had been criticized fiercely in Vienna for his caution, and rumormongers had blackened his name. Now his stock was rising again. Half a victory only, the battle yet put the Spaniards on the defensive.

Considering the state of her affairs a year earlier, Maria Theresa had ample reason to be grateful to her Maker. She did thank Him profusely but also asked Him for more. Frustrated in Naples, she had come to the conclusion that the "loss of Silesia can be compensated for only by the acquisition of some other adjacent country."[20] Adding to the girth as such of the Habsburg patrimony was not the ultimate goal; new territory within the *Reich* must be acquired to nip in the bud the theory (as formulated in an English pamphlet) that Austria was but one of the Empire's "members" and no longer its "head."[21] Even though her troops by now had been squeezed out of Bavaria, she hoped that Charles VII could be compelled to swap his ancestral land for Belgium*—the last place on earth where her allies, the Maritime Powers, would tolerate a prince allied with France. She was to learn that the last thing King Frederick might acquiesce in was an aggrandizement of the Habsburg compound on the Empire's soil.

Frederick cautioned Carteret, who had won over his king and Parliament to the plan of direct intervention on the Continent. As Marshal Stair, the aged commander, began to form an army of Hanoverian and Hessian mercenaries in Belgium, Frederick let it be known that although he would not interfere with Anglo-French hostilities even on *Reich* territory, he would not stand by idle if Stair's "Pragmatic Army" should attack the emperor's forces. At the same time, the king was exhorting the Ratisbon Diet to raise an army for the defense of the neutrality of Charles VII.

He also, several times, offered his good services to Maria Theresa as a mediator between her and Louis XV. She spurned the proposal. The court of Versailles had not learned its lesson yet. It had permitted the transit of Spanish troops through French territory. Led by Don Philip, they had entered Savoy; and Charles Emmanuel, to defend the Alpine passes, had called some of his regiments home from the Austro-Sardinian army.

Marshal Stair, having received orders to "march into Germany,"[22] stood close to the River Main when Maria Theresa set out for Prague to have herself crowned as Queen of Bohemia. She entered the city on April 29. As the long train moved through the narrow medieval streets, past the massive town hall, across the ancient stone bridge, and up to Hradschin Castle—the aldermen riding ahead, and the mounted heralds of Bohemia, Hungary, and the Austrian lands sounding their trumpets over the din of the church bells—many of the great nobles of the kingdom, and not a few of its prelates, the archbishop of Prague among them, were conspicuous through their absence. The defectors had been exiled to their estates.

May 11 had been set as the day of the coronation. Kinsky, who thought the haste inappropriate, was set right in a billet from the queen: "The Elector [afterwards Charles VII] gave even shorter notice. . . . I expect to be in ill humor anyway. Must not be worsened. Everything remains as laid down. Nothing will be postponed for even an hour's

---

* This project had cropped up first in the days of his father who, married to a Spanish Habsburg, held the Belgian governorship for many years.

time."[23] When Kinsky suggested some minor changes in the coronation oath she roundly bade him keep his counsel. St. Wenceslas' venerable crown was taken to her apartments from the vault of St. Vitus's with great ceremony. "Crown came," wrote Maria Theresa to Kinsky. "Tried it on. Heavier than the one in Pressburg. Looks rather like a fool's cap."[24]

She could afford to flaunt her foul humor. Though the first prince of her race to rule the kingdom had been duly elected by its estates, the Bohemian crown had been proclaimed hereditary in 1547. Bohemia was deprived of her constitution eighty years later. The Bohemian Chancellery was in Vienna. Unlike the Hungarian Diet, the Bohemian estates could not come forward with any *gravamina*. However, the great lords had come by certain powers surreptitiously. "After Ferdinandus [II] had quelled the Bohemian rebellion [of 1620] he showered gifts and benefices on those ministers who had remained faithful to him, and on others as well," wrote Maria Theresa in her memoir of 1751. "And these men, in drafting subsequent laws, made use of the credit they had gained [with the sovereign]. Rather than his interest, they furthered the kingdom's, even though his arms alone had regained it. . . . The power of the Bohemian chancellor, which had been built up underhandedly in the first place, was neither compatible with royal authority nor with the exigencies of the administration."[25]

Although the Maria Theresa of 1743 might not have put it that clearly, she assuredly felt that she must not be reminded of any privileges that the big landowners—and thus the estates—had known how to secure. Accounts with the traitors were still far from being settled. Worse, settling them was a vexatious business. Many of the nobility had employed subterfuge to remain in her good graces; in not a few instances the head of the family had left Bohemia on Charles Albert's arrival, while a son or brother had sworn allegiance to him.

As the French had threatened to put the town to the torch, Lobkowitz, granting them the honors of war, also had pledged freedom of prosecution on political grounds to anyone in Prague at the time of its surrender. Maria Theresa had no intention to honor the pledge extorted from her field marshal. Throughout the occupation, informers had kept the court au courant; and by the time of her entry, an investigating committee had been working for some time in Prague. Sitting under a titled chairman who himself was not past suspicion of duplicity under the usurper, the committee divided the accused into three groups— "careless men," "men bent on innovation," and those "actually averse [to the rule of the queen]." No distinction was drawn between officials who had curried favor with the occupier and others who had simply carried on. Irreverent jokes about the queen, such as many nobles had bandied about, weighed against them. On the whole, the great were saved from being labeled "actually averse" and having to stand trial. Kinsky saw to that. Those who were arraigned pleaded duress, spoke of the example set by the archbishop, or referred to a landowner's natural concern for his property. "I cannot but laugh," one high-placed noble-man wrote in reply to the writ of indictment. Yes, he had gone to kiss hands. But how, pray, could he have abstained, his estate being situated in an occupied part of the kingdom? Yes, he had accepted an office in Charles Albert's court. But he "could have helped that as little as being given a title by the Grand Mogul."[26] The deeper the investigators dug into the murky records, the more often did they support a defendant's plea for mercy, or even recommend the reinstallment of a suspended official of proper extraction. Kinsky himself sponsored a number of these proposals. "I have to admire the suggestion," the queen wrote in one case, trying to sound sarcastic. It was "one thing to acquit a person out of *clementia*; to do him favors is an entirely different matter again, especially as men who have deserved them by their loyalty are still to be found, I suppose."[27] And: "I have made up my mind once and for all to withdraw my good graces from any of my subjects who, even in peacetime, enters a foreign army without my permission, takes service in a foreign court, or so much as accepts a foreign title of honor. . . ."[28]

Some latifundia owners who were not her subjects were banished from all Habsburg lands and their properties confiscated. The Bohemian nobility fared better. Many of them were fined and the names of a few stricken from the rolls of the herald's office. One noble was, *in absentia*, sentenced to death. But the memory of the executions and the whole-sale expropriations of 1620 that ever since Prague's liberation had haunted the titled collaborators was but a past nightmare. In fact, the landowners triumphed over a danger they had been dreading as much as the traitors among them had the queen's vengeance.

Charles Albert had in some valleys distributed muskets to peasants, inciting them to partisan action in the rear of the queen's troops; and his handbills were far more explicit than the promises *she* had made to the Moravian peasants. The new king of Bohemia undertook to release from their vassalage all men who were fighting his war. The sweeping decree appalled the nobility everywhere in Maria Theresa's lands. Her ministers impressed upon her that "there is no country where the dis-tinctions between manor lords and their subjects do not obtain. To free the latter from his obligations to the former would turn the peasants utterly irresponsible, and the landowners deeply dissatisfied. At all events it would not be consonant with justice."[29] As soon as Prague was freed the conference urged drastic measures. The queen did not tarry. She de-clared that "the emperor's edict and Belle-Isle's ordinances for its execution" had constituted a "criminal attempt to suborn my subjects."[30] After having ordered the documents to be burned by the hangman in public, she thought better of it, to be sure. "Crowned heads must treat one another with respect under any circumstances"; and though the decrees would have to be destroyed, they "must not be touched by the unworthy hands of the executioner."[31] She had no second thoughts about the gullible peasants who had accepted muskets. Although their activities had been negligible on the whole, their villages were razed and the inhabitants dispersed. One of Belle-Isle's native agents who had been caught handing out firearms and handbills had to stand trial and was sentenced to decapitation. His life was spared in a last-minute display of royal mercy.

Surely Maria Theresa—who would not for another thirty years bring herself to abolish torture in interrogation—had no compunction about the rough treatment to which many humbly born suspects were exposed during these spring days. But no culprit lost his life in reconquered Prague; and her feelings were hurt deeply as a very different story, spread by the pamphleteers of Frederick, found credence in foreign countries.

Charges against the Jews of Prague had been discussed in Vienna even before the court's departure. A sizable number of Jewish traders had been accused of dealings with the French army. At the queen's entry the notables of their community were nevertheless allowed to take their traditional place in the cortege. As became known, she had allowed the Jews to make a "voluntary gift" of fl. 150,000 to the treasury in expiation of the transgression.[32]

The coronation was postponed for "an hour's time," after all. A courier from Prince Charles arrived in the small hours of May 11 and brought word of an engagement near Simbach, on the lower Inn. The Bavarian regiments had been routed, and the prince was advancing toward the Isar valley, driving the French before him. (It was Khevenhüller who had led Charles's army out of Bohemia and restored its spirit, while the prince himself sojourned in Vienna.) A "paroxysm of happiness" took hold of everybody at Hradschin Castle, the Venetian ambassador reported. "Whoever thought himself entitled to do so, stepped into the apartments of the queen, while a huge crowd flooded the gardens and gave themselves up to unbridled outbursts of jubilation."[33] Maria Theresa had a *Magnificat* and a *Te Deum* sung ahead of the act of coronation.

Kinsky, having prevailed on this one point, led her to the high altar. Instead of the disgraced archbishop of Prague, the primate of Moravia put the crown on her head. At the banquet she toasted "the men who had, and still have, the welfare of the Arch House and its hereditary

Bohemian kingdom at heart."³⁴ The crown was not restored to the vault of St. Vitus's. Maria Theresa had made up her mind, two years before, to take it to Vienna.

The grand duke had been on her side when she entered the city. In the coronation ceremonial there was no place for him, and he watched the proceedings, as did little Marianne, from the rectory of the cathedral. It was in Prague, indeed at St. Vitus's, that his comely person had for the first time come into Theresa's presence. He was still a good-looking man, though the lower part of his face had grown heavy. Sometimes a veil of melancholy seemed to dull his eyes. His mother was said to be lost in thought for days on end at Commercy. The queen of Sardinia, his elder sister, had died. But in Padua, a Gonzaga princess related to Francis also had died, and in Florence the electress Palatine had breathed her last—and each had bequeathed her vast fortune to him.

Francis no longer pursued the thought of a French peace. A plan of pushing the French armies back across the Rhine and advancing beyond it had come into being at the Hofkriegsrat. It could not but appeal to Francis. Ever since Alsace had fallen victim to French aggression, and throughout the decades the Bourbons held Lorraine in their grip, the Holy Roman Emperor had bound himself to reunite these lands with the crown. Charles VII, obliging his French masters, had omitted the pledge in his oath at Frankfurt. Maria Theresa, then, fighting for the Empire's claim, would shoulder imperial duty, shame the Empire's princes, as well as its pitiable head—and if God willed it, return to Lorraine its rightful ruler!

But how was she to raise the moneys needed for that campaign, or the Italian operations, for that matter? As the ministers—some new men were among them—set about to "improve matters in internis,"³⁵ they submitted that two millions would have to be raised. Why, retorted the queen, "last year's expenditures for the Bohemian army alone amounted to fl. 450,000 per month!"³⁶ It would seem that Bartenstein was the architect of the new tax it was hoped would produce the sums that were necessary. The decree instituted a levy on income to be computed on its average in the past six years.* The peasantry was excluded. Not so, to Rome's displeasure, were ecclesiastics. Assessed and collected by the individual estates, the levy was to remain far behind the expectations of the court. The lack of any statistical service handed the estates a means for whittling down the demands. Only in Bohemia did they support them; having seen their kingdom ravished, they had begun to appreciate the necessity of defensive operations, no matter how far from their own land.

Nothing goes to show that the ministers, in drafting the levy, con-

* Hungary, Lombardy, and Belgium were not subject to the levy.

sulted the grand duke, even though his financial acumen could not have been unknown to them. Yet he was not altogether idle. His recent presence at his brother's army—he was even with it on part of its march—had brought him close to the generals. They tended to voice their complaints in long letters to him, asking him to arbitrate in their squabbles or plead their cause with the Hofkriegsrat and the queen. He, in turn, reserved one of the prerogatives of supreme command to himself: word of the outcome of any engagement must be given to him first. He would pass it on to the queen.

As the beautiful May days drew to their end in Prague, her determination to punish the Bohemian traitors gave way to a stance more lenient. Some of the men who had paid homage to Charles Albert could be seen, with their jeweled ladies, at the receptions their untainted peers arranged for her in their palazzos and gardens, or on some of the boats in the wake of her own as that little flotilla was being rowed up and down the river. In the last week of her sojourn she even accepted the hospitality of some lords whose names had been cleared through *clementia* only. On June 16 the royal party quitted Prague to travel to Linz.

The exemplary retribution she had wished to descend on the Upper Austrian estates had come to naught. Only a handful of the defectors had been found guilty; their penalties had been commuted to token fines. In March, 1742, a message apprised the estates of the queen's "merciful willingness, under the circumstances, to let the affair fall into oblivion." She hoped that they would "not be less cooperative in the future than some of them were when, overriding the law, they swore fealty to [Charles Albert]."[37] After their vote on the *contributionale* had satisfied her she wrote from Prague that "the Estates proved their loyalty and zeal so well, I can safely expect them not to tolerate any suspects in their midst, or any person I would not welcome."[38] No such men were in appearance on her arrival in Linz.

Even without Bartenstein's counsel she would have understood that the men indispensable for the success of her new fiscal measures had to be dealt with softly. She delivered her speech to the estates "with that well-known sweet voice of hers and a charming mien, restricting herself deliberately to the customary generalities. She avoided any remark referring to, or likely to call to mind, the malpractices and illegalities that had occurred in the course of the late revolution."[39] Her new lord marshal, who put down this observation in his diary, was highly gratified that the estates had paid homage to Maria Theresa *"antiquo ritu."*

Prince Charles's optimism had been justified. Supported by Khevenhüller and Browne, he kept advancing. Economizing his resources, he came up with the French only when he so wanted. Their generals had but one desire—to reach the upper Rhine.

There was better news still. Fleury had died, Louis XV's new minister of war, D'Argenson, was said to be lost in a miasma of cabals, and Paris itself was on the brink of panic. Directly Maria Theresa's army had retaken Munich, the imperial generalissimo (none other than Seckendorf) offered Bavarian neutrality to Prince Charles. "Plain humbug" the queen called the proposal; and the prince should accept it only if it "facilitated endeavors to come to the assistance of the allied Pragmatic army."[40] Had not Charles Albert had the nerve to make the offer "in his usurped quality of the head of the *Reich*"? And did not "the Empire and the whole world know very well that the war started through the invalid election, and is carried on against him solely in his quality as elector?"[14] She relented within ten days; while she could not ever recognize the elector's emperorship, she would not engage his forces outside Bavaria, "as my paramount concerns are to restore peace to the Empire . . . and cleanse it of French troops."[42] The Duke of Noailles, who had replaced Belle-Isle, hindered that task. Belying the tales about turmoil within his country, his large army was well diciplined and in good spirit.

The Pragmatic Army, comprising sixteen thousand British troops and an Austrian corps, besides German mercenaries, was heartened by the arrival of George II, who had joined his son, the duke of Cumberland, early in June. But royal ardor alone could not surmount the obstacles Noailles's strategy put in the path to success. On the twenty-sixth Stair found himself outmaneuvered in the vicinity of Frankfurt. Maria Theresa, learning in Linz about the impending disaster, was so dejected that she canceled her farewell reception.

Two days later the world looked entirely different. Stair had broken Noailles's ring of troops on the narrow plain of Dettingen; the Austrian corps had repelled a furious counterattack; and King George himself had led his cavalry to the charge with a bravery mocking his years. The days of Marlborough seemed to be back!

For the trip to Vienna Charles Albert's river yacht had been requisitioned. The Bohemian crown in its hold, the sleek craft sailed down the Danube, past the ripening wheat fields of Upper Austria and its orchards, past the Lower Austrian vineyards and pastures, its towering monasteries, and the crumbled strongholds of the valley's medieval robber barons. Robinson was present when the royal party went ashore at Nussdorf. "The queen . . . was hailed by multitudes of people who, pouring from Vienna, crowded the banks of the Danube for the space of nine miles." The grand duke by her side, she rode "through a delirium of joy"[43] into the city. As the open carriage approached the Hofburg the two-year-old archduke could be seen, held aloft at one of its windows, waving a diminutive flag.

The following morning, returning from the cathedral, Maria Theresa, "in making a eulogium of George the Second, expressed with a mixture of humiliation and pride a modest sense of her own unworthiness to deserve these favors from heaven otherwise than [as] an instrument in the hands of Providence to raise the House of Austria in proportion to its recent depression."[44] Yet, as she remembered—or thought she did— two months after, premonitions of the sterility of the victory had been assailing her even in Linz. "I was close to tears . . . and as I do not cry easily, I wondered whether my being with child was to blame."[45]

The glorious day of Dettingen was not followed by energetic action. King George had come to like Neipperg (who had succeeded the wounded Austrian commander) and was spellbound by his counsel of caution. Moreover, the royal victory had not silenced the opposition to Carteret's policies of Continental involvement. "To tell the truth," Prince Charles wrote his brother from a visit to the king's headquarters, "this seems to me like a republic, for everyone speaks out and appears to have a different opinion. . . ."[46] Stair resigned in disgust.

Maria Theresa's new chancellor, Count Ulfeld, complained to Sir Thomas Robinson (as he now was) about the inactivity of the Pragmatic Army and asked eloquently for more generous subsidies from London. Robinson, changing the subject, brought up, first, the plight of Charles VII and his court at their refuge in Frankfurt, and then "the cessions promised to the king of Sardinia . . . which the queen was evading by every possible pretence."[47] "This must have been a captious entretien," she wrote Ulfeld. "Not that I imagined it to work out better. I certainly did not since I talked to [Robinson] myself, and felt how greatly he was enjoying his own air de satisfaction. Alas, how often have I seen this expression on his face when he delivers himself of an untoward message. I know it only too well. . . . I have always been of the opinion that France must be paid greater attention to, instead of being shrugged off. Unfortunately, this was considered as merely a flare-up of my vivacious temper. I wish I had been wrong."[48]

On August 18 Maria Theresa was delivered of another girl. She knew by then that King George had agreed at length to concert his actions with Prince Charles's. Leaving her confinement, she had to learn that Holland's failure to support the Pragmatic Army, as promised, was hampering the execution of its plan. And within the week she had to give up the hope that her brother-in-law would, as he had undertaken, take his army across the upper Rhine. Maurice de Saxe was mounting guard on the far bank of the river.

"I still say that only resolutions arrived at on first blush ever gave me satisfaction," she wrote to the chancellor on August 25, returning to her recriminations. "I always would have liked to get on a better footing with France, and keep the door open, following the example of the court of Turin. How often did I ask Bartenstein for a memorandum along these lines. One time I was told that it would be *contre la bonne foi*, at some other . . . that we would be taken advantage of, or that the moment was not propitious, conditions having changed, opportunity passed. Now he is falling back on the idea. But it is too late, for I believe absolutely we are going to get the worst kind of peace. Yet we must try by all means, as things may get worse still. I for one will do my work, and exert my strength. I will support any feasable solution. . . ."[49] Had she forgotten the French overtures passed on to her by the burgomaster of Strasbourg in July, and not acted upon? Hindsight—not for the last time—blurred Maria Theresa's recollection.

The bad tidings had reached her at Schönbrunn Palace, where the court had moved soon after her lying-in. The buildings were not at all in good repair. Work on them had been desultory for decades.* On her return from Prague and Linz the queen had informed the chancellery of her wish to have "something really beautiful result from the blueprints. . . . One must not worry about fl. 20,000 more or less."[50]

At about the same time, the twenty-six-year-old commissioned the monument to be erected to Francis and herself in the vault of the Capuchins. "It is not composed of marble, but of a species of bronze or metal," writes an English visitor in the late 1770's. "Unlike the generalities of tombs, where the persons whom they commemorate are commonly laid recumbent, their hands joined in prayer, here the two figures . . . are represented in a half reposing attitude. Francis, partly raised on one side, is regarding his wife with an expression of fondness, while the genius of immortality crowns them with a wreath. . . . The posture of [Francis] which, it must be owned, is a little equivocal; the tenderness displayed in the looks of both the figures, added to the warm attachment which, it is well known, Her Majesty always felt for Francis, who was then young and handsome; these circumstances have given rise to many ludicrous or sarcastic remarks upon the tomb itself. Persons who are disposed to see the ridiculous rather than the serious side of every object have thought, not altogether without reason, that it bore more resemblance to a couch where the lovers are crowned by Hymen than to the gloomy solemnity of a mausoleum destined to contain the ashes of the dead."[51]

Also in 1743 Francis purchased a five-story building on one of the quiet streets of the city. Rumors, to persist for many years, sprang up

* See pp. 198 ff.

that some "chemists" were at work in the room of the inconspicuous townhouse. Even though Francis *was* interested in natural-science experiments, as well as mechanical inventions, it was not alchemy he banked on to make money. At the desks of his *Kanzleihaus* a staff of experts, Lorrainers and Italians, were busy investing his personal funds.

VIII

"Le Monstre!"

UPON SINZENDORF'S DEATH early in 1742, it had been assumed
widely that the chancellor's office would go to Count Frederic
Harrach. This Bohemian magnate had served with distinction, if little
fanfare, at Turin, in Ratisbon, and at Brussels. Forty-six years old, he
was of winsome appearance and conspicuous through the affability of
his manners. He was possessed of an easy grasp of the most varied problems and known for his efficiency at whatever he set his mind to. His
very gifts, however, stood in his way. For Bartenstein was loath to serve
under a man who would not be dependent on him. Having watched
Maria Theresa dealing with her co-regent, he was confident that the
streak of jealousy in her nature would play into his hands. His own
candidate was Count Anthony Ulfeld, who "would not presume to urge
his opinion in opposition to the will of the sovereign."[1] Being a "pleasure-
seeking cavalier and short of money," he would be "easy to keep close
to the flame, like a moth."[2]

As ambassador to the Porte, Ulfeld had been given credit for the
smooth ratification of the Peace of Belgrade, and was sworn into the
conference upon his return. His father, the descendant of a Danish
family, had stood high in the esteem of Charles VI since the days of
Barcelona; and the monarch's gratitude had transferred itself to the son,
who was pushed up the diplomats' ladder with speed. He had proved to
be well-intentioned and scrupulously honest. Apt to impress foreigners at
first sight, he would soon repel them through brusqueness. His defective
hearing "embarrassed those who negotiated with him."[3] He was tall and
husky of stature, dark-haired, and swarthy of complexion. Having grown
a patriarch's beard in Turkey, he looked far older than his forty-three

years. One of the foreign envoys in Vienna, writing in 1747, suggested that Maria Theresa at the time of Ulfeld's appointment knew "full well that his capabilities did not at all qualify him for the office."[4] She had not much choice, however. She had begun to be of two minds about Kinsky, whose talents might have been equal to the task. Also, Ulfeld was willing to serve at a salary half that of his predecessor. So Ulfeld moved in at the chancellery.

But Frederic Harrach had a great friend in Vienna—Tarouca. And the queen, yielding to her "little pedagogue," gave Harrach a seat in the conference and gradually turned over to him some of the powers of the new chancellor. Whereas Ulfeld was "as submissive to Bartenstein as he was overbearing to others,"[5] Harrach did not seek Bartenstein's friendship. He also "refrained from currying favor" with Maria Theresa. "He makes a point of appearing at court only when he is summoned."[6] She in turn was reluctant to summon him. The lightness of his conversation, verging on flippancy, upset her only a little less than did his occasional lack of discretion or his rumored penchant for gallant adventures. She did not care for Harrach's wit and sophistication—or anyone's, for that matter. She might have said even then what she wrote to her first-born nearly a lifetime later: "High time you started ridding yourself of your fascination with bon mots and those pointed phrases which only serve to ridicule others and hurt their feelings."[7] Susceptible as she was to men's charm, she preferred it tempered with stateliness, as it was in Grassalkovich, with modesty, as it was in Tarouca, or with manly exuberance, as it seemed to be in Prince Charles.

The man she chose as her lord marshal in 1742,* Count John Joseph Khevenhüller (a first cousin of the field marshal) if soft-spoken and polite, was anything but a charming person. Looking at his portraits— at the curiously elongated face, the popping eyes beneath beetle brows, the small hooked nose, the thin-lipped mouth, and the pointed chin— one cannot imagine a smile on John Joseph's visage. Born into a land-owning family in 1706, he added to his holdings by a wise marriage. His father, vice-chancellor of the Empire, sent him to Ratisbon, the customary launching place for diplomatists. Subsequently John Joseph filled a succession of minor embassy posts. Sometime during the troubled 1730's he granted a loan to Charles VI. He was knowledgeable and also educated, albeit not brilliantly so. Although concerned about his holdings, he was not rapacious and was untouched by corruption. He was an exemplary family man, a believer as sincere as he was observant, and a benevolent master to his peasants. Khevenhüller frowned and some-

---

* In the course of his long career he also became Lord Chamberlain and Grand Master of the Household. For simplicity's sake, he will be referred to only as lord marshal in these pages.

times fumed, at the merest shadow of change. "Extraction" determined his view of the world. But, alongside his petrified views and a ritualism that might have done honor to the court of Byzantium, there was in the undersized, skinny man a prosy practicality that at times did service for wisdom. His daily contacts with the sovereign from the first influenced her judgment despite the caution with which he at first would give voice to his own.

Although she encouraged candidness, it was not always easy sailing for men whose frankness got the better of the courtier's prudence. The third of her conference appointees of 1742, Count Leopold Herberstein, was least fortunate in that respect. Attached to the grand duchess' household as its Grand Master, he was regarded as a "*surveillant* and *éspion*"[8] by the young couple. On the journey to Florence Countess Fuchs dispelled those suspicions. But Herberstein was plagued by some bilious disorder which shortened his temper and made him appear to "berate you even as he paid you a compliment."[9] As Maria Theresa had turned to him for some advice at the time of her accession, he counted on promotion. The delay on her part—perhaps due to his friendship with Harrach—made Herberstein indiscreet as well as impatient. One day in her antechamber he vented his indignation in an outburst whose din penetrated the inner apartment. But for Tarouca, who managed to mollify the queen, the "old grumbler"[10] would have lost out. After his untimely death, in 1744, she would speak with warmth of "that utterly honest and also capable man."[11]

Ulfeld, Frederic Harrach, Kinsky, and Herberstein, then, formed the cabinet, along with its old men—Starhemberg, Joseph Harrach, Königsegg—the "half ministers," as she was prone to call them. "I have nothing to read, and time is hanging heavy on my hands," she wrote to Ulfeld from her lying-in in September, 1743. "Send me the circulars as usual. But pass them on to me ahead of the ministers, that is, the half-ministers . . . among whom I also count our Königsegg."[12] She had not, of course, any compunction about discussing affairs of state with Prince Charles or Tarouca, that "species of Portuguese *maître de plaisir*," as Khevenhüller came to call him, "who has insinuated himself more and more into her friendship,"[13] or with Ignatius Koch, her private secretary.

A trained jurist originally employed by the Hofkriegsrat, Koch had been known to Maria Theresa even in the late thirties as a "man of honor, integrity, and matchless discretion."[14] When she decided impetuously to send a secret message to Fleury in December, 1740, trying to dissuade him from breaking faith—a fool's errand—she chose Koch for the task. Minuting for her all memoranda "pertaining to domestic business,"[15] and all petitions as well, he influenced her judgment as a matter of course, although he had not, it would seem, any intention to do so. He took care of her personal correspondence and before long also became something like a one-man secret service for the young sovereign. "Certain private persons [*particulares*] . . . brought many many things to my attention through Koch, as I was trying surreptitiously to procure myself secret informations both here and in the provinces. . . ."[16] Koch's father had become a well-to-do man as Prince Eugene's secretary—some people had spoken of him as a crook—and the son's financial independence enhanced Maria Theresa's trust in his selflessness. He also was "exceedingly devout."[17]

Unlike most ruling queens, Maria Theresa did not talk business with her mistress of the robes or her ladies-in-waiting. However, she was not above eliciting from them, and even from the *Kammerfräuleins*,* gossip about court and town. Soon her appetite for it was growing.

In foreign affairs Bartenstein had the final word. He "opened my eyes,"[18] she said with telling brevity at a time his star was waning. She hardly ever called on Kinsky's firsthand experience among the inscrutable men in London or consulted Liechtenstein about matters French, as he had come to know them.

Negotiations with Sardinia had dragged on for a year and a half. To soften Vienna's resistance to the Lombard cessions D'Ormea had advanced various schemes in his talks with Kaunitz—this man who, in Tarouca's words, seemed "alone destined by Divine Providence to give it reasonable support."[19] One of these concerned an Austrian annexation of Bavaria. The British were quick to dampen the enthusiasm of the queen. "I wish I had not been in Schönbrunn," Ulfeld wrote to Bartenstein. "I went through a lot. Her Majesty was beside herself about Wasner's report. Never have I seen her more upset. With tears in her eyes, she reproached herself with not having listened to her enemies. She said that she had a good mind to dispatch someone to France this very day. . . . Believe me, I was not spared. She said that we had been doing nothing, while her enemies had been most active. . . . Her language was as passionate as one can image. It came straight from the heart."[20] Some days previously, on September 13, the Treaty of Worms had been drawn up by her allies; and persistent rumors of a clandestine Franco-Sardinian understanding left her no alternative but to bow to what amounted to a British dictate.

The sacrifices that treaty imposed on her were second only to the surrender of Silesia. All Lombard territory on the right bank of the Ticino and south of the Po were to be ceded to the little king in Turin, together with a slice of Piacenza and the title deed to Finale. (Someone in the Vienna chancellery dug up "evidence" that the margraviate had

* In general, *Kammerfräuleins* were unmarried women from the petty nobility.

been mortgaged, rather than sold, to the Genoese republic.) In return, Britain pledged to keep a flotilla in the western Mediterranean and to enable Sardinia, through subsidies, to raise forty-five thousand troops.

Maria Theresa's sense of humiliation was capped by her conviction that she had been shortchanged. True, the Maritime Powers had spoken at Worms of their intention to depose King Carlos in Naples. But the validity of her claims to his kingdoms—indeed, the principle of *dédommagement*—was not spelled out in the treaty, and had been dealt with only in nebulous words in an exchange of letters between Carteret and Wasner. And only after lengthy discussions did the British promise to continue the annual subsidy (three hundred thousand pounds) for the duration of hostilities.

As if to salve her hurt pride, Maria Theresa provoked a conflict with the Empire's Diet by setting precedent aside in a matter of some importance. She likewise denounced the Diet's transfer from Ratisbon to Frankfurt, and in an acrimonious note referred to the "*Nullität* of the election, so called, of the Bavarian Elector."[21] At about the same time, she directed the lord marshal to have all of the traditional splendor of an imperial court displayed at the wedding of her sister.

Cavalierly as Prince Charles had courted Maria Anne, she still was enamored of him; and Maria Theresa had obtained her mother's consent to the match after some spirited altercations. As for the prince's future glory, new plans, including Traun's transfer to Charles's army, were raising new hopes. As Traun's successor in Italy, the conference nominated Lobkowitz, who happened to be the brother-in-law of Ulfeld. Both the grand duke and his brother thought Lobkowitz the right man, and the Hofkriegsrat expressed their differing view with little force. By the time the Treaty of Worms was signed Lobkowitz, portly and pompous, had been in command for some weeks. In December (1743) he received orders to march on Naples.

The threat to Bourbon rule in Naples prompted the court of Versailles to renew the "family pact" with the Spanish king; and Elizabeth, his termagant queen, was plying her son in Naples with exhortations to defend his throne against the octopus of Vienna. Technically Don Carlos was still neutral when Lobkowitz got his orders. To join battle with the Spanish army the field marshal would have to invade the Papal States. He asked for instruction and was told by Maria Theresa herself to cross the border. The Habsburgs had learned long before how to distinguish between the Church and Christ's Vicar on earth.

Habsburg championship of the Counter Reformation had not secured Rome's love to the court of Vienna. When, in the late 1620's, its religious policies became inextricable from its power struggle in the *Reich*, the specter of imperial aspirations of yore alienated the Holy See from the deeply devout Habsburg monarch. The outcome of the Thirty Years' War softened the antagonism. The great Turkish peril removed it. But the issue of the Spanish succession brought it back with a vengeance. Innocent XII was horrified by the thought of Habsburg (and hence, imperial) dominance in Italy; and, also anxious to end Rome's long conflict with France, he fostered the Bourbon cause at the deathbed of the last Spanish Habsburg. Upon his death, Clement XI made haste to recognize Philip V. A declaration of neutrality in the war did not keep Vienna's troops from camping on papal territory on their march to Naples. Joseph I, defying the threat of excommunication—as was Eugene —answered protests with warlike actions. With the French unable to heed the pontiff's call for help, he had to make his peace with Joseph and to acknowledge his brother's Spanish kingship.

That humiliation was not forgotten in Rome. Nor, in Vienna, was a snub dealt by the Holy Father to Charles's bride on her way to Barcelona. He was not invited to send a legate to Charles VI's coronation in Frankfurt. Clement, in turn, was conspicuously tardy in recognizing the Pragmatic Sanction. His insistence on Sicily's status as a papal fief made for friction up to the day of the loss of the island by Charles VI. Other incidents kept that friction alive.

The election of Cardinal Lambertini as Benedict XIV in the summer of 1740 did not improve matters. His sympathies for the Bourbon courts were, if anything, more pronounced than those of his recent precursors. A friend of Cardinal Tencin, a member of the council of the French king, Benedict also was prone to listen to Alberoni, who, though banished from Spain, still pleaded the cause of her queen. One of the first acts of the new pontiff was the settlement of an old controversy with the Neapolitan court.

Maria Theresa had solicited the support of the new pope in the earliest stage of her tribulations. Benedict, hinting at some claims her father had refused to negotiate, roundly turned down her plea. "One asks for much in Vienna," he told her Orator at his court, "and does nothing for me."[22] When the Spanish expeditionary force violated his territory, he showed no enmity to its commanders. "I cannot comprehend," Maria Theresa wrote to the Holy Father, "that the service of our Lord, the welfare of the Faith, and the defense of papal rights, should demand a complete lack of consideration for the weaker party, and on the other hand forgiveness for the worst iniquities on the part of the stronger."[23] In his reply Benedict evaded the issue and chided the queen for the indifference she had, allegedly, shown toward ecclesiastic rights in the Treaty of Breslau. Whereupon her chancellery declared that the queen well remembered the alacrity with which His Holiness had recognized the lawfulness of Charles Albert's election and that she hence doubted his professed zeal for the Catholic cause. "Anyone reading these communications," the pope observed in a letter to Tencin, "would . . . take them for the forgeries of some fool. Yet this is also the way the Orator talks."[24] The boorishness of this cleric, Count Thun, aggravated the irritation of Benedict, a man of refinement and erudition. Susceptible to the lay thought of his day, he corresponded with Montesquieu and Voltaire. Fond of good conversation and hilarity, he did not mind receiving Casanova. His nuncio at Vienna was not a benevolent observer of its court, whose philistinism, though coupled with great piety, could not recommend it to a person of Benedict's cast of mind. He blamed the two Lorraine princes for what he considered the self-righteousness of Maria Theresa's policies. At the time her troops entered his states, she was embroiled in still another controversy with the pope, who had ignored her wish to elevate a certain favorite prelate of hers to the purple.

Lobkowitz, unchecked by papal protests, started operations and dislodged the Spaniards from some of their encampments. But as De Gages took his troops into winter quarters before winter set in, Lobkowitz followed suit. The disappointment in Vienna should have been mitigated by the Sardinians' success in repulsing the Franco-Spanish ("Gallispan") army under Don Philip. It was not. While the queen was anxious to see the common enemy engaged by the Sardinians, she hoped for her own army to decide the fight before they ensconced in the territories they had gained at Worms.

Meantime preparations for the wedding were proceeding at Vienna. Metastasio had delivered a drama, *Ipermestra*, a glorification of marital bliss, which pleased Maria Theresa so greatly that she decided to take over the leading part herself even before Hasse, her old teacher, delivered the score from Dresden. No sooner had she begun to rehearse than heads were wagging, "as though the appearance of a queen regnant" were *contra* decorum." Khevenhüller did not join those critics; there were precedents, he observed—"Louis XIV used to perform a dance in comedies arranged in his court"—and "surely one was not always all that *austère* in other respects."[25] What about those carnival visits to the *Mehlgrube*, for instance? Still, we can hardly doubt that the lord marshal felt relieved when Maria Theresa withdrew from the opera cast.

The ceremonial that he had worked out for the nuptials with many sighs and great gusto was breached on one point. The queen walked by the side of her sister, holding her hand. The published account of the wedding carefully listed the jewels worn by the two ladies—perhaps to give the lie to stories that would have a good many Habsburg gems in pawn with Genoese bankers.

On New Year's Day, the eve of the wedding, Maria Anne and Prince Charles had been appointed to the joint governorship of Belgium. They were not until Ash Wednesday to set out on the journey to Brussels. For the wedding celebrations blended with carnival—its supper parties, dances, masquerades, "peasants' balls," and those sleigh rides that had become all the rage.

Only one lady was seated in the daintily painted one-horse sleigh, the gentleman driver standing behind her. What with the handpicked animals, their colorful caparisons and ostrich plumes, what with the liveried runners by the vehicles' sides, what with the furred gowns and hats—to say nothing of the feats of skill on the part of the drivers— those rides through the streets and around and around the town's squares enthralled the crowds of spectators as much as they amused the participants. The teams being decided by lot, fortune favored the grand duke, giving him regularly one of the prettiest ladies as a companion, and that too was a cause for general mirth.

Some time during these gay weeks Maria Theresa, having second thoughts about the gubernatorial duties of her brother-in-law, recalled Kaunitz from Turin and attached him to the young couple at Brussels. "A man of honor has to know himself and his strength of mind and body. . . ." Kaunitz wrote to Tarouca upon the summons. "I for one do know myself, and neither selfish considerations nor misplaced ambitions could ever become the main spring of my actions. Young as I am, my health is poor. Treatments I underwent brought me as little relief as does my strict regimen. I have to take care of myself. Winter is always dangerous for me. Your Excellency must realize what it would mean if I fell ill."[26] Belgium was certain to become a trouble spot soon, as little conducive to Kaunitz' taking care of himself as was the winter journey. It needed the concerted efforts of Tarouca and Ulfeld to make him budge from Turin.

Dire portents were driving home to the court the consequences of the failure of the past year. The French had recouped their losses with astonishing vigor; intelligence spoke of four armies they had ready, amounting to one hundred thousand troops. The Pragmatic Army, on the other hand, while awaiting replacements from the Dutch, had been weakened through the withdrawal of some of the British regiments. De Saxe was assembling an invasion force at Dunkirk, and the young Pretender was in the camp.

Most probably the French were not in earnest about the invasion. Yet, widely publicized, it transformed the sullen discontent of the British public into a sanguine determination to teach a lesson to the competitors across the Channel. The government were spared a decision, as Louis XV on April 26 declared war on George II and the Queen of Hungary. The French troops who had fought her as "imperial auxiliaries" for three years exchanged the Bavarian colors for white Bourbon cockades.

Even as hopes for massive British assistance in the field were waning in Vienna, Robinson pressed for reinforcements to the Pragmatic Army. The queen would not hear of drawing so much as one regiment from her army on the Rhine, which, after Lewis Khevenhüller's sudden death, had been retrained by Traun. Sir Thomas and his Dutch colleague, admitting to the dearth of experienced generals in their countries, also asked her to put Prince Charles in charge of the Pragmatic Army; but the prince demurred, fearful of being outranked should King George come again to the Continent. Moreover, he had his own ideas about the campaign he wished to fight, and these were anything but displeasing to Maria Theresa. He arrived at headquarters on May 19 and reported presently that his troops were *"magnifiques."*[27] The court was buzzing with an exhilarating tale: in a letter to his wife in Brussels, he had announced that he would write her soon from Paris.

For once he seemed to be as good as his word. During the last four days of the month he took his entire army, seventy thousand men, across the Rhine without enemy interference. "At last, my dear brother, we are in Alsace,"[28] he notified Francis, whose consort lost no time bestowing the victor's laurels upon Prince Charles. "In emulating the august exemplar of your grandfather . . . [she wrote] and adding to the immortal fame that you won on earlier occasions, you have deserved well of me, of the Arch House, the Empire, and the whole of Christendom."[29] Strasbourg was within Charles's reach,* and the false ruler of Lorraine, Leszczyinski, was packing his bags.

And Lobkowitz? Tarrying on the Adriatic coast, he had been plying the court and the Hofkriegsrat with letters. He stressed the Gallispan threat, which hindered his moves no less than did his shortage of funds. Only after Francis advised him, with unwonted curtness, that the "conquest of Naples has become imperative to the queen"[30] did the field marshal break tent to march his army across the peninsula and advance south along the Tyrrhenian coast. As he led his troops past the walls of Rome he took himself and a glittering suite on a call on the Holy Father; and to believe Lobkowitz—as Maria Theresa appears to have done—the populace gave him a rousing welcome. Some days later a regiment of his hussars penetrated Neapolitan territory, and their colonel issued a proclamation in the name of his sovereign, "Queen of the Two Sicilies." It promised freedom of assembly to the city of Naples and to the kingdoms' barons and ecclesiastics, all those privileges of which Bourbon rule had shorn them.

King Carlos had abandoned neutrality in March and himself led his

---

* In the later seventeenth century Alsace had come under French dominance step by lawless step. The most brazen of these coups was Louis XIV's occupation of the Free City of Strasbourg, in the midst of peace, in 1681.

army of twenty thousand men north for a junction with De Gages. Their combined forces, after some skirmishing, entrenched themselves at Velletri, some twenty miles south of Rome, while Lobkowitz took up positions between that old town and Lake Nemi. The two armies commenced bombarding each other; and this they continued to do, intermittently, for six weeks. Cassanova, who happened to stumble into this little war, affords us in his memoirs a glimpse of its comic-opera aspects.

But if Lobkowitz invited ridicule, his second in command, Maximilian Ulysses Browne, did not. His father was an Irishman priding himself on a long pedigree, who, like a good many of his fellow Hibernians, had entered the Habsburg service. In due course a patent of nobility was given to him, a conscientious soldier. Marriage into a family of the old Bohemian peerage bestowed social status on the son. He saw action first, in 1731, in Corsica where Charles VI, heeding Genoa's call, had dispatched an army to quell a rebellion against the republic. Since these days Browne had acquired the reputation of an officer of bold spirit and cool judgment in the backwaters of the Turkish campaigns and in Silesia, and had come into his own during the campaigns in Bohemia, on the Danube, and in Bavaria. He was thirty-nine years of age in 1744, and as Prince Charles, recommending Browne's transfer to Italy, put it, "capable of standing up to Prince Lobkowitz, something which is rather necessary."[31]

Lobkowitz' most vehement critic was Thun, Maria Theresa's Orator in Rome. Visiting the encampment regularly, this meddlesome bishop was appalled by the levity of the officers and the misery of the common soldiers. A Spanish surprise coup which resulted in the loss of the foremost Austrian outwork so exercised Thun that he urged the queen to sack Lobkowitz and replace him with Browne. The unbidden advice was rejected out of hand. For one thing, Lobkowitz had been "one of the few when few were to be had" in 1741. And, then, he believed, as did Maria Theresa, in the zeal of the pro-Habsburg faction in Naples and its strength. He contended that two thousand of his crack troops, put ashore by a British squadron, would, together with the threat of its guns, suffice to bring about an upheaval in the city of Naples and return the kingdoms to the Habsburgs in King Carlos' absence. Lobkowitz was about to entrust this mission to Browne when a French move in his own rear compelled him to devise a maneuver promising quicker results. His plan was to confuse the enemy in and around Velletri through a diversion and give Browne the chance to lead six thousand troops under the cover of darkness up to the walls of the town, force its southern gate, and kidnap King Carlos. The Neapolitan garrison, bereft of their royal commander, were expected to lose their nerve, while the Spaniards, encamped outside Velletri, would be taken on by another Austrian force.

And Naples itself, stunned by the king's capture, would be easy prey for the partisans of Maria Theresa. Lobkowitz, writing to Ulfeld on August 8, announced the imminence of a decisive action.

On the night of August 10–11 a Neapolitan deserter guided Browne across the valley, through its vineyards and *macchia*, and up the slope toward Velletri. The Spaniards' Irish brigade was nearly annihilated in a ferocious melee under the southern ramparts before Browne's Croats broke down the doors of the gate at dawn. By the time they had begun to pillage the buildings, as well as search them for their royal quarry, Don Carlos was out of their reach. Clad in his nightshirt only, His Sicilian Majesty had jumped from one of his lodgings' windows, grabbed and mounted a horse, and escaped through the northern gate, which the Austrians had not succeeded in blocking. As more and more of them poured into the town from the south they were set upon by irate inhabitants and Neapolitan soldiers. Toward noon De Gages was approaching. In vain did Browne, who had not himself entered Velletri, plead with Lobkowitz to throw in his reserve. The Croats and hussars, heavy with wine and loaded with plunder, and soon lost in the town's crooked alleys, were nearly all of them hacked to pieces. King Carlos returned at sunset.

Lobkowitz refused to admit to the failure of his harebrained scheme. As Browne had taken some prisoners in the pre-dawn fighting and seized some enemy flags, Lobkowitz claimed the traditional honor of the victor, his courier's riding into Vienna with twenty buglers. The request was treated with scorn. At a reception that same night Maria Theresa berated the papal nuncio within earshot of a group of courtiers, accusing the Holy Father of giving aid and comfort to her enemies. She was in a savage humor. Count Dohna, the Prussian *chargé d'affaires*, had notified Ulfeld that a state of war existed between the Queen of Hungary and his own king and master.

The Treaty of Worms had worried Frederick greatly even before Augustus of Saxony became a party to it. One of its secret articles was said to reaffirm the Pragmatic Sanction with no qualification regarding Silesia. As early as March he started clandestine talks, through one of his best agents, with the Duke of Richelieu* and one of his four beautiful nieces, the mistress of Louis XV. At the same time, he unleashed his most aggressive pamphleteers.

Maria Theresa had never ceased mocking and vilifying Charles VII.

---

* A grandnephew of the celebrated cardinal, Richelieu had been ambassador to Charles VI in the 1720's. His victory over Ripperdá in a precedence squabble, as well as diplomatic success, had brought him advancement in Versailles. So had his pimping for the king. A monumental debauchee, Richelieu had been bored to excess in Vienna and had formed a passionate dislike for its court.

She had refused to disgorge the archives of the *Reich*. By "scandalous, underhanded means"[32] she had tampered with the proceedings of the Diet. A Prussian memorandum delivered to the Empire's sovereigns castigated the "presumption of the Queen of Hungary,"[33] who—so a later pamphlet put it—acted as if the court of Vienna and the Empire were synonymous."[34]

Dohna had blown hot and cold. In December he made representations about troop movements in Bohemia "under the pretext of tales devoid of any truth."[35] In February he assured Ulfeld that the king would always act in accordance with the Treaty of Breslau. The queen herself was so little troubled by the barrage of his hostile propaganda that, in April, she ordered Traun to move toward the Rhine. "And do not worry about the Prussian king; I have stopped thinking of him."[36] As late as July 30 Bartenstein opined that the king would not start hostilities if operations on the Rhine went well.

It was precisely Prince Charles's progress that did away with any scruples on the part of the king. He had renewed the alliance with Louis XV in June. But, having left him twice in the lurch, Frederick could hardly bank on loyalty in disaster. An Austrian march into France might well prompt her court to rescind the agreement and make peace with Maria Theresa. Would she then withstand the temptation of hurling her army into Silesia? On August 15 one of the king's armies invaded Bohemia as auxiliaries of the emperor, Charles VII. "*Le monstre!*" the grand duke exclaimed when the news came to Schönbrunn.

His wife rushed to Pressburg. Although the Diet was not in session, Pálffy assembled a group of magnates and county nobles. Rumors of Prussian agents busy in Constantinople were afloat, and the Hungarians had become mindful of their security. Besides, the queen had kept faith with them. In spite of her need for money, she had not touched their tax laws. Their self-importance had thriven on the honors bestowed upon some of their own in Vienna. A score or so of them boasted a general's rank, and Count Charles Batthyány was in command of an army (and, in fact, on the road to Bohemia from his Palatinate camp).* Count Nicholas Esterhazy—incidentally, a jolly gentleman—was ambassador in Dresden. Hungarian troops had been in the thick of the fighting everywhere; and if people in Bohemia, on the Danube, on the Rhine,

---

* Malicious gossip, never scarce in Vienna, had dubbed him "Prince Eugene's Codicil." His widowed mother had been a close friend of Eugene's, and people who discredited the persistent rumor of his homosexuality thought her to be his mistress. Most probably Mme. Batthyány also sold favors to be gained from Eugene. Her two sons, brought up in Vienna as loyal supporters of the court, were not injured by the tittle-tattle. They were rare birds: bearers of a prominent Hungarian name, they also were, on the distaff side, grandsons of Emperor Leopold's chancellor, a man of German stock who had served the Habsburgs exceedingly well.

and in Italy had come to dread their presence, their countrymen high and low gloried in the prowess of those hearty warriors. Thus Maria Theresa faced an assemblage ready to give her what she wanted. As she wound up her address, shouts of "*Ad arma, ad arma!*" rose to reverberate from the rafters of the castle's great hall. (Forty thousand fresh troops were, in fact, levied within two months.)

Only too soon was the queen, back in Schönbrunn, to realize the extent of Frederick's aggression. His main force had demanded transit through Saxony and met only a weak protest. His Prussians were streaming into Bohemia. With nary a day's hesitation Maria Theresa ordered her brother-in-law to break off his advance on Strasbourg, recross the Rhine, and hasten to Bohemia's rescue.

The Hofkriegsrat trembled for Charles's army. A stroke of good luck assisted him in the hazardous passage of the river under the eyes of Noailles and his superior numbers. Louis XV, egged on by his mistress, had taken it into his head to lead the army himself; and as he happened to fall ill at his headquarters, Noailles had to stand by and watch all of Prince Charles's troops reach the right bank with their horses, guns, and baggage. Four weeks later they were on Bohemian territory. Prague by that time had surrendered.

The nobility, having learned their lesson, had left the kingdom in droves. The clergy was openly hostile to the Lutheran invaders. The peasants had buried their crops and taken to the woods with their cattle. Count Nadasdy, the boldest of hussar generals, was raiding the Prussian magazines. Frederick's soldiers, arriving hungry and ugly of mood before Prague, had descended on the prostrate town like a swarm of locusts. As they continued to sack it, their vaunted discipline went by the board. "I cannot find the right words to tell you how grievously the suffering if the population affects me, the queen wrote to Batthyány. "I can find solace only in recalling that everything was done to save them. . . ."[37]

Bavaria was lost once again. The Pragmatic Army was fumbling in Flanders. Don Philip's Gallispans were moving into the Lombard plains, and Spanish and French men-of-war, cruising off the Tyrrhenian coast, mocked any attempt to execute Lobkowitz' plan of a seaborne attack on Naples. And Noailles had crossed the Rhine. That flood of bad news made Maria Theresa yearn for a spectacular victory over Frederick. She was weary of the cautious maneuvers of Traun, into whose hands Prince Charles had let slide the initiative even on the march to Bohemia. She was "sick with sorrow and irritation. . . ."

"The other day I was pestering *mon vieux* for so long, he came down with a fever," she confided to her sister, who was expecting her first child. "Imagine, he had set his heart on going to the army [in Bohemia]. . . and did not tell me so until his traveling coach was ready. I treated the matter as a joke at first, but as I realized he was in earnest, I had recourse to my usual stratagems, that is, tears and caresses. But what power do *they* have after nine years of married life? . . . Finally, I resorted to an outburst of anger. It served my purpose so well that we both felt a fever coming on. . . . Now, instead of fighting his idea, I am putting him off from one day to the next. Should he insist, I am going to go with him, or retreat to a convent."[38]

Poor Francis. More patiently than any other man in court he had worked for bringing about peace with Prussia; now the Treaty of Breslau was a scrap of paper. It was not least he who had helped Lobkowitz to his command; now the field marshal, his authority undermined, was even failing in the retreat of his army. Francis had been looking forward with bated breath to his brother's march into their Lorraine; now Leszczynski was back in Nancy snugly enjoying life.

For all that, Francis did not venture forth to tempt, once again, his fortunes in battle. His wife was pregnant, and (as he said in a similar situation to one of his *intimes*) her "extreme excitability might throw her in a fit which would affect her health, and disrupt the conduct of affairs."[39] Proofs of her short temper were not wanting. Khevenhüller in his journal frequently mentioned her "*fumo*." But neither he nor her Francis seems to have realized the deliberate use she made of the notoriety of her proneness to anger.

Shortly after she dissuaded Francis from going to the wars the war itself came closer. Frederick had turned south from Prague to unite his army with Noailles's, crush Prince Charles, and lay siege to Vienna. The *Diarium* gave no news of the peril, but "bits of information leaked out," and the Viennese, "who recalled previous unhappy experiences, were seized by consternation. Signs of this may be noticed even in court. Today the midday meal was not served until four o'clock. . . . I do my best to counteract the disorder and such breaches of custom."[40] Preoccupied with the tendency of the "young court" to let "things get out of their groove,"[41] the lord marshal was slow to appreciate the turn that events in Bohemia were taking. So, strange to say, was the queen.

Noailles was not in pursuit of Prince Charles. Nor was Seckendorf, with his Bavarians, eager to concert his strategy with the king's. Frederick decided to go to battle without either of them. But Traun could not be provoked. Employing all the skills of old-school warfare, he confused Frederick's generals by marches and countermarches whose purpose eluded them. He relentlessly harassed the Prussians' overextended lines of communication, burned down their magazines as soon as they had been set up, and isolated their fortified camps one after another. Dysentery and the shortage of food and forage played havoc with Frederick's battalions in the autumnal countryside. The number of desertions increased with every day. Early in November the king ordered withdrawal. As his army was dragging itself toward Silesia he was pinning his hopes on the approaching winter, which might prevent the queen's troops carrying their activities past Bohemia's border.

By the middle of December not a single Prussian was in the kingdom. But there was no celebration in Vienna. Maria Anne, after delivering a stillborn child on December 1, had died on the sixteenth. "I can discern the Will of the Almighty," Maria Theresa wrote to Gerhard van Swieten, the Dutch physician who had attended the princess in her long agonies. "In His Grace, He keeps me alive to tread the path of trial and grief that He has designed for me. Throughout the great adversities I have encountered in my reign, the thought of establishing these two families, who would support each other, was my sole comfort."[42] With this allusion to dynastic dreams wrecked she broke off her laments. Van Swieten was known to have disagreed with Dr. Engel, her own physician-in-waiting, who had been rushed to Maria Anne's sickbed in Brussels. Maria Theresa sympathized with men who dared to speak their minds vis-à-vis their honor-laden elders. She invited the Dutchman, a Catholic of Jansenist leanings, to join her court and make Vienna his home.

Maria Anne had died without seeing her husband again. Prince Charles was not a sentimental lover. Moreover, he had been unwilling to leave the scene of the triumph of his army. After New Year's he asked for permission to take it into winter quarters. The Hofkriegsrat, however, overriding Traun's judgment, bowed to the desire of the queen, and ordered advance. As soon as the vanguard was on Silesian soil the court had a manifesto ready. Distributed wherever the king had held sway, this proclamation declared null and void any oath of fealty sworn him.

A series of spirited counterblasts issued from Berlin. In a circular note to his fellow sovereigns in the Empire the king declared that it was the Queen of Hungary who had breached its peace. He had taken up arms only as the loyal liegeman of Charles VII and for the defense of the imperial crown. Even as that paper war was being fought, Charles VII lay ill in Munich.

He died on January 20, while Batthyány's army was about to overrun Bavaria again. No one in Europe doubted but that Charles Albert's misfortunes had undermined his health and hastened his end. Looking back at his pathetic career on Charlemagne's throne, a Frenchman wrote some years afterward: "We have come to know the power of the House of Habsburg. At the time of its greatest affliction, it was strong enough virtually to dethrone a lawfully and unanimously elected emperor, and oust him from his hereditary dominions."[43]

IX

The Highest-Placed
Couple in Christendom

MARIA THERESA GAVE BIRTH to her second son twelve days after the demise of the "mock emperor." Erizzo, the Venetian ambassador, surely was not the only man to observe that "Divine Providence has manifested itself in the queen's favor, and well she deserves it."[1] The Viennese thought so. Who among them gave a hoot for the news from Silesia, where Schwerin had turned the tables on the troops of the queen? All over Vienna, up went, alongside the flags and the bunting, gay placards extolling the nativity of Archduke Charles and the vacating of the imperial office. One of the paintings on display showed the imperial eagle spreading its wings over the nine electoral coronets in the foliage of a tree, with the two little sons of Maria Theresa standing in its shade —Charles urging the firstborn to "catch grandpa's birdie," and Joseph replying that he was too small, and they had better ask papa to catch it.

While the Viennese may have looked forward above all, to seeing the imperial residence reestablished in their town, "together with the profit certain to result,"[2] they were far from being alone in the wish for Francis' election. It was favored by such public opinion as there existed in the *Reich*. In its westernmost parts, where the depredations wrought by Louis XIV's aggressions were still spoken of with shudders, Frederick's French alliance had been shocking people. The cynical use he had made of the imperial cause had been open for all to see. His miscarried Bohemian campaign had palled his fame even in his own dominions. His own officers no longer trusted his lucky star and looked blank when he asked them whether they proposed to "show less courage than a woman who did not despair as her enemies overran her most flourishing provinces and stood at the gates of Vienna."[3] His exchequer depleted, he was reduced to sending his plate to the mint. The Berlin bankers refused him credit. To "renew his accommodation with the House of Austria," Frederick (or so he relates in his memoirs) made "overtures to George the Second."[4]

Prince Charles's retreat from the Rhine had created a crisis in London and compelled Carteret to resign. Yet, the new cabinet—with the Duke of Newcastle conducting foreign affairs—began to tighten what in effect was an anti-Prussian confederation. Distributing their habitual largesse, the British prevailed on the Saxon elector to declare war on Frederick and co-sign the recent Union of Warsaw, which had reaffirmed their status as belligerents in Maria Theresa's struggle. In fact, the new instrument envisaged no less than a partition of the Prussian kingdom. "Before parcelling out the skin of the bear, we had better think first of how to kill him,"[5] the queen wrote to Esterhazy in Dresden. She had become doubtful of her allies' exertions although new bounty arriving from London gave her a breathing spell.

The mourning for her sister had struck carnival festivities from the calendar of the court. The young widower would come to Vienna on shorter or longer visits, would talk about his resolve never to remarry, and more than once moved Maria Theresa to tears. Talk he also would about Traun, who "cannot cope with details, and seems to be a tyro in the métier."[6] As had King Frederick, so the Hofkriegsrat had nothing but admiration for the campaign that Traun had fought, avoiding battle; and his new fame got on the nerves of Prince Charles. His chance to disembarrass himself of the "tyro" was not long in coming.

The Italian war had bogged down. King Carlos had entered Rome, greeted as a "true son of the Church"[7] by the pope; and Lobkowitz, on his snail-paced retreat, his supply service in greater disorganization than ever, eschewed all opportunities of attacking the enemy. Browne had been transferred to Batthyány's army. Stopping over in Vienna, he spoke his mind. "She has grown tired of intrigues and maneuvers employed to keep Lobkowitz in his post," Erizzo wrote, "and her will prevailed in the teeth of all remonstrances. . . . This is how this princess, who verily must be called great, acts in all matters. There is nothing she does not examine, nothing she does not direct, herself. Even though she entertains the most tender feelings for her consort, she does not permit him to make any decisions, and not infrequently decides . . . against his opinion."[8] Erizzo should have withheld for a while his unqualified admiration. When Traun, to King Frederick's delight, was given a command in the western theater of war, Lobkowitz was picked to replace him in Bohemia.

Liechtenstein went to Italy. His requests for fresh troops to fill the gaps that mass desertions had torn into his battalions were as futile as were his demands for funds. The Hofkriegsrat had neither to spare. At the same time, Charles Emmanuel, harassed by the Gallispans, kept urging Liechtenstein for reinforcements. And the Genoese had thrown in their lot with the Bourbons. The Finale deal, sealed and signed in Worms, had inflamed the republic with anger from the first, and the presence of French frigates off its shore emboldened its senate. Maria Theresa's fortunes on the peninsula, then, were at a low ebb indeed. Nor could she presume that Cumberland and old Königsegg, with their fifty thousand troops in Flanders, were a match for the one hundred thousand under De Saxe. Yet all the tribulations on the fringes of her dominions did not impinge on her determination to destroy the foe who aimed at their heart.

On May 15 word of the bloody day of Fontenoy reached Schönbrunn. Königsegg, who blamed the Dutch contingent for the defeat, warned that it opened Belgium to the French victors unless the discord within the leadership could be healed with dispatch.

The court had not yet recovered from the shock when Prince Charles—he had been advancing across the Bohemian mountains into Silesia—advised his brother of the "vexatious *affaire*" of Hohenfriedberg. "The Prussians attacked and gave us chase [he wrote]. We lost part of our colors and cannon, and many men, especially generals. . . . The disaster pains me all the more as our soldiers behaved like swine. Pardon the expression. But I am hopping mad."[9] It was true that morale in some regiments had broken down under the impact of the unexpected assault. It was not the whole truth, however. The king had decoyed the Austrian generals in the dead of night, and in the small hours attacked the detached Saxon corps before Prince Charles rose from his bed, only to realize that his men were in their billets, the horses unsaddled. Outflanked though he was, he hurled his army into a hopeless slaughter. Had he not, in his slumber, heard the din of the Prussians' cannonading the Saxons? Oh, yes, he had heard an echo but had mistaken it for the clatter of a Saxon advance. His sound sleep was the topic of some crude lampoons that appeared on the walls of public buildings in Vienna; and accounts of Prussian ruses were bandied about with so much gusto that some tavern gossips were put under arrest in an attempt to suppress the scandal.

The name of the victor of Hohenfriedberg was absent from Prince Charles's long letter to Francis. Nor did Königsegg waste any ink on giving De Saxe his due. Maria Theresa, talking to Erizzo three months later during a ball at Schönbrunn, did talk about Frederick. "Nobody can deny that he is a prince of great perspicacity and far-ranging talents," she said after she had taken the ambassador into the recess of a window.

"It must be admitted that he devotes himself without respite to his duties as a ruler; and on the battlefield, these qualities are joined by that never-slackening alertness that is indispensable in the leader of an army."[10] These observations were the first of their kind on the part of the queen. To her own mind they were not novel. In the days before Hohenfried-berg, so she told Erizzo, she had not "been able to rid herself—my ministers are so many witnesses—of forebodings, although everything looked so auspicious. . . ."[11]

As Frederick did not seem intent on pursuit, Prince Charles estab-lished his headquarters in the border mountains; and thither the queen sent her lord marshal. He reported that the lesson of Hohenfriedberg had been lost on His Royal Highness. Instead of relying on "men of merit and mature judgment," he still surrounded himself with people whose "incompetence, arrogance, and boorishness" should render them "unworthy of his trust."[12] Having delivered himself of his candid opinion, Khevenhüller proceeded to Dresden to stiffen Augustus' back-bone and have a friendly chat with Count Brühl, the maker of Saxon policies and a venal man if ever there was one.

As Hohenfriedberg had driven fear into Augustus' heart, so the butchery of Fontenoy had appalled the British public. A note from Bartenstein's hand went out to the allies: did they not see that Prussia and France would continue to "stir up unrest, fish in troubled waters, and aggrandize themselves at the expense of their neighbors, to lord it over all and sundry"?[13] To Wasner in London Maria Theresa herself wrote: the "well-known Count Gotter" was said to be on his way to Hanover; was it true that some British emissary was waiting for him to discuss peace? "Obnoxious negotiations"[14] these would be. When Wasner opened this letter, he no longer could expect the cabinet to listen to his inquiries or to the queen's passionate plea "not to be urged to abandon the recovery of Silesia."[15] The Stuart prince, Charles Edward, had landed in Scotland.

The Vienna court learned of the event on August 2. On the fourth Robinson came to Schönbrunn. On the same day the electors' special envoys in Frankfurt went into their first session at St. Bartholomew's.

Thriving between the realities of power politics and the residual mystique of the crown, excitement over the election had been mounting. Nor was it confined to the courts and their chancelleries. Charles VII's teen-age son was not a candidate.* The French court spoke of Augustus

---

* Concluding a separate peace in April, he had pledged his vote to the grand duke and surrendered all claims to the Habsburg dominions. Maria Theresa, on her part, restored all conquests to Bavaria and, if reluctantly, also recognized the legality of Charles VII's emperorship.

despite his alliance with Vienna. But the Saxon had no intention of risking the British friendship recently gained in the Union of Warsaw.

A flood of Prussian and Prussian-inspired pamphlets descended on the Germanies, all of them inveighing against Maria Theresa rather than Francis. Inordinate ambition and lust for power, obscurant bigotry, and base vengefulness were imputed to her. She would take advantage of her do-nothing husband and strive to rebuild her ancestors' tyrannical rule in the *Reich*. Neither did Vienna's pamphleteers bother to extol the candidate. They fired away, praising his wife—an "angelic spouse," a queen regnant who "had weathered all tempests with the fortitude of a true king."[16] A handbill printed in Frankfurt exhorted the electors to "uphold the freedom of the election against France and Prussia."[17]

In fact, its freedom had been in great danger in May and June. A French army under Prince Conti stood on the right bank of the Rhine, less than a two-day march from Frankfurt. Batthyány's forces amounted to barely half of the French, and contradictory orders from Vienna were hampering his dispositions. "For God's sake, no interfering with Batthyány's advance!" a panicky Bartenstein wrote to Ulfeld, "or else the imperial crown is gone, gone. . . . I can foresee that everything will go awry again. My heart bleeds!"[18] Traun, who commanded the troops still in Bavaria, was instructed to unite them with Batthyány's. Slowly, as was his wont, the old field marshal led his regiments toward the junction. As soon as it was effected, Francis, in Vienna, grew restive, declaring that he "would not stand by idle"[19] while his own fortunes were being decided on the field of battle. His wife raised objections before she appointed him commander-in-chief of the Traun-Batthyány army. Then she went with him to one of the Marian shrines on the town's outskirts and bade him Godspeed.

The Virgin this time heeded the royal supplications. Two days after Francis' arrival, Traun ousted the French from the vicinity of Frankfurt, and Conti took them across the Rhine. The grand duke wished for their passage to be obstructed, but Traun persuaded him easily to drop the venturesome project. Frankfurt was safe.*

Now the French raised a hue and cry about the armed hosts of the Queen of Hungary which were supposed to bring pressure to bear on the conclave. They also had their puppet, the elector Palatine, lodge a protest against the candidacy of the Grand Duke of Tuscany, who was not a

---

* This was Traun's last action in the field. About a year later he became commander of the small body of troops in Transylvania and the head of the administration of that remote province. He died there in 1748, in his seventy-first year, after having horrified the court by his marriage to a commoner. Maria Theresa, as a rule openhanded to the point of extravagance toward old servants, does not appear to have been moved by the fact that Traun—he never had been a good householder—had almost no personal funds to fall back on in the end.

prince of the Empire. But English money had found its way to the electoral courts. As Robinson stood before Maria Theresa on August 4 in Schönbrunn, she could be reasonably certain of her Francis' election.

Sir Thomas commenced his speech by pointing out that his government "this year furnished one million seventy-eight thousand seven-hundred and fifty-three pounds, not to mention the [sums] expected by the Electors of Cologne and Bavaria." His nation was "not in a condition . . . to maintain the necessary superiority in the most essential parts, and, by endeavoring to provide for so many services, will fail in all." Therefore "the force of the enemy must be diminished; and as France cannot be detached from Prussia, Prussia must be detached from France. This return the English nation expects from all its exertions in favor of the House of Austria. The question is not whether the king of Prussia shall be reduced, but whether the prosecution of the war against France *and* Prussia will not reduce the allies to accept any terms. . . ."

According to Robinson's report the queen listened to him "with more than ordinary patience and complacency."

He continued: "By the king's voluntary retreat Your Majesty may [be enabled to] dispatch effectual succors into Flanders to check the rapid progress of the French which not only threatens [Belgium] but menaces the very existence of the Maritime Powers, in whose fall the House of Austria will be involved." He implored the queen to "consent to an immediate accommodation with the king of Prussia. This is the only inducement of the Maritime Powers to continue the war; and by this alone the election of the Grand Duke can be secured . . . and France reduced to honorable and solid terms of peace."

Maria Theresa did not reflect on the ambiguous reference to the election. She protested her feelings of gratitude toward the ambassador's nation and its king and promised to consult her ministers the following morning. "But whatever may be determined in my council . . . I cannot spare a [single] man out of the king of Prussia's neighborhood. Perhaps a regiment or two of horse, and as many of infantry, may be sent to Italy; but the rest, in time of peace as well as in time of war will be necessary for the immediate defense of my person and family."

Robinson said that "amongst 70,000 men who were affirmed to be employed against Prussia, enough might be found for all purposes." And if Her Majesty's troops were "so necessary for her personal defense, those of England would be found too soon necessary at their own home."

"Why are there less hopes of detaching France than Prussia?" she asked.

"Because the king of Prussia would more easily make a peace to preserve what he has than France to give up, as she must, what she has acquired, and is in a fair way of acquiring in [Belgium]."

The queen "expressed her eagerness for another blow with the king of Prussia; and upon my showing the just diffidence of the Saxons, she affirmed 'that Prince Charles was able alone to give another battle.' "

"That battle, Madam," Robinson answered, "if won, would not conquer Silesia; if lost, Your Majesty is ruined at home."

"Were I to agree with the king tomorrow," she exclaimed, "I would give him battle this evening! But why so pressing now? Why this interruption of operations by no means to be despaired of? Give me only to October, and then you may do what you will."

"That October," said Robinson, "will be the end of the campaign in all parts, and will be that very fatal moment when we have reason to fear we shall be obliged to accept the conditions France and Prussia shall think proper to impose upon us."

"That might be true," she answered, "were the . . . time to be employed, as you propose, in marching from Bohemia to the Rhine, and from the Rhine to the Low Countries. But as for my troops, I know none of my generals who would not refuse to command such marching, or rather inactive, armies; and as for the Grand Duke and Prince Charles, they shall not. The Grand Duke is not so ambitious as you imagine of an empty honor, much less to enjoy it under the tutelage of the king of Prussia. . . . The imperial dignity! is it compatible with the fatal deprivation of Silesia? Good God! give me only till the month of October; I shall then, at least, have better conditions."

Robinson did not respond to the disparagement of the imperial dignity, which had been an obsession with her for three years. He "delicately touched on the discontinuance of the subsidies," and then—not too delicately, one may surmise—requested an "immediate and specific answer."

"I see what will be concluded," she said, "with or without me."[20] And this acrimonious remark concluded Sir Thomas's audience. Before twenty-four hours were up Ulfeld informed him that the queen could not act on the proposal of his king.

Wasner, who had followed George II on his journey to Hanover, could procure no information on the Anglo-Prussian pourparlers. The conference in Vienna was kept guessing at Frederick's terms. British pressure reduced them; and the understanding arrived at, on August 26, aimed, in brief, at obtaining Maria Theresa's guarantee of the Silesian status quo in return for Frederick's guarantee of her dominions within the *Reich*. As Newcastle wished to keep the French court unaware of the impending pacification—and of what he hoped would be the end of their Prussian alliance—he instructed Robinson not to divulge the contents of the Hanover Convention unless the queen promised on her honor to keep the secret. She refused to give any such pledge.

Frederick was less secretive than the British statesmen. While spreading rumors to the effect that peace terms were settled, he invited Prince Charles to discuss an armistice. But meantime the Vienna court had cemented its ties with Saxony, whose master, in turn, had received a firm assurance from Russia that he could count on armed assistance should Prussia attack him. Consequently, Prince Charles was directed to turn down Frederick's invitation.

Maria Theresa chose to ignore the Hanover business in the audience she granted Robinson on September 9. In high spirits, she told him of a letter she had sent her brother-in-law. She expected him to "add luster to the Frankfurt coronation through a victory in the field, even as he had added luster to her coronation in Prague through the victory in Bavaria."[21] Everybody in Vienna, Robinson, somewhat mystified, concluded his dispatch, was looking forward to a grand battle and counting on its happy outcome.

Everything went off smoothly at Frankfurt after the envoys of Brandenburg and the elector Palatine had departed in protest against the reactivation of Bohemia's suffrage. Its envoy disarmed objections to the candidate's status by reminding the electoral representatives that the grand duke, though as Tuscany's ruler not a prince of the Empire, could still claim a seat in its Diet. He could indeed: he had retained it as the titular sovereign of a pocket margraviate that had been ceded to France when he was deprived of his Lorraine; and was not Tuscany herself, from way back, one of the Empire's fiefs? The conclave welcomed the solution.

As the envoys proceeded to cast their votes on September 13, none of them denied that the grand duke was, as an emperor must be, *bonus* and *justus*, and none rose to disprove that he would be *utile*. Custom required that the result of the election be made known to the crowds in front of St. Bartholomew's. When the secretaries inside seemed to be taking their time, a couple of bystanders climbed up to the windows and, having peered into the chapel, cried out: "It's the Queen of Hungary's husband!"[22] This way of putting it was in tune with how she herself felt, as a matter of course, as word of his election reached her at Linz.

Her decision to travel to Frankfurt had ripened in the first weeks of August. Erizzo pretended to know that the expenditures of the state journey were estimated at three million florins, "and people ask, under their breath, whether, in these calamitous days, all that money had not better be spent on the exigencies of war."[23] She herself found it necessary to admonish the president of the Hofkammer: "Watch out. Not one farthing must be diverted from the army funds. And keep an eye on the Hungarian revenue. Otherwise, there will be plain misery in Bohemia."[24]

Determined, then, to go to Frankfurt, she was at the same time unwilling to let herself be crowned. Francis, writing from Heidelberg, asked Ulfeld to intervene. "Your Highness certainly know how it is once Her Majesty has made up her mind," replied the chancellor. "The only response I could get was that she did not wish to be crowned, and if she had to assume that someone was going to force her into it, she simply would not go to Frankfurt. I did my best to discover her motives, but failed. . . . Perhaps Her Majesty considers this coronation beneath the dignity of the two crowns she wears. . . . Today she told me that being crowned in Frankfurt would be no more than a farce and that she does not intend to play it."[25] The ancient ritual did not constitute an actual coronation of the Holy Roman Emperor's wife; the archbishop only held her husband's crown, for some minutes, against her right shoulder.

Francis asked her to reconsider. Being four months with child, she pleaded advanced pregnancy. When in still another communication he reminded her of her grandmother's coronation robe that must be taken along, she informed him curtly that the garment "will not be needed."[26] She was equally sparing of words in some other matters he broached. He wished to wear the Lorraine cloak? Fine—"if you have got one." Presents would have to be made? "If only I had money, but I haven't got any [and would not have any even] if I sold my jewelry."[27] Much of it was still in pledge. Apparently she was intimating that Francis ought to dig into his own funds.

The paraphernalia of the Habsburgs' imperial display, which had gathered dust for nearly five years, were taken out of storage and shipped to Frankfurt—the crimson doublets and breeches of the halberdiers, the yellow liveries of outriders and coachmen and their plumed headgear, the caparisons with the double-headed black eagle embroidered on yellow baize. Teams of Kladrub horses were sent from their Bohemian stud, and along with the gilded state coach and the gilt-spoked coaches of the privy councilors, teams of Lipizza stallions from Vienna. On September 15 Maria Theresa set off on the journey with a cortege of sixty-eight carriages.

It was joined, upon leaving Habsburg territory, by Count Rudolph Chotek, her ambassador to the son of Charles VII. The young count had no mean story to tell: his French colleague in Munich had approached him and spoken of a *rapprochement* between their courts. In Passau the archbishop sang a *Te Deum*. On September 30 the cavalcade entered Nuremberg. "I wish I could have talked to the wives of all the patricians," the royal traveler wrote to a former lady-in-waiting, "but I had been on the road for thirteen hours without changing."[28] The warmth of the reception wherever she went compensated for discomforts. Not all of it was mere curiosity about a queen regnant in the flesh—a spectacle seen never before in the Reich—or the pleasure that her handsome person or the suite's splendor afforded the populace. The valleys through which her progress moved had seen their lives disrupted by marching and countermarching armies; and common folk were looking forward to the new emperorship as a guarantee of peace. Agitation also had seized many educated men, among both Catholics and Protestants, who were praising the electors for having bested the French meddlers. The itinerant court of Charles VII and its low estate had been an embarrassment to most of the petty sovereigns, who also had grown concerned about the tangible benefits their younger sons or nephews used to attain in imperial Habsburg service. Princes and princelings, sovereign bishops and abbots, alongside the aldermen of Free Cities, made haste to pay their respect to the wife of the emperor-elect. Even King Frederick's favorite sister, the Margravine of Bayreuth, came to kiss hands. The *Diarium* did not exaggerate in calling the journey a "species of triumph."

Reaching the River Main, Maria Theresa boarded a ship (decked out in the colors of her, not Francis', dynasty) for the last lap of the voyage. An often-repeated story has Francis, who wished to surprise her, arrive too late at the embarkation point, jump into a row boat, and catch up with her craft. Frankfurt's most illustrious son, Goethe, tells the tale as told him by his elders and describes the "great joy of the loving couple at the unexpected reunion." No doubt Maria Theresa was elated to see her Francis hale and hearty and out of the reach of Conti's cuirassiers; as Lobkowitz' plan of Velletri went to show, kidnapping royalty was not entirely unheard of.

The next morning they both went to the encampment of Traun's and Batthyány's armies at Heidelberg. Never before had the queen set foot in a camp or seen in a body the men who did her fighting. Reviewing their regiments, she "was not, as one had expected, on horseback in the Hungarian fashion, the physicians having counselled against it on account of her pregnancy. Instead, she had herself carried in a small sedan chair. The grand duke on his horse was by her side, and pointed out regiments and officers by name. At dinner, which was served under canvas, she had a courteous word for everybody. . . . All the talk is about that princess."[29]

Hohenfriedberg was not forgotten during these festive days. But it would seem that the expectation of a great victory had drowned out the dire warning implicit in Khevenhüller's report from his mission to Bohemia. And if Chotek was not mistaken, the court of Versailles was planning to desert the *méchant homme!*

The coronation had been set for October 4, Francis' name day. It turned out to be an unseasonably warm, sunny morning. Multitudes crowded the streets as Francis rode to the cathedral on a white charger. He wore the ancient mantle of the dukes of Lorraine, and on his head the crown of Jerusalem's Christian kings of yore. From the balcony of the Frauenstein House, a private building, Maria Theresa saw the solemn procession advancing. As soon as it was out of her sight she rushed ahead of it to the church to take a seat in its oratory. The ceremonial over, she returned to Frauenstein House, from whose balcony she watched the new emperor's progress toward the town hall—much as he, in Pressburg, had been watching her, from a mansion's window, canter up the Royal Hill. But unlike Francis at Pressburg, the royal spectator at Frankfurt did not restrain her emotions. Nor did Francis, as she had done in Pressburg, for solemnity's sake pretend to ignore the presence of the consort. "As he returned from the cathedral in his strange disguise, showing himself to her, as it were, as Charlemagne's ghost, he is said to have lifted his hands as if in a jest, displaying the orb and scepter and the marvelous gloves. Whereupon she is said to have broken out in loud laughter, and this occasioned great joy amongst the people who were privileged to witness this sign of the good and natural relationship of the highest-placed couple in Christendom." Maria Theresa— so Goethe tells the story—waved her handkerchief, and called "Vivat Emperor Francis!" at the top of her voice.

Medieval tradition denied any woman a place at the coronation banquet. The Empress-Queen (as henceforth she was styled)* made short shrift of some sticklers who tried to exclude her. If, for this once, she was seated to the left of Francis, the precedence she thus gave him did not betoken her view of the new situation. "She made it clear," Erizzo wrote, "that what she planned for the Empire would be achieved more by using clemency than stressing authority."[30] Even before Chotusitz, Khevenhüller had noted that the "disasters had turned her more humble, and had . . . dampened her well-known fumo."[31] Had they? An informant of Frederick's related that she was "treating princes of the Empire as though they were her subjects, and carried her pride to the point of rudeness toward many private persons, and Prince William of Hesse as well."[32] But, then, she may well have been courteous and curt within one and the same half hour. Moreover, Frankfurt was alive with stories of new disaster.

The battle she had so fervently wished for had taken place on September 30; and "to call a spade a spade," as Prince Charles did in a

---

* The style was never to become popular. Outside Hungary (where she remained the Queen) her subjects, high and low, would call her the Empress. So did people in the Reich and abroad, unless engaged in official business.

This led to a curious confusion. It lasts to this day. In general books, and even library catalogs, she is more often than not referred to as "Maria Theresa, Empress of Austria." The title was unknown in her own day, as indeed was an "Austrian Empire." It was to come into existence only in 1804, two years before her grandson laid down the crown of the Holy Roman Empire, which had given up its ghost.

letter that may have reached his brother on the very day of the coronation, "we have been thoroughly beaten."[33] To counteract the Prussian
infiltration of the hilly borderland, the prince had advanced with his
superior forces, keeping the king unaware of his maneuvers. During the
night the Austrians had succeeded in encircling the enemy camp in a
valley surrounded by rocky heights. How Frederick had turned the tables
on the prince, unnerved his generals by unexpected swift moves, and
driven his own grenadiers up the inclines under fire—this was a kind of
warfare that Charles could explain only by saying that the Prussians were
"unlike all other enemies."[34]

His sister-in-law was, "because of the circumstances, more dejected"[35]
than she had been after Hohenfriedberg. Three regiments had "turned
tail without firing a shot, or using their sabres once."[36] Lobkowitz, "after
killing three officers for cowardice, was jostled by his own men into a
ditch . . . and the only corps of hussars who reached the camp of the
enemy were, during the heat of battle, busy pillaging the baggage."[37]

The Viennese had erected three triumphal arches for the entry of the
homecoming couple, and there was much rejoicing as they passed under
these wooden structures with great panoply. In the small hours of the
following day a motley crew set about dismantling the grandest of the
arches, a structure as flimsy as it was colossal. It took the authorities
some hours to realize that the populace did not want Prince Charles to
pass under an arch of triumph on his return from the defeat of Soor.

Robinson had of course been in Frankfurt. After the news of Soor
arrived he had an audience of the empress; and his own king's Hanoverian envoy found himself "moved to compassion" when she described
to him the "vehemence and the downright despotic tone with which
Robinson had presented his demands."[38] She had to face him again on
October 31 in Schönbrunn.

We have an account of this interview from the facile pen of Erizzo,
to whom she talked within the week. Robinson had "dwelled on the
events in Scotland, and they afforded him a fine pretext for trying to
force me into a reconciliation with King Frederick, irrespective of terms."

As it was, the ambassador had no reason to minimize those "events."
The Young Pretender, who had entered Edinburgh on September 11,
was marching on England. True, his hopes for French assistance appeared to be vain. But the situation in the Low Countries was most
perilous in that De Saxe had entrenched himself on the Channel as far
north as the Scheldt.

Now, Robinson said, was the moment for Her Majesty to concentrate
all of her strength against the Bourbon powers. Now was the moment
to recall that her cause alone had embroiled his nation in war with
France. Her Majesty must end the war with Prussia. She had to end it.

Four times the king had trounced her armies, four times! Of course, he had broken the Treaty of Breslau. "But if settlements with all princes guilty of similar conduct were to be ruled out, war would become permanent." And why did not the empress-queen think of the most culpable court of all? "No power has more often than France betrayed the House of Austria. Indeed, history knows of no betrayal more vile than hers upon the death of Charles VI!"[39] Most probably the British had got wind of Chotek's conversations with the French ambassador in Munich.

Conversely, they did not know that a bizarre highway incident had furnished the Vienna court with a complete text of the Hanover convention. Maria Theresa might have thrown her knowledge in Sir Thomas's face and told him that his appeal to the spirit of their alliance was disingenuous. As he went on to say that unless she ceased chasing the Silesian will-o'-the-wisp, she no longer could count on financial aid, she merely rejoined that those moneys had not of late been of decisive importance; having had to raise twenty-two million this year, she simply would raise twenty-four in the next. In these very weeks the court was "unable to raise the money for the expenses of its own household.[40]

Robinson's parting words were a warning of the calamitous consequences Her Majesty's inflexibility was bound to bring down on her head. Inflexible she was. But she was also enterprising again. She refused to be panicked by Charles Emmanuel's dealings with France, of which she had word. Liechtenstein must wait until "the end of January or the beginning of February . . . [for] an adequate number of troops."[41] Overriding Prince Charles's representations, the empress had decided on another blow with the king. Every last man was needed for its execution. If doubts about her troops' worth in battle, or Charles's, clouded her determination, she gave no indication of them.

Frederick may have been in the dark about the operations mapped in Vienna and Dresden. Of what was brewed in St. Petersburg, his intelligence kept him abreast. The czarina's long–drawn-out controversy with Vienna had been resolved;* and "in a four-hour meeting of her council" she had declared with great passion that it was "necessary, and indeed high time, to check Prussia."[42] Two Russian corps were being mobilized. Speed was of the essence for Frederick if he wanted to forestall an embroilment with Russia. On November 11 he left Berlin.

Ten days later two Austrian armies entered Saxony—Charles's to effect a junction with Count Rutowski's forces, Count Grünne's to head straight for Brandenburg and Berlin.† This double thrust was made to coincide with a diplomatic offensive. The Hanover convention was said,

* See p. 175.
† Rutowski, one of the numerous bastard sons of Augustus II, had played a minor role in the coup by which De Saxe forced Prague in 1741; the growing fame of his half-brother was a thorn in his flesh. Grünne was one of the few Austrian generals who had kept his sangfroid at Hohenfriedberg.

in Vienna, to have brought the French king up in arms. Frederic Harrach was journeying to Dresden to meet M. de Vaulgrenant, Louis XV's ambassador to its court.

Harrach had risen in the esteem of Maria Theresa, if not her affection. When Kinsky had been put at the head of the treasury on Starhemberg's demise, Harrach had been appointed chancellor of Bohemia. His felicity of speech and his firsthand knowledge of Belgium should stand him in good stead in the talks with Vaulgrenant.

On his road toward Dresden Harrach learned of a setback that the Saxon contingent in Prince Charles's army had suffered on the Silesian border. The contretemps had forced the prince to turn about and abandon Saxon territory. (Grünne, who had been intercepted by the enemy, was retreating.) Complying with new instructions, Harrach called on Charles. He listened to his surly recriminations, interviewed some of the junior generals, and then composed a report for the empress. Its unvarnished truth had a peculiar effect in Vienna. "It is regrettable," Ulfeld submitted, "that no one can bring himself to inform His Majesty betimes of conditions as they prevail in the army, and [tell him] that all its misfortunes are blamed on the prince."[43] Yes, yes, the empress answered, "in many instances it would be preferable . . . to talk to the emperor instead of letting me withhold the truth." In fact, she had spoken to him now, and he had had a brief talk with Bartenstein, who "thinks that there will be no battle."[44]

The perplexity in Vienna was, in Dresden, matched by a "confusion" Esterhazy was "at a loss to do justice to."[45] Augustus and his fatuous premier had betaken themselves to Prague, where the liveried servants and blooded horses and the plate and choice wines arriving from Vienna assuaged the eloquent anger of the elector as little as did Maria Theresa's assurance that the "just cause will triumph sooner or later."[46]

Prince Charles led his army back into Saxony in the first days of December. Although he found Rutowski "a man after my own heart"[47] on first blush, they were soon to squabble about a concerted plan. Meanwhile Frederick moved up the Elbe valley, and Anhalt-Dessau was approaching Dresden. To stop him, Rutowski chose a ridge between the river and the village of Kesselsdorf. On December 15 Anhalt-Dessau, giving way to his king's exhortations to throw caution to the winds, attacked, leading his battalions across the ice-covered gorge into the fire of the Saxon guns on the heights. Rutowski repulsed the assault and sent part of his force down into the Prussian camp. The resulting melee compelled him to halt his cannonade. The Prussian dragoons, riding roughshod over the men on the slope, breached the left wing, and as Rutowski had failed to prepare a second line, precipitated a panic. Anhalt-Dessau's son Maurice hurled his troops across terrain judged impassable by the Saxons, against their center. As they were thrown back, the commander of the right ring, which consisted mainly of Austrian troops, offered assistance. Rutowski ordered him to stay where he was. Not until the victors pitched tents in the dusk did the Austrian corps begin to withdraw.

Where had Prince Charles's own army been all the while? Afterward he blamed his inactivity on the Saxon quartermasters, who had billeted his troops at a three-hour distance from their own in scattered hamlets. The Saxons, on the other hand, declared that widespread hostility toward the Austrian soldiery had restricted the choice of billets. But, such post-mortems aside, Charles could not deny that he had been adamant in his refusal to split his army and had waited for all its regiments to reach the rallying point. By that time Rutowski's mauled divisions were streaming past Dresden into Bohemia. And thither Prince Charles too was leading his army.

Harrach arrived in Dresden in time to sit in at a meeting of the beaten generals. Late at night he wrote to Ulfeld: "Henceforth it will not be advisable to entrust Prince Charles with the command of an army that has to fight the king of Prussia, who, so help me God, is just too smart for him. Now, if I had any say, I would give Traun an army of 80,000 Germans and 20,000 hussars . . . Croats and Slavonians and take them to Moravia. If there should be other troops to spare, I would attach them to the Saxons to [re-]enter Saxony. . . . What with Bavarians and Hanoverians[?] and from a third side the Russians, that Tamerlane we have to grapple with would find his head spinning."[48] How far from reality was this clever man!

How close to it was Maria Theresa! On the day she learned of the first setback she had dispatched a courier to Harrach with authority to treat, in case of emergency, with the King of Prussia. Harrach felt "like tearing out my own eyes as I see that I am about to . . . forge shackles of permanent bondage for our august empress and her descendants."[49] Three days after the battle he no longer could doubt the imminence of a Prussian-Saxon armistice, as recommended to Augustus eloquently by the British envoy. Nor, rushing to present himself to Vaulgrenant, could Harrach misjudge the chances of a satisfactory settlement with the French. Belgium, his main bargaining object, was at their mercy; the British had evacuated their last troops from the Continent; and Don Philip, Louis XV's son-in-law, had taken Milan. Vaulgrenant's tentative proposals, in actual fact, were a far cry from what had been intimated to Chotek in Munich. Worse, the Frenchman barely concealed his mistrust of the court of Vienna.

On the twenty-first of the month Harrach received directives to arrange for preliminaries with Prussia on the basis of the convention of

Hanover. It would be futile, the empress added, to let one's mind dwell on the irretrievable past. "Delay is fraught with dire peril."[50] This was not how Ulfeld and Bartenstein looked at delay. Why should not Harrach settle with the king without breaking off the talks with Vaulgrenant? The ratification of the Prussian treaty might be postponed. Maria Theresa wanted none of it. "It is true that the others made us weep often enough, and it only would be just to make *them* weep, for a change. But [your scheme] would cry to Heaven."[51] Morality apart, the fear of "falling between two stools"[52] had been haunting her for a long time.

Frederick, who had entered Dresden with his troops, received Harrach on Christmas Eve. "A pox on all negotiations!" Harrach exclaimed in his report to Ulfeld. "Those that were close to my heart had no success whatsoever. Those I dread are proceeding most successfully." The king had suggested immediate cessation of hostilities. "He is a brilliant and sanguine prince, but does not dare look you in the eye, either because he is squint-eyed, or on account of a bad conscience. I was seated opposite him at dinner, and he was talking to me nearly all the time. As he has a caustic turn of mind, I was hard put to it to avoid the capital sin [of pride] in replying. If I were his equal, a talk between him and myself would assuredly amuse you ten times as much as did those I used to have with our late lamented Herberstein."[53]

The king was no stickler for minor points. But he insisted on ratification within ten days. If he was wondering about a possible change of heart in Vienna, events proved him right. A new set of instructions was delivered to Harrach two days after peace terms had been settled. The count was convinced by then of Vaulgrenant's disingenuousness. He took it upon himself to sign the instrument of ratification. Frederick renewed the Peace of Breslau, recognized Francis as emperor, agreed to the reactivation of Bohemia's electoral vote, and bound himself to evacuate Saxony. He had not bothered to consult his French ally.

On New Year's Day—five years to the day on which Gotter, standing before Francis, had announced the rape of Silesia—Erizzo reported: "The mortification at court, among the ministers, and also among common people, is greater than it was even upon the disastrous events of the late campaign."[54] The empress retired to Schönbrunn despite the cold season and buried herself in memoranda on Italian affairs. She also corresponded, through her private secretary, with the head of her administration in the few Silesian counties left her, a man with very special ideas. She may or may not have learned that people in Berlin had taken to calling their king Frederick the Great.

Harrach stopped over on his return trip to pay his court to Augustus. Although let off lightly by Frederick, the refugee in Prague could not be mollified. His particular ire was directed at Frederick's sardonic idea to have his own singers perform Hasse's *Arminio*, which had been commissioned in anticipation of victory over the Prussians.

A note from the empress was handed Harrach in Prague. She approved of what he had done, thanked him in measured tones, and went on to say: "However remote the thought of signing so calamitous a treaty may have been from my mind, and no matter how little I imagined, at the start of the campaign, that things would ever come to this pass, I nevertheless am resolved, as is my wont, to live up to this agreement as a hallowed obligation."[55]

Her resolve to stand by the Treaty of Dresden was also written into the pact of alliance she concluded six months later (June, 1746) with Elizabeth of Russia. Lord Hyndford, now ambassador to the czarina, suggested that the new treaty was, to the mind of the Habsburg empress, primarily a means to "take Silesia away from the king, and bridle his dangerous ambition."[56] The suspicious Scotsman was ignorant of the treaty's *article secretissime* by which Maria Theresa was guaranteed military assistance in the recovery of Silesia if Frederick ever should violate her own or Augustus' dominions. Hyndford gauged her emotions with greater accuracy than she herself cared to apply.

Two months after the Peace of Dresden a daughter was born to the empress.

X

Ruler and Ruled

In April, 1746, Count Otto Christian Podewils, a nephew of King Frederick's foreign minister, was posted as Prussian ambassador in Vienna. His instructions were "(one) to explore the sentiments of the imperial court, and whether it intends to live with us in peace, (two) to mollify the empress-queen's spirit little by little . . . (three) to deliver . . . character sketches of the empress, the emperor, the most important ministers, and all persons who influence the conduct of affairs without holding office."[1]

Podewils had not an easy time in Vienna. High society snubbed him. "Inasmuch as I am the envoy of a prince looked upon with mistrust . . . no one dares make friends with me, lest he displeases the court. If I do find people who with due caution confide in me, I surely cannot give full credence to information which passion may distort, or lack of discernment truncate or cast the wrong light on." He tried to "arrive at as accurate a picture as possible" in his pen portraits "by comparing character traits as they are related by different people, and checking the former against the actions of the personages I describe."[2] He was not altogether isolated in the diplomatic corps. For one, Erizzo, who entertained good relations with the ministers, appeared to have talked to Podewils regularly.

The ambassador was not above pandering to his king's curiosity. But whenever a piece of intelligence was based on hearsay he said so. And he fed him what we should call human-interest stories primarily to gloss over the failure of his political mission. For Maria Theresa paid little attention to Podewil's presence in Vienna, since she was convinced that "the king decides everything by himself anyway."[3] Not until late in June was he invited to present himself at Schönbrunn.

"She is above rather than below average height [he wrote on January 18, 1747]. The numerous confinements and the native ampleness of her figure . . . have made her very heavy. Still, her gait is easy, her posture majestic, and her appearance distinguished, although she harms it by the way she dresses, particularly by the little English hoop skirt. Her round-shaped head has a full face with high forehead. An expression of gentleness enlivens her large eyes. The small nose is neither aquiline nor turned-up. Her mouth, while a bit on the large side, is well shaped. White teeth make her smile pleasant. Her throat is formed well; arms and hands are most beautiful. So must have been her complexion, if judged by what still can be seen despite the poor care. . . . Her mien is frank and serene, her speech graceful and kindly. One cannot deny that she is an attractive woman.

"Upon her accession," Podewils went on, "she discovered the art of winning everybody's admiration and love. Her sex, her handsome appearance, as well as her misfortunes, contributed not a little toward the favorable response. . . . She took pains to show herself in the best of lights. Affable, pious, generous, charitable, simple in manner, courageous and high-minded, she soon conquered the hearts of her subjects, who indeed reproached themselves bitterly with having shown sympathies for the Elector of Bavaria, afterwards Emperor Charles VII. Anybody could gain admittance to her in the general audiences. She read petitions herself, and made inquiries about the administration of justice. She would gratify people by a kindly smile, or a felicitous phrase, and try to buffet the blow when she rejected a plea. She made big promises . . . stressed her compassion for the poor, established hospitals, and distributed money among soldiers [on duty]. . . . 'Inconsolable' was a word she used time and again to express her grief at having to make her subjects share her tribulations. . . . Defying ill luck, she tried to imbue people with her own fortitude.

"The praise lavished on her, and her own well-developed *amour propre* as well, soon inflated the opinion she had of her efficiency and talents. She became high-handed, impatient of advice, and no longer brooked contradiction. . . ."[4]

She had matured. Maturing, she also had hardened. As early as October, 1743, Khevenhüller made a note of the "overly despotic ways of the otherwise so praiseworthy woman."[5] Back in the dark winter of 1740–41 her subjects, high and low, had nearly all of them doubted that she would ever be able to reign. As she now tried to rule, they found fault with her increased vigor.

"Her mind being lively and keen, her memory excellent, and her _judgment sound, she is perfectly capable of dealing with affairs of state . . . [and] ambition has instilled her with the desire to govern herself. She is more successful in that respect than most of her ancestors were. However, her ministers and the personal entourage try to keep accurate information from her. They do not want her to interfere with certain malpractices which afford them and their families no small profit. Thus her efforts, if not entirely useless, bear little fruit. . . . She has stopped a goodly number of abuses, and curtailed some unnecessary expenses. She plans many changes in the treasury and the army, often referring to Your Majesty's system."[6]

Rumored innnovations had begun to disquiet people, who also were quick to speak of a lack of appreciation. Twice Mme. Fuchs was said to be on the verge of dismissal, and much sympathized with even among townsfolk. But this kind of gossip was only incidental to the creeping dissatisfaction. "People grumble about taxes. . . . They no longer crowd the streets to catch a glimpse of her. Her pictures are no longer sought after in the shops."[7] But how could she possibly live up to the exalted notion people had formed about her in the first years? Its very perfection, Podewils suggested, had been bound to create disillusionment sooner or later. "Of course she is not possessed of all the fine qualities she displayed so dazzlingly in the beginning. But this is no reason for blame. . . ."[8]

Even before limning the character sketch, the diligent Prussian had collected material about "the finances of this court." They were "in the most appalling disorder. One lives on credit and subsidies, from hand to mouth, as the saying goes. . . . A few weeks ago, the court raised a fl.-300,000-loan in Holland. The army in [Belgium] is paid by England. That country is supposed to have sent paymasters of its own there, asserting that subsidies had been used for less pressing purposes. . . .* The Italian army is paid miserably. Officers have gone without pay for eight months, and the well-to-do among them have advanced some money to their regiments or companies, as the soldiers, too, are given their pay with great irregularity only. . . . The lack of cash here is unbelievable. I was told that one officer asking for his arrears was brushed off with the words: 'What do you expect us to pay you from? We have exactly 36 florins on hand.' . . . It seems to me that twenty years of peace and exertions would not suffice to rebuild the finances if one wanted to clear up all debts. . . . Still, what with the subsidies from the Maritime Powers and the present taxation—and if the empress-queen succeeds in raising more and more loans, and continues to pay her troops poorly,

* English suspicions on that score had been evident even a generation before. In 1706 a remittance from London to Eugene's Italian army reached him "via a financial house in Venice which had received it from Frankfort, thereby satisfactorily circumventing the imperial court." (Henderson, op. cit., 124.)

denying them even the necessaries—she can carry on the war for several more years."[9]

Apart from irregulars, Maria Theresa's army consisted of men the individual regiments recruited for lifetime and (to a much smaller extent) of those mustered by the individual estates through rudimentary forms of conscription. Soldiering held little glamour for penury-ridden men who had been lured into the ranks; it held even less for peasant boys who had failed to evade the levies of the estates. The rigors of the service diminished rather than enhanced the respect that the soldier commanded among civilians. His sacrifices in battle did not make him a hero. Desertion did not necessarily brand him a villain.* Looked upon with suspicion by the rural population and often maligned, he reciprocated, at best, with callousness, with cruelty at worst.

In the summer of 1746 the court-martial of Francis von der Trenck was the talk of the army, indeed a *cause célèbre*. At long last this colonel of pandours had been called to account for atrocities known to the court since the days of Neipperg's Silesian campaign. "He used to send out special detachments to kidnap twelve- and thirteen-year-old girls, including well-born ones, who he then violated. . . . He would force his own officers to give him part of their booty by putting them into irons. . . . In Bavaria and elsewhere he took people from their homes, shipped them to his estate [in Slavonia] and kept them as slaves, summarily hanging anyone who attempted escape."[10] When Prince Charles tried to pry Trenck loose from his judges Maria Theresa admitted to her troubled conscience—what extraordinary services had Trenck rendered during the war!—and asked Ulfeld for his opinion.** He answered promptly: "I consider it my duty to draw Your Majesty's attention to the fact that many of the weaknesses of the members of the Arch House stemmed from their very virtues." Had not her father carried the virtue of gratitude to the point of depriving himself, for the benefit of his Spaniards in Vienna, of the moneys needed for the troops in Naples and Sicily? And what, if not his shortage of funds, had been responsible for the loss of those splendid kingdoms? Having thus played on Maria Theresa's mourning for Naples, Ulfeld continued: "It is out of a sense of gratitude only that the emperor and his brother have intervened in Trenck's behalf with such vigor.† Its degree may be gauged

---

* Though apprehended deserters were punished mercilessly, wholesale amnesties for those still at large were frequent in all armies of the period.

** Until 1748 the chancellor was at the head of the administration of justice.

† The Chancellor wished to give the lie to an ugly rumor about their motives. "I have been told," Podewils wrote, "that Trenck, to secure the intercession of the Prince of Lorraine, returned to him an I.O.U. for fl. 20,000 that the latter had given Trenck for a gambling debt." (*Diplomatische Berichte,* 111.)

by His Majesty's summoning the prosecutor, and by what His Majesty told him. . . . Your Majesty will not find many men who [as the prosecutor did after that audience] would ask for a sentence of death notwithstanding an emperor's prejudging the defendant not guilty. Your Majesty can change the laws. But as long as they are on the books, they alone must guide decisions in a court of law."[11] Maria Theresa commuted the sentence to life imprisonment. Trenck died two years later, after much breast-beating, and was buried in the habit of the Capuchins, one of whose friars had led him to repentance. This aftermath of the scandal pleased Maria Theresa no less than it did the more sentimental among her subjects.

War, one of the normal hazards of the countryman's life, was part of royal business. Its horrors in battle weighed less on Maria Theresa's conscience than did the excesses of troops on the march. Punishment for men who "overdid it" was discussed in Vienna long before and after the trial of Trenck. But the generals, to a man, objected to stringent measures: once the peasant knew that any soldier guilty of "some small transgression" was in for a flogging—and any officer culprit for loss of his rank—the peasants would "get insolent" and make life miserable for the troops, who then "would either lose heart completely, or pick quarrels likely to result in some outrage."[12]

The countryside was, in general, spared such wanton destruction as had laid waste entire valleys half a century earlier. Regimental commanders, alert to the troops' propensity for desertion, tried to keep them from wildcat foraging. The peasant could claim payment from the estates for requisitions, but chicaneries delayed his indemnification sometimes for years, and billeting left him at all events the loser. As the army increased in numbers and brought with it men from the four corners of the monarchy—and their babel of tongues—billeting grew to be the most dreaded of visitations. Looting was one of the privileges of the ranks on enemy soil; with their pay growing less and less regular, they did not trouble to distinguish between enemy land and Habsburg territory. Hungarian and Croat irregulars in Italy never had.

Thus Maria Theresa's marching armies compounded the everyday misery of the peasants. Whether the manor lord held them as serfs* or ruled them as "hereditary subjects," his juridical and administrative functions gave him practically unlimited power over his peasantry. Labor-service regulations were lost sight of in days of seasonal work. Peasant boys were pressed into unpaid full-time service. While the manor lord was obliged to keep his peasants out of want when the crops failed,

* Their status must not be confounded with that of serfs in eighteenth-century Russia; for one thing, the lords in the Habsburg dominions could not sell their "Leibeigene."

no system existed for enforcing that duty. "Only a handful of my parishioners have bread all year round," a Styrian priest reported shortly before Maria Theresa's accession. "To pay their rent and taxes, they sell what wheat and rye they harvest, and live on maize, oats, and millet. . . . Many go to bed in damp clothes, and have neither sheets nor blankets."[13] The army endangered the last resort of their self-reliance—the ownership of a cow or a team of horses. Virtually without any education, the peasant had all the gross tastes of his medieval forebears and none of their sense of security under the manor. Ridden by superstitious fears, he could derive small comfort from religion. A decree issued in 1741 forbade him the possession of firearms. Rendering him helpless against highwaymen and wild beasts, it also struck a blow at what little self-respect the peasants had salvaged from two centuries of oppression. Dispirited, many of them may well have been as indolent, slothful, and loose in morals as the landowners' bailiffs in certain areas contended all of them were. Townsfolk, taking the churls' lot for granted, loved to tell stories about their coarse holiday feastings.

Although few barracks existed in the 1740's, the army abstained in general from requisitioning quarters in city dwellings. Instances of rapine were all but unknown. The provincial levies seldom got hold of town boys. More wordly-wise than young rustics, they also were not easily trapped by the recruiting officers of the regiments. Unless, then, the enemy stood at the gates or occupied a town, its daily life, except for taxes, was hardly encroached on by the sovereign's war. To Vienna, war had restored some of the prosperity of the 1720's.

In 1728 a Hanoverian traveler noted that "they overdo eating and drinking in Vienna, and this is true of the lowly classes as well as the high, of clerics as well as laymen. They know of no better way of spending their time than at table, a glass of wine in hand."[14] Nineteen years later Frederick's envoy was amazed that "burghers and common people live as opulently as ever, and masters in the crafts spend as much money here as do noblemen elsewhere. . . . In spite of the huge sums extracted [by taxation] there is a great deal of money in circulation."[15] The financial misery of the court profited moneylenders. "Some of the bankers here are able to raise a million or two within a week or so."[16] Although "the great are slightly reducing their retinues,"[17] their love for ostentation still sustained a vast class of builders, artificers, and luxury-goods importers. It was estimated that half of Vienna's two-hundred thousand inhabitants were dependent for their livelihood on the court and the aristocratic households.

But the affluence of the masters in the crafts did not seep down to the lower rungs on the social ladder. Repeated attempts of the authorities to breach the power of the guilds had barely begun to dent it. Journeymen were paid poorly. Homeworkers lived in grinding poverty. Winter threw laborers in the building trades out of work. The public pawnbroker shop, a *monte de pietà* set up in the day of Maria Theresa's grandfather, did not want for business in her own. Workhouses for destitute people willing to earn their bread had been planned; they were never established. Beggars, "licensed" or not, swamped the neighborhoods of churches, defying a stream of ordinances. Petty crime was rampant. An element of shiftlessness had entered Vienna and its sprawling suburbs. Two bodies of police—their duties overlapped, and both were hated fiercely—did not know how to cope with these conditions. But economic insecurity did not change the Viennese bent for amusements.

Nothing was more indicative of it than the vexation of the *publicum* as, in the winter of 1746–47, the empress took it upon herself to interfere with carnival pleasures. A spate of decrees subjected localities, hours, fancy dresses, masks, and the mode of dancing to strict regulations; one of these "little laws"[18] (as Khevenhüller was to call the unenforceable injunctions of a later period) made it a punishable offense for people of opposite sex to talk to one another while dancing. In the autumn of 1747 a "special security commission" came into being, in effect, a vice squad. "The empress issued the most stringent orders *in puncto sexti* [*sic*] . . ." Khevenhüller wrote in his journal, "in order to prevent, and intrude on, all clandestine trysts. . . . The commission, facetiously referred to as '*la commission de chasteté*,' has been made sport of freely in foreign newspapers."[19]

This petulant puritanism shocked people all the more as it was at variance with Maria Theresa's own much-talked-about delight, but a few years earlier, in carnival merrymaking. Such "*divertissements* have ceased to attract her," the lord marshal remarked. "The youthful high spirits have vanished."[20] Besides, amorous dalliance had always been loathsome to Maria Theresa.

Thirty years before, Lady Mary Wortley Montagu, never averse to generalizing, observed that "'tis the established custom for every lady to have two husbands, one that bears the name, and another that performs the duties. . . . These submarriages generally last twenty years together. . . ."[21] Such liaisons had kept unmarried young (and not so young) noblemen within their class. They "do not only scorn to marry, but also to make love to, any woman of a family not so illustrious as their own; and the pedigree is much more considered by them than either the complexion or features of their mistresses."[22] High-society mores had changed. The traveling companies that took the place of the disbanded opera troupe of Charles VI had brought with them a type, new to Vienna, of female singers and dancers, an international of entertainers on stage and off who set about to seduce wellborn men—or so Maria Theresa chose to assume. In 1747 two companies were expelled on account of such scandals—incidents which prompted, of all people, the papal nuncio to "remark that he doubted very much the empress could find young women willing to come from Italy to Vienna only to lead the lives of Capuchin monks."[23] Mlle. Santini, a widely admired soprano, was seized and escorted all the way down to the Venetian border by two *commissarii*. Things had come to a pretty pass, to the mind of the empress, if even a Frederic Harrach was "carrying on intrigues with lowly women."[24]

"Strict in her own mores, she may well be too rigorous a judge of those of others," the Swedish minister at her court observed in 1756, adding: "She has often been dealing with details that are beneath her, which has caused some people . . . to say that this princess is great in great affairs, and small in small ones."[25]

Indeed, an *ésprit policier*, hardly becoming her station, had come to the surface in Maria Theresa. "She made it the duty of the *commissaires* to search houses as they see fit . . . and arrest every man entertaining a lady of the opera, or a woman of like mores. The empress has also decreed that every opera singer who receives a young man in her lodgings will be shipped to a convent . . . and her visitor removed from Vienna, and banished for good."*[26]

Surely the "submarriages" of society folk had not been broken off upon the death of Charles VI. What annoyed his daughter was a tendency to carry those affairs beyond the customary bounds of discretion. One young nobleman eloped to Switzerland with his *inamorata*, a married woman of exalted lineage. (The refusal of the cantonal authorities to extradite the couple prejudiced Maria Theresa for the rest of her life against Switzerland, a "refuge for all profligates and criminals.")[27] Count Francis Esterhazy, nicknamed "Quinquin," seemed to enjoy parading his *commerce d'amour* with a Countess Althan. The Hungarian aristocrats were the least manageable of the lot. Podewils, giving a spirited account of Nicholas Esterhazy's debauches in Dresden and his uncouth pranks, observed that "everybody is astonished at Emperor Francis' devotion to that man."[28]

Francis clung to men who amused him, and nothing amused him more than practical jokes. To dissuade one of the most frolicsome of his

* "The files of the 'Chastity Commission' occupied, down to our own day, considerable space in the archives of the Palace of Justice in Vienna. They went up in smoke in the fire that destroyed this building on July 15, 1927." (Egon Cesar Conte Corti, *Die Kaiserin*, 121.)

own "Lorrainers," an Irish exile who went by the name of Ogara, from leaving the court, he made him grand master to the household of Princess Charlotte, who had moved to Vienna after the death of her mother. Even though this unmarried sister of Francis', a woman overly tall, gawky of movement, and horsy of face, was well past her prime, Ogara was spoken of as her lover. By the mid-forties some prurient stories about Francis himself were abroad in Vienna.

"The emperor is below average height, but fairly well built [writes Podewils]. His habit of carrying his head low impairs the posture, and he does not care about his gait. He has a squarish face. His dark-blue eyes, beautiful as they are, lack luster. The slightly aquiline nose is not big. His mouth is small, and his smile engaging. He has a youthful and regular complexion. The details should combine to give him a handsome face; but many people think it to be slightly vulgar. . . . He is courteous, if rather cool, toward persons he meets for the first time, and appears to be somewhat shy in contacts with foreigners. He expresses with ease whatever he wants to say. His demeanor is, to say the least, informal. . . . As he treats people he knows with familiarity even in public, he is often taken advantage of, and not shown due respect. He hates ceremony, and tries his best to abolish it. . . .

"He has a lively imagination, a good memory, and a good deal of common sense. Being lazy by nature, he cannot apply himself to anything thoroughly. He dislikes work, is not ambitious, and pays as little attention as possible to official business. All he wants is to enjoy life, have a good time, and he willingly leaves to the empress both the glory and the anxieties of government. The empress and her ministers also guide him in the conduct of the Empire's affairs, of which he has little knowledge." But he "is perfectly conversant with financial problems, and actually does apply himself to this one field. He has organized fiscal matters in his state [of Tuscany] very well. He even submitted to the empress divers projects for re-organizing her own [finances] showing her how sorely mismanaged they were. . . .

"He has a gentle disposition; I have heard of no instance of his losing his temper. It is generally he who gives in during the little quarrels with the empress. He detests gossip, and would like all people to get along with one another. . . . Because of the small influence he wields, he cannot do much for a man's career, and is reduced to asking the empress, at a skillfully chosen moment, for favors she might bestow on people he is kindly disposed to. Meetings he attends only as a matter of courtesy, and is harkened to but rarely, even though he sometimes comes out with sound advice. Small as his aspirations may be, he is sensitive to the by no means brilliant position in which he finds himself. But congenital lassitude . . . and his desire to stay out of trouble will keep him aloof from any attempt to change his situation.

"He is fond of all kinds of amusement, without pursuing any with passion. The hunt and the stage are his main diversions. . . . Formerly, he had a penchant for Countess Colloredo, the wife of the vice chancellor* and also showed affection to Countess Pálffy, a lady-in-waiting of the empress-queen, who subsequently married Count Canalis [the Sardinian ambassador]. And there were others. He used to dine with them in secret. But the jealousy of the empress has compelled him to restrict this sort of thing. No sooner does she see him paying attentions to a woman than she turns sulky and starts making life miserable for him. Moreover, his own goodheartedness prevents him exposing a woman to the vindictive moods of the empress, who is not likely to forget such affronts. As she began to realize his weakness [for the fair sex] she grew doubly suspicious. He is still said to have his little escapades, pretending to go hunting some miles away. . . . However, if there were any truth in these stories, the empress would remedy things in no time; and, having surrounded him with her creatures, she certainly would learn of such trysts."29

The great shock to her self-assurance as a woman lay still in the future; Neipperg's daughter was still a child in 1747. But Maria Theresa's dream of owning Francis body and soul was already clouded by the pleasure, however innocent, he took in the company of attractive young women. She did not question his devotion to her. What menaced her marital happiness was man's innate concupiscence. She must bridle it—in all places—by the kind of Christian morality she had always believed in and the kind of propriety she was resolved to enforce wherever her arm reached. So she went out of her way to find transgressors.

Podewils related some pertinent anecdotes, true or half true. One of these had the empress order "Count Königsegg to make sure officers did not frequent houses of ill fame; advancement would be withheld from those who were apprehended in such places." As the story went, Königsegg replied that he praised his good luck, for if that order had been in force in his youth, he would still be an army ensign. "One of the commissaires tried to persuade the valet of a certain young gentleman to let him know when his master expected a lady caller. The servant informed his employer, who then asked him to tell the snooper to come at such-and-such an hour. The commissaire came and found the young man entertaining a woman. The gentleman feigned panic, implored the commissaire not to denounce him, offering a bribe of one hundred ducats. After protracted coy refusal, the fellow took the money. No sooner, how-

* Count Rudolph Colloredo, a son-in-law of Gundakar Starhemberg, had become vice-chancellor of the Empire in 1737. Upon Charles Albert's election, Colloredo sold the office to the lord chamberlain of Bavaria. Having bought it back when Francis became emperor, he was shortly thereafter sworn to the conference by Maria Theresa, even though she resented the amorous adventures he engaged in and boasted of.

ever, had he turned to leave than he was set upon by the young man, who dealt him a hundred strokes with the cane, and forced him to return the gold coins. The fellow has not dared lodge a complaint."[30] No doubt the nobility relieved their discomfort by ridiculing the militancy of decreed virtue.

To the population at large it appeared as the harbinger of police rule.* The plain-clothes squad roved the streets day and night. Unaccompanied women risked being taken to the stationhouse, and after exposure to sundry indignities, shipped to a town in eastern Hungary. Adulterous wives or women denounced for adultery by some neighbor were jailed irrespective of the husband's wishes. "A number of vituperative anti-government pamphlets are in circulation; they deal mainly with the commission set up to watch over the chastity of the public."[31]

But neither fear nor anger appears to have stifled the Viennese *joie de vivre*. The favored stage fare of the populace was still the kind of *commedia dell'arte* whose ribald pantomime had made Lady Mary's hair stand on end and whose topical jokes no supervision could suppress. In a spacious arena situated two miles from the Hofburg, bear baitings attracted large crowds. Fireworks drew hosts of onlookers. And there never was a dearth of incidental spectacles—religious processions, the entries of foreign ambassadors, the passing through of army formations from Hungary, Croatia, or Slavonia, the funeral of some field marshal or grandee with its dark pomp and mournful music, or the arrival of some exotic beast for the menagerie of the court. The very narrowness of the streets afforded diversion. Points of precedence created traffic snarls, which erupted in profane altercations between coachmen or fisticuffs between the running footmen who, wielding a staff, pushed ahead of the carriage, singing out the name of their noble master. There was always some commotion in the wine shops and coffeehouses. The *Lotto di Genoa* (a kind of numbers game farmed out by the treasury to a succession of operators from the petty nobility), offering a chance to the smallest bettor, was a font of continuous excitement. Except for clandestinely produced handbills, the *Wienerisches Diarium*, appearing twice a week under censorship, still constituted the only printed source of information. Rumors sprang up by the hour, were embroidered, and broadcast with gusto—manna to people whose pleasure in talking and hearing others talk was only heightened by the climate of scandal the vice ordinances created.

They did not fail to misfire. Casanova, who stayed for some months in Vienna in 1747, was not served well by his memory when he contended that the pleasures of Venus were hard to come by. The number

---

* In fact, veterans of the "chastity commission" were to form the nucleus of the corps of informers of the secret police established in the 1760's.

of prostitutes grew by leaps and bounds. Unlicensed entrepreneurs arranged dances in remote localities. Secret nudists' associations met in the cellars of suburban vintners—and, as came to light in some raids, not all the participants were common people.

In 1748 an "English riding master by name of Hyam,"[32] who had won the favors of a string of titled women, was deported from Vienna. Indeed, Maria Theresa's enthusiasm for the imagined purity of an earlier day only served to encourage infringements on its hallowed structure of caste. She did not discern the connection between puritanical legislation and deteriorating mores and was blissfully ignorant of the raillery whose butt the former was among sophisticated people. Not by any stretch of her imagination could she have imagined the scurrilous revenge the lowly born were to take on her good name.

Peccadilloes on the part of Francis had been whispered and chuckled about for some time, along with his alleged ruses to evade the watchfulness of his spouse. Now people wondered, or pretended to wonder, whether she did not repay the straying husband in kind. It was fun to imagine her committing the very sin for which she hounded down her subjects. Strongman stunts were known to amuse her. On the river wharf of Prague she had challenged a Herculean stevedore to lift Prince Lobkowitz, and been seized by a fit of laughter when the fellow carried the obese field marshal up and down the pier. Now smutty tales about such Samsons performing feats of virility in her bedroom were made up by wags and passed on with relish. Other, more refined stories solicited actual credence. Some of them were based on the memory, still green, of Maria Theresa's *Mehlgrube* dances. Some others, more maliciously still, capitalized on the impetuosity with which she was reported to interrupt an after-dinner card game to beckon a Tarouca or a Grassalkovich into her study. All of that gossip was a tissue of nonsense. Not even Frederick at his most sardonic ever so much as hinted at any illicit romance.

Early in 1748 the lord marshal noted that the special vice squad was "being abolished *via facti* because the *commissaires* had gone too far."[33] More likely, popular reaction to their activities had revealed a disgruntlement that went far deeper than people's vexation at police surveillance of lovemaking and frolics. It also went far higher.

Ill-humored and morose, the empress often seemed to welcome opportunities of giving rein to her *fumo*. And who was there to suggest that she control her temper? Surely Francis, himself its victim at times, was not the man to do so. And Bartenstein, growing more and more irritable himself as he was aging, now tended to break into tears in their talks, or even to "raise his voice to such a pitch, one could hear it in the emperor's apartment."[34]

At length—late enough—Tarouca spoke up. The redundance of his long letter did not detract from its trenchancy. What emboldened him to go as far as he did was not only the assurance given him "even back in Pressburg" that his mistress would not "bridle at a bit of chiding in my honest representation." It also was her having asked him to explain the "cooling-off of feelings" she had noticed among those who served her, as well as among her "good subjects."

"Every human being has some imperfection," Tarouca wrote, "some weakness, some streak of smallness. If he does not tolerate these in others, how can he flatter himself that others will make allowance for them in him? Love and trust will cool off. . . . There is something called reciprocity. . . . I cannot deny that certain complaints have reached me, some resentment of Your Majesty's lack of confidence in men who have served you for a certain time. It may stem from weariness on your part, or from an inability to compromise with their shortcomings. They may still do justice to the essential goodness of Your Majesty's character. But your treatment of them affects the feelings of their families, their friends, their servants. . . . Man automatically tends to have regard for those who have regard for him. Conversely, he is wary of those who seem to mistrust him. True, respect veils the ensuing resentment. One lowers one's eyes before the sovereign and holds one's tongue. . . ." But must Her Majesty "call an overcautious or overly suspicious, sensitive minister 'just a fool' or some such name?"* Would she not do well to "at least show the wish to restrain yourself?"[35]

After returning again and again to the "necessary reciprocity," Tarouca assured his mistress that he for one had never discovered in Her Majesty anything even coming close to malevolence. "I am not, however, equally certain of how others feel." And what remedy did "the little pedagogue" suggest? "Unlike simulation . . . dissimulation is not a vice. Rather, if guided properly by prudence and patience, it is a virtue. But it asks for restraint and [I know that] Your Majesty hate it."[36] In fact, Maria Theresa had never given a thought to the royal art of *disimular* and the advantages it might bring her. It does not appear that Tarouca hoped that she ever would.

Yet he took even a step beyond recommending self-discipline. "When Your Majesty, as gloriously as painfully commenced a reign whose duration your very subjects doubted, some men rose to the height of noble-minded endeavors while some others showed a kind of circumspection that surely originated in feelings less than lukewarm. . . . The former (to use a phrase Spaniards employ) acted like faithful dogs that do

* In August 1747 Podewils reported "on the strength of a good source" that the empress in a conference had called Ulfeld "a jackass who'll most probably remain one." (83)

not hesitate to leave the building to follow the person; the latter behaved like cats that remain in the building to live in comfort under its new owner. . . . One can appreciate the deep resentment of men who remained true to you, as they find themselves pushed aside for the sake of men who had the fidelity of cats."[37]

We may assume safely that this allusion was not at all to Maria Theresa's liking. Did not Tarouca see that a ruler must not be guided by ordinary gratitude alone? Unfamiliar with the subtleties of the history of her house, this foreigner obviously knew little of the claim on un-ending gratitude with which her predecessors' supporters had managed to shackle the government. The strictures passed on her lack of affability did not touch her closely. The accusation of ingratitude did. She was ready to bear it wherever it came from. "Whosoever knows that the Almighty in His grace endowed me with a nature not entirely evil," she was to say some years later, "can imagine with ease how deeply the decline of my subjects' affection grieved me. . . . But their fierce criticism, known to me only too well, failed to confuse me, or deflect me from what I had embarked on."[38]

XI

A Royal Revolutionary

Picking at random some of Maria Theresa's financial instruction of the mid-forties, one is in for pathetic reading. "The banker Ochs must be rendered a statement, and paid fl. 150,000 by Wednesday in order to prevent a further deterioration of our credit. . . . A certain Burckhard, lessee of the mines in Anterior Austria, has offered to advance money again; I must be informed, and will decide whether he ought to be given a new lease, and his terms accepted. The Phillippsburg bridge must be sold. . . . The fl. 675,000 remittance from Styria, Starhemberg will make available at once; but he must at the same time be given the Styrian bonds to lay hands on fl. 42,000 for horses in Italy. . . . Ask Prandau if he can swear that fl. 200,000 were on hand at the tally. . . . First of all, fl. 160,000 must be disbursed to the infantry regiments as an installment. . . . Fl. 96,000, from the Bohemian contribution can be fetched from Koch; they are for the hussars.[1] . . . Another meeting should be held soon, with Salburg and Bartenstein present, and if necessary, Kinsky, too, in order to find out what funds are still available.[2] . . . As soon as payments from the levy come in, I must receive a specified daily report on who paid and how much. Nothing whatever of these moneys must be used even for the most urgent military purposes without my or the emperor's signature.[3] . . . As I am close to confinement, I [instruct you] not to publicize the resolution on the copper mines before I return the memoranda.[4] . . . It is illegal to discharge [tax obligations] through delivery of cloth or wheat, the latter being of inferior quality, in the first place, and charged to me at twice the current price. . . . I know how difficult it is to find any money, but all the greater will be the merit of those who do.[5] . . . How about the beer and wine excises?[6] . . . Tonight, at seven at the latest, I must be informed how much can be paid to the [Lower Austrian] Estates in interest on their fl. 800,000 advance.[7] . . . No supply officer, supervisor, baker, or whatever name such men have, will be sent to Italy, Belgium, or the Empire. . . . They are to be dismissed, as I cannot afford them.[8] . . . I want to know where those fl. 900,000 can be found in Koch's statement, and whether they arrived, to begin with. Dates!"[9]

In 1745 it proved impossible to put up collateral for loans that were being negotiated; "I would not dream of mortgaging the [lands'] contributions,"[10] the empress wrote after such a transaction had been recommended to her by a self-styled financial wizard new in her service. "If only some order could be brought into the interest payments. . . ." Bartenstein wrote. "I could well restore our credit, if it were not for the various chicaneries, and the discrimination employed toward wealthy creditors out of envy and spite. . . ."[11] "Some of the principal ought to be repaid from time to time, besides interest,"[12] Maria Theresa suggested wistfully. When Ulfeld announced to her in 1746 that Bartenstein would make a survey of all funds to be counted on before drawing up the budget, she said to the chancellor: "He *is* the soul of my service, is he not?"[13] He was—and she knew it—the soul of all makeshift solutions. For by then their sworn enemy, Count Frederic William Haugwitz, had begun to prove his mettle.

His father, a Lutheran, had been a general in the Saxon service. He himself turned Catholic as a young man and secured a position in the monarchical administration of Silesia.* Instead of "merely signing the notes prepared by a secretary,"[14] as was the wont of titled officeholders in such jobs, Haugwitz attended to the details of his work himself. His diligence did not go unnoticed. In 1739 the treasury in Vienna, challenged by the comparative affluence of Silesia, started contemplating a reform of the contribution of her estates. Haugwitz was entrusted with preparatory work. The Prussian invasion put an end to it. He went to Vienna, a penniless refugee, and was kept out of misery only through a loan granted him by a friend. He had not many of them. He was not, at first sight, an engaging person. Ugly to the point of grotesqueness, he also discomfited his interlocutors through a facial tic. His manner, while polite, was deficient in refinement. "He looks more like a fool than a great man,"[15] a foreign official observed after meeting Haugwitz at the height of his power.

It would seem that his interest in financial matters brought him into Francis' presence some time before the Peace of Breslau. "God's

* As in most other lands, this administration, separated from the estates' magistracy, collected excise taxes and certain tolls and supervised the mines and royal domains.

Providence made Count Haugwitz known to me after he left Silesia out of loyalty and a desire to serve," Maria Theresa wrote in 1751. "It was His Majesty the emperor, and then Count Tarouca, who brought him to my notice. . . . In order to break through, I needed precisely such a man— honest, free from self-interest and bias, without personal aspirations, and belonging to no clique."[16]

In September, 1742, Haugwitz was sent as governor into the queen's little Silesia. He set out to introduce some startling innovations. More surprisingly still, he did not restrict himself to the affairs of the province. In a memorial submitted to Maria Theresa he offered to "wager my head"[17] that King Frederick, not satisfied with having annexed most of Silesia, would try to conquer Bohemia as well if given three or four years of peace. As the prophecy came true within two, Haugwitz' subsequent memoranda found Maria Theresa an increasingly attentive reader.

He proceeded to review the whole melancholy story of the recent past. Why had Silesia been lost overnight, as it were, to begin with? Because her garrisons had been insufficient, her fortresses crumbling, and above all, the bulk of the army stationed in the farthermost counties of Hungary. And why had it been? Why had no adequate numbers of troops been kept in Bohemia and Moravia? Why indeed were none in those lands now? Because the estates dreaded the burden! He realized, Haugwitz went on, that large sums of cash had to be on hand to keep a steady army of the size he envisaged. They would not be available so long as the high nobility remained exempt from the land tax. Neither could Her Majesty sustain such a military establishment so long as she had to haggle, from year to year, with the lands over their contributions.

Some months later Haugwitz asked for permission to practice in his little province what he was preaching. He was told to go ahead. By February, 1744, he had reduced the local estates, a dispirited body, to virtual powerlessness in fiscal affairs. The significance of that change did not escape a Kinsky or a Harrach. They did not at all like the idea that the Silesian system might become a model in other lands. It had indeed caught Maria Theresa's imagination, opening to her the vista of a financial basis for the army she needed. "As I saw that I had to make peace at Dresden, I changed my whole way of thinking. I directed my undivided attention to domestic affairs, to take the measures necessary to preserve and protect, as best I could, my Hereditary Lands against those two powerful enemies, the Prussians and Turks. . . ."[18]

Unlike most reformers, who start out with a grand design, Maria Theresa opened her reforms by tackling a limited project of immediate concern. In December, 1746, Carinthia and Carniola (two lands of Interior Austria) found themselves once again in a financial crisis. She dispatched Haugwitz as *commissarius regis* into the mismanaged duchies.

His powers, termed "investigative" by the hesitant chancellery, were a matter of interpretation, and the legality of his mission was debatable. Confronting the estates with the imminent danger of their bankruptcy, he prevailed on them to sign a four-year agreement with the court, regulating their annual money grants to Vienna.

Here, then, was a model more drastic than anything Haugwitz had done in Silesia. And barely had the empress, on his recommendation, set up in Vienna a permanent commission for the financial administration of the duchies than a storm broke loose in the estates of some other lands. "I had always thought of my lands with an affection and *tendresse* greater even than the love I felt for my children. One can imagine easily how inconsolable I was when I met, if not with hatred, still with ingratitude on the part of the lands."[19] The Carinthian experiment ran into the opposition of her ministers and their clerks and even provoked criticism among common people, who knew little what the excitement was all about. The hue and cry only served to invigorate her sympathies for Haugwitz' ideas. She instructed him to prepare individual blueprints for ten-year agreements with all the Austro-Bohemian lands. He also was to submit a system that would secure the funds necessary to establish, equip, and maintain an army of one hundred and eight thousand men, not counting irregulars.

Belgium and Italy on the morrow of Dresden had not, in her own words of some years later, been "worth prolonging the war. . . . We had to search for a good way of extricating ourselves, whatever the price."[20] The price, however, was forbidding, and the man who was hiking it up appeared to Maria Theresa as devil incarnate.

Marquis d'Argenson was a person of great book learning, a friend of Voltaire's, and the darling of the salons of Paris. The younger brother of the minister of war, he had been put in charge of foreign affairs in 1744 despite his total lack of experience. He became enthralled by the utopia of a "European republic." As a first step toward this visionary goal D'Argenson devised the plan of a federation of all Italian states under the chairmanship of the King of Sardinia—and the patronage of his own king. In other words, he proposed to expel the house of Habsburg from the peninsula.

Ever since Francis' election Charles Emmanuel had been talking with France about accommodation. He distrusted D'Argenson but also had little confidence in the army of his ally, the empress. "The men are almost naked, without shirts, shoes or stockings. . . ." the British envoy at his court wrote at about the time of the Peace of Dresden. "The officers [are] several months behind in their pay, and Prince Liechtenstein, when he came to Turin, had neither funds nor credit [to supply] the current and ordinary subsistence to the common soldiers from the first day of the next month forward."[21]

But the King of Sardinia, flexible man that he was, bided his time—and was soon to protest undying loyalty to his alliance with Vienna. Liechtenstein had begun to use his personal funds to supply the army; and Browne was crossing the Alps in midwinter with ten thousand fresh troops.

Now Charles Emmanuel withdrew from his parleys with the French and mounted an attack on their army which, under Mallebois, stood at the Piedmontese border. Browne, on his part, went into action as soon as he had reached the plain. He swept Lombardy clean of all Spanish garrisons; Don Philip had to abandon Milan; and Parma surrendered on April 19. As De Gages led his army of twenty-six thousand toward Piacenza, Liechtenstein, now in command of fifty-six thousand, pressed on toward that fortified town. Its strong defenses ruled out frontal attack; and as Don Philip was known in Vienna to be urging Mallebois to relieve De Gages, Liechtenstein's postponing the assault from one week to the next was censured by the Hofkriegsrat and even the empress.

The French did arrive on June 14. But so, on their heels, did the Sardinians. And by the early afternoon of the following day victory had been gained, under the walls of Piacenza, over Mallebois and De Gages, Liechtenstein directing the combined operation.

Everybody in Vienna agreed that, next to Browne's tactical inventiveness, the cool-headed dispositions of Liechtenstein were to be given credit for the triumph. In truth, the common man had decided the day. Mallebois, who had watched Maria Theresa's spiritless soldiers in Bohemia four years before, could not believe his eyes as they withstood assault after assault under the ramparts of Piacenza. Even the cavalry—whose lack of discipline had been notorious in so many engagements—counterattacked in perfect order. Well taken care of and inspired by the competent leadership of the two generals, the rank and file had done more than their duty. "I hope," Maria Theresa said to Erizzo after dwelling with pride on their heroism, "that this event will turn my enemies' minds from the idea of chasing me out of Italy."[22] What, nevertheless, soured her joy was less the thought of the Gallispan garrison still within Piacenza than her fear that the Sardinians, having fought bravely in the victorious battle side by side with her soldiers, now would press doubly the demand for the pound of flesh adjudged them at Worms. Neither was this the only blow to her gratification on the morrow of Piacenza: Liechtenstein resigned on the grounds of poor health.*

---

* He led a very active life in the following twenty-five years, and particularly as the reorganizer of the Austrian gunnery, proved ingenuity and devotion to duty. Unless one assumes that Liechtenstein shied away from further financial sacrifices, his resignation in 1746 remains something of an enigma.

The empress might have replaced him with Browne. He was familiar with Italian affairs from earlier days. He had also been used in special missions to King Frederick and George II and thus was possessed of the kind of experience that should stand the commander in good stead in dealing with the court of Turin. Perhaps the zeal of Browne's admirers rubbed the Hofkriegsrat the wrong way. Perhaps his extraction seemed, to the court, not exalted enough for the top post. And at any rate Maria Theresa was hoping for Liechtenstein's return to the field after he had taken the waters. She let the command devolve on Browne's senior in rank, Marchese Botta d'Adorno.

He came from a line of Genoese patricians whose fortunes had been broken when his father, accused of some political crime, escaped vengeance by flying the republic. The son took service in the army of Charles VI but after some years decided on a diplomatic career. He acquired the reputation as a "tricky Italian"[23] at the Berlin legation, where he presumably also met the crown prince. He happened to be back in Vienna when the emperor died, and Bartenstein chose him for the thankless mission to Frederick. Subsequently he was posted as ambassador to St. Petersburg, where a child of eight weeks had been declared czar as Ivan VI. As Botta paraded his sympathies for the clan of the infant ruler—Brunswick relations of Maria Theresa's—the coup by which Elizabeth drove him from the throne after scarcely a year's time put the ambassador into an embarrassing position. He asked for recall and was appointed minister to the court of Berlin after the Peace of Breslau.

At about the same time, Elizabeth learned of a conspiracy that was supposed to have aimed at the return of the child czar's family to power, indeed at her own life. The alleged ringleader, put to the torture, named Botta as one of the originators of the plot; and the French ambassador, who had been supporting Elizabeth's aspirations all along, swore that the accusation was justified. The czarina was beside herself in her thirst for revenge. She demanded that Botta's sovereign punish him with the utmost rigor. Frederick, never loath to aggravate Vienna's troubles, declared him promptly *persona non grata*, and Maria Theresa had no choice but to withdraw him from Berlin. Then she asked Elizabeth to furnish proof of Botta's guilt. While the request was not complied with, new and increasingly peremptory notes arrived at Vienna. Maria Theresa's pointed answer to the effect that she was "not above the laws, but bound by them."[24] made no impression on the czarina. So Botta was put under arrest and a special tribunal set up to try him. When its members repeated the request for evidence, Elizabeth ordered her ambassador to leave Vienna. Nothing short of a miracle could prevent an open break between the two courts.

Something like a miracle did come to pass. A flippant *mot* of the

French ambassador came to Elizabeth's ears and destroyed his influence. When Maria Theresa offered to accredit a "grand ambassador" to Russia —her choice was Count Philip Rosenberg, a levelheaded Bohemian magnate—the czarina was game. Still, she let fly at him with vulgar vituperations as soon as he stepped into the audience chamber.[25] Her grand chancellor, Count Bestuzhev-Riumin, received Rosenberg in an entirely different manner.

Elizabeth was prematurely weakened in body by her dissolute life* and robbed of her peace of mind by fears of a palace coup that might do to her as she had done to her baby predecessor. Incapable of attending to regular work, she yet was wide awake to Russia's "natural" objectives—expansion at Sweden's, Poland's and Turkey's expense. Bestuzhev had early on shown her that the attainment of these goals was contingent on close cooperation with the Vienna court and its allies. Frederick's aggression had fortified him in his apprehensions of far-reaching plans on the part of the king. This fear provided Rosenberg with a lever for clearing up the Botta imbroglio.

The agreement worked out by the two men stated that the Queen of Hungary abhorred Botta's crime, would advise Europe's courts of her feelings, and keep him detained at the pleasure of the czarina. Rosenberg's report sent Maria Theresa into a tantrum. Was this the "modest stance of steadfastness"[26] she had instructed him to assume? Why had he neglected to put on record that Botta, while accused of a heinous misdeed, had not been proven guilty? She ordered Bartenstein to make this crystal clear in his notes to the foreign courts.

By then, however, Elizabeth's fury had run its course, and Rosenberg was involved deeply in discussing the Prussian menace with Bestuzhev. Some months later the "grand ambassador" touched on Botta's fate, and the czarina raised no objections to his being given his freedom.

He had protested his innocence throughout the bizarre affair. Whatever Maria Theresa's thoughts may have been about his apparent lack of discretion at St. Petersburg, she pitied him as the victim of political necessity. Released in March, 1745, Botta applied for reemployment in the army and was given a field marshal's baton despite his spotty experience in the field.

Commanding the right wing of Liechtenstein's army before Piacenza, he had been about to yield ground when Browne came to his rescue. Relations with the Sardinian generals deteriorated as soon as Botta had taken Liechtenstein's place. Highhandedly rejecting their plans, he boasted of the wonders his own strategy had wrought. In reality, the

---

* We can no more than guess at Maria Theresa's abhorrence of Elizabeth's messy private life and her uncouth court. Not even at the height of the Botta crisis did the pious empress ever refer to either.

Spaniards had no longer much stomach for fighting. Their king had died; Ferdinand VI, his successor, had no desire to exert himself for his half-brother, Don Philip; and the power of the Farnese woman had gone into eclipse. On August 11 Botta could enter Piacenza. In his account to the Hofkriegsrat he made much of the engagement that had preceded the seizure of the fortifications.

Meantime Browne was advancing toward Genoa. The republic, abandoned by the French and the Spaniards, capitulated to him on September 5. It availed its Senate nothing to declare that Genoa was not at war with the empress-queen and had sought the protection of the Bourbon powers only after the Treaty of Worms violated its sovereignty. Directly Botta arrived in his native city, he demanded that "the doge and six senators . . . repair to Vienna to implore forgiveness, and four senators . . . be delivered as hostages for the fulfillment of the articles"[27] of surrender. The empress spared them the indignity. She did not lower the huge contribution Botta imposed on the vanquished or object to his bringing pressure to bear on the bankers who held some of her jewels in pawn. Where money was concerned, she could not afford to be squeamish.

To the Pragmatic Army the summer of 1746 brought nothing but ill luck. Cumberland had returned to the Continent with the laurels of Culloden, and Prince Charles begrudged him his seniority, as well as his new fame. He himself tried to protect the key fortresses on the roads to the Dutch border. Bewildered by the maneuvers of De Saxe and his lieutenants, he also was hampered in his dispositions by an increasingly hostile population. Not until October 12 did De Saxe force a decision on the allies, giving them battle at Rocoux, northwest of Liège. Charles was cut off from the Dutch and British contingents and could not deploy his battalions. All he could do was to cover the retreat of the allies as night was falling. His skill in that operation came in for praise in the Hofburg, where Cumberland's leadership had been denounced throughout the months of the campaign. At Rocoux he had not been present.

Public opinion in England, still shocked by the Pretender's rebellion, did not take kindly at all to the reverses in Belgium. To reduce French pressure in that area the government revived a plan which, originating with Marlborough, had dragged Prince Eugene to defeat in 1706. They proposed that an Austrian army invade southern France, and lay siege to Toulon, supported by a British squadron.

Maria Theresa's consistent aim was to attack territory she could claim as her own. Not by the wildest stretch of the term could a Habsburg claim be advanced on Provence. To fritter away her strength on a campaign there, while Naples, all but denuded of troops, seemed to be easy prey, was to her mind the height of folly. Never mind the king of Sardinia, who would not hear of an Austrian march on Naples! "You had better know," she wrote to Wasner, "that I have no intention to let my hands be tied, even if I should announce that I will desist from taking Naples. . . ."[28] To be sure, her Neapolitan dreams were no longer shared by any man in her council. Bartenstein warned her of the "likely imminence of . . . the greatest of evils, a hasty French accommodation of the Maritime Powers on the basis of D'Argenson's scheme."[29] In an ill-humored directive the empress ordered Botta to drop preparations for the expedition to Naples, for, in order to "prevent the Maritime Powers from deserting me, and salvage *summa rerum*,"[30] Browne would have to cooperate with the British in Provence.

He crossed into France late in November with a combined Austro-Sardinian force of fifty battalions. He began to maneuver successfully, found the naval ally cooperative, the war-weary French population less antagonistic than expected, and Mallebois an adversary of scant determination. At the time Belle-Isle arrived to take up command, Browne stood before Antibes, which would have to be reduced before pushing the advance further. Short of artillery even after the British landed a number of guns, he had asked Botta to send him some pieces from occupied Genoa. But there was a man there who was "jealous of Browne's merits . . . [and] he leaves no art untried to dog and disappoint him in every thing."[31] Even as the British minister to the Sardinian court wrote thus from Nice, disaster had struck in Genoa.

Botta had established a harsh regime in the prostrate city. His every decree breathed the pleasure he took in humbling the community that had driven out his father. He treated its patricians with cutting haughtiness, its lower classes with petty chicanery. As payments on the contributions began lagging, he seized the funds of the bank that held the savings of middling people. This spirit transferred itself to his subordinates and even the ranks, and excesses on their part went unpunished. At the same time, he was careless of security. No guards had been posted at the arsenal. Contemptuous of the Genoese army, Botta had neither disbanded it nor stripped it of its weapons. Nor did he give much thought to the able-bodied men who, having slipped from the town ahead of the capitulation, were all over the countryside.

Ironically, it was his belated compliance with Browne's requests for guns that led to Botta's undoing. Some soldiers dragging a heavy mortar from the arsenal to the harbor got stuck in one of the narrow streets, and their demand for help elicited only jeers from the lookers-on. One of them started to scuffle with the cocky Austrian sergeant, and in no time the growing mob was pelting the soldiers with paving stones, and forced them to abandon the piece. An attempt to retrieve it at night ran into even greater violence, and some of the soldiers were knocked down and wounded. The spreading disorders unnerved Botta. Taking the advice of an officious Jesuit priest, he appealed to the Senate, and a five-day truce was arranged.

Probably the padre was double-dealing. At the very moment the truce expired, all the church bells started ringing, and the population, plebeian mobs and proud nobles alike, descended on the occupiers. Botta's men, outnumbered everywhere, their officers thrown into confusion by changing orders, beat a hasty retreat from the city—only to be set upon beyond its walls by armed bands which French officers in disguise had been organizing for weeks. The Austrians were chased from the republic's territory with the loss of all artillery and baggage. Twenty-five hundred men were in the hands of the Genoese. As Browne wrote to Ulfeld some days after, "nearly everybody foresaw the catastrophe, save the man who should have foreseen it."[32]

Despite the towering rage of the empress as word of the uprising reached her, she did not turn with violence against Botta, who could continue for five weeks to sow discord in the command of the peninsular army. He was not court-martialed upon his return to Vienna or even banished from court. The wrong she had done him in the Russian affair —or had she?—still weighed on her conscience.*

The wrong done the Genoese at Worms did not. According to Erizzo's successor, Antonio Diedo, "even the most sober men think it necessary to avenge the foul deed with fire and sword"[33]—or, as Robinson phrased it dramatically, "punish . . . the perfidy, perjury, and rebellion of the natives more atrocious than even the massacre of the Sicilian Vespers."[34] The sensation that the revolt caused throughout Europe, as well as wild rumors current in Vienna about mob rule in Genoa, fired the empress' desire for retribution. However, when Browne inquired whether he should tempt Antibes's garrison out "by very easy terms, and then make them prisoners of war in reprisals for the sufferings of the Austrian prisoners in Genoa . . . Maria Theresa absolutely forbade this monstrous project."†[35] Shortly after New Year's, Browne began evacuating Provence.

* An illness, which allowed Botta to live in virtual retirement, vanished overnight when the empress sent him to Brussels, after peace was restored in 1748, as minister plenipotentiary and grand master to Prince Charles, who "did not wish to deal all by himself with the discontent" in that province. (Aufzeichnungen des Grafen William Bentinck, 79.) Botta's activities in Belgium aroused the displeasure of the British and Dutch governments. When Count Bentinck finally complained about him in 1750, Maria Theresa said: "He is an Italian, and Italians always seek crooked ways." (Ibid.) In 1753 he was transferred to the Tuscan administration—and upon the emperor's death, caused trouble, as indeed much heartache, to Maria Theresa.

† Prisoners of war were, as a rule, exchanged or ransomed in the eighteenth century. This is why the fate of men in captivity, or trapped in a fortress, exercised the imagination of people.

It was in these weeks that Podewils composed his character sketch of Maria Theresa. "She has no love for Your Majesty," he concluded, "but she respects you. She will never be capable of forgetting the loss of Silesia, which, as I learned from a good source pains her all the more for the loss of renown suffered by her troops at the same time. She also looks upon Your Majesty as an obstacle to the growth of her power and prestige in the Empire. As did her forebears, she wishes to aggrandize both."[36]

Her personal success on the journey to Frankfurt had done nothing to further Habsburg business. Requests on the part of Francis for an "Army of the Empire" had been smothered by French protests in Ratisbon. Worse, the Reich's very structure seemed to be under discussion in France. D'Argenson had come forward with a double-pronged scheme: the Empire's Catholic princes should form a federation under French protection, and their Protestant peers band together under the leadership of Prussia. Frederick's separate peace with Maria Theresa had not destroyed D'Argenson's reliance on him as a makeweight to Habsburg power.

The consequences of Prussia's ascendancy were noticeable also in England. Frederick's spectacular victories had made him a popular figure, and the Jacobite troubles had turned the nation resentful of the alliance with the Catholic princess in Vienna. Even before the miscarried campaigns strengthened the hand of her adversaries in London, the empress, writing to Wasner, wondered whether the British did "not intend to weaken my Arch House more and more, and . . . use in its stead, the King of Prussia as a counterweight to the House of Bourbon . . ."[37]

As it was, Britain was ready for a breathing spell in the maritime struggle. From the early summer of 1746 on, Lord Sandwich had been discussing, in the Dutch town of Breda, a general settlement with a succession of emissaries from the court of Versailles. George II had assured Maria Theresa that her plenipotentiary would be welcome. Yet Count Ferdinand Harrach (Frederic's younger brother), whom she dispatched, was denied admission upon Holland's protest.

The Hague was a hive of so-to-speak clandestine bilateral discussions between foreign envoys sharing the fate of Harrach. The Spaniard Melchior Macañaz was at the center of these intrigues, and, as Harrach discovered, was bandying about the great secret of his own court—its negotiations, some months before, with a Spanish emissary over the heads of its allies. Once Macañaz had elbowed his way into the conference rooms at Breda, Harrach thought it wise to sound the aged man. The Spaniard saw no obstacles to peace, if only the emperor renounced the grandmastership of the Golden Fleece and his consort agreed to having her Italian possessions divided between Don Philip and Charles

Emmanuel. Maria Theresa, who declared Macañaz to be "out of his wits,"[38] was soon to learn that Sandwich, after talking him out of his demand for Gibraltar, did not at all think so. Louis XV, by dismissing D'Argenson—and thus burying his Italian grand design—had drawn the court of Madrid closer again to his own; and pacifying Spain was uppermost on Sandwich's agenda.

He had begun drafting an agreement with Macañaz when the empress advanced a scheme of her own: Genoese-owned Corsica should go to Don Philip, in lieu of Parma, and the Riviera di Ponente, Genoa's also, buy off the Lombard claims of Sardinia. These proposals were taken no note of at Breda. "Mark my words," she wrote to her ambassador at The Hague, "just as the protest of that famed republic played havoc with the vaunted steadfastness of the English in the matter of Harrach's admission, so it will be in the matter of the peace terms. One would have to be very stupid or entirely blind to misjudge the trend."[39] The war must go on. Sixty thousand troops would be ready in Belgium by spring, and Browne, now in command on the peninsula, should count on a fresh army seventy thousand men strong.

Before Genoa, Count Schulenburg was in charge of operations. He depended for supplies on the Lombard administration; and its head, Count Pallavicini—no Botta, he—disliked the thought of seeing his native Genoa chastised.* While the French, barely molested by the British navy, landed troops and food in the city, misery stalked Schulenburg's camp. On April 15 he notified the Senate that the empress would hate to doom one of Europe's most flourishing towns to destruction; solely surrender could save it from bombardment. "The right of self-defense has been given by Nature to all men alike,"[40] the Senate replied; and this was the right they availed themselves of; no one on earth could possibly have a higher opinion than they had of Her Majesty's sense of justice, and no one therefore would ever convince them that either their earlier or their present actions excited her wrath.

The eyes of the whole of Europe were fastened on the defiant republic, whose citizenry had done the prestige of the empress greater harm than even De Saxe. Schulenburg, deficient in artillery—and, perhaps, also mindful of public opinion everywhere—did not bombard the city. He exasperated the Hofkriegsrat by the slowness of his preparations for its capture by maneuver. Yet his patience seemed to bear fruit. He was on the verge of taking the key outwork of the town when Belle-Isle stayed his hand.

With Macañaz practically disavowed by his own government and

---

* Originally Genoa's ambassador to Charles VI, Pallavicini had negotiated the Finale transaction. Having entered the Habsburg service, he became very popular both at court and among his subordinates.

De Saxe's supporters gaining the upper hand at Versailles, all of Sand-wich's efforts at Breda had proved vain. A sudden Franco-Spanish thrust at the Piedmontese border opened a new campaign. Belle-Isle's advance and the failure of the British frigates to stop it threw Schulenburg into panic even before the Sardinian king recalled his battalions from the enterprise before Genoa. His heart had not been in it; Finale was in his hands; he had received no share in the Genoese booty; and unlike Maria Theresa, he did not worry about bargaining counters at the conference table. Browne declared that the "seizure of Genoa can no longer be thought of."[41]

By the time Schulenburg started withdrawing troops and cannon, the Pragmatic Army was bracing itself against De Saxe's great push. None of the allies had lived up to his pledge. For one moment, valor, where it was expected least, had promised to make up for inferior numbers. The French march toward Holland had united her factions, and early in May the seven provinces each elected Prince William of Orange stadtholder and generalissimo. But his ancestors' spirit was not alive in the prince; and Holland's domestic dissensions, which had not been done away with by the show of unanimity, combined with the low morale of the Dutch army to turn it into a liability for the allied leadership. Cumberland ignored the advice of his more competent lieu-tenants. Neither got along well with Batthyány, who had taken the place of Prince Charles.

The battle fought at Laufeldt on July 2 was a costly victory for De Saxe. But for Batthyány's strong and sudden intervention, French casualties would have been lighter by far, and the allied retreat might well have turned into a rout. The outcome was not considered a crush-ing defeat at Vienna. Maria Theresa nevertheless authorized Batthyány "by these lines, done in my own hand, to negotiate and sign peace with the Most Christian King and his allies. Formal powers will reach you as soon as possible, but I do not wish to retard in any way so beneficial a work, and am well content to have it taken up with Count de Saxe, whom I esteem greatly. . . ."[42] It was high time to ward off further set-backs on the peninsula, as well as in the Low Countries.

Browne had concerted his plans for counterattack with Charles Emmanuel while Schulenburg's battalions (no longer under his com-mand) were still on the march to the Piedmontese mountains. But even before that countermovement could be executed, Belle-Isle's younger brother, Chevalier de Belle-Isle, broke loose with his shock troops to storm the Colle dell'Assietta. The Sardinians, entrenched on this forti-fied elevation, held off the onslaught until Austrian forces reached its heights to join the murderous fray. The chevalier himself perished by their bullets and bayonets.

"Ambition has always been the ruin of any scheme in which the Belle-Isle brothers have had a hand,"[43] De Saxe, getting the news, wrote to his royal half-brother in Dresden. To Maria Theresa the chevalier's death must have appeared as poetic justice. It was a Belle-Isle who had unleashed the French war and proposed to carve up her realm. Along with the captured enemy colors, a full account of the victory was brought to Schönbrunn on August 7. There were many stories of personal heroism to warm the heart of the empress. Khevenhüller echoed her sense of jubilation as he recorded: "The *affaire* of the Colle dell'Assietta has altered circumstances most fortunately *in respectu* Italy."[44] It had at any rate spared Lombardy a Gallispan invasion.

But it also had whetted the appetite of the Sardinian king for carry-ing the war into French territory: and the British once more wanted to try their luck in Provence. The empress, after talking about Naples again, bowed to Bartenstein's urgent advice and directed Browne to "exert the utmost industry to reduce Genoa soon . . . [and] desist from getting embroiled in any other *entreprise*, be it against Dauphiné or . . . Provence."[45] As Charles Emmanuel refused to cooperate and seemed to be convincing Browne of the merits of his own strategy, a letter from Maria Theresa put the field marshal in his place. "In order to make you pay heed to my instructions [she wrote] . . . I admonish you in full earnest to conform with them. You will execute them, as prevailing circumstances permit, and stop reflecting [on my instructions] with un-seemly criticism."[46] Even though Browne was not the first of her field commanders to be called back from the brink of insubordination, none had been rebuked with similar sharpness. In her core Maria Theresa had never been very fond of the self-willed Irishman. And, then, she penned that letter while another of Robinson's calls was imminent.

He came to Schönbrunn to harp, as he had throughout the recent months, on the fact (if such it was) that "both in Italy and in [Belgium] the Austrian army amounted to scarcely half the stipulated num-bers. . . ." The Maritime Powers "therefore proposed that in future only half of the subsidies should be paid at the commencement of the year, and the remaining half reserved until the Austrian contingents were ascertained to be complete and effective by the inspection of British officers." The empress "did not refrain from expressing her high indigna-tion at so degrading a proposal." She also "remonstrated against the unfairness of estimating the numbers in the middle of the campaign, when the army must have experienced a considerable diminution from action, sickness, and desertion. . . . Disgusted likewise with repeated de-tails of the annual subsidies, she indignantly asked, 'Has one farthing . . . ever been diverted? And have I not, in every campaign, exerted my whole force to the utmost?' "[47]

For all the valor proved on the Colle dell'Assietta, the morale of Browne's troops was deteriorating in step with the growth of their hardships out of battle. On a visit to headquarters, the supreme commissar for war, Count John Chotek, had found himself helpless to improve supply. A large group of Croats had deserted in a body, and only a regular battle fought with them had coerced them back to duty. Chotek's "deeply saddened report" did not fire the inventiveness of the conference. In its meeting of September 20 the empress told them that "speedy and extensive *media* must be found to tide over [the troops] in Italy with a prompt remittance of two million. Some of it may go to the Low Lands, though."[48] Four days before, the French had taken Bergen-up-Zoom, the great Dutch fortress on the Scheldt. The scandalous story of its loss by a garrison roused from sleep only as its bastions were being stormed was capped by reports on the massacre the enemy had engaged in. Hundreds of Austrian soldiers had been stabbed or trampled to death, alongside two thousand Dutch troops and many of the inhabitants of the town, by the pillaging Frenchmen.

Late in November "the ministers talked to the empress with great passion about the *misère* of her soldiers, but did not advise her on how to help" in Holland, in Browne's Lombard winter quarters, or the new camps in the Genoese countryside. She "had been in a rotten humor for some time," and "the one thing the ministers thought of was to extricate themselves without losing face." As the meeting dragged on, she ordered each of them to put his suggestions in writing within twenty-four hours, while she was jotting down her own "on a little quarto sheet" to be shown them only after they delivered their homework.[49] The resulting excitement abated only when the emperor intervened. As she tore up her notes, it was in a gesture of morose disgust rather than *fumo*. She had grown to be a most trying mistress indeed.

Batthyány's peace mission after Laufeldt had not even come to a start. De Saxe himself, on his king's orders, had arranged for a meeting of the new foreign minister, Puysieux, with Cumberland; but these talks too had broken down almost at once. Augustus of Saxony, who had married one of his daughters to the dauphin, impressed on the Vienna court that Louis XV was thirsting for peace. He was. On October 14 Admiral Hawke had captured six of the eight ships of a French convoy on its way to the West Indies. French ocean trade was crippled, and want, and even unrest, were growing in the kingdom from day to day. But De Saxe and his lieutenants had their hearts still set on another campaign and the conquest of Maastricht, which they swore would enhance the king's prospects at the settlement.

To meet the menace in Holland, the allies pledged one hundred fifty-six thousand troops, and hired thirty-six thousand from the czarina.

These strange auxiliaries had crossed Poland by mid-December; and the dread their approach gave rise to in the Empire—and Frederick's likely reaction to their march westward—was a matter of no mean apprehension in the Hofburg.

The peace conference which had adjourned at Breda in May, had reassembled in early autumn at Aix-la-Chapelle. Kaunitz, appointed the empress' plenipotentiary, was admitted forthwith. Certain members of the British government had grown alarmed by the rise of the national debt. The war must, it had to be, put an end to. Not even the most sanguine Englishman could hope for victory on the Continent; and nobody gave a fig for whatever the stubborn woman in Vienna hoped to gain by prolonging the fight.

As it was, Kaunitz' instructions were to make peace before the French would open the spring campaign. Peace at any price? Maria Theresa said so. When Bartenstein submitted to her a résumé of his talks with Augustus' emissary, she added to her *"Placet"*: "May the Almighty bring about the end soon. The situation will not be better in two months, and not even so good [as now]."[50] Yet for many weeks, indeed months, her ministers had to watch her raising issues that were out of tune with her desire for peace *"coûte que coûte,"* and way out of tune with the troops' plight in the field and the specter of bankruptcy at the treasury.

It was a weary Ulfeld who wrote to Kaunitz on April 9: "I trust this will be the last courier—that is, if one really has the intention to spare the lives of many good men who would be doomed to no purpose."[51] On this same day De Saxe, who had fooled the allied command for weeks, commenced the march toward Maastricht. Twelve days later he could bring his siege guns into position. Five thousand Austrians were in the fortress. "I would not like to be in the shoes of Puysieux," wrote Ulfeld, "and have all those men in Maastricht and Italy on my conscience, while having the means of making peace with a stroke of the pen."[52]

As Maria Theresa saw Robinson on April 30, she had just received word of the stroke of the pen that Puysieux's envoy had made at Aix-la-Chapelle. He had signed preliminaries with Sandwich.

She barely allowed Robinson to "execute his commission."

"You, sir," she exclaimed, "who had such a share in the sacrifice of Silesia; you who contributed more than any person in procuring the additional cessions made to the king of Sardinia—do you still think to persuade me? No! I am neither a child nor a fool. Your accounts about the Dutch are exaggerated. . . . If you [wish] to have an instant peace, make it. I can accede [or] can negotiate for myself. And why am I always to be excluded from transacting my own business? My enemies will give me better conditions than my friends. At least they will not refuse a peace, they want as much as I do, for any dispute, between me and the king of Sardinia, about a little territory more or less, or for the interpretation of [the] treaty [of Worms]. And who tells you Spain so much as desires Parma and Piacenza? She would rather have Savoy. Place me where I was in Italy before the war, and I will establish the Infant [Don Philip]. But your king of Sardinia must have all without one thought of care for me! The Treaty of Worms was not made for me, but for him singly! Good God, how have I been used by that court! [And then] there is your king of Prussia! Indeed, indeed, all these circumstances at once rip up too many old, and make new, wounds."

After Sir Thomas had borne her outburst, he gave an account of the utter helplessness of the Dutch. As he went on to "explain the Treaty of Worms," she listened "with sullen indignation." What else did he wish to lecture her on, she implied when he had finished; perchance the Genoese funds that the emperor had impounded in the Palatinate?

The ambassador was impervious to the irony of her broaching so trifling a matter. He carried a letter from Newcastle's hand and proceeded to read to her a passage that dealt with Don Philip.

Her resistance to yielding Parma and Piacenza to Louis XV's son-in-law had been eroded long before this hour. Occupied by Sardinian troops, the duchies were out of her grasp. But they were fiefs of the Empire; and Newcastle, ignoring that claim, declared that they would have to "revert to the present possessors, should Don Philip succeed to the kingdoms of Naples and Sicily in consequence of the accession of [King] Carlos to the crown of Spain on the death of the present ruler without issue male."

This intimation of another boon to be delivered to the rapacious king of Sardinia was more than Maria Theresa could bear with even the pretense of royal restraint. "What?" she cried out. "Revert to the *present* possessors? No! No! I will rather lose my head!" As Robinson described the scene in his dispatch, she "accompanied her words with a significant gesture."[53] For once he does not seem to have overdramatized his story.

She was thirty-one years of age, approaching middle age by her day's standards. She had stood up to the men about her. While she could not convince all of them of the merits of her decisions or compel their critics to carry them through with enthusiasm, none of her counselors would so much as dream of brazenly forcing her hand. In these very days she was lecturing the most truculent of Haugwitz' opponents on the supremacy of her will.

It had been disregarded before by her creditor-ally. Nor had the British, at Aix-la-Chapelle, for the first time acted behind her back; they certainly had at Hanover (and it was on them, rather than on lost battles, that Maria Theresa would blame the Peace of Dresden). But 1748 was not 1745; and she knew she was at the end of her tether, even though the Anglo-French preliminaries were not in theory binding for her. She had dragged out the Italian campaign to get a bargaining counter against the French; she had none against her allies. The feeling of being cornered fired her moral indignation. Sincere as it was, it scarcely would have reached the pitch it did, had she seen a way out of the vise the British appeared to have thrown round her neck.*

She never forgave Robinson for having delivered the news. Four months after the stormy audience he came to take his leave. Never, in Ulfeld's words, had "a foreign minister been bidden Godspeed with less grace. The empress really applied too strong a dose."†⁵⁴

Disputes over the definitive treaty continued in Aix-la-Chapelle. Points of disagreement between the allies outnumbered their controversies with the Bourbon powers. One of the empress' most dogged demands concerned the arrears of the British subsidy payments. The Barrier Tractate of 1716 was the subject of interminable inter-allied wrangles.

In this famous treaty, which was based on two previous agreements, the imperial court had granted the Dutch the right to secure their territory by manning a chain of fortresses on Belgian territory. These fortifications were kept in repair and their Dutch garrisons maintained out of the revenue of Belgium. The financial burden had rankled Charles VI to his dying day, as had the limitations set his sovereignty in these places. Moreover, the tractate closed the Scheldt to seagoing vessels and made any changes in Belgian import duties contingent on British and Dutch approval. Thus controlling Belgium's trade, it had been strangling its economy for well over a generation. Attempts to revise the Barrier Tractate had remained futile. Maria Theresa, more so than her father, had also been irritated by the Calvinist services of the Dutch troops in the Barrier towns. The provisional Franco-British agreement at Aix-la-Chapelle provided for Belgium's evacuation by the French. The question as to whether the Barrier fortifications were to be razed, returned to the Dutch, or handed over to the empress assumed an overweening importance.

---

* Five years later Sir Charles Hanbury Williams (see p. 228), after several talks with her, reported that "she was the only person left in Europe who was not of the opinion that the signing of those preliminaries had been the salvation of the house of Austria." (Arneth, *Maria Theresa* IV, 540.)

† He replaced Sandwich at Aix-la-Chapelle. In 1761, he was elevated to the peerage, as Baron Grantham. "When he played the orator, which was too often, even his friends could not keep their countenances." (*Directory of National Biography*, Vol. 49, 49.)

Suddenly, amid proliferating conflicts, Maria Theresa declared that she would not be a party to a general settlement. Ignoring what amounted to an ultimatum of the British government, she instructed Kaunitz to negotiate bilateral treaties only. She had taken alarm at the resolution of both her enemies and her allies to spell out in the treaty a European guarantee of Frederick's possession of Silesia. While friends and foes alike accused her of "cavil and delay,"[55] her "hope for having matters sped up" in Aix-la-Chapelle made life miserable for her ministers. "You would not believe me," Ulfeld wrote to Kaunitz, "if I gave you a description of what we have to suffer through her impatience to see the troops return, so she can put her economic program into practice, and [introduce] the system of Haugwitz. . . ."[56]

This system was of revolutionary simplicity. It envisaged ten-year agreements with the individual Austro-Bohemian estates. The sum total of their money grants, to be paid in monthly installments, was budgeted at fourteen million florins per annum. (The average sum of the contributions heretofore had amounted to nine.) In return, the lands would be freed from the obligations to deliver recruits to the army and defray its upkeep on their territories. Blueprints for a uniform land-tax assessment completed the bold plan.

It awoke Maria Theresa to the magnitude of the crisis into which Haugwitz proposed to plunge her. But his was the first methodical project ever submitted of meeting the needs of her army. Again and again she had urged the conference to "suggest a system," and "not a single *idée* had come ·forth. I actually noticed a wish to contradict and procrastinate, rather ·than any intent to put the shoulder to the wheel. . . ."[57] She realized how "distasteful innovations as such were to the *publicum*," and even more so to "the men who were to pay higher taxes, and had to expect a curtailment, nay, the stamping-out, of all those malpractices, illegalities, and inequities so firmly entrenched, and engaged in for so long, both at court and in the lands . . . that none of my predecessors, wise rulers all, ever planned—or, speaking correctly, dared—to attack the deep-rooted evil."[58]

Before taking the great step, she had several talks with Harrach and Kinsky and had Haugwitz discuss his system with them. Noncommittal at first, the two ministers next expressed doubts about its legality. This challenge turned her—or Haugwitz—inventive. She stated that the famous rights of the estates were based only on customs and traditions that had been "tolerated and confirmed" by a succession of sovereigns. Inasmuch as those royal acts invariably had referred to "well handed-down customs," surely "badly handed-down ones"[59] could not claim legal protection. She did not recoil from what her critics might call a semantic sleight of hand. Neither did she stop to consider that she was setting herself up as the sole judge of what was bad in the "form of government that," to quote Khevenhüller, "has been customary for many *saecula,* indeed from the very beginning of the Arch House."[60]

As she herself was to reminisce, "a great clamor went up, particularly . . . in the estates, and among the nobility and their hangers-on. But the most vociferous protest was heard in the court itself, from men who either lived on my bounty, or had attained riches and prestige through the leniency and munificence of my forebears toward their own."[61] How "small was the number of men on whose lack of prejudice" she "could rely, and who at the same time knew enough about the lands' business to be of use in so delicate a matter." For she *was* beset by scruples— scruples about the lands' capacity, "which the loss of Silesia had so sadly reduced, to . . . sustain in peacetime an army almost double the size of that which the late emperor, of blessed memory, had deemed possible to keep after the first Turkish war."[62]

Nothing embittered her critics more than her turning for further advice to "quilldrivers . . . rather than men who were animated by noble sentiments, love of honor, and a concern for true *gloire.*"[63] In January, 1748, Harrach emerged as the spokesman of the opposition. A reform plan of his own, brought before the conference, proposed to secure the fourteen-million-florin contribution by turning all excise taxes over to the lands. This change, so far from diminishing the powers of the estates, would have enlarged them. Did Harrach not realize that the plan of the empress had outgrown its initial aim? Its pursuit had opened to her the vista of "God-pleasing equality"[64] in the distribution of the tax burden—as well as the vista of its exclusive control by the sovereign's government.

The thought of reorganizing the estates as such by altering their composition did not occur to Maria Theresa. Centralized government had been the lodestar of Haugwitz from the first. It appealed to her temper. Within a few years it would dawn on her that there were dangers inherent in the new order. "I would neither think it advisable myself nor advise my successors to tamper . . . with those of the estates' prerogatives that were honestly gained and are beneficial. . . . I cannot possibly repeat often enough that I would have gladly submitted my authority to theirs, if I had been convinced of the unequivocal nature of their privileges, or if their administration had been more in accord with equity than my own."[65]

The individual estates had no common representation. They could be dealt with one by one. The conference, banking on a storm of opposition in the estates themselves, proposed to have Haugwitz' system submitted to them. But when the empress asked first Harrach and then

Kinsky to do the job, neither was prepared to take it on. "Yesterday a certain bishop had an audience of the empress," Podewils reported in March, 1748, "and she opened the talk by asking impatiently whether he, too, wished to complain about Count Haugwitz. As the bishop said he did not, the expression of her face changed at once (so I have been told) and he was treated with signal kindness."[66] The great clans came to loathe Haugwitz. Unlike them, he owed nothing to the liberality of the crown or the patronage of well-placed cousins or in-laws. Some speculative ventures had made him a well-to-do man in a brief span of time, and these new-fangled ways of financial advancement scandalized high society. The restitution of some funds that Haugwitz had had to leave behind in Breslau in 1741 set nasty rumors afloat.

It had been decided that the estates of Moravia would be negotiated with first, and the task was entrusted to Haugwitz. His success, as swiftly achieved as it was complete, came as a shocking surprise to the landowning grandees, who had failed to realize that their own predominance in the estates had for a long time been weakening their vigor. "All the ministers condemn the project most fiercely,"[67] Diedo wrote after Haugwitz also gained the consent of the Bohemian estates to a ten-year agreement.

Harrach happened to hold *pro tem* the land marshal's office in Lower Austria.* The sense of independence of its estates dated back to the time of the great Bohemian rebellion, and some of that spirit had survived the Counter Reformation. Haranguing them, Haugwitz reviled "those men who put their notions into Her Majesty's head, and act as though there were no God, and justice had been banished from this earth."[68] The empress relieved him from his duties in Lower Austria and installed Haugwitz as *commissarius regis*. Undaunted, Harrach advanced new counterproposals to the hated system and informed Maria Theresa that their rejection would force him to resign. "I was less surprised by his communication than grieved at seeing Harrach willing to lose his own self [reads the draft of the letter she wrote to Ulfeld]. I give him ten more days to make up his mind as to whether he will remain his queen's loyal subject, or persist in his wrong-headedness. The only solution I can think of in the latter case is his departure for Spa, which would be consonant with an earlier thought of his, and seem a good pretext. Afterwards, I would carry out my intention of [returning Harrach to his former office in] Brussels. Thus one year would be gained, and his absence would protect me from the ugly thoughts I admit I could not suppress were he to remain here. I consider him honest enough to rid himself . . . of all resentments once he understands him-

* The incumbent, his brother Ferdinand, had succeeded Pallavicini in Milan.

self more fully. . . . To reject a plan outlined over my signature, this is really too much! I have been deeply hurt by his remark about posterity. Wherever my name will be found, it will reflect credit on his, and I never would have imagined that the Harrachs could forget that so soon. Whatever may happen, I shall stick to my decision. Whoever cannot obey may desist from doing so. But he never must come into my presence again. I felt like replying to Harrach directly. I thought better of it, and will not expose my signature to another humiliation. You are a great friend of his. Use this letter as you see fit. But he must be talked to with clarity. The matter must not suffer any delay. I know what I can and will do."[69] She may have mellowed the draft in her final note to Ulfeld, who, in turn, transmitting its gist to Harrach, may have watered it down. At all events, Harrach did not depart to take the waters at Spa and did not resign from the conference.

The campaign in Holland was over on May 10, with De Saxe granting the defenders of Maastricht the honors of war. An armistice had been signed the day before.* But this news reached the belligerents in Italy only in conflicting bits of information. As Robinson conjectured, the empress had still "meditated some brilliant enterprise in Italy, which she sanguinely hoped would be crowned with success."[70] But Browne's plan to gain control of the Genoese coast to the south of the city had come to nothing. Genoa itself, well provisioned under French command, had been sending out partisan bands to harass her troops. The last shot was fired on June 15. Never would Maria Theresa forget the resistance of the purse-proud republic. (Nor, for two centuries, would Italians.) When twenty years later her firstborn was traveling in those parts, she forbade him to set foot on Genoese soil.

On September 18 the empress was delivered of a girl that died after a few minutes. She was deeply alarmed by the thought of an infant snatched away unbaptized, until her ladies dissipated that fear through a lie. Khevenhüller, increasingly disturbed by the *ésprit de nouveauté* in the court, as well as in the administration, blamed the death of the newborn on Her Majesty's indifference toward imperial lying-in protocol.

Up to the day she went into confinement she had dictated instructions for Kaunitz in Aix-la-Chapelle. On September 21 she resumed the correspondence. Her protest against the Sardinian acquisitions in Lombardy had not been put on the agenda? It must be registered in the treaty nevertheless! A Prussian guarantee of the Pragmatic Sanction was forthcoming? Why, "judging by the king's latest letter to Podewils"—

* Its signatories had agreed earlier on keeping the Russian corps away from all operations. They were interned on the island of Walcheren.

had it been intercepted?—she knew that he considered himself betrayed by France on that score, and "while having no choice but to give his pledge now . . . will care little about living up to it later."[71] Time and again she exhorted Kaunitz to gain revisions of the Barrier Tractate; and when he had failed, she ordered him to sign the peace documents only some days after the other signatories had done so "in order to drive it home to the whole world that I am only under duress joining in this bad and faulty work, which has turned out to be as monstrous as were the preliminaries, and in some respects even worse."[72] Count Philip Rosenberg, returning to Vienna from a mission to Lisbon, was struck when he saw her. "I found Her Majesty changed greatly indeed," he said to Ulfeld. "It seems to me as though everything disgusted her, and the crown sat heavy on her head."[73]

The instruments of peace were exchanged in Aix-la-Chapelle in October and November. They included a European guarantee of Prussian Silesia, confirmed the Austrian cessions to Sardinia, and turned over the Parmese duchies to Don Philip. The treaty brought the north Italian aspirations of the French to nothing and eliminated them from Belgium. It dented Maria Theresa's patrimony. But it also gave her a general guarantee of the Pragmatic Sanction.

The breakup of the Habsburg realm, which nine men out of ten everywhere had thought inevitable on her father's death, had not come to pass. She had defied all portents and mocked countless disasters. But neither had the Fates served her altogether badly. She did not feel beholden to them. When the new British ambassador, Robert Keith—a "soft-spoken and sensible man,"[74] in Kaunitz' opinion—asked for permission to offer congratulations on the return of peace, Ulfeld was directed to "observe that compliments of condolence were more proper than compliments of congratulation, and [he] insinuated that the British minister would oblige his mistress by sparing a conversation which would be highly disagreeable to her and no less unpleasing to him."[75]

By the time the treaties were ratified, the Austro-Bohemian estates had all of them signed agreements in accord with Haugwitz' system.* The size of the pledged annual money grants had grown in the course of the negotiations; and the estates had also acquiesced in having part of their contributions applied toward the upkeep of the court and the civil service. To expedite the proceedings, *commissarii* had been dispatched into some of the lands. In Carinthia, which had reneged on its earlier understanding with Vienna, the empress restored its validity *"jure regium."* She had covered the road from reformatory planning to authoritarian practice within three years.

* The Tyrol, whose free peasantry had its representatives in the estates, agreed only to a one-year, if renewable, obligation.

The new system of tax assessment was introduced in May, 1749. It was still a far cry from "God-pleasing equality." But to Maria Theresa's mind that notion lifted the reform of taxation above its actual purpose. Haugwitz had convinced her that the fourteen-million-florin revenue could never be collected unless the nobility and high clergy paid taxes. This is why their age-old privileges were breached. As the innovation— furthered, however feebly, social justice, she felt confident that the Almighty guided her work.

The reform did not greatly lighten the burden of the peasant. Defeated in their opposition, the landowners took recourse to chicaneries. Particularly in Bohemia they managed to extract more labor services than before from their "hereditary subjects," and protection, practically unobtainable from the estates, was slow in coming from the central government. Given the attitude toward reform on the part of the lower clergy and the religious,* the peasant had but the most nebulous notions about the faraway monarch and her striving for "God-pleasing equality." Centuries of exploitation had made him suspicious of the goodwill of any authority.

In Vienna the lower classes were openly hostile to the new legislation. For well over a hundred years a large part of them had profited from the corruption that pervaded the world of "middling and small people,"[76] as well as that of the great. The "chastity commission" was giving them a taste of the lengths to which authority might go. They considered the empress, at best, misguided. In July, 1748, disorders broke out. A mob pelted Haugwitz' mansion with offal and stones. "Four cuirassiers have been assigned to him. . . . He nevertheless is in danger of becoming a victim of the general dissatisfaction. Most of the great are thoroughly embittered, make common cause with one another, and surreptitiously incite the rabble against him."[77]

A new wave of violent protest swept Vienna in May, 1749. On the seventeenth, the *Diarium* published two decrees: a central government was established for the Hereditary Lands (*Directorium in publicis et cameralibus*) and a newly created Supreme Office of Justice was to effect a "complete separation of the judiciary from the *publicis* and *cameralibus*."[78] The estates were to be deprived of their judiciary functions and the higher courts removed from the province of the chancellery.†

* Cf. p. 232.
† The lower jurisdiction remained in the hands of manor lord or town. In Bohemia the former retained capital jurisdiction well into the 1750's.
The rudimentary separation of powers, as decreed in 1749, was the result of practical considerations rather than any influence of Montesquieu's *L'Ésprit des lois*, published the year before in Geneva, on government thought. The censors in Vienna (see p. 236) got the book banned in 1750. There is nothing to show that Maria Theresa gave it even a cursory reading. Except for devotional literature and Italian poetry, she never, for all we know, read a book.

The strictures passed on the empress grew malicious when Frederic Harrach died on June 4 in his fifty-third year. "The public, always eager to attribute premature death to a special cause," Diedo reported, "asserts that the liquidation of the Bohemian chancellery, whose head Harrach had been, to say nothing of all the other changes . . . afflicted his heart, corrupted his bloodstream, and brought about his decease."[79] In truth, Harrach succumbed to the smallpox. It so happened, however, that Philip Kinsky, a man even younger than Harrach, and but slightly less outspoken in his hostility toward reform, had died five months previously; and people's superstition and their discontent now were feeding each other. Looking for scapegoats closer to them than Haugwitz, the *publicum* turned against the "Silesian quilldrivers," those hardworking clerks—not all of them necessarily Silesians, many of them recent converts—whom Haugwitz had put at the desk of his *Directorium*. They were the target of much spiteful gossip among common people. The privileged classes joked about and took exception to the grand style of living in which the upstart Haugwitz indulged. The costly redecoration of the Bohemian chancellery building, which now housed the *Directorium*, outraged society folk.

The sea of popular dissatisfaction lapping against the throne baffled Maria Theresa far more than did the outcries of the nobility or the whisperings and cabals with which they tried to sabotage change. Outside the "general audiences," some cursory talks with soldiers on guard, or servants' gossip, she scarcely ever hand an opportunity of listening to what her lowly subjects were saying. According to her lights, she loved them. Never would it have occurred to Charles VI to think of himself as their "father"; his daughter saw herself as their mother—a mother who knew best. "Do you really think that the King of Prussia, or the Grand Turk, is beloved by his subjects?"[80] Tarouca once asked her. This daring allusion to absolutistic rule can hardly have touched Maria Theresa; political theory was a matter of indifference to her. As her subjects refused to requite her love, she forced them to accept what was good for them—as well as her house. But even as she seemed to succeed, she could not rid herself of the suspicion that God had denied her one of his great blessings.

In the autumn of 1749 Count William Bentinck, one of Holland's delegates to the late peace conference and an influential person in London, came to Vienna, ostensibly on personal business.* The imperial couple came to enjoy the company of the cosmopolitan nobleman. Some weeks before his departure, Francis, "having joined the empress and myself in the park of Schönbrunn, said . . . that he ought to make me listen to a singer who, to be sure, had not appeared on the stage

* See p. 200.

but sang very well indeed, and that I should report on this to the Princess of Orange who was a great lover of music. The empress at first was trying to beg off, saying she was out of training, and no longer sang anything worth the while. The emperor insisted that she fix a day. Finally she consented. . . . "[81] Five days later Khevenhüller sent Bentinck a billet, asking him to be at Schönbrunn at half past four with Mr. Keith. "The chamberlain on duty led us to a room where the emperor alone was present. He took us himself, up a staircase, to the apartment of the empress where we found her with Wagenseil and her clavecin. The empress was quite self-conscious and said so, adding: 'I must be a great friend of yours, or else I wouldn't do what I am doing.' But then she sat down, and sang an aria. She did better singing another, and the third one was better still. She wanted to stop, but the emperor urged her so long to go on till she consented, and sang two more arias. I was greatly surprised by what I had heard, and no less enchanted. So fully did the gracefulness of the empress enthrall me, I could not help saying that she reminded me of those story-book princesses . . . on whom a good fairy bestows, at birth, all kinds of fine gifts and all charm. 'Don't forget,' she rejoined with a smile, 'there is always an evil fairy around, too, and she spoils everything.' "[82]

XII

The New System

EATH CAME for Charles VI's widow in December, 1750. Life had
not been good to Elizabeth Christina, the "most beautiful princess upon earth," the courageous woman who had gone through the
motions of governing a kingdom for her husband while the whole of
Europe knew he could not hope to retain it.

In the ten years since his decease, cascades of fat had destroyed the
classical features of her face. A persistent case of erysipelas gave a
purple color to it. She was afflicted by dropsy, short breath, and in-
somnia. As her legs could no longer carry the dowager empress, "a
machine was invented which lifts her into and out of the berlin in
her sedan chair."[1] She spent her days in idle talk and card games with
her ladies, whose sufferings would appear to have been talked about
much. "Your Majesty know better than I do whether your august
mother . . . was particularly beloved,"[2] Tarouca told Maria Theresa
boldly as he was preaching tolerance toward *her* entourage.

"Ambition is her main passion," Podewils wrote as late as 1747, "and
the wellspring of most of her actions."[3] Frustration was her lot from
the day of her daughter's accession. Whatever the relationship of the
two ladies may have been since Theresa returned from Florence, the
anxiety of the young queen to forestall interference must have lessened
what had survived of the intimacy grown up between them in the final
years of Francis' difficult courtship. Certainly the matter of Elizabeth's
widow's portion was not conducive to keeping them close to each other.
For no sooner had Charles been laid to rest than the dowager empress
came forth with her demand. The aged Starhemberg had to enlighten

her on its futility, even though he could not deny that the emperor on his deathbed had made provisions for his widow.

Her money-mindedness became noticeable again as she kept objecting to the marriage plans for her younger daughter. "An emperor's daughter, mind you," must be given an appropriate dowry, she wrote to Starhemberg. True, "one would not have to worry, if Maria Theresa were immortal, for her love and generosity would offer surety enough" to Maria Anne in the marriage to a landless prince. "But such is not the case,"[4] the dowager empress went on with little delicacy—Maria Theresa was mortal. The Belgian governorship, with its large emoluments, smoothed over that point of friction. One may wonder about Elizabeth's thoughts after tragedy had struck in Brussels: had she not all along been feeling that Heaven was not in favor of that union? Did she ever remind Maria Theresa of those presentiments? Or Francis? He rarely joined his wife on her almost daily calls on her mother.

The older she grew, the more rigidly did she adhere to the protocol of Barcelona (whose fine points used to amuse the Englishmen in the "Archduke's" court). At one time a question of precedence involving a Brunswick relation of hers led to a heated altercation with Maria Theresa, rumors of which even seeped down to the *publicum*, who had been taught to take her filial devotion for granted.

In Maria Theresa's letters one would search in vain for a word of tender remembrance of her mother. More revealing still is her children's neglect ever to reminisce about the grandmother. Certainly they were taken to her apartments regularly. Was Elizabeth, looking at the young archdukes, able to suppress the memory of her own failure to give the Arch House a male heir? Podewils was certain he had been informed well by people who "assure me . . . that she never loved the emperor, her consort, although she always was acting as though she loved him very much."[5]

While Elizabeth's haggling over her widow's portion had brought her no success, she wanted for nothing throughout the ten years of widowhood. Her establishment in the Leopoldian Wing was incomparably more luxurious than the convent retreat of the widow of Joseph I. A large staff was at her beck and call. A commodious summer residence for the old lady was commissioned in 1741, when the lack of money was, to her daughter, a concern second only to her struggle with the Hungarian Diet. Schloss Hetzendorf, situated at a short distance from Schönbrunn (whose use the queen contemplated only in a vague manner when deciding on the site of the widow seat of her mother), was built and furnished with a speed uncommon in the court of Vienna. It was ready within three years.

Simple in its lines and economical in the decor of the façade, it was different from the summer dwellings of the aristocracy, and strikingly so from whatever the Habsburgs had built in the preceding decades. The first royal building to go up in Maria Theresa's reign, this charming château has remained the finest example of what a much later era, with a self-consciousness totally absent in herself, was to dub the "Theresian" style.

The heroics of the late baroque, as the exuberance of victory it breathed, could scarcely appeal to a young queen set upon by rapacious princes abroad and betrayed by faithless nobles at home. But even after she had overcome the mortal peril, her personal taste did not agree with the showiness of that style. Representational architecture was never to engage her interest. The passion for large-scale building projects which had animated the three last emperors of her race was not alive in Maria Theresa.

The reconstruction of Schönbrunn—though not of course its ultimate glory—was owed to her aversion to the New Favorita. She never once sojourned there after her father's remains had been removed from that palace. Her love of fresh air also made her dislike the cramped Hofburg compound, whose walled-in garden afforded no leeway for the brisk walks to which she was partial. In 1741 Tarouca suggested that the royal residence be removed altogether from the vulgar bustle of the city and its offensive odors. Prince Eugene's niece and heiress was willing to part with Belvedere, still by far the most magnificent of all the suburban estates.* Tarouca foresaw a merging of its grounds with those of the adjacent New Favorita and Salesian convent. This area of lawns, formal gardens, with water works and statuary, English parks, sprawling meadows, and well-tended woods, was large enough for another Versailles. But the asking price for Belvedere was beyond the means of the court.† The idea of moving the court out of the city was dropped and substituted for by the search for a residence suited for prolonged summer sojourns. The alternative to Schönbrunn was Laxenburg Lodge, which indeed was favored by Francis. But it was neither spacious enough to house the big staff required for government work nor sufficiently grand to impress foreign ambassadors.

The grounds of Schönbrunn had belonged to the Habsburg family as early as the middle of the sixteenth century. The small hunting lodge

---

* Its celebrated two palaces were the work of J. Lucas von Hildebrandt, probably the most remarkable of the period's Austrian artists. He received his training in Rome and came to Eugene's notice as a field architect in the imperial army.

† Anne Victoria of Savoy, a spinster of fifty-five when she came into the inheritance, had shortly after married Saxe-Hildburghausen. A few years later she moved without him to Turin, to whose court she sold the bulk of Eugene's art treasures. Charles VI had purchased the fabled library of the prince.

Anne Victoria waited for about ten years for a bid at her price. As no such offer came her way, she sold Belvedere to Maria Theresa for a much lower sum.

that stood there was somewhat enlarged in the 1650's; and after this structure had suffered heavily during the Turkish siege, Emperor Leopold considered rebuilding the place for his son Joseph, who recently had been elected King of the Romans. Fischer von Erlach was ordered to submit a plan and in 1690 came forward with a project so gigantic it gave pause even to the monarch. The blueprints were revised on a scale more modest. Around 1700 the main building was completed and a royal garden enclosure laid out. Joseph I stayed but rarely in Schönbrunn. Charles VI was content with Laxenburg as a rural retreat. Nevertheless, some years before his death he turned over Fischer's blueprints to Niccolò Pacassi for another revision. Obviously the work he was doing at ·Hetzendorf for the dowager empress pleased her daughter, for it was he who in 1743 was commissioned to rebuild Schönbrunn.

Although the main part was still surrounded by scaffoldings in 1745— a story has the boy Haydn climb about them with some fellow choristers on Whit Sunday of this year, and being scolded by the empress as she caught sight of the little band—she had begun to live in the apartment two years earlier. As the original space did not suffice for the family and their various establishments, the younger of her children were in those years left behind in the Hofburg when their parents moved to Schönbrunn. The construction of galleries and ceremonial halls progressed but slowly, the latter being put to use only in the autumn of 1749.

Whatever personal instructions Maria Theresa may have given to Pacassi, none are on record. But she made very clear what she wanted done about the décor of reception rooms and living quarters. To her dying day she was to indulge her taste for furniture, Venetian mirrors, *objets d'art*, and bric-a-brac. *Chinoiseries* delighted her. "I own many things from the Indies . . ." she wrote at one time to Liechtenstein, who had presented her with some choice Far Eastern piece. "All the diamonds of the world are as nothing to me. Only objects from the Indies, such as lacquer work and wallpaper, give me pleasure."[6]

The empress loved Schönbrunn. Refined beholders found fault with the "squatting structure" of the palace, its "glued-on fourth story," or the "truncated"[7] pilasters of the central façade. They wondered about the location of the palace at the foot of a slope rising up to a hill. The Viennese, who, hungry for fresh air, flocked to Schönbrunn on summer Sundays were enchanted, and doubly so after a large section of the grounds had been thrown open to them in 1750. Wide avenues, carved through the wilderness of pine and oak, invited to rambles. Exotic shrubbery, whimsical arboriculture, waterworks, Grecian statuary, and pseudo-Roman "ruins" would all be added only at a later period. But the very rusticity of the landscape with its shadowy stretches impressed common folk as *gemütlich*, as indeed did the lack of ostentation about the palace buildings. Moreover, a "licensed cook, by imperial appointment, served meals and beverages"[8] in a pavilion.

Robinson had not neglected to report on the building activities in Schönbrunn. As the empress one day was strolling with Bentinck through the Kammergarten—an enclosure that Dutch and Lorraine gardeners had embellished—she told him she knew quite well that some people in London loved to speak of the British money that had been spent on her Schönbrunn. They did not really believe it, did they? She could show the records to prove that every remittance from London had gone in full to the troops in the field. Or did one wish to ridicule her?*

His country had asked Bentinck to discuss in Vienna the unresolved problem of the Barrier Tractate and also to hire one of Maria Theresa's generals for the Dutch army. Informal conversations about the general situation of the Habsburg realm and the Empire developed as a matter of course.

~ She began by complaining about the Empire's princes. They were shortsighted men whose love of luxury made them susceptible to the lure of the highest bid. She did not have the means to compete with the French court. Her fiscal reforms would not show results before another four or five years. Bentinck had no conception, she went on, of the indignities her husband had to put up with in the Empire. And did Bentinck know of the humiliations that her ministers and she herself had to endure from France and Prussia? But all that was preferable to a new war! It was said in London—was it not?—that she was bent on re-capturing Silesia. God was her witness that nothing was farther from her mind. She had learned her lesson. Both her officers and the rank and file simply dreaded the Prussians. Some day her son might think of squaring accounts with them. She herself would never pick a fight with King Frederick, even though the rise of this prince, the magnitude of whose gifts was matched by his appalling lack of scruples—an adversary more dangerous than France and Turkey combined—had put her in a position far worse than that of her forebears. A firm alliance with Russia was the only way of checking the king's ambition. "She was certain that subsidy payments for several years would result in a commitment on Russia's part to keep a sizable corps ready for England, and that one hundred thousand pounds, and probably much less, would suffice."[9] Only a year previously she had written to Kaunitz that it would be

---

* The construction funds for Schönbrunn came from a succession of loans granted the court by Diego d'Aguilar, a Portuguese Jew who held the title of comp-troller in the Council for Belgium [Niederlandischer Rat]. (Arneth, IV, 142.) Con-sidering Maria Theresa's notorious hostility toward Jews (see p. 230), Englishmen in the know may in fact have been amused by her dealings with that financier. Some time around 1760 D'Aguilar departed from Vienna under pressure and moved to London.

"better to rely on our strength alone, and not go begging for money abroad."[10]

Bentinck encouraged her to discuss the idea with the British government but warned her of their discordant views. Well, she retorted, did not her allies share her own wish for continued peace in Europe? And was it not plain that nothing short of Prussia's containment could make for a lasting peace? As Bentinck's reply was inconclusive, she remarked that she on her part would never betray the grand alliance of old.

In an audience he had of Francis, he broached another, more delicate matter. There had been an epidemic of smallpox in Vienna three years before, and it had taken its toll among the nobility, as well as ordinary people. Bentinck submitted that the Maritime Powers were not indifferent to what might happen in the Empire should His Majesty die before his time. Probably France and Prussia would attempt to thwart the election of his firstborn. Why not have the archduke elected King of the Romans? The emperor did not take this reminder of his mortality amiss but failed to reflect on Bentinck's proposal. As the Dutchman subsequently took up the matter with Maria Theresa, she at first made light of the possible contender for the imperial crown, which "was an honor, but also a burden, as the House of Bavaria knew well." She "admitted that to have that crown assured for the lifetimes of two [men] instead of only one made for no mean difference, but that one could not pay more for that advantage than its worth." Surely some of the electors would try to extract a high price for their votes in territorial concessions and money. "She has made up her mind not to cede a single acre of land . . . and would not give even this house of Schönbrunn" for the Roman kingship. Moreover, the archduke had "not yet had the smallpox and scarlet fever," and therefore she considered the project premature. "It was up to its originators, not to her, to see how it could be done. Of course she would be pleased, and beholden to them, even though she knew the Maritime Powers were thinking of themselves, also."[11] When Bentinck returned to the matter in a subsequent talk, she expressed doubts about the election, whatever Britain's assistance, unless the czarina's goodwill was assured beforehand. She had learned much of the diplomat's trade at the time its future master was coming into his own.

Wenceslas Kaunitz had gone through varied experiences in Belgium. As the *de facto* commander of Brussels, he watched the preparations for its siege in February, 1746, and was to "hang out the white flag"[12] before De Saxe had fired a single shot. He took himself to Antwerp, and then to Aix-la-Chapelle, where he received word of his release from further Belgian duties; in his whole life he had "not felt a more vivid pleasure."[13] The empress wished to send him to Breda, but Kaunitz kept himself out of the "assignment bound to overtax my physical strength"[14] and what he correctly foresaw would be an unpleasant situation. The following year he accepted the mission to Aix-la-Chapelle with alacrity. Although neither his skill nor his industry salvaged much of the wreckage of his sovereign's aspirations, her ministers could not but admire his composure in the face of her far from consistent directives. He returned to Vienna in January, 1749, thrown into mourning by the death of his wife, who had given him a bevy of children. Maria Theresa appointed him to the Privy Conference.

⌐ In March—at the height of the crisis over the policies of Haugwitz— she surprised her ministers by asking for their individual views on the future conduct of foreign affairs. Ahead of this move she asked Francis to put down his views in writing.

His reputation had continued to go down in the court. His disinclination to take sides in the matter of the new taxation angered its enemies, while even his *intimes* wondered where his sympathies lay. His brother's failures in the field, and what transpired of his attitude toward duty, reflected, however unjustly, on the picture the *publicum* drew of Francis. As atrocity stories from Bergen-up-Zoom and Maastricht were exercising them in the last stage of the fighting, they blamed him for not having raised an army in the Empire.

His own imperial job had been burdensome to Francis from the beginning. Its ceremonial duties bored him to excess. A high Prussian official has left us a description of one of these, the investiture of German princes. The ambassador extraordinary of the fief's recipient would come "at eleven o'clock in the morning, in a carriage-and-six, to a certain building near the Hofburg. . . . He proceeds, as soon as such is the emperor's pleasure, to the courtyard, and betakes himself to the Knight's Chamber, the doors of which are being closed behind him. At the same time, the emperor and his great suite, who all wear the Spanish cloak, walk into the throne hall. Hat on his head, the emperor takes his seat. . . . The ambassador steps into the hall, and before reaching the rug, genuflects three times. On his knees, he delivers his [Latin] speech, asking for investiture. The emperor gives a sign to the vice-chancellor, whereupon the latter replies, saying that it has pleased His Majesty to grant the request. After having approached the throne, the ambassador kneels down again to swear the oath of allegiance (as read to him by the vice-chancellor) keeping his right hand on the Gospel which the Lord Chamberlain and Grand Master are holding aloft above the emperor's knees. Then the Lord Marshal hands the sword to the emperor, who proffers it to the ambassador to kiss it. . . ."[15] Maria Theresa and those of her children who could be relied on to keep silent posted themselves regularly at small holes bored in the wall to watch the medieval proceedings. They were not altogether empty of value for Habsburg business. But they made no impact whatever on the view Maria Theresa had formed of the emperor's co-regency in the Habsburg lands.

To bear out Francis' dilemma in this shadowy office of his, Podewils passed a juicy morsel of gossip on to his king. "She loves the emperor with all of her heart [he wrote]. I have heard it said that her love is, partly, conditioned by her passionate nature and the qualities with which he gives it satisfaction. The scanty influence he has on her thinking, her love notwithstanding, would appear to support that theory. One day, so I learned from a good source, the empress, who had been defending with ardor her own opinion against the ministers', asked him sharply to keep his counsel, implying that he ought not to mix in affairs about which he knew nothing. In his sulky mood, which lasted for several days, he opened his heart to one of his favorites, a Lorraine colonel by name of Rosières. 'Sire, permit me to submit that in dealing with Her Majesty your method is all wrong,' this man said. 'If I were in your shoes, I would know . . . how to make her pliable as a glove.' 'What would you do?' asked the emperor. 'I would sleep separately,' the officer replied. 'Believe me, Sire, this is the hub of her love, and, doing as I suggest, you could assert your will in everything.' The gist of this conversation came to the knowledge of the empress, and she has been making life miserable for Rosières ever since. He intends to quit service."[16] (The story may have had no basis in fact. However, judging by the repeated warnings against separate bedrooms Maria Theresa addressed to one of her married daughters,[17] the problem appears to have turned up in her own marriage.)

Asked to speak up, as he was in March, 1749, Francis showed surprising firmness of judgment. Someone undoubtedly helped him with the grammar of his memorandum. The thoughts it expressed were his own. "The means to win the respect of adversaries . . . keep friends, and gain new allies, are a beautiful large army and the funds to maintain it ready for operations. Hence, the domestic strengthening of the Monarchy is to be considered the very foundation of future policies." Yet no matter how strong, one still would need friends. And who but the Maritime Powers had since time immemorial been Austria's friends? "We must treat them with forbearance, accommodate to whatever may result from the peculiarities of their constitutions, and prevent their gradual estrangement." Neither France nor the Porte was to be feared for the time being. The king of Prussia alone was to be guarded against. And only a strong Russian alliance could foil his propensity toward mischief and force him to "keep the peace *malgré lui*."[18] The preservation of peace, not war and conquest, must henceforward be the goal of Austrian policies.

The empress left her ministers uninformed on the views of her consort until they had turned in their own homework.

Harrach, out of her graces by then (and destined to die within three months), was passionate in his defense of the "old system." He reminded Maria Theresa of the pride of the British. She needed them more than they needed her. The more justified complaints about their conduct, the more likely were such recriminations to hurt their feelings. The chancellery must stop irritating London through nagging notes and innuendos which breathed their author's pleasure in raking up old dissensions. High time Her Majesty diminished the influence of those men in Britain who would love to see Prussia occupy the place of the Arch House on the Continent.

While Harrach's critique may well have aimed at the empress herself, Bartenstein was its ostensible target. When the secretary protested the accusations, Maria Theresa asked him to remove the draft of his vehement note from the files. "Pray, make this sacrifice. . . . Rest assured I know that whatever was salvaged [at the peace conference] is due to the concern and toil of the two men who did the actual work."[19] Bartenstein must have caught the implication—Harrach's opinion no longer counted. And along with Ulfeld, Khevenhüller,* Colloredo, and Königsegg, Wenceslas Kaunitz had delivered his memorandum, one hundred and twenty-seven folio pages of it.

Its opening was brilliant in its tactics. Dividing the European powers into three categories—friends, enemies, and those that might become either in consequence of the policies Her Majesty chose to follow— Kaunitz pretended to take it for granted that freedom of choice was as feasible in world affairs as it was in domestic business.

He did not waste any time discussing the Anglo-French competition overseas. He simply stated that Britain, being in conflict with France, was predestined by her own interest as Austria's ally. However, the island kingdom and its enviable resources could no longer be counted upon as a matter of course in the case of another Prussian attack. After having brushed aside Holland with scorn, he warned against reliance on Russia, whose actions depended on the whims of personalities—and no one knew who would happen to have the czarina's ear in a moment of crisis. Nor could anyone foresee Turkey's future decisions, Kaunitz declared with cavalier brevity before, with deceptive emphasis, he began listing the "crimes of France . . . all of them capped by her recent attempts to despoil Your Majesty of crown and scepter."[20] That pursuit alone had saddled the Arch House with a new enemy, who in his turn had alienated the Empire's princes from their liegelord. True and true again. Yet Her Majesty might deign to take a close look at this day's France—her decay as a naval power, her exhaustion, and the increasing lack of wisdom, finesse, and experience in her leadership. Her king had

* He had been appointed to the conference in 1748.

ceased hankering after martial glory, and Puysieux was a man pacific by nature. As to the Prussian alliance, could one not assume that France, deserted three times by King Frederick, was growing weary of him? It was not unknown that fear of his duplicity had been at the root of her halfheartedness in assisting the Jacobite rebellion. Similar situations might well arise again, and Her Majesty should be ready to turn them to her advantage, unencumbered by the memory of her dynasty's centuries-old struggle with the house of Bourbon.

"Regarding the king of Prussia, he indubitably belongs in the category of natural enemies. . . . He has to be considered the worst and most dangerous neighbor of the All-Highest Arch House." Inasmuch as he surely did not doubt its wish to undo the loss of Silesia, Her Majesty on her part could not question *his* desire to frustrate that intention by weakening her whenever occasion arose. Thus, the two courts would "continue to live, in mutual jealousy, as each other's implacable foes."[21]

From this statement Kaunitz turned to the heart of the matter. The traditional system of alliances had ceased serving the interests of the house. A novel system must be constructed, based on the determination "not merely to be on our guard against the king, and contain him, but also undermine his power to a point where we can regain that which has been lost." To make war on him single-handed was out of the question. Not by any stretch of the imagination could the Maritime Powers be expected to proffer help against Prussia. The "sole way of reaching the great goal" was to prevail upon France to "abstain from obstructing our undertaking, and indeed lend it support, at least indirectly, and thus tip the scales."

Touching on the means of his "New System," Kaunitz mentioned a number of alternatives to predispose the French court toward it, notably an aggrandizement of Don Philip and his ambitious French consort, Madame Infanta. Parts of Sardinia-Piedmont or Lombardy might be held out as inducements, or even an exchange of Parma for Belgium. "I admit that my thoughts are not well arranged as yet in that respect." The main task was to hold fast to the conviction that the New System was no pipe dream. He, Kaunitz, urged Her Majesty to put it into practice forthwith.

The "folly of imagining that France would assist in the recovery of Silesia" did not originate with Kaunitz; Keith called it the "bait constantly held out by Bartenstein."[22] What was new was the young minister's analysis of the European situation—an early example of the "political algebra" he soon was to praise as the hallmark of his work. It appeared to turn a marginal idea—a thought Maria Theresa had played with whenever the British tried her endurance—into the cornerstone of necessity. The prospect of regaining the initiative enthralled

her no less than did the vista of *"primo* recovering Silesia, *secundo* sepa-
rating France from Prussia, and *tertio* raising our prestige in the
Empire."[23]

These were the words in which Batthyány summed up the *desiderata*.
He had been recently sworn to the conference, and like the rest of its
members, was invited to judge the merits of the New System. Although
the field marshal extolled the "inexpressible blessings"[24] that the system
might bring about, he spoke in the same breath of Frederick's reaction
should he get wind of the project. So long as both army and treasury
were unprepared to cope with a Prussian attack, even overtures to France
would entail a grave risk.

The other ministers likewise fought shy of tendering clear-cut advice.
Only Colloredo spoke unequivocally. What on earth made Count
Kaunitz assume that the Bourbons' envy of the Arch House was a thing
of the past? If it was not, he for one could neither believe nor hope
that the court of Versailles would ever embark on a course charted to
strengthen Habsburg power.

Maria Theresa had told Bartenstein that she would "assent to such
measures as the ministers agreed on, and side with the majority on
points of division."[25] The performance of the conference left her where
she had been. Her dilemma worried Khevenhüller. To detract Kaunitz'
mind from foreign affairs—and the empress' from the New System—
the lord marshal suggested that the youngest of her ministers be put in
charge of *internibus*. Maria Theresa was certain that Kaunitz would not
see eye to eye with Haugwitz; and he was neither experienced nor interested in home affairs. No, no. The embassy in Paris was the right spot
for Count Kaunitz, even though the post might strain his delicate health.

No one quite knew what were his afflictions. They tended to become
virulent in times of crises. Shortly after the death of Charles VI an enigmatic malady had compelled Kaunitz to seek the salubrious climate of
his family's country estate. Another mysterious ailment had delayed his
journey from Turin to Brussels. And in some quarters the suddenness of
Brussel's capitulation was ascribed to Kaunitz' allegedly febrile condition.

Impatient as Maria Theresa was of any kind of pretense, she pitied
Kaunitz for the sufferings that his indispositions, true or imagined, inflicted on him. She herself was anything but a hypochondriac. A fresh-air
fiend, she insisted on keeping one of the casements open irrespective of
the weather, wherever she happened to be. She made no fuss whatever
about childbirth; after one of her *accouchements* she was heard saying
that she wished she were six months' pregnant again. "She takes few
pills, and relies on her strong constitution. . . . Her physicians tell her
she will live to regret it, but she shrugs off their warnings."[26] Feverish
migraines she took in her stride, as she did the fact that outbursts of ill
temper might bring them about.

Good news was a nostrum. Down with a fever one day in May, 1750, she was studying a memorial on the Barrier question from Kaunitz' pen. "I can truthfully say," she minuted, "that what cured me was my elation at having such a unique man in my cabinet. The more I come to appreciate the worth of Count Kaunitz, the more I tremble for his health, and realize keenly how much I will miss him."[27] Five months later Kaunitz took up his post at the court of Versailles.

His instructions were a far cry from the spirit of the New System. "You will avoid any action that might give the Maritime Powers cause for complaint [they read, in part]. On the other hand, you will take no step that might lead to a new crisis in our relations with France." Kaunitz' most pressing task was to "offset the Prussian king's notorious endeavors to foster French mistrust of the court of Vienna, and make himself indispensable to the court of Versailles."[28] Meanwhile the empress was doing her bit in Vienna. She showed signal affability to the French *chargé d'affaires*, a vain little person by the name of Blondel, and even told him of her intention to ask the Most Christian King to stand godfather to the next son she would give birth to. When Marquis d'Hautefort, as ambassador, replaced Blondel, she received him immediately after arrival. Within a few weeks D'Hautefort found himself exposed to some surprisingly forthright talk on the part of the empress-queen. She admitted that she might give some thought to Silesia's recovery should favorable circumstances develop in the course of time. "But I repeat that I do not so much as dream of it for the time being. . . . About your king, I have no apprehensions. What I fear is the influence of those men who wish to separate us as far as possible from each other."[29]

Kaunitz' first reports from Paris were not apt to dispel that fear. He saw not the slightest hope for divorcing the French court from Frederick. Worse, France and Britain were both resolved to uphold him in the mastery of Silesia—France because he was her only ally, Britain because he was Hanover's dangerous neighbor. "What other means is left of gaining security, then, but to forget the loss of Silesia at long last, rid the king of Prussia of all misgivings, and sooner or later draw him into Austria's alliance with the Maritime Powers?"[30] The empress, passing Kaunitz' letter on to Ulfeld, remarked ill-humoredly that the emperor had "had it all day long yesterday," but had not told her "whether he read it or not."[31] She did not reply to the ambassador, and when Koch reminded her of his communication, she rejoined that Count Kaunitz had his instructions. "But write him anyway," Koch quoted her as saying, "that . . . nothing would be harder for me than to follow his advice."[32] Shortly thereafter, Kaunitz informed Koch that he had had to take to the sickbed.

But good news, as it had for her migraines, had a curative effect on her ambassador's ailments. He wrote to Koch: "Should Mme. de Pompadour take a hand in foreign affairs, I have reason to assume that she could render us no mean services. . . . My establishment in Compiègne gave me the opportunity of making myself agreeable to some prominent courtiers who are her friends and also belong to the close entourage of the king. I know that I can count those gentlemen among my friends now, and that the king is pleased. I even was given to understand that he would welcome me in his inner circle, if he were free to so honor a [foreign] envoy. . . . All that, I admit, does not influence actual business. However, such personal relations, so far from doing any harm, certainly will bear fruit under propitious circumstances."[33] It was not long before Kaunitz assured Koch that he had never in earnest thought of an alliance with Prussia. The empress does not appear to have resented the brazenness of his turnabout. She had no qualms about his budding friendship with the king's mistress. She did not object when Kaunitz proposed to solicit Mme. de Pompadour's intercession in behalf of her own sister-in-law, who, planning to move back to Lorraine, wanted certain prerogatives restored to her.

The royal favorite was not the only unusual intermediary to be sought out abroad by Maria Theresa's envoys. Nicholas Esterhazy, now in Madrid, was hand in glove with the *castrato* Farinelli, whose influence on both the king and his wife was well known in all the courts of Europe. Such methods, however undignified, turned out to produce results.

Although Spain was one of the signatories of Aix-la-Chapelle, her nobility had not yet despaired of the Italian dreams. The Vienna court was as good as isolated. Its negotiations with London were at a standstill, its Russian treaty lacked a financial basis, and Kaunitz' social success was meager solace. A treaty of friendship with Spain might guarantee at least peace in Italy and bridle the greed of the King of Sardinia. In January, 1751, the Neapolitan ambassador had proposed to Maria Theresa a "true union" with his king, the heir presumptive of his half-brother, the ruler of Spain, whose incapacity to father offspring no one doubted. The ambassador then suggested that the empress-queen give one of her daughters in marriage to the crown prince of Naples, whose eldest sister would make a perfect consort for Archduke Joseph.

"You will easily imagine that the project is far from displeasing to me," Maria Theresa wrote to Esterhazy. "What prevents me from dealing more closely with it is the thought of future contingencies. Yet full attention shall be paid to the proposal when the persons involved . . . have reached maturity."[34] A letter she wrote to the Spanish queen, a Portuguese-born cousin of the empress'—Esterhazy delivered that missive, together with a draft of the treaty of friendship—was less ambiguous.

In fact, that letter committed Maria Theresa to the Neapolitan marriage projects. It was the first step on a road she was to tread with exemplary energy. Her house, having failed on the battlefields, would yet succeed in the conjugal beds of Europe's great princes.

Farinelli had fostered the scheme from its inception. As it began to arouse suspicions in the Sardinian court, the most dexterous of all men in the service of the empress was dispatched to Turin from Milan. His name was Beltrame Cristiani.

"He is a *subjectum* of a sort rare in Italy. He is industrious, erudite, far-sighted, and quick of mind . . . and, to my knowledge, has never been accused of seeking advantages for himself."[35] With these words Kaunitz, writing from Turin in 1743, brought Cristiani to Maria Theresa's notice. Born in the Genoese countryside, the son of a poor lawyer, Cristiani had attained a post of some consequence in the administration of the duchy of Piacenza at an early age. He was very useful to Traun in the Italian war, never permitting its crises to impinge on his loyalty to the Vienna court. When the Duke of Modena decamped to side with the Gallispans, Cristiani was put in charge of the affairs of that small but strategically important duchy. He was transferred to Milan in 1745. The memory of his equitable government was still green in Modena in 1748, and after the duke's return Cristiani became his friend.*

As Pallavicini's subordinate in Milan he had often made Browne angry. His total indifference toward handed-down methods and his perseverance in devising new ones irritated Ferdinand Harrach, Pallavicini's successor. Thus Cristiani did not lack enemies. When Harrach sent him to Vienna in the spring of 1750 he presumably expected him to make a fool of himself on the parquets of Schönbrunn. In fact, Cristiani was the strangest of birds among its courtiers. Stocky of figure, he was utterly careless of his appearance. Bits of snuff constantly stuck to his upper lip and peppered his clothes. (The empress detested the habit of snuffing.) The expressiveness of his pockmarked face robbed it of even the semblance of poise. Afflicted with a stammer, he yet was a great talker. Innocent of etiquette, he remained unconcerned about its pitfalls and blind to any obstacles it might put in his way.

The vigor with which he put forth his ideas—and more so, these ideas themselves—had an enormous impact on Maria Theresa. For the first time, Lombardy was shown her as more than a bastion to protect the southern approaches to her Hereditary Lands; Cristiani had worked out a scheme whereby thirty thousand troops could be raised and maintained

---

* During the campaign of 1744 the duke held the title of generalissimo of all Gallispan forces. He was in Velletri when Lobkowitz attacked, and much like King Carlos of Naples, escaped in the nick of time.

through Lombard money alone. "He is all the rage here," wrote the Venetian ambassador, "particularly with the empress and her consort. Everybody wants to deal with Cristiani only. They will end up by killing the man, so many responsibilities are they heaping upon him."[36] In the meantime, Ferdinand Harrach had lost the taste for gubernatorial duties; and Maria Theresa, listening to Cristiani's counsel, buried her grudge against Pallavicini and returned him to the Lombard governorship. The appointment was destined to give wings to the *"génie supérieur"*[37] of Cristiani, his "grand chancellor."

As the story of his success in Vienna reached Kaunitz, he was quick to remind the sovereign of his foresight. He himself was achieving little in France. Contrary to expectations in Vienna, the conclusion of its treaty with Spain did not predispose the court of Versailles toward Kaunitz' ideas. Now as before, its marked coolness kept him even from hinting at them. Maria Theresa did not blame him or allow his pessimistic moods to mislead her. As day by day she herself was forced to probe her tenacity at home, she more and more keenly sensed the hardness in Kaunitz despite the pose he adopted.

Frederic Harrach's death had not written finis to the nobility's opposition to reforms. Reduced to petty intrigues in Vienna, they still could bank on apathy and the momentum of custom in the lands. Under the newly created "Representations and Chambers" of each, "Circles" had been set up to supplant the various administrative bodies in the towns and the rural districts. The authority of the "Captain of the Circle,"reaching down to the local level, extended from the supervision of religious observances to the enforcement of stable prices, or from the control of labor services to cooperation with the army in its recruiting and billeting. However, the dearth of trained personnel compelled the central government to put many of the former executives of the estates into the new jobs; and direct instructions from Vienna were a strange novelty to these men. Attempts to follow the letter of orders frequently ran afoul of animus on the part of the very people they strove to protect. The Supreme Office of Justice proved particularly ineffective. It barely managed, now and then, to dent the entrenched powers of inequity and procrastination. It was presided over by Count Seilern, one of the drafters of the Pragmatic Sanction, now an octogenarian notorious for pedantry and inertia.

Even as exalted lineage was a prerequisite for army command, so noble breeding remained indispensable for the top positions in the new government departments and their proliferating "commissions." Indubitably, some of these aristocrats were intelligent men with some interest in government theory or even foreign methods. But the pride of their families, as well as religious scruples, had denied most of them a modern education abroad; and the universities on Habsburg soil—Vienna, Prague, Innsbruck—had been dominated for well over a century by the Jesuits.*

Educated commoners were not rare in Lombardy or Belgium. They were at a premium in the Hereditary Lands. The new order opened the road to government service to those few, and they took it, avid for reaching the higher rungs of the immutable social ladder. Toiling under superiors averse to daily grind, these new bureaucrats were often competent and sometimes imaginative men. They were faithful to a fault in practicing the policies laid down in Vienna—those reforms grumbled about and not seldom resisted by the very class from which they themselves had risen. They were to grow estranged from it within one generation. Comparatively speaking, these bureaucrats were an intellectual elite. As they began to form a caste of their own, they filled the vacuum that the absence of a cohesive middle class had left in the social fabric. At the same time, they paved the way for the authoritarianism that was to characterize the officialdom of the monarchy to the end.

The court's search for what we should call junior executives could not fail to invite favoritism. Baron Wiesenhütter, the son of a Frankfurt banker and a Catholic convert who had married one of Bartenstein's daughters, was put at the head of the royal copper and mercury mines after granting the court a substantial loan. He mismanaged them within three years, losing in the process the collateral for the money he had advanced. Love of luxury did the rest; and even though the empress ordered that "fl. 50,000 must be paid to him . . . the *camera* will suggest from which funds."[38] Wiesenhütter had to go into bankruptcy. Shortly thereafter he was made governor of the port of Trieste, whose development was as close to Maria Theresa's heart as it had been to her father's. Wiesenhütter's tenure was short-lived. Count Chotek had no use for men who did not share his own passion for work.

Rudolph Chotek had been among the prominent traitors of Prague. One of the first to desert Charles Albert, who disappointed the turncoat's hopes for high office, he had also been one of the first to be forgiven by Maria Theresa. He became her envoy to Munich after Charles Albert's son made his peace with the court of Vienna. Chotek was not part of the anti-reform clique, was initially on good terms with Haugwitz, and indeed headed the commission that reorganized the Bohemian administration. On the death of Kinsky, his brother-in-law,

---

* An English traveler, visiting Vienna about twenty years later, still observed that "the Austrian nobility of both sexes, a few excepted, seem never to read, and appear equally destitute of an acquaintance with the polite as with the abstruse branches of study and literature." (N. W. Wraxall, *Memoirs of the Courts of Berlin, Dresden, Warsaw, and Vienna*, II, 127.)

Chotek was entrusted with the management of most of the financial affairs and in addition put at the helm of the Universal Directory of Commerce, a new agency for trade and related matters.

According to a high Prussian official who had dealings with him in Vienna, Chotek was, "to do him justice, one of the most capable of the ministers of the empress. A man of the world . . . he tries to appear courteous, but one cannot help feeling his innate hauteur. He is stubborn, sacrifices everything to the goal he has set himself, and will not listen to anybody once he makes up his mind."[39] High tariffs were the arcanum that Chotek prescribed for the ailings of manufacture, trade, and agriculture.* That policy was bound to raise the cost of living and jeopardize the collection of Haugwitz' taxes. Soon the two men were locked in a dispute which, outlasting the merger of their departments, offered occasion for some gleeful mirth to the critics of any reform on their slow sullen retreat.

Apart from the fiscal benefits that Chotek foresaw through the implementation of his theories, it was also supposed to make industry flower. Even before his tariff laws were enacted many different projects were taken up and scores of specialists imported from foreign countries, as well as from Lombardy and Belgium. The indigenous artisans, still fairly secure behind the walls of guild regulations, did not on the whole hanker after new ventures. Whatever factories were established owed their existence to a combination of private and government initiative. Few of these enterprises were destined to prosper.†

In the winter of 1750–51 it became poignantly clear that the fiscal innovations in the Hereditary Lands could not alone alleviate the chronic shortage of funds which encumbered the reorganization of the army. The eyes of the empress turned, not for the first time, toward Hungary, whose financial contributions had remained paltry. Those Hungarian magnates who lived in Vienna encouraged the plan of asking the kingdom for an additional yearly contribution of 1,200,000 florins. Maria Theresa convoked the Diet and arrived in Pressburg on May 9 in the company of her husband and five of their children.

The six-year-old Archduke Charles had been taught some Magyar words—the first Habsburg prince to use, however poorly, the tongue of the nation. The pleasure of the reception committee at his surprise performance was still reflected in the mood of the two chambers as they assembled for the opening session. In her speech from the throne the

---

* Interstate tariffs were an old institution in the Habsburg realm.
† It was different with the large-scale production of textiles on which many Bohemian landowners embarked in the 1760's without government participation, mobilizing, on the whole, unfree labor.

queen praised the genius of the Hungarian generals and the valor of their troops rather than the benefits that her own rule had brought the kingdom. She did not mention the administrative changes that had been discussed in Vienna and which proposed to do away with what a foreign observer called the "barbaric and downright Ostrogothic"[40] conditions in some of the counties. But rumors about her intentions soon percolated to the Diet.

Pálffy had died in November, and the impending election of his successor had revived some of the old fears in Vienna. To Maria Theresa's satisfaction, an undivided Diet let the Palatine's office go to Count Lewis Batthyány, the field marshal's brother. They also confirmed her choice of the crown guardians—Nicholas Esterhazy (an absentee in Madrid) and Grassalkovich, her old confidant. But this spirit of deference did not extend to the reception accorded her fiscal demands. The Diet did not even consider a change in the tax privileges of the aristocracy. They took it for granted that the peasant would have to carry any new burden. But they feared lest this new obligation should interfere with the discharge of his duties to the landlord. At all events, the queen was told that her request would not be debated in either chamber ahead of the settlement of the *gravamina*. (One of these dealt with Hungary's cattle export to Venice, which was being crushed by transit dues collected on the Austrian border.) Many weeks passed before it was decided that the crown's request could be discussed only concurrently with the demands of the Diet. At length they offered the queen a raise of the contribution by seven hundred thousand florins. The reply of the Diet, while "overflowing with sweet words,"[41] reminded the queen, in unambiguous language, of the unresolved *gravamina*, well over a hundred of them, and practically made the new money grant contingent upon their settlement. That memorial was delivered to Maria Theresa even as news from a trouble spot of old injected a novel element of crisis into the debates at Pressburg.

The kingdom of Croatia was autonomous under the crown of St. Stephen. Its relationship with the "mother kingdom" had undergone many changes, as, in the course of the past two centuries, had the Croats' sentiments toward the house of Habsburg. Their estates had ratified the Pragmatic Sanction twelve years earlier than had the Hungarians; in fact they had one year prior to its promulgation suggested to Charles VI themselves that he introduce female succession. The recent battlefield exploits of the nation's sons, whatever their ill repute in foreign parts, had enhanced its sense of independence. Although Hungarian demands for a curtailment of the kingdom's prerogatives were of long standing, they had not alarmed the Croats. The mild government of the viceroy, Charles Batthyány—or his absenteeism—had softened anx-

ieties. The proceedings in Pressburg revived them. The Croats persuaded themselves that the foremost *gravamen* of the Diet was their
country's reduction to a Hungarian province. As their smallholders had for
decades suffered from encroachments on the part of acquisitive Hungarian magnates, they feared that these, squeezed by the queen for
money, would in turn squeeze the Croatians. This climate bred indignation. In a number of valleys local authorities met with defiance. Ineptly
handled, the unrest erupted in riots by the end of June.

The men in Pressburg did not itch for a blood bath among the
rebels. Loudly as they denounced them, they were content when the
queen, rather than order Batthyány to restore peace, asked Saxe-Hildburghausen to take on the mission. This easygoing general had done
service in Croatia and enjoyed some popularity. There were no Hungarians among the troops he started moving into the insurgent counties
by mid-July.

Maria Theresa's spirits were very low indeed. A heat wave aggravated
the discomforts of the castle of Pressburg. She packed the five children
off to Vienna and departed for Pest with Francis and Prince Charles.
Before setting out on the Danube voyage—scheduled originally for after
the adjournment of the Diet—she advised them that she would return
on August 18, expecting the bills to be passed by that day.

The royal craft put in at Pest on August 4 after nightfall, and the
queen and her party were driven in state to the archiepiscopal palace
through streets lightened by thousands of torches. The *Diarium*, which
had spared its readers any account of the empress' tribulations at
Pressburg, went into raptures, describing the reception offered by Hungary's true capital, a city reborn. On August 6 the visitors rode out to
Liechtenstein's army camp. Two days later they ventured across a pon-
toon bridge to Pest's twin city, Ofen, and up its hill, where the new
royal palace was yet to rise over the gutted foundations of the old. In
the palazzos of the magnates, which had lain in ruins only two decades
before, sumptuous dinner parties were arranged for the queen. Not a few
of these hospitable grandees had been anything but subservient in
Pressburg; and while they loved to lecture the petty nobility on her strained
situation, the blessings of peace, or the needs of defense, they themselves
were still unbending in their refusal to follow the example of their
Austro-Bohemian peers and acquiesce in a change in the tax laws. Maria
Theresa appears to have enjoyed their fetes nevertheless.

The town was awash with country people who had come to catch a
glimpse of their "mistress and king." Its streets and the shores of the
Danube resounded with their songs and the tunes of their bagpipes.
One afternoon the royal couple were invited to watch a group of
fishermen haul in their nets on the bank of the river. And, lo and

behold, some enormous carps and pikes were brought in. "One cannot but surmise [the *Diarium* reported on September 1] that the Danubius . . . this prince among Europe's rivers, in order to emulate the heartfelt devotion that the honorable Council of Pest and its burgesses proved to Their Majesties, found himself moved to show his own respect and devotion to these great monarchs by yielding up such extraordinary fishes."[42]

On August 10 Maria Theresa visited Gödöllö, the "country seat worthy of a ruling prince" that Grassalkovich had built at a twelve-mile distance from Pest, "complete with elaborate gardens, an orangerie, and a pheasant preserve." Many new honors had been bestowed on the old friend of the queen, including the presidency of the Hungarian exchequer. None of the ailments troubling the kingdom had diminished his personal revenues. He received his queen with truly Oriental splendor. "A hundred mounted county nobles, with standards flying and trumpets sounding, were posted at every relay stop. A wide avenue had been hewn out of the stretch of woodland the royal cavalcade had to cross; and as night was descending when they entered the woods, the road was lined by the count's own heiduks who held burning torches aloft. Grassalkovich and his son met the queen half-way with an abundant retinue. . . . About 70,000 lanterns illuminated the palace. The banquet hall was flooded with light. . . . Twenty-four squires waited at the table of Their Majesties, who themselves were waited on by two magnates. The following morning they were guided through the palace, its theater building, and the indoor riding school. They heard Mass in the new chapel, whose walls are covered with Italian marble. Forty carriages followed the berlin of the empress as she was driven through the park. . . . A ball in the great gallery, assembling over a thousand gentlemen and ladies, concluded the festivities [of August 11]. . . . 20,000 country people were camping near the little village, and 2,000 of them were fed on the grounds of the estate."[43] On the same day, the lower house voted that the "royal reply to the *gravamina* contains nothing that can be used as a basis for new bills."[44] In order to save the taxpayer further expenditures, the Diet requested prorogation.

Maria Theresa came back to a Pressburg seething with wrath. During her absence the Diet had been presented with a demand whose offensive nature she herself had not grasped. She had proposed that Baron Koch (as he now was) and Baron Toussaint, her husband's foremost financial adviser, who both had acquired property in the kingdom, should be granted the privileges of its native nobles. The contrast between such concern for familiars of the court in Vienna and the queen's alleged indifference toward Hungary's urgent problems raised tempers to a boiling point in the lower chamber. Not even the reports on Saxe-Hildburghausen's progress in pacifying the Croat revolters assuaged the violent anger.

"My very name has been reviled," the queen wrote in a message to the Diet delivered by Grassalkovich amid bedlam. "Sorrow fills my heart as I see the Estates treat me in a manner never experienced heretofore by any of their kings."[45] Only in its sixty-first meeting, on August 27, did the Diet agree to let their seven-hundred-thousand-florin offer stand despite the number of *gravamina* the crown had not settled. Not one farthing had been added to the contribution.

When the members of both houses called on Maria Theresa, she did not hide her displeasure. Stony-faced, she listened to the oration of the primate. Her reply was of cutting brevity. "Desist from mistrusting your mother," she said, "so you might regain her loving benevolence, which you have lost." At dawn the next morning she boarded the ship to Vienna, where the *Diarium* was to inform the public of the prorogation of the Diet "to the great pleasure of the reigning monarch and her loyally obedient Hungarian Estates."[46]

XIII

A Teeming Nursery

M ARIA THERESA had given birth to twelve children by 1751. Nine had survived infancy, three boys and six girls. They were seen and heard far more frequently than Habsburg youngsters used to be outside the nursery. Once, writing to a former lady of hers, the empress apologized for the careless form of her letter, which was "done in four installments, with six children in the room, and the emperor, too."[1]

Archduke Joseph was in his seventh year when Podewils described him as "handsome and well-built, if not very tall for his age. In general, he resembles his father, but he has his mother's eyes. . . . His countenance reflects pride and haughtiness, and so does his behavior. . . . He has the most exalted concept of his station. I have been assured that one day in a room hung with ancestral portraits he said to someone: 'This is my grandfather the emperor, and that is such-and-such an empress,' and then, turning to the other side, added with derision: 'Over there you can see some duke of Lorraine and his duchess.' The emperor tries to rid him of such airs, but his own great love weakens these attempts. . . . [The archduke] is obstinate and mulish. Rather than ask for forgiveness, he will accept being locked in, or deprived of certain dishes. . . . It is hard to say whether he will grow up to be an intelligent man. That he will ever prove genius, I doubt."[2] There was a story abroad to the effect that a certain person, being received in the course of the empress' general audiences, had "offered his services as a tutor . . . boasting of his knack for giving an extraordinary education to children who had no talent at all."[3]

Joseph was removed from the care of women in his eighth year, and his first tutor, a Jesuit, replaced by P. Weber, an Augustinian pedagogue.

The prince was given his own establishment, complete with lord steward, equerry, six chamberlains, and a bevy of servants. When Charles Batthy-ány was appointed his *ayo* about two years later—shortly before the trip to Pressburg—the choice was considered a flattering gesture toward the Hungarians. Actually Maria Theresa hoped that the crusty old field marshal would succeed where women and tutors had failed. Above all, she wanted her firstborn to grow up under soldierly discipline.

Lack of military talent had been conspicuous in the latter-day Habsburgs. They were aware of this shortcoming and did not allow it to embarrass them. Their keeping themselves away from the battlefield did not, to their subjects, betoken deficiency in princely valor. When Emperor Leopold departed from Vienna in undignified haste at the approach of the Turks, to take himself farther and farther away from what he himself did not tire of proclaiming as Christendom's battle, even those Viennese who could not follow suit had not criticized his prudence. Nor had army men found fault with his absence from their encampments throughout the long years of campaigning against Turks and Hungarian rebels.

Times had changed, however. In the course of Maria Theresa's warring, five kings had taken the field—George II, Louis XV, Frederick, Charles Emmanuel, and Carlos of Naples—besides such princes of the blood as Cumberland and Don Philip. Whether or not Maria Theresa actually hoped that her firstborn might grow up to be a soldier of mark, the story of Frederick's formative years persuaded her that soldierly qualities could be grafted on a prince not made to obey by nature. And was not obedience the first virtue to be implanted in a future soldier? Instead, Joseph was taught to command, or at least to put up a show of commanding. Created colonel proprietor of a grenadiers' regiment at the age of eight,* he would march it past his parents, the soldier uncle, and a press of courtiers, himself in a trim uniform on horseback, saber drawn. This sort of play did not fail to go to his head. "Recently Count Haugwitz called on [him] and was promptly asked whether he was the man dealing with the [new] order in the army. The count replied that he followed the empress-queen's orders in the discharge of his duties. 'But did you ever do service in the army?' the archduke inquired, and, as Haugwitz said he had not, Joseph continued: 'Why, then, do you meddle in matters you do not understand? I warn you not to extend your reforms to my own regiment, for I would not tolerate them.' When the story came to the mother's ears, she tried to get the archduke to tell her who had put those words into his mouth. He refused steadfastly, referring to the word of honor as an officer on which he had promised

* See p. 239, note.

not to divulge the name; and neither entreaties nor threats could elicit the information from him."[4]

Maria Theresa was not at all blind to the problematic side of the boy's makeup. She may or may not have discerned in it the strange mixture of skittishness and languor she took for granted by then in his father. No doubt she also wondered as to how much of her own obstinacy might have come down to Joseph. The ideal of princely forbearance she set up in her lengthy instructions for his *ayo* carried an echo of Tarouca's warnings against her own intolerance.

His "wishes and requests have been paid much too much heed to all along," she wrote. The archduke loved "being honored and obeyed," while finding "criticism . . . well-nigh unbearable. Tending to indulge his whims, he is deficient in courtesy and even rude." Yet "signs of a good heart" could be noticed. "But, as youth wills, he scarcely listens when he is being admonished." Even though P. Weber seemed to have awakened a "remarkable vivacity" in the prince—"the last thing one assumed in him at first"—he still could "be made only with great difficulties to apply himself." "My son does not lack intelligence," the mother continued. But it was precisely this fact that enabled him, "particularly when he is animated, to come out with vehement protests, and engage in arguments apt to confuse a superior who has to avoid unseemly scenes. . . ." What was to be fought against most in the archduke was the "pleasure he is prone to take in descrying the shortcomings, physical or otherwise, of everyone, and dwelling on them with scorn. . . . The *ayo* will strive to remove from his presence men who flatter him too much, give him ideas bigger than necessary of his birth, or try to divert him through laughter, grimaces, jokes and malicious gossip. He must be disaccustomed from amusing himself at the expense of others—a habit especially reprehensible in the great, as they are at liberty to embarrass and vex men who cannot possibly repay in kind." The archduke must "win the affection of people through affability and a consistently kind language, pardon their mistakes, and plead their cause whenever allowed to do so." Such intercessions, however, "must not be motivated by favoritism, but come out of goodness of heart such as distinguished so many of the prince's forebears, and which makes it his duty to set a good example to the run of mankind."[5]

Batthyány did not search for subtle solutions. "Everything depends on the impression the prince will gain in the first days," he wrote to Weber's successor. "If you manage to make him respect you, and convince him of the steadfastness with which you follow your principles, as well as of your affection for him, you can be certain that you will solve your task. If you yield to his little whims, or allow him the upper hand by showing irresolution, you will fail." Leniency would be misplaced.

Nothing short of severity could curb the archduke. "Considering his station, this is a saddening fact."[6] To combat the blend of surliness and shyness in the child, Batthyány introduced him to the company of some army officers; and promptly we find the empress admonishing Joseph's chamberlains to "avoid all profanity in talking to him, and tolerate none in his own language."[7]

As Batthyány was anything but a lettered gentleman, Bartenstein was asked to supervise the curriculum of the archduke and attend his monthly oral examinations. After one such test Bartenstein wrote: "Sometimes I feel that there is more in him than he has been credited with, and this raises my hopes that with God's help everything will turn out well." "It assuredly will," the mother confirmed. "But how to find the right system? Has not been found yet."[8]

The emperor—who himself had caused his tutors many a troubled hour—suggested one "system." Why not have two or three youngsters join the classes of the prince? "But care must be taken to pick boys of a lively disposition, so that my son is drawn out of his sluggishness and indifference, and made to see with his own eyes how such people work."[9] This method, long adopted in many German courts, was not to the liking of Maria Theresa, and the proposal went by the board. Francis, inured to rebuff, continued to advance proposals for the heir's education. At one time he instructed Bartenstein (who was out of conference office by then) to let someone "make excerpts from the well-known history textbooks, and relate current events to these accounts." That man also must "point out the mistakes of the rulers mentioned, besides the good they did," and thus teach the archduke "how to avoid the former and try to achieve the latter."[10] Bartenstein, soon despairing of finding a savant to meet these qualifications, was to take on the job himself, writing one verbose tome after another for the overburdened, lonely student.

According to her lights, Maria Theresa did her best in trying to mold the character of the heir. In years to come she never wondered whether her best had been good enough. Whatever she found intolerable in Joseph or fraught with dangers for himself and the realm she would blame on the changing world and its noxious influence on a young man. Not that she did not come to know remorse as an aging woman. She was to know plenty of it, even as she could, without self-righteousness, look back at her work with some satisfaction, along with regret at happiness gone. But in her many conflicts with the heir grown to manhood, remorse never entered her thoughts. Her favorite son-in-law relates in his memoirs that Joseph's first wife, a young Italian princess adept at judging people (as we know from her writings), "espied the hardness at the bottom of [Joseph's] character."[11] Maria Theresa was never to ask herself where she had failed to touch the heart of the adolescent.

Marianne, the eldest archduchess, had been ailing from the first. Growing into pubescence, she developed a curvature of the spine. A talent for drawing afforded her some diversion. The girl closest to her in age (and one year Joseph's junior) was Maria Christina, the darling of the empress, her "Mimi." Born while half of Europe was making war on the queen, who did "not know where to prepare in peace for the confinement,"[12] Mimi saw the light of day three months before Charles Albert's coronation. She grew up to be as quick-minded a child as she was pretty. There was a porcelain sheen about the complexion of this granddaughter of the White Liz.

A French tutor who, in days still remote, took up his duties with the youngest of Mimi's sisters (and most ill-starred of Maria Theresa's daughters) was to remark on her "inability to concentrate," adding that her mind was "much keener than people here have assumed, but . . . nothing whatever has been done to develop it."[13] While the mother did better by some others of the princesses, that "inability to concentrate" was to mark all of them save Mimi; and scant attention was paid to finding a remedy. Maria Theresa, delighting in her male progeny, could assume safely that the Habsburg dominions would never again have to fall back on a distaff ruler.

"Getting up at 7:30," reads the schedule submitted by the *ayah* of two of Mimi's younger sisters. "From 8:30 on, penmanship, reading, spelling. Holy Mass at 10, French lesson at 11. Dinner at noon. Three times a week [irrespective of holy days, as the empress wrote in the margin] from 2 to 3, Father Richter. On other weekdays, this hour for maps, some history, some books of fables. Needlework and the like till 4. At 5, Rosary in church (every day). Evenings: games, callers, sometimes theater."[14] Maria Theresa in her directives reminded the *ayah*, among other points, that "conversations with doorkeepers and stokers must not be tolerated. Nor must [they] give orders to such people." Her daughters were "born to obey, and have to learn to do so betimes. . . . Under no circumstances must they be permitted to feel fear, be it of thunderstorms, fire, spooks, witches, or similar nonsense, and the servants must neither discuss such matters among themselves, nor tell any ghost stories. As [the princesses] must not be afraid of illnesses, you will talk to them about any of these quite naturally, even of smallpox. And of death also, for it is well to familiarize them with the thought of it. . . ."[15]

Save Lent, hardly a fortnight passed without some ballet, comedy, or musical drama staged by the children and some handpicked coevals. "*Pour diversifier le plaisir* . . . the little Highnesses changed several times.

For the wind-up, they supped at small tables, places having been decided by the lot."[16] Khevenhüller, keeping track of these affairs, one day
asked himself whether directing the fancy of the young Highnesses
toward the stage at so early an age, in preference to almost all other
activities, did not detract the mind from serious studies. But Maria
Theresa could not get enough of displaying her big brood of children.
Their sight amid the glittering décor of Metastasio's productions enchanted her stagestruck consort. Their reciting, acting, singing, and dancing, or merely their appearing in formal or fancy clothes, afforded the
parents a pleasure they could share wholeheartedly. And such pleasures
were becoming less and less frequent in the early 1750's.

Less and less frequently could the empress be seen on horseback.
She had long ceased joining Francis on the chase in the surroundings
of Vienna. More and more often did he occupy the royal-theater box
without her. "In the early morning hours he took care of his personal
business affairs, working with Pfütschner and Toussaint."[17] He loved to
slip out of the Hofburg with his sister in the afternoon to take a stroll
on the glacis or watch, recognized, he thought, by no one, one of the
Punch–and–Judy shows on a public square. His delight in carnival
pleasures had been stifled. From 1745 on Maria Theresa had been frown-
ing on *Mehlgrube* visits. The court's own carnival fetes had become
monotonous affairs, barely different from formal receptions. She relented
in the winter of 1752–53 and allowed fancy-dress parties to be arranged
in the redecorated Redoutensäle of the Hofburg. She even made some
attempts to enter herself into the carnival spirit by catering to Francis'
irrepressible taste for practical jokes. But such prearranged hilarity remained awkward as a rule. She would withdraw at an early hour, escorted
by Francis, who afterward might turn up again, as likely as not to tell
his *intimes* stories they had heard before or invite them to a game of
faro, which they tended to stay out of, afraid of the high stakes to which
he was partial. He no longer seemed to seek the company of attractive
young women.

A chatty correspondence with Kaunitz had become part of Koch's
routine. Writing to the ambassador in the Holy Week of 1752, he
quoted the empress as saying that the "vertigo-plagued head of Count
Kaunitz is worth more to me than all those [in Vienna] in their good
health, put together. . . . She has entirely lost the taste for Conference
meetings."[18] In fact, she missed Kaunitz sorely. Sir Charles Hanbury
Williams, who the year after was in Vienna, summed up the accounts
given him of her temper in the summer of 1752 by suggesting that she
looked forward to Kaunitz' return from France "with the same impatience as Henry VIII looked for the return of Cranmer when he was
tired of Wolsey."[19]

On October 31 Khevenhüller made the following entry in his journal: "After Divine Service I had a long talk with the empress about forthcoming changes in the chancellery. . . . Some time ago she had spoken to me of her intention to put Count Kaunitz at the helm of the chancellery, give Count Ulfeld the post of Grand Master [vacated by Königsegg's death] and let him continue as chairman of the conference with the salary of fl. 45,000. . . . Today she told me that she had talked to him, and broached the subject. Ulfeld, far from expressing his gratitude, had turned down the proposal with a few dry words. He had written her soon after, saying that all he wished for was to spend the rest of his life in tranquillity and remote from business, but that he must be indemnified for his personal expenditures in her service. . . . The empress, telling me all that, broke out in repeated complaints about the contempt with which Ulfeld was treating what, after all, was a favor proffered. No sovereign could remain indifferent toward such lack of appreciation. And was not she alone, of all sovereigns, compelled by misfortune to pay those huge salaries, while having to hire new men all the time, and double and treble the payroll? In fine, *elle avait le coeur si gros*, as the saying goes, that she ended by admitting she did not know what to do. . . . I tried to advance one thing and another in favor of Count U., mentioning his integrity and the length of his service. Touching on human frailties, I also remarked that his surly ways had, after all, been known for a long time. . . . Then I spoke of the generosity, forbearance, and goodness of heart, she had always shown her servants. I flatter myself that I did rather well by that honest man. . . . The talk then turned to Count Kaunitz, and we discussed at great length his qualities, the contradictions within human nature, and how one person *peut allier les qualités d'un génie supérieur avec des ridicules qui frisent même l'extravagence.* The empress agreed that that was true. But she could see no alternative. . . . Concluding the interview, she said that she no longer could bear the sight of Count Ulfeld, and was determined to try out Count Kaunitz, even though she foresaw difficulties on the part of the emperor, and was aware that Kaunitz's ailings, as his eccentricities, did not augur well for the length of his tenure."[20]

Having received the summons, Kaunitz protested the pitiable state of his health. Neither, as he went on to say, could he picture himself attending to important business while being swamped by the flood of minor matters such as were bound to turn up in the chancellery. Thus he could not consider himself the right man for the post so graciously offered him. Yet he felt it to be his bounden duty to assist Her Majesty in putting the conduct of foreign affairs on a new footing, serving for a limited period of time. . . . He was to stay in office for forty-one years.

Perhaps the empress was sufficiently inured by now to his quirks and conceits. At all events, she declared herself content with his taking over on a temporary basis and made haste to give way to Ulfeld's demands, which included a new mansion and the settlement of his debts to the tune of (so it was said) 160,000 florins. She ordered a speedy remittance of 100,000 florins to Kaunitz to pay for his formal entry into Paris, which he had had to postpone for a year and a half for lack of money.

Four days after that *entrée*, Kaunitz gave Koch a glowing description of it. "Among the friendly comments of the populace, as I rode by in my state coach, some people exclaimed 'Vive Monsieur l'ambassadeur,' and such acclamations would have become general in a hundred different places but for lack of daring"[21] on the part of the Parisians.

The Fates enjoyed sending Wenceslas Kaunitz on midwinter journeys. He set out on New Year's Day on the long trip to Vienna. "It did not dawn on him how much of a laughing stock he had been in Paris," a Prussian diplomat on the spot reported. "He departed from the town, filled with passion for a nation caring little for him, and whose ways, which he had tried to copy . . . he never had understood." After amusing the royal addressee with accounts of Kaunitz' foppery, hypochondria, and tightfistedness—and throwing in, for good measure, some anecdotes about the ambassador's abortive amorous exploits and his mingling with uncouth tax farmers and their wives when high society gave him the cold shoulder—Herr von Ammon continued: "For all his eccentricities, Count Kaunitz is neither deficient in intelligence nor in insight. He is knowledgeable and not without talent. A coxcomb in his manners, he is not superficial in his propositions. Whatever he says is thought through well. No nonsense comes from his lips, no rash observation. Expressing himself with ease, he yet talks little, preferably about inconsequential matters. Only seldom does he give tongue to any personal sentiment, or opinion. His conversation is neither interesting nor diverting. Experience has taught him to adopt a jargon all his own, as it were, and a stance that may indicate anything. . . . He is consistently serious, assumes a grave mien, and strives to impress people by the grandness of his bearing rather than any brilliance in his speech. Capricious himself, he does not yield to the caprices of others. He is so hardened in his prejudices that he cannot agree with any view differing from his own." Venturing into prophecy, the Prussian thought Kaunitz sufficiently ambitious to earn fame in his tenure through some sensational coup and foolhardy enough to leave anything to chance. "He has not enough genius to prefer a plan that is merely safe to one that is only brilliant; not enough sagacity to foresee all obstacles; not enough skill to overcome them; and not the brains to change [his own approach]. His first failure will destroy all his projects, play havoc with his notions, and reduce him to groping along, living from one moment to the next."[22]

Had Maria Theresa read this report, it would have disturbed her as little as had Kaunitz' virtual failure in France. The attraction he had begun to exert on her was beyond analysis. She needed a hand to guide her in foreign business with firm purpose and subtle tactics such as a Bartenstein could not winnow from his nature. Nor was this all. Married to a prince far from being subtle, who was anything but firm, she could not help longing for the companionship in council of a man who was both.

If ridding herself of Ulfeld had been only a matter of money, dismissing Bartenstein preyed on her conscience. "To him alone do I owe the preservation of the realm. . . ."[23] Even Kaunitz marveled at how Bartenstein had "all those years carried the whole burden."[24] But as the old man tried to cling to his office—he promised to "subordinate himself, to agree, to concur"—Kaunitz said no. "Two pipers won't do in one tavern,"[25] he wrote, rudely. So Bartenstein had to go. The empress offered him a seat in the conference—a unique distinction in view of his modest birth. But unable to conceive of himself as one of the members of that body whose virtual master he had been for so long, he turned down the proposal. "I shall be in town tomorrow the whole forenoon to say my prayers in the crypt," the empress notified him on the eve of the anniversary of her father's death. "I asked a number of people to call on me after that. To see you would be too hard on me. I know how the emperor, of blessed memory, felt about you. I also know how you are still feeling yourself. Hence I am unable to look at you as coolly as I do at others. Let us postpone our meeting for a week or so."[26]

With Königsegg's death and Bartenstein's enforced resignation, only Joseph Harrach remained of the ministers of Charles VI. For all of her gratification at the change, it made Maria Theresa acutely aware of the passage of time. Getting older, she felt that she was getting old. "Perhaps I won't last long, after all . . ."[27] she wrote to a former lady of hers. Of the entourage of the early years of her reign, only Tarouca was left. And it was he who, at this juncture, once again talked to her in his old avuncular fashion. It happened to be autumn as he put pen to paper, but in the reference to the season with which he opened his letter the double entendre was obvious. Her Majesty, he wrote, was likely to say: "Now that the leaves are turning, the days getting shorter, and the evenings longer, what am I supposed to do?" She should do, Tarouca countered the hypothetical question, "what people everywhere do." Why not act "as Maria Theresa did eleven years ago, when she was twenty-four and twenty-five, had many enemies, very little money, scant help, and hardly any experience"? In those days, "when Your Majesty were thrown back on your own devices, studying the ABC of sovereignty, and did as much work as four men might have done, Your Majesty yet found the time to relax, and give us the pleasure of your company. You almost overdid horseback riding, danced . . . had fun, entertained at both meals, and sometimes made a little trip, even though you gave birth to a child every year. Your Majesty had the same, indeed greater reasons, or rather pretexts, for keeping to yourself as you have today. . . . Your Majesty are still young and full of vigor."[28]

"I am tied down by work," she replied, "and my attempts to attend to it as well as I formerly did put a great strain on me. I cannot concur in your assertion that I might still amuse myself the way I used to. I am no longer the same person. Amusements no longer exist for me. I must not think of them. Let us try to make shift of life [à vivoter]."[29] The tone of resignation on the part of the thirty-five-year-old may have been designed to help Tarouca bear his own decline; the influence of the "over-subtle and alembic" man (as Bentinck called him)[30] was waning in step with Cristiani's ascendancy and Khevenhüller's. Still, the endless succession of festivities which the lord marshal recorded does not disprove the small attraction the social whirl was holding for her. More than once did he note that she was "glad it was over."[31]

Ever since she had made it her habit to move to Schönbrunn in early spring, and from there to Laxenburg in autumn, many of the great families had established summer residences in the vicinity. They went hunting together, fleeced one another at the gaming table, carried on their amours with more or less circumspection, and together engaged in dances, masques, music-making, and theatricals. Despite mutual jealousies and political intrigues, they formed as closely knit a group as had ever surrounded a Habsburg monarch. Consisting of barely more than a hundred clans, this group within a decade also grew far more dependent on the monarch than their forebears would ever have cared to imagine. Even as Maria Theresa curbed their privileges as a class, she continued to bestow honors and gifts upon them. What was more, she made their personal concerns her own and offered them her friendship. She was a meddlesome friend. But a genuine interest in these families—an interest in what might benefit their "houses," as well as her own—tempered her meddlesomeness.

In 1749 she opened a boarding school for young nobles, turning over to it the buildings and grounds of the New Favorita. "Nothing will be more conducive to the welfare of my dominions," read the preamble of the deed, "than my offering to the nobility . . . the opportunity to give their sons the kind of education, both in refined comportment and all the branches of scholarship, that will enable them to render useful services to the commonweal, and to me and my successors."[32] Although the great lords were not contemptuous of high office, its glamor and its perquisites, they had never been seeking these posts. They used to come to them. They were not eager to enroll their sons in the *Collegium*

Theresianum, whose semimilitary discipline might harm their sense of feudal independence. But as the rise of new men in the administration began demonstrating the advantages of a methodical education, the landed aristocracy relented in their bias. At the same time, the lower nobility—whose sons had frequently been reduced to taking employment with the great—were quick to grasp the benefits of the new institution. The young men of both classes came under the spell of collegiate living; and even those of the proudest lineage, as they entered adult life, tended to accept royal authoritarianism, much as they had the strict rule of the Jesuit teachers at the *Theresianum*.

As for the boys' sisters, the empress arrogated a virtual veto power in the choice of husbands. She also secured mates for young ladies of impoverished families, and many a *fräulein* of little attraction. Not a few unwilling bachelors were cajoled and bullied into marrying maidens not of their own picking. Thus Prince Trautson, the man whose "odalisque" affair had scandalized the court in the mid-1730's, found himself tied to the former *ayah* of the two eldest archduchesses, a spinster of forty-three, although his "disposition does not seem to sympathize with an old maid."[33] Count Enzenberg, who had courted one of Maria Theresa's favorite ladies for fifteen years with varying fire, at long last made her his bride; he was given the governorship of the Tyrol. When another of these ladies, a Countess Berchtold, formed a liking for a certain gentleman, off went a letter to her uncle: "I am all against it. [He] has not a penny to his name. In fact, he is in debt, and has never known how to manage. . . . He is a great hand with the ladies, who all adore the fellow. My good Berchtold girl is neither young nor pretty, and she tends to be moody. . . . His suit must have some ulterior motive."[34] Or: "I understand the daughter of Dietrig wishes to marry a certain Brentano, a Genoese who is involved in several lawsuits. . . . I could never agree to her taking this foreigner. Therefore the whole affair must be stopped. . . ."[35] Naturally Maria Theresa wanted young noblewomen to marry good men, find contentment in marriage, and raise a flock of children. This, after all, was the only kind of happiness she herself had ever experienced. However, like the suit of the debt-ridden Brentano, her matchmaking too had an ulterior motive. She strove to consolidate the circle of noble families who, beholden to her from the cradle to the grave, would trust her motherly feelings and, hence, could be trusted.

The company of these people did not always divert her, unless she sat down with them at the gaming table (a pastime she could not do without even while she issued decrees against it). She appears to have complained to Tarouca about the boredom spoiling her work-free hours. Yes, he wrote facetiously, "good princes may forgive errors and transgressions on the part of their subjects, but not the tedium they impose on them."[36] It is futile to ask why she never ventured beyond that circle and its endless talk about the decoration of mansions and estates, about births, marriages, anniversaries, spectacles, and, perhaps, music-making. The gulf between the sovereign and untitled people, or even the petty nobility, was unbridgeable on a social level. The general audiences, which used to afford her a glimpse of the concerns of common people, had been discontinued after a deranged petitioner one day precipitated an unpleasant scene in the antechamber.

But Maria Theresa's social confinement to a miniscule section of society did not warp her mind. The directness with which she tackled whatever demanded her attention—or sometimes did not—was not contaminated by the supercilious circumlocutions of those men and women who cultivated their estrangement from practical life as a mark of distinction. Sir Charles Hanbury Williams, who attended one of her small parties, observed that the countenance of the empress was "filled with sense [and] spirit. . . ."[37]

"Chevalier" Williams, as he had been nicknamed on the Continent, was at that time accredited to the court of Dresden. He had been sent to Vienna after both Keith and Hyndford failed to further what New-castle referred to as the "great system, the great object of my life in foreign affairs."[38] Not even a letter from the hand of his king had diminished Maria Theresa's resistance to the archduke's election. It had only grown when the British, in an arbitrary first step toward winning over the electoral college, concluded a subsidy treaty with Bavaria, Maria Theresa's recent enemy and Frederick's recent ally.

An incident going back to Bentinck's sojourn in Vienna dampened the hopes with which Williams had set out on his mission. A citizen of one of the Dutch-garrisoned Belgian towns, accused of some crime, had been maltreated by his captors. "It almost seems as though the commanders of the Barrier towns made it their business to pile one outrage on another," she wrote to Prince William of Orange, "in order to scoff at my sovereignty. . . . No monarch on earth would have toler-ated such excesses for so long as I did. . . . Now they have been driven to a point where . . . in a manner without example in history, a citizen of Namur, my subject, was twice put to the torture, and flogged by the hangman, for an alleged misdemeanor which, even if he had con-fessed to it, could have been penalized by no more than a fine in any court of law. I am at a loss to express my grief, nay, my horror. . . ." Her "demand for a reparation commensurate to the ignominy"[39] had not been met. Of course, what galled her was the underlying conten-tion that the Barrier Tractate nullified her jurisdiction in the Dutch-garrisoned fortresses. Williams told her just that. "This Her Imperial Majesty seemed also to take very ill," he reported, "and insisted loudly, so loudly that the people in the next room heard her, that she was sovereign in the [Austrian] Low Countries, and that it was her duty to protect her subjects, who had been so long oppressed by the Barrier treaty, and deprived of the natural privileges which all other nations enjoy."[40]

Kaunitz, whose return coincided with Williams' arrival, went out of his way to persuade the Englishman that the empress had no intention to alienate his government. "He was extravagant upon the necessity of the strictest alliance between the House of Austria and the Maritime Powers." Sir Charles was rather taken by the new chancellor. "[He] has already put the office of foreign affairs on a new footing, in imitation of those of England and France, and all his commis and clerks are persons of his own, very little known at Vienna."[41] Keith at about the same time wrote that Kaunitz "has no confidants, nor even intimates, and therefore his designs are impenetrable."[42] And this was to be Williams' opinion too once he was back in Dresden.

From there he also had some comments to make on one particular feature of Maria Theresa's rule. "I am sorry to say [he wrote to Newcastle] that the spirit of persecution still reigns in Vienna, which is push'd and encouraged by the empress-queen's confessor, for it is known in Vienna that in a council held upon the affairs of Protestants in Upper Austria, the emperor's confessor declared that he knew of no lawful methods for bringing the lost sheep back to the flock but argument and persuasion. On the other hand, Her Majesty's confessor declared loudly for the legality of violent measures, and compelling to come in by force, and this advice prevailed."*[43]

Actually, religious unity had always been the lodestar of Maria Theresa's policy. Coercion had been used from at least 1750 on. Lutherans in the Alpine lands were "persuaded" to sell their holdings for a song and take themselves to Transylvania. As many of them, unable to purchase land in that principality, came back home in 1752, they were hounded down with no mercy. Families were split up and widows "under suspicion regarding religion"[44] forced to divest themselves of their property, on whose proceeds their children were subsequently brought up in Catholic homes. A number of injunctions made it illegal for Protestants from non-Habsburg territory in the *Reich* to settle in the Hereditary Lands. Rather than acquiesce in the migration of Calvinist Dutchmen to her Belgium, Maria Theresa denied that much-tried province the benefits it would have reaped from the activities of such merchants.

* According to Khevenhüller, this meeting took place on March 17, 1753.

Freedom of worship was guaranteed in rump Silesia, Hungary, and Transylvania. Yet the rights of Hungarian Protestants had been infringed surreptitiously throughout the 1740's. A deputation of their notables came to Vienna in the summer of 1749 and was promised redress by Maria Theresa. However, the Protestant nobility must cease turning their peasant coreligionists against her. And had not both Lutherans and Calvinists vented their gripes even abroad? "Burmania, the Dutch ambassador, came to see me in your behalf, as did the Hanoverian envoy, and even the ambassador of the king of Prussia!"[45] Some weeks after that audience a Hungarian prelate attacked his Protestant countrymen in an abusive pamphlet. They invoked the help of King Frederick, who gleefully ordered the bishop of Breslau to bring the affair to the notice of the Holy See; and Benedict XIV prevailed on the empress to prohibit further distribution of the booklet.*/The incident fortified her conviction that all non-Catholics were, as such, enemies of her house. It annoyed her no less for coming on the heels of defeat in the war she had waged, singlehanded, against the Jews of Bohemia.

Expediency had tempered the Spanish bigotry of Charles VI. Faced with the scarcity of military talent, he put a Protestant into high command. He had had no compunction about dealing with Jewish bankers in his continuous search for money. His daughter's anti-Jewish sentiments dated back to childhood; bearded Jews in their special garb were said to have frightened the little princess whenever she caught sight of them on the way to a church situated close to their somber quarters. In 1741 Robinson reported from Pressburg that the queen, riding past the ghetto at the foot of the castle's hill, had not been able to suppress signs of disgust.

She inveighed against the Jews of Breslau, who, alongside its Protestants, seemed to prefer Frederick's rule to her own. The "voluntary gift" extracted from the Jewry of Prague in 1743 seemed inadequate to her. When after the Prussians' withdrawal from that city in 1744 some of its Jews were again denounced for having done business with the occupier, she ordered the wholesale expulsion of their community. Kinsky besought her to rescind the order. Robinson intervened, only to be told that Jewish money seemed to have greased some palms in London. Nor did demarches on the part of Holland, Denmark, and the Porte shake

* In these very weeks the Jesuit P. Parhammer conducted in Vienna one of his celebrated missionary drives, preaching on a public square to children, who would "break out in ear-splitting shouts against Luther and his successors." The conference held that "the padre should be commended for his zeal, but advised that, for important reasons, non-Catholics who have found it necessary to reside here must not be abused in public." (E. Guglia, *Maria Theresa*, II, 73.) The empress followed the advice, availing herself of this opportunity to strike a blow at the lower clergy (see p. 232). She subjected their sermons to government censorship.

her determination. As the provincial authorities sabotaged the ordinance, she instructed the army to implement it. The exodus began in January, 1746; and as the midwinter search of the expellees for shelter disrupted the countryside's life, she made it known that the entire kingdom must be cleared of Hebrews.* The Bohemian administration procrastinated. Haugwitz pleaded with the empress, pointing out that "the Christian artisans of Prague themselves are clamoring for the return of the Jews."[46] It was the Moravian estates that came out with the blunt request for a revocation of the decree in the talks about the contribution; and Haugwitz was certain that their Bohemian peers would follow suit. Of course Maria Theresa was anxious to keep the negotiations with the estates free from new complications. But she also wanted to avoid the appearance of tolerance as the motive for a repeal. Thus a special commission was set up to investigate the contention that the elimination of Jewish traders had resulted in a rise of the cost of living. Assured on that count, she gave way "solely because the lands have asked for it with such passion."[47] The Jewries of Bohemia and Moravia paid three hundred thousand florins, and in the autumn of 1748 started returning to their homes with permission to reside there for the ten-year duration of the general agreements with the estates. However, as the limitation of these lapsed into oblivion, so did that proviso.

Although Maria Theresa never revived the project—it also had envisaged expulsion from the Austrian lands at one turn of the bitter controversy—her bias did not weaken to her dying day. As late as 1777 she objected in the most vehement language to the migration of a handful of Jews to Vienna.† The disabilities of them all, as their debasement, appeared to her as a just punishment for their refusal to accept the Saviour.

Her adviser on church affairs at this period was the archbishop of Vienna, Count Trautson, who, in Khevenhüller's censorious words, was "more of a politician, and more greatly devoted to the court, than is suitable for a religious leader."[48] His insistence on Biblical rules for day-to-day life made him the object of contumacy among the lower clergy and religious. In a pastoral letter of 1752 he reminded them of the untold harm suffered by Christendom two centuries earlier and the blame that the priesthood had had to bear for the great rift. They had been censured for drawing people's minds to the worship of saints and holy

* In 1743 her proclamation distributed in Neopolitan territory had, among other changes, promised the expulsion of all Jews from that kingdom.

† The Jews had been driven from Vienna in 1669–70, when fear of the Turks drew more than the usual attention to non-Christians within its wall. The quasi-legal repeal of the expulsion decree compelled Jews desirous of settling in Vienna to apply for a *privilegium*, which could be withdrawn at the sovereign's pleasure.

images and to the blessings of pilgrimages and indulgences rather than to the eternal substance of Christ's word—faith, charity, hope. Were not these tendencies apparent again in the pulpits? Miracle-working images were eulogized, while the Saviour Himself was all but forgotten. . . .* Repeatedly the archbishop berated the rural parish priests for spicing their sermons with coarse jokes and irreverent talk about the empress.

"After I have told your Grace that her Imperial Majesty is showering down riches and favors upon the whole priesthood," wrote Williams to Newcastle, "you will be surprised to learn that in general the priests are not her friends. They talk loudly and openly against the government, and this is done in so barefaced a manner as would not be tolerated in the most free government in Europe."[49] The Englishman overrated Maria Theresa's munificence. She had begun dismantling the tax exemptions of prelates and monasteries as early as 1742. The poll tax, decreed early in 1746, imposing an annual payment (of four *kreutzer*) even on servant girls, stipulated a six-hundred-florin obligation for archbishops and prince-bishops. In her Political Testament, so called, Maria Theresa admonished her successors to think of "the common good" in dealing with the clergy. And "as God in His Grace made the Catholic religion flourish . . . and ecclesiastics are numerous and provided for well, it would not be praiseworthy, and indeed highly objectionable, to give them more. They do not need it, and do not, alas, make the right use of what they own. They oppress people. . . ."[50]

But people by and large did not at all applaud that check on royal bounty or what their padres and the mendicant friars, who were all over the countryside, told them about it. Voices that common folk had been taught to listen to in awe joined their chorus of grumblings. "[The empress] is far from being so well loved as she was in the early years of her reign," observed a Prussian functionary who happened to be in Vienna, and "there is a general outcry against all innovations."[51]

Perhaps the most unpopular of these was the government's interference with holiday leisure. Since time immemorial about three score of holy days had been on the calendar. An entire week was set aside for Christmas; Easter was marked by a three-day break in work; and the veneration of local patron saints had swelled the number of the days of leisure. To believe reports from the Circles, unbridled merrymaking at rural holiday feasts had been on the increase ever since the end of the war. The conference, encouraged by reforms in Naples and the em-

---

* In that year a sizable number of Moravian parish priests was engaged in clearing churchyards of "evil spirits" by exhuming the corpses of "witches and warlocks" and burning them with ritual solemnity. An ordinance that was issued in 1755 declared these "exorcisms . . . unlawful unless undertaken by permission from the [secular] authorities." (Ignaz Beidtel, *Geschichte der österreichischen Staatsverwaltung 1740–1848*, I, 40.)

peror's Tuscany, had discussed a change in 1750. "Self-evident!" the empress scrawled in the margin of the minutes. "Letter to pope must not be postponed. Draft by Bartenstein."⁵² The papal breve, issued the following year, abolished twenty holy days; and Maria Theresa added another four.

Enforcing the decree was something else again. Trautson's enthusiasm⁻ for it only served to bring new censure down on the head of the empress. Parish priests openly condemned the "outrage," and such was their language that Maria Theresa had three of these clerics summarily arrested and shipped to a remote abbey. When, on Easter Monday, 1754, the workmen at a building site close to the Hofburg stayed away from work, she demanded their immediate return. Within an hour a crowd had gathered, and its protests grew so violent that she thought it prudent to rescind the order. Now the rioters, flushed with victory, started attacking some shops kept open in compliance with the new law; and the police, who had been hesitant to interfere, could restore order only after a good deal of scuffling. On subsequent "former holidays" mounted military patroled the city, and shopkeepers were forced to keep open for business. (They sabotaged the law by overcharging customers.) To make the new ordinance palatable in the countryside, landowners were enjoined from asking for labor services on "former holidays."

The pontiff had cooperated in the question of holy days after being⁻ persuaded that their profusion put the economy of Maria Theresa's dominions at a disadvantage to that of Protestant countries. Fulfilling her wish also was in accord with his lessened hostility to the court of Vienna. Thanks to Cristiani's skill, the consolidation of its Italian power had proceeded with surprisingly little friction, and Benedict's misgivings as a sovereign were proving unfounded. This changed climate did not, however, impinge on the empress' determination to curtail the rights of the Holy Father in her realm. She blocked the visits of his legates to episcopal sees, modified the right of asylum given by churches, denied the ecclesiastic courts jurisdiction in matrimonial disputes and "deflorationes," and pressing an earlier request for financial accounting on the part of certain religious houses, went so far as to style herself "suprema advocata ecclesiarium."⁵³

Gerhard van Swieten, the doctor who attended Prince Charles's young wife in her hopeless struggle, had gone places since coming to Vienna on her sister's invitation in 1745. Physician-in-waiting to the empress and her family, he also taught at the medical school and held the directorship of the court library. Yet he had met nothing but enmity on the part of his fellow professors at Vienna.

An opportunity to challenge Jesuit control of higher learning was first offered in Prague. Stagnation there had for decades been appalling. The deftness of the Jesuits in dealing with secular authority had emasculated opposition. In 1747 Maria Theresa signed a series of edicts "for the improvement of studies"[54] in Prague. Under the threat of calling in secular teachers, these decrees compelled the faculty of the law school to revise their curriculum. The reform plan for philosophical and divinity studies paid no attention whatever to the rules of the Jesuit order. Although Van Swieten had not drafted those decrees, he was widely blamed for the enforced changes. The following year Rudolph Chotek, who happened to stay at Innsbruck on his own department's business, was ordered to initiate there the reforms being tried out in Prague. The Jesuit faculty protested vehemently and in a pun referred to their university's "deformation."[55] As they appealed to the empress directly about one particular change, and she appeared to waver, Chotek reminded her of her initial resolve and convinced her that the methods of Innsbruck "only serve to further idleness"[56] among students.

Her paramount concern was, of course, Vienna University, whose "lectures surely are of little worth,"[57] but whose privileges were as great as they seemed unassailable. Twice under Charles VI attempts had been made to breach them, only to be repulsed. The shortcomings of higher studies had become glaringly manifest in the public health service, which was staffed by graduates of the medical school. As Van Swieten brought to Maria Theresa's attention, 580 children out of 600 delivered at the municipal hospital within a certain period had perished. The edict of February, 1749, bore Van Swieten's stamp. It reserved to the sovereign the right of appointments to the medical school; and while its faculty would continue to elect the dean from their midst for the traditional one-year tenure, their choice could be vetoed by the government, which would also appoint a person to control him. The first appointee was Van Swieten. But the university was "just not accustomed to obey orders. . . . Rather than participate in the dean's election" under the new proviso, "some of the professors stayed away from the meeting." They had, had they? Maria Theresa answered Van Swieten's complaint. Well, such absentees will "in future . . . find their names stricken [from the roster]."[58] Royal authority was "unconditional," Prague University was informed in 1752, "and therefore includes the power over institutions which, based on handed-down customs, have proved to be harmful."[59] She had advanced this principle to justify the virtual dismantling of the Austro-Bohemian estates; it came in handy as she started wrecking the autonomy of the universities, along with their Jesuit domination.

Maria Theresa's interference with the society's time-honored rule over education did not spring from any hostility toward the Jesuits. Much less did it signify any change in her detestation of religious indifference.

Doctoral candidates had still to confirm by oath their belief in the Immaculate Conception. Physicians were enjoined, under the threat of losing their license, to urge extreme unction on any patient who was "in some danger,"[60] and in fact were at liberty to discontinue treatment if the admonition went unheeded.

Higher learning as such was a matter of no concern to the empress. She could see no merit in the suggestion of a foreign celebrity that she establish an institution on the model of the Académie Française. She wanted her universities to turn out God-fearing and competent medical practitioners, efficient civil servants, knowledgeable judges, and clerics who would be neither obfuscated by superstition nor prone to cast any doubt on the wisdom of her government. Intellectual debate was the last thing she wished for in the lecture halls (or anywhere else, for that matter). As it happened, some of the new teachers were to carry controversy into the divinity school, and a breath of the new legal thought was to touch the budding bureaucrats at the law school.

No law school in Europe, she declared in 1752, must boast scholars of greater eminence than those she would assemble in Vienna. To attract such luminaries she offered them tenure and titles, along with respectable salaries.* After the administration of Vienna University had been transferred to the *Directorium* the teachers became for all practical purposes government employees. While this dependency did not necessarily corrupt those scholars, it tended to breed servility in many of them. The empress was not blinkered to that fact. Once she objected in no uncertain terms to a particularly fawning dedication with which one of those savants had garnished a book of his. She also was careful to preserve the trimmings of autonomy at the university. When Kaunitz asked for precedence at the opening of its new building in the summer of 1755— incidentally, one of the architectural masterpieces of the period—she did not want to hear of such an arrangement, as "the Rector Magnificus . . . is the ranking person there."[61]

Not the least complaint about the Jesuit teachers had been their method of dictating lectures and denying printed texts to the students. Thus, textbooks assumed great importance—and so did censorship. In 1747 Haugwitz had proposed that Jesuits should continue to censure philosophical and theological works. In 1753 Van Swieten offered his own services as censor of philosophical writings and recommended Trautson

---

* Officials were vexed. She was told that big emoluments would turn the *Herren* professors into arrogant idlers. Trautson, who by that time had been given supervisory powers over all theological and philosophical studies, argued that even ten thousand florins per annum would be a good investment if paid to an illustrious savant, who was bound to draw foreign students and their money to Vienna. "I own that I wholeheartedly share the view of the archbishop," the empress minuted. (Arneth, *op. cit.*, IV, 121.) Migration of Austrian students to foreign universities had been curtailed by making it unlawful for them to take a degree abroad.

as censor of divinity books. Adopting these proposals, the empress attached a rider to them: no "general book" must be passed without the approval of a Jesuit scholar. And to forestall any shadow of misconception, she decreed that "no secular, let alone any religious, work must be printed or published . . . without approbation of the *censoribus* and a permission issued in writing."[62] Moreover, a "revising commission" was set up to give the final word; and as its presidency went to a succession of more or less hidebound aristocrats, Van Swieten found himself embroiled in not a few controversies with Maria Theresa. The conflict was to gain momentum—as was her dilemma—when the very existence of the Jesuit order was put in jeopardy in the late 1760's throughout the Catholic world.

Censorship, as the empress saw it, must keep rationalist doctrine at arm's length while giving room to common sense within the framework of revealed truth. It must prevent religious indifference reaching her subjects from foreign parts. It must draw man's mind to the practical tasks of his life. And it must stifle opposition to reform. Maria Theresa never said in so many words that the government must strengthen its hold on thought, as indeed on people's taste. She took it for granted as a goal.*

Nothing looked innocuous or trivial enough to lower her guard against the cynicism she espied in the wake of foreign immorality. Once Van Swieten proposed that a monthly published in Bavaria, and "which ridicules good-humoredly . . . the dialect and other characteristics of the population" be admitted to her dominions. "The world is so frivolous nowadays," she replied, "so little well-meaning, and everything is made sport of and looked upon as a *bagatelle*." No, those "booklets" must not be imported. Van Swieten was bold enough to disagree: had not "sarcasm" since time immemorial helped people grow aware of their own shortcomings, and had not many religious authors themselves made use of "irony and fables" to that end? "I for one have no love for whatever smacks of irony," she declared. "Rather than improve men, it irritates them. It is inconsistent with the love of one's neighbor. Why should people waste their time writing such stuff, or reading it?" Austrian speech, she went on (involuntarily puncturing the myth of her great familiarity with it), did not lend itself to "that kind of light joke," and anyway, some scribblers "might hit on the idea of publishing similar little stories here under the cover of a Bavarian imprint, and that I could not possibly tolerate."[63]

* The Captains of the Circles . . . maintained that a private person, having no access to the files, could not as a rule form a well-founded opinion. . . ." (Beidtel, *op. cit.*, I, 86.)

XIV

Ascendancy of Wenceslas Kaunitz

THE REORGANIZATION of the army had got off to an unauspicious start in 1748. Even enlargement was in jeopardy for three years. Shortage of funds, but also the end to wartime hope for plunder, foiled the regiments' efforts to fill their numbers. New methods of drill, not easily coped with by old soldiers—or green recruits, for that matter—caused an increase in desertion.

In 1751 the central government asked the estates to levy each a certain number of men, even though the "absolute separation of military affairs from the administration of the lands"[1] had been the main incentive for them to sign the ten-year agreements. A solemn promise to the effect that compliance with the request would not constitute a precedent did not mellow their objections; similar pledges had been made in respect to wartime taxation, only to be breached by Haugwitz. The estates, having yielded after lengthy negotiations, plainly showed their distaste for the renewed obligation: foreign deserters, vagrants, and minor felons were delivered as recruits, and much ink was shed to determine which crimes disqualified men for army service. A plan for local militias fared even worse. Although the estates agreed to this "Prussian" scheme, the landowners, jealous of the peasants' working hours, did not cooperate; and the rural population, who had forgotten the local-defense institutions of a much earlier day, tended to make sport of the village drill, and were soon to stay away altogether.

The stillborn project, as many viable ones, had been drawn up by the "Military Committee" set up by the Hofkriegsrat, whose president was still Joseph Harrach. Much as Maria Theresa was looking forward to his resignation, she did not dare force the issue. Apparently she was wary of indiscretion on his part. Upon Frederic Harrach's death she had asked Count Joseph to express her sympathy to the widow, for "I will not send her [a note] myself, as it would only aggravate her grief." And "if the family . . . will gain merit, they may all of them be certain of finding in me not only their mistress, but a mother and friend as well. . . . [Frederic] Harrach had many important, confidential, and highly secret, communications from my own hand in his possession, some about personal matters. I am anxious to keep this fact from everybody except Koch. I rely on you to straighten it out with him."[2] Surely the old man had perused those letters.

His laxity kept paralyzing all attempts to check the Hofkriegsrat's most strong-willed and least reform-minded member, Augustus von Wöber. Originally one of its clerks, he had climbed to a place of influence in the 1730's, thanks to the inertia of Charles VI and Eugene's sinking powers. The Turkish debacle made him a target of popular wrath, being accused of the indiscriminate sale of army commissions for his own profit. Wöber survived the scandal, his power undiminished. A past master of day-to-day solutions and a man addicted to work, he was irreplaceable to the young queen. His dexterity in keeping track of the complex money transactions of the army gave him a key role in grand strategy. No less a man than Haugwitz admired Wöber's accountancy system. For all his power, however, he had not attained the goal of his ambition, an army officer's brevet, and the resentment of the unsoldierly man combined with his pedantry to hinder the proceedings of the Military Committee.

Prince Charles was its chairman. Neipperg, past seventy now, would take his place whenever the prince was in Brussels. Browne was conspicuous through his absence; like Traun before him, the opinionated field marshal had been sent to Transylvania. A man far more easy to get along with, Count Leopold Daun, was the homme de tête. He was the descendant of a family of soldiers and the son of a field marshal highly esteemed by Eugene in the field and as viceroy of Naples. Count Leopold, born in 1705, had seen action first as a boy of thirteen. He served against the Turks, was present at Chotusitz and Prague, and led the advance guard of Lewis Khevenhüller's victorious army. In the Bohemian campaign of 1744 Traun relied heavily on the younger man, who in the following year was promoted to a full general's rank. Many veterans of Rocoux maintained that only Daun's skill had rescued Prince Charles from disaster. He was a generous, soft-spoken man, and his amiable disposition kept him out of the intrigues and the backbitings of his fellow commanders. Married to a daughter of Countess Fuchs, he was known as an exemplary husband—a repute to the taste of the empress. The emperor, who was fond of the other son-in-law of Mme. Fuchs, Count

Adam Losy, the "music director" of the court, thought Daun an agreeable companion as well as a fine soldier. In fact, few men had failed to approve of his appointment to the committee.

Its work was based on the assumption that the training methods of King Frederick's father had been the wellspring of the victories of the son. The drill and firing manuals that Daun set about to compose adopted those Prussian methods. The large-formation peacetime maneuvers that he advocated followed, likewise, the Prussian model. The empress was enthusiastic about that project. Undeterred by the great expenditures involved, she agreed to and pressed for the establishment of permanent army encampments in Hungary and Bohemia. Daun proceeded to draw up a code of tactics. He began to organize regular staffs on the army level—an innovation devised to put to an end the haphazard ways that so often had shaped operational plans and the bickerings that nearly always had bedeviled the revisions in the field of the Hofkriegsrat's orders.

To Maria Theresa's joy, no Frederic Harrach or Kinsky arose among the generals to argue against the reforms or retard their progress. Only Wöber raised objections. Outvoted in a succession of meetings, he offered his resignation in return for a lieutenant field marshal's rank and its perquisites. His elevation, which gave him the "grande entrée" at court, shocked the nobility. Yet it was not the first blow dealt the court's hierarchical order.

"To give the military men new proof of my special affection," read an edict issued in February, 1751, "I have at my pleasure resolved that any officer of my armed forces wearing his uniform may attend court. . . ."[3] This decree did not bridge the social gulf between the aristocrats in higher command and the colonels,* let alone subalterns, from petty-nobility or commoner stock. But it lifted the army officer *qua* army officer high above the common run of Maria Theresa's subjects. It bestowed on him the prestige that his profession (or the insistence on a special code of honor) had never won him. For better or for worse, his "being admissable at court" was to further the formation of an army officers' class. But, unlike Prussia's miltary caste, which grew from one matrix only, that class was destined to cut across the whole social fabric.

The wish of the empress to raise the social status of the military —men paid miserably on the lower echelons—did not betoken egalitarian ideas. Yet the nobility thought so. To their minds the newly established military academy endangered their sons' customary road to higher com-

---

* "Ownership" of a regiment went to men of high birth or, in rare cases, to older officers of extraordinary distinction. The colonel proprietor was free to appoint the commanding colonel; not infrequently money passed hands. From the mid-fifties on the privileges of the former were gradually modified.

mand, a kind of apprenticeship in the field, and seemed to cast doubts on their inborn virtues as leaders of men. Although Maria Theresa, to soothe that irritation, ordered that blue-blooded cadets have segregated living quarters and dining halls at the academy, the aristocracy remained averse to seeing their offspring trained and examined side by side with their social inferiors. Daun, the originator of officers' methodical education, complained about the apparent bias. "It is beyond belief that nobody wants to avail himself of my good graces!"[4] the empress minuted on one of his reports. A prospectus of the academy, distributed to the landowning families through the estates, had little effect. Not until the end of the decade—and the outbreak of a great war—would the arrogant prejudice vanish.

From 1750 Maria Theresa journeyed regularly to the army camps and often followed the maneuvering troops on horseback. No longer riding astride, she succeeded in concealing her corpulence beneath the wide folds of an English habit. Few of the soldiers ever had seen a woman on horseback,* and the empress, who had not of late been spoiled by public ovations, must have relished the joyful surprise of the men ringing out their acclamations. And there was more than parades and fanfare in these visits. She learned at first sight something about the rigors of army life, its austerity, its dullness. Everywhere she asked to be shown the magazines and bakeries. She never would try to make men see glamour in hardships. One of the medals struck in her honor called her *"mater castrorum"*; as epithets given to royalty went, she was not entirely undeserving of the title of the "army camps' mother."

⌣ Sentimentality did not enter her concern with the rank and file. She insisted on the necessity of corporal punishment. Overriding contrary advice, she decided that the lash was the only adequate penalty for excesses in the countryside. "Innocent men will have no cause for complaints. . . . I am the mother of my lands, and all [of my subjects] are equally close to my heart provided each stays within the limits drawn him."[5] At the same time, she impressed on officers that "soldiers must not be treated as if they were slaves"—"the greater the freedom they are given, the more trustworthy will they become"[6]—and rescinded an old regulation that compelled regimental commanders to put up a bond for men granted a furlough.

Soldiers were paid with regularity from the mid-fifties on. They found

*Khevenhüller disapproved thoroughly of the fad the sovereign had started in Vienna. "Ever since our gracious mistress began to show her great passion for horseback riding, our womenfolk, including some elderly ladies, have developed a craze for following her example. . . . In general, they do so under the pretext of salubrious exercise. But did they ever think of it before? No. . . . In the beginning, street urchins would gape at the extraordinary sight of such an amazon, and run after her." (Podewils, *op. cit.*, 51, note.)

their reputation improving in step with the lessening of the regiments' demands on the peasant. As the musketeers started to grasp the new firing instructions, a feeling of self-reliance came to the fore. The new, uniform clothing, while bothersome in the beginning, tended to breed in the soldier a special vanity which often did duty for genuine professional pride. To all appearances, the enlisted men were more greatly devoted than before to the subalterns, whose social advancement seemed to cast a glimmer of respectability on the ranks.

In one instance the effort to create a disciplined body of fighting men led to a bizzare event. The "Military Frontiersmen" of southern Croatia boasted a tradition going back to the middle of the sixteenth century. Originally they constituted a defense force against Turkish raids (and also a *cordon sanitaire* against the plague endemic in certain parts of Turkey). As the Turks posed less and less of a peril, the Hungarian nobility pressed the dissolution of the frontier corps. Charles VI enlarged their number.* In lieu of pay, the frontiersman was given the hereditary tenancy of a patch of crown land, and each of these pocket fiefs furnished an able-bodied man to the corps. Prior to 1741 it had not as a rule been employed outside its native region. The frontiersmen had been the fiercest of irregulars in Maria Theresa's campaigns. Their sharp-shooting and ambushing exploits were legendary thoughout Europe. So was their ruthlessness. Attempts to tame them without impeding their spirit had proved futile even after regular-army officers were put in command of the battalions in which they were reorganized. Among the measures devised after the war to turn them into modern soldiers, the order to exchange their semi-Oriental garb against uniforms surely was not the most drastic. But the frontiersmen saw in it another token of Vienna's determination to crush their group independence. The empress, ill-advised by Saxe-Hildburghausen, did not appreciate the extent of their vexation until it burst out in one particular valley, whose Orthodox population had long been harassed in their worship. A hastily assembled force was marched there but had to withdraw before the savagery of the muti-neers. As rumors about impending changes in Turkish policies made it imperative to prevent the rebellion from spreading farther, Maria Theresa, in the teeth of Hungarian protests, received a deputation of the insurgents, who submitted a list of their grievances. Then she sent no less a person than Neipperg to the frontier, while a small army took up positions at its northern border. In return for his pledge to spare the frontier a "foreign" occupation, the rebels turned some of their leaders

---

* In the wake of Hungary's liberation the army had established a similar "frontier" along the entire southern border of Hungary proper. Its semiautonomous regime of peasant settlers, including many runaway serfs, was an eyesore to the Magyar nobles. Correspondingly, it was coddled by the Vienna authorities.

over to him as hostages. Though he had them hanged summarily, the revolt did not regain momentum. As Neipperg began to redress some of the wrongs the frontiersmen had aired in Vienna, these warriors, no less naïve for all of their cruelty in battle, grew proud of their special relationship to the queen. They accepted a good many changes and finally also donned regulation uniforms.

Withal, the army was still deficient in numbers by the time Kaunitz began flexing his muscles. It was far from being ready for an emergency. There was none in the offing. The instructions received by Count George Starhemberg, who in October, 1753, was posted in Paris, did not carry a breath of the New System. He was to inform the French that the Christian conscience of the empress-queen enjoined her from considering any move that might conceivably lead to bloodshed. He had better not mention King Frederick at all. Should any of the French ministers bring up his name, the ambassador might remind them of the Prussian's notorious fickleness as an ally. For the rest, "truthfulness, probity, an equable demeanor, fairness, and avoidance of ambiguities"[7] were the means to gain the confidence of the Most Christian King.

Kaunitz' draft no doubt gratified Maria Theresa. She would have been surprised, as well as indignant, could she have read the directives of the French court for its new ambassador to Vienna. Austria and Britain, he was told, "are constantly occupied with inventing pretexts for attacking the king of Prussia. . . ."[8] Sanguine as she had been in 1749 as Kaunitz first showed her the vistas the New System would open, she had long come to regard them as remote. She did not probe her chancellor's view on their remoteness.

He made it easy for her to look upon him (as Williams suggested she did) as "her handiwork . . . her creature,"[9] a man trained under her own eyes by her own directions. "If Your Majesty will give me the slightest hint of your disapproving my ideas," he would write, "I will dispatch them immediately to eternal oblivion."[10] Yet no shadow of servility tainted the gravity of Wenceslas Kaunitz. His affectations should have annoyed Maria Theresa, who herself was so natural of manner. His unabashed rationalism seemed made to shock her, and she might well have recoiled from his concept of a "political algebra," which left no room for the will of the Almighty. But Kaunitz' serenity, or the pose of it, enthralled her, as did his patience—a quality she herself had not an ounce of. His singleness of purpose, which yet was alert to a hundred different stratagems, filled her with wonder.

Starhemberg was given little opportunity to put the empress' high-minded instructions to the test in Versailles. He was treated with indifference. Only Mme. de Pompadour received him kindly. Shortly before

Kaunitz' departure from France she had asked him to come to the assistance of Mme. de Marsan, a close friend of hers and the governess of the king's children. Through an accord between Francis' father and the descendants of *his* father's natural son, that lady had fallen heir to vast estates in Belgium, only to find her claim contested by the authorities, who maintained that the properties had reverted to the crown. Mme. de Marsan refused to abide by any decision of a Belgian court. Now, in a letter that Starhemberg delivered to the royal mistress, Kaunitz proposed that she change the mind of Mme. de Marsan and promised indemnification should the law courts decide against her. His thoughtfulness pleased Mme. de Pompadour; and inasmuch as his pledge involved the empress herself, it could not fail to flatter the marquise.

Seen from Kaunitz' vantage, her appreciative sentiments turned out to be sterile. Although "the portfolios were distributed by Mme. de Pompadour"[11] when Louis XV reconstructed his cabinet in July, 1754 (thus Starhemberg reported), two of Austria's inveterate enemies, Belle-Isle and the younger D'Argenson, were in office again. There was "no hope that an understanding, or any genuine friendship, can ever be established between the courts of Vienna and Versailles, however far the former might go in the pursuit of that goal."[12]

The colonial conflict had not been resolved at Aix-la-Chapelle, and the founding of the Ohio Company had stung the French into action.* They assumed that the outbreak of large-scale hostilities overseas was but a matter of time and did not doubt but that repercussions on the Continent would find Maria Theresa on the side of the British despite their present disagreements. The war party at Versailles welcomed the prospect, looking forward to the seizure of Belgium, that never-plucked fruit of the victories of the late De Saxe. And the surprising consolidation of Habsburg power in Italy disturbed even men who were not avid for revenge and conquest.

In Lombardy the uncompromising rigor of the punishment inflicted on some conspiring nobles in 1746† had not been forgotten by any means. But heavy taxes, rather than hurt pride, had been the most burning issue in the province. Cristiani, whittling down papal resistance to the taxation of church lands, took some of the wind out of the opposition's sails. At the same time he stilled Sardinia's displeasure about Vienna's new Spanish treaty; in fact, Charles Emmanuel took a fancy to the empress' lively emissary on his visits. And capping these achievements, Cristiani had secured for Maria Theresa the virtual pos-

* Washington had been forced to surrender at Great Meadows some weeks before Starhemberg sent his pessimistic report.
† One of them, despite Cristiani's plea for mercy, had been executed on a public square in Milan.

session of an entire duchy. Here, at long last, was a tangible piece of the *dédommagement* she never had ceased talking about. No matter how small the territory, its acquisition was bound to raise the prestige of her house on the peninsula

This is what had happened. Francis III of Modena was bored in his humdrum capital city. A pleasure-seeking man, he had no bent for affairs. Uncertainty about the succession disquieted his ministers and impaired the loyalty of his subjects. He had fallen out with Prince Hercules, his only son, who, himself no mean pleasure-seeker, had banished his wife from his presence. Unless one chose to bank on her premature death and a second marriage of Hercules, the only child of the estranged couple, Maria Beatrice d'Este, was the last sprig of the ancient dynasty. Cristiani went to work by prompting the empress to ply the duke with promises of honors and pecuniary advantages, and step by step prevailed upon him to exclude Hercules from the succession and pledge Beatrice's hand to the emperor's third son, Peter Leopold. The princess was three years old, the archduke six. But no thought of the tender age of the "personages involved" presented itself to the mind of the boy's mother. The duke, recalling a dynastic quirk that made George II the head of his own house, submitted the project to him; and the king blessed the match, and sealing Modena's fate as a Habsburg adjunct, removed it from the influence of his French adversary. The emperor created Cristiani a count.*

The Modena compact gave a new weapon to the anti-Austrian faction at Versailles. Whether Mme. de Pompadour did anything to counter that clique in 1753 and into the following year—this has remained a question to tease us. Starhemberg did not in those months wait on her frequently; there was talk of another lady who was likely to replace the marquise in the favor of the king. The ambassador had some talks with Rouillé, the new foreign minister, and came to think of him as a timorous man.

As the New System appeared to be lost on the becalmed sea of French listlessness, Kaunitz veered his boat to sail it to the windward. He informed the conference of his plan for an "innocent defensive alliance" with Britain, Hanover, Saxony, and Russia. While the czarina was itching for an attack on Frederick, Kaunitz of course knew that such a move would be doomed without British money. Count Charles Colloredo, the new ambassador to the court of St. James's (and the imperial vice-chancellor's younger brother), had no encouraging news. The note he received, late in July, 1754, over the signature of the empress was designed to give new impetus to an appeal to the British.

---

* Certain "dark spots" in Princess Beatrice's maternal extraction kept worrying Khevenhüller, who also looked with a jaundiced eye on the rise of a lawyer's son to what for all practical purposes were viceregal powers in the Italian dominions.

Archduke Joseph, the heir,
at eight or nine years of age

"Mimi," Maria Theresa's
favorite daughter
at nine years

Count Wenceslas Kaunitz

"Every nation is anxious to avoid needless expenditures in peacetime [it read] and keep its finances in good order. . . . But illusions should vanish. Reasonable men must not be blind to undeniable danger. . . . Is it not common knowledge that we are the only ally England can count on? The mighty crown of France entertains the closest relations with Prussia, Sweden, the armed princes of the Empire, and the Sublime Porte. Should war break out, the French will try to overrun Belgium, blockade the British in their island, subdue the all but defenseless Dutch republic . . . [and] march an army into Westphalia to keep the whole of Germany, and above all, Hanover, in an iron grip." Had His Britannic Majesty forgotten the Jacobite revolt? Colloredo must alert him to a greater peril, for "with the Low Countries lost, and England cut off from any assistance from the Continent," the French would carry the torch of war into the island itself, and enslave its nation. . . ." While it was true that the Russian court asked for too much, "and does not always present its demands in the proper manner," it was equally true "the English court . . . should grant substantial subsidies to the czarina."[13] Nothing was said about Prussia's containment in this communication.

At about the time Colloredo must have perused it, the imperial couple were sojourning with Batthyány on his Bohemian estate. Ostensibly the empress traveled to Prague to lay the foundation stone for a "ladies' abbey"* and visit an army invalids' home whose construction had taken nearly two decades. The actual motive for the midsummer trip was her desire to draw the Bohemian aristocracy still closer to herself.

A number of German princes came to pay their court to Francis. There also arrived Seckendorf, the old deserter and quondam generalissimo of Charles Albert, and the archbishop of Prague, who had crowned him at St. Vitus's. Maria Theresa was most gracious to both and even invited Seckendorf to accompany her and her consort as they went to watch the troops maneuvering nearby under the direction of Browne. (Recalled from Transylvania some months before, the field marshal was in command of all troops in Bohemia.)

On August 21 Princess Charlotte, who was on her way to Belgium, joined the swarm of Batthyány's house guests. Having never felt at home in Vienna, she had of late also come to resent the precedence that her little nieces had over her; and much as Francis besought her to stay on, she had decided to leave Vienna for good. As the party set out for Prague, the emperor's melancholy silence was commented on widely. Nor, apparently, had the *battues* in Batthyány's preserves afforded him

* Such semireligious houses for unmarried and widowed noblewomen had existed for a long time in Belgium and some Rhenish principalities.

the right pleasure. After entering Prague, he withdrew to the castle while his wife and sister drove through the gaily lit streets.

"Audiences started at six o'clock in the morning" for the empress. In the course of the following ten days she "visited the Jesuits' House, and every single convent, and said her prayers at the tomb of St. John of Nepomuk, Bohemia's martyred saint, whose remains had been lifted from their repose to offer the queen a relic."[14] She also was present at the consecration of the chapel that she had vowed in commemoration of the discovery of a cross-shaped piece of wood in 1741 in the course of defense constructions. At night the nobility entertained the monarchs. The rehabilitated archbishop offered a concert, for which King Frederick had sent him his musicians from Berlin. The university students staged a Latin drama "which was less tedious than such affairs usually are,"[15] and Maria Theresa sat through the entire performance, no doubt to the satisfaction of the Jesuit teachers, who still smarted under the indignity of the reform. Francis managed to divide the daytime hours between pilgrimages to local shrines and shooting in the woods around Prague. He did not, moreover, neglect to visit two royal domains he held as surety for one of the loans granted the treasury during the war.

On September 3 the court heard mass at the sepulcher of St. John's. "Tears stood in the eyes of both the empress and Princess Charlotte,"[16] who set out on her journey immediately after service, escorted by Quinquin Esterhazy and Ogara, the pleasant grand master of her household. Francis' spirits remained subdued on the first lap of the return trip. Incessant rains turned the roads almost impassable. And Archduke Joseph had been taken ill in Schönbrunn.

Thirteen years old by now, he was a handsome boy, although narrow of chest. His longish face but rarely broke into a smile. His teachers were still at a loss to keep his undivided attention and to evade irrelevant questions on his part. Although the number of facts they forced on him overtaxed the strength of the prince, these cramming methods had begun to train his memory well. He spoke French fluently, knew how to express himself in Italian, and even had acquired a smattering of "la langue esclavone," which he was taught "because of the close and true friendship between the empress and Her Russian Majesty."[17] To judge by his writing style as a grown-up, he was also, unlike his mother, being trained well in using his native German. It was said that he had a good head for mathematics. Natural sciences, the only field of learning that attracted his father, "have their place among other pastimes."[18] In March, 1752, the archduke had been led to First Communion ("as the nuncio opened the ciborium, he dropped one of the wafers, and many Viennese thought that this boded ill for the future well-being of the archduke").[19] In the course of Holy Week the following year the emperor took him to eighteen different churches.

The fever with which the archduke had come down could not but raise the fear of smallpox. On September 12 Joseph's two eldest sisters were brought to Hollitsch—the emperor's Moravian hunting lodge, where the party had interrupted their progress—along with their nine-year-old brother Charles, an impish child, no less inattentive to studies than the firstborn, and the favored son of the empress. Better news from Joseph's sickbed and lovely weather lifted Francis from his brown study. The arrival of a group of young courtiers put him in excellent humor. He had a great deal of fun dragging Khevenhüller through the forests for hours on end. "The empress spent the forenoons at her desk, reading and minuting."[20]

From Hollitsch the company traveled to Schlosshof, Eugene's famous *plaisance* on the Hungarian border, of which his heiress, parting ways with her husband, had made him a gift. Saxe-Hildburghausen had made extravagant preparations. "After the mid-day meal the large party walked, through the park, toward the open-air theater, behind which the plain could be seen stretching to the hills of Pressburg. The overture to *Il vero imaggio*, composed by Bonno to Metastasio's lyrics, welcomed the visitors. . . . The closing duet, sung by Mmes. Tesi-Tramontani and Heinisch, was given an echo by a mixed chorus which, coming from the woods, repeated the aria's concluding words, '*Tutt' in omaggio il cuor!*' At night another drama by Metastasio was performed. . . . The second day, a great shooting match took place on the banks of the River March. A two-story structure, on nine arches, had been built on the farther shore, and there were rifle ranges, decked out with foliage and flags, on both shores and in mid-stream, connected by bridges. The river was crowded with small barges, and a splendidly decorated ship modeled after [Venice's] *Bucintoro* brought Their Majesties to the first range, where beaters had driven deer and other game down to the water. . . . At night, *Le Cinesi* by Metastasio and Gluck. . . .* The sets were in Chinese style, the lighting magnificent. . . . Later there was dancing in the courtyard, which was flooded by light. . . . A supper ended the pleasurable evening. The next morning, we strolled through the vineyards, shot partridges and hares. . . . In the afternoon, a water carrousel was executed on the great pond in whose center a platform had been erected. Owls, bears, and wolves had been chained to rocks jutting out of the water, and these beasts accompanied the music with horrible noises. Two teams of four boats each, manned by gentlemen and rowers in harlequins' costumes . . . advanced on each other and tried to fend off

* Gluck had stayed in Vienna for some months in 1748 and returned some years later. In 1754 he became conductor of the court theater, and a number of his comic operas and concert pieces were performed there. After the première of *Il rè pastore* (December 8, 1756) Khevenhüller noted that "the music of Signor Gluck, who recently has been made *cavaliere dello sperone d'oro* [by the pope] met with no special applause."

the opponents by hosing them. . . . In the end a floating isle with flower beds and allegorical decor approached the place where Their Majesties were sitting. Some of the 'gardeners' stepped ashore to invite the illustrious couple, and boys and girls in fishermen's garb asked its children to try their luck. . . . At night there was target shooting indoors, and good marksmen were rewarded by bursts of fireworks."[21]

Archduke Joseph, having recuperated, arrived at Schlosshof the next day in time to see the great pageant. The first float, "preceded by heralds, warriors, arm-bearers, and trumpeters, and drawn by white oxen with gilded horns and wreaths around the neck, carried a load of wine casks, and Silenus and Bacchus atop them. Musicians disguised as satyrs, and girls appearing as nymphs, were walking behind. . . . Another float represented a ship, musicians playing below, and the sides hung all over with fowl, and loaves of cheese and bread. Three hundred peasants in fancy dress followed. . . ."[22]

Maria Theresa had had more than her fill of spectacles as the days of Schlosshof came to their end. Khevenhüller observed somewhat sourly that "our host had been doing his best to entertain us."[23] Overwhelmed by debts, Saxe-Hildburghausen had arranged the whole affair with an eye to selling the property. The empress bought it some months later and presented it to her husband, who at once set about to embellish its grounds, stock its ponds with carp and pike, and replenish the vast game preserves.

He felt lonesome in Vienna. Gone were the hours he used to while away with his sister. The loyal Pfütschner had died; and in January, 1755, the decease of Mme. Fuchs destroyed the routine of Francis. It had been his custom to call, in the late afternoon, on the old countess, the confidante of his wooing days, and listen to her and her daughters' small talk or exchange stage gossip with her son-in-law Losy. Her death also robbed the emperor of the only person who "knew how to restore harmony"[24] between him and his increasingly irascible Theresa.* His loneliness turned Francis restless during this winter. But his uneasiness did not stem only from boredom. Simple as his reasoning was, he could see only too well that his wife's budding dependence on Kaunitz was different in kind from her reliance on a Haugwitz or a Cristiani. The New System might be an unworkable scheme, but its apparent failure did not diminish her admiration for its author. Francis had never dreamed of dominating her mind; Kaunitz' ascendancy over it irritated him more and more. And Kaunitz' airs rubbed him the wrong way.

The chancellor was careful to ignore what he divined of these feelings, and masking his superciliousness, kept the emperor abreast of for-

* They paid an unprecedented honor to the countess by having her remains entombed in the Habsburg crypt—a sensation among townsfolk.

eign affairs by direct communications. Francis may have perused some of these memoranda. More of them, he presumably turned over to Colloredo. In the autumn of 1756, at the height of the great crisis, it would be said at home and abroad that he had been ignorant of what his wife and Kaunitz had been up to. There was a kernel of truth in that story. Surely Francis was not privy to the ultimate goal of Kaunitz' design. But neither did Maria Theresa grasp the extent of the plans of Wenceslas Kaunitz, in whose fantasies Prussia's dismemberment was only the first step toward the resurrection of Habsburg greatness. Once the Prussian menace had been disposed of with the help of the French, the Arch House must cast them off, resume its hallowed imperial duty of holding their power in check, and at the same time shoulder again its own storied mission as Christendom's bulwark against the infidel.

The slow decline of Ottoman strength was not visible from the vantage of Vienna. A decade and a half of peace with the Porte had not sufficed to undo the nightmare of Turkish aggression. Even though Starhemberg's original instructions called the aged sultan a man whose "love of peace . . . will not allow [French] intrigues to draw him into their net,"[25] his death some months later revived the old fears. They grew more poignant still as it became known that Frederick had sent a special envoy to the new ruler in Constantinople.

At the same time, her allies more and more puzzled Maria Theresa. She could make no sense of Newcastle's determination, reiterated over and over again, to "preserve and maintain the old alliance and system"[26] on the one hand, and the pressure brought to bear upon her in Belgian affairs on the other. New tariff regulations introduced in that province, on Kaunitz' advice, had envenomed that question. The Maritime Powers contended that Belgium, "conquered with their blood and treasure, [had been] delivered to the House of Austria as a deposit, on the condition of defending those territories against the French; that, according to the principles of the grand alliance, the natives were debarred from the exercise of their trade, and the sovereign had no right to extend their commercial privileges. Those countries formed the only cement of the connection between the House of Austria and the Maritime Powers; and by breach of the Barrier Treaty that cement would be dissolved."[27] Even while the Vienna court was exposed to such threats, it found itself still appealed to as the ally of old against the Bourbons. The "disagreements that have become increasingly evident between the London cabinet and the French court *ratione* their establishments in America"[28] were impressed once again on Kaunitz in March, 1755. As an inquiry in France about the empress' intentions closer to home in case of open war with Britain had produced no conclusive reply, Kaunitz suggested that the empress offer herself as a mediator in the "American squabbles." In

April he warned her that she must under no circumstances split the armed forces. Five weeks later he made Maria Theresa pledge twenty thousand troops for the defense of Belgium. In June the conference, on his motion, declared that "the conflict over the American colonies is a matter of indifference to the House of Austria."[29] Keith did not tire of urging Vienna to prepare for operations against France. Late in July he hinted at his government's expectations to secure the neutrality of King Frederick.

For the first time since Kaunitz had moved into the chancellery his self-assurance failed to sweep the empress. Bartenstein was asked to offer his view; the reserve with which the old man had been watching the virtuoso performance of his *de facto* successor might temper his own anti-English bias. Maria Theresa's final words in the conference meeting of August 16 reflected Bartenstein's opinion. Prudence, she said, "always recommends the lesser evil. Hence, to sit tight in the war, which no longer seems avoidable . . . and leave Belgium to her fate, will be preferable to risking perdition by participating as an auxiliary, and weakening our strength."[30] Koch, in a letter to Christiani, put it more clearly: a campaign "of that kind could only result in a total exhaustion of manpower and funds . . . [and] would incapacitate the monarchy, for many years to come, to tackle its most dangerous, its mortal enemy."[31]

"Sitting tight" in the likely war was one thing; inactivity was another. "If the Arch House is to prevail, Prussia has to be knocked down!"[32] Thus Kaunitz had written in March, 1749. Thus he said, on August 21, 1755, in a conference meeting whose delicate nature the participants recognized, even as it was coming to order, by the decision to keep no minutes.

On adjournment Maria Theresa with her own hand copied Kaunitz' draft of a document to be sent to Starhemberg, attached to new instructions. "Upon my honor as empress and queen [she wrote] I pledge my word that nothing will ever be divulged of the propositions Count Starhemberg will submit to the Most Christian King in my name. Whether the parley bears fruit or does not, the deepest silence will be kept about it forever, provided, to be sure, the Most Christian King delivers the same declaration and pledge."[33]

Also in the ambassador's pouch was a letter from Kaunitz to Mme. de Pompadour, whose "correct address is unknown to me," and would Starhemberg "please put the address on the missive"—in case, that was, he decided on her, in preference to Prince Conti, as the intermediary to Louis XV. "Madame, I often felt the desire to remember me to your memory [Kaunitz wrote]. Judging by what I know of your feelings, the occasion that now presents itself cannot possibly displease you. Count Starhemberg has to impart to the king matters of momentous importance. Their nature is such that none but a person His Most Christian Majesty honors with his unqualified trust can deal with them. I feel that our proposals will not make you rue the pains taken in asking the king to assign someone to negotiate with us."[34]

In offering Starhemberg the choice between Conti and the marquise for the mission, the chancellor may well have intended to buffet Maria Theresa's shock at getting involved with the sinful woman. If such was his concern, he need not have worried. When the ambassador reported, somewhat sheepishly, that he had called upon the marquise, the empress wrote him: "I by no means disapprove of your having chosen . . . la Pompadour, who enjoys the king's maximum confidence. If one had passed her over, she might well have done the maximum harm."[35]

XV

"Try to Amuse Your Husband..."

THE ONLY VOICE RAISED against Kaunitz' hazardous step had been Colloredo's. He submitted that secrets had their way of leaking out in the French court and that the King of Prussia might get wind of Her Majesty's proposals. Surely her army was not ready for war. Kaunitz, who could not help assuming that the emperor shared the cautious view of Colloredo, nevertheless brushed it aside.

Starhemberg's initial success appeared to vindicate the chancellor. It so happened that some men in the French cabinet—which was nearly unanimous in anti-Austrian feelings—were hostile to Mme. de Pompadour. No longer the king's mistress, she was anxious to consolidate her power as his indispensable friend and more suspicious than ever of threats to her position. She looked at Starhemberg's overtures as a lever for eliminating her enemies. This, rather than vanity at her being approached by Maria Theresa's envoy, seems to have prejudiced the marquise in favor of his confidential message. She presently informed the king, and playing on his fancy for being his own premier, persuaded him that Starhemberg ought to be given a hearing. She also recommended the man he should be allowed to talk to.

The abbé de Bernis was one of her oldest and most pliable friends. Four years earlier she had procured him the ambassadorial post at Venice. His present attempts to be sent to Madrid were running into objections at the foreign ministry, which had no high opinion of him. His very guilelessness, however, made him, to Louis's mind, a good choice as the recipient of what looked like quixotic news.

Bernis met Starhemberg, in Mme. de Pompadour's presence, in a bowered pavilion on the grounds of one of her country estates, and the very place where she used to receive the king in the years of his amorous ardor. Its pentagonal hall, adorned with a statue of Love in those days, now boasted a chaste marble statue of Friendship.

We may assume that Bernis's credentials complied with Maria Theresa's request for a pledge of secrecy from the hand of the king. Yet Starhemberg followed Kaunitz' instruction not to relinquish his letter. He read it to the abbé and allowed him to take notes. An expression of sympathy on the empress' part for France opened the communication: the setbacks suffered in America were a matter of deep regret to her. Even though she must live up to her obligations toward the Maritime Powers, she expected the Most Christian King to appreciate the defensive nature of her treaties with them. Moreover, she had reason to assume that the British, those treaties notwithstanding, aimed at weakening her house, as well as the house of Bourbon—in other words, the Catholic cause—with the help of the Protestant Prussian.

Kaunitz was not wide of the mark in blaming London's coolness, partly, on the religious sentiments of public opinion. He could not foresee that the religious concern he put into his sovereign's mouth would have a special appeal to the marquise. Even though she had abandoned her sinful life, the priests at court, intent upon seeing her depart from it altogether, still denied her the sacraments. Whatever the sincerity of her faith, she could not but love visualizing herself as an instrument of policies that aimed at strengthening Catholic power.

To foster a reconciliation with the house of Bourbon for the sake of the right faith, as well as of peace, the empress-queen—so Kaunitz' letter ran on—would not recoil from great sacrifices. She would offer Don Philip a slice of her Belgium in exchange for Parma, and indeed agree to a French occupation of two specified Belgian ports upon the signing of a treaty that assured her of the king's neutrality in an Austro-Prussian conflict. The proffered Belgian barter attracted Bernis on the spot. Visiting Parma from Venice, he had struck up a friendship with the duchess and learned of her passionate desire for a more glamorous place in the world.

Bernis's account did not carry away the king. Although loath to give up the Parmese foothold of Bourbon power, he was neither contemptuous of the advancement held out to his favorite daughter nor blind to the advantage of entrenching himself on the Belgian coast; for all practical purposes, he was at war with George II, and some two hundred French ships were in the hands of the British. Louis could hope to widen the rift he knew existed between Vienna and London and deprive his great enemy of his "Continental soldier." Moreover, he was not insensitive to the image of a Catholic coalition. He had never disliked, and often admired, Maria Theresa, and Frederick's caustic remarks on life at

Versailles had annoyed him often enough. True, and true again. But the Prussian was his only major ally—the treaty was not due to expire for another year—and he was not prepared to risk isolation. Thus the message Bernis handed to Starhemberg after two more meetings did not go past the statement that the Most Christian King hoped for lasting peace with the house of Habsburg.

The ambassador got new directives from Vienna. They appeared to withdraw the Belgian offer, and at any event shifted the initiative to the French.

What seemed to be a windfall had come Kaunitz' way in the last days of December. The subsidy treaty with Russia, which the Vienna court had urged on the British government for so long, had been signed in St. Petersburg by Williams. As events were to prove, Newcastle, by having "a strong Russian army on the frontiers of the king of Prussia's country,"[1] only followed his old idea of forcing Frederick, as he could not draw him, into the "Old System." Kaunitz, however, saw his anti-Prussian coalition taking shape. He increased the pressure on France.

Now Bernis, warming up to his role, asked for his king's permission to draft an Austrian treaty. Mme. de Pompadour saw his handiwork before Louis perused and approved it. Its contents—in effect, a mutual guarantee of the two dynasties' European possessions—fell disappointingly short of Maria Theresa's expectations. But, as Kaunitz was to recall, "this first period of the negotiations was marked by suspicions, doubts, irresolution, and agonizing suspense. . . . We had to convince a great power that its entire policy, as practiced theretofore, contradicted its true interests. We had to prove [to France] that the means she considered the only feasible way of extricating herself from her English troubles, did not serve the purpose, and that she was taking the wrong path in continuing to support the king of Prussia as the linchpin of her alliances. . . . Providence alone could inspire, guide, and crown with success that work. . . ."[2] Providence and Mme. de Pompadour's ambition? It would seem so. Late in October—the empress was about to go into confinement—Kaunitz had better news from Starhemberg. The French king had appointed a "secret committee" to discuss a *rapprochement* with Vienna, and neither Belle-Isle nor D'Argenson, the minister of war, belonged to that body. Rouillé was its spokesman.

Maria Theresa was delivered of a daughter on November 3, and at noon the following day the princess was christened, Archduke Joseph and Archduchess Marianne acting as proxies for the godparents, the King and Queen of Portugal. The newborn, destined to enter history as the most storied victim of the New System, was named Maria Antonia. As the mother was not feeling well at all, the customary *Hervorgang* was postponed until November 14, and the public, contrary to tradition, not admitted to the church. Robbed of the spectacle, the Viennese once again engaged in gloomy talk about the portents of a royal birth: on its eve, All Saints' Day, an earthquake had struck the capital city of Maria Antonia's godparents, reducing it to a heap of rubble, and some ten thousand people, as they were worshiping God and His saints, had been buried beneath the collapsing structures of Lisbon's churches. The Jesuits in Vienna, as elsewhere, discouraged speculations about the "reasonless" catastrophe. To believe them, as did Maria Theresa, it was a manifestation of the wrath of the Almighty at the spreading sinfulness of the world. When in January some tremors were felt as close to Vienna as Munich, the empress "set aside two days for fasting and prayers . . . to thank God for having spared her lands, and beseech Him to protect them," and forbade "all spectacles and masquerades, as such affairs would not be in accord with our spirit of penitence."[3]

Originating in London, the first rumblings of another kind of convulsion were felt in those weeks.

So long as Frederick knew that the czarina's coffers were empty, neither her bellicose talk nor her friendship with Maria Theresa had been disturbing his peace of mind. The subsidy agreement with Britain threw him into near panic, and he rashly offered the British his guarantee of Hanover's borders. Believing that nothing on earth could alter the enmity between the houses of Habsburg and Bourbon, he gave scant thought to the impact his offer might have on the court of Versailles.

Newcastle jumped at the Prussian proposition—he probably had counted on it—and the convention was concluded at Westminster on January 20. It obligated the signatories to act in concert if foreign troops should ever imperil Hanover. As it was, the French had suggested to Frederick that he seize the electorate; and after he rebuffed that "invitation" with a show of outraged morality, they began contemplating an invasion themselves and even raised the question of passage for their troops through imperial territory. "It is beyond belief [Maria Theresa promptly advised Starhemberg] that His Majesty, and the premier prince of the Empire [she herself] should be expected to condone its invasion by a French army. . . . Suppose we brought ourselves to act in this manner against law and propriety, would not France be justified in forming the worst possible opinion about our good faith, and in mistrusting whatever pledges we might give in the future?"[4] According to Kaunitz, "Their Majesties in the delicacy of their judgment" were not even certain of the propriety of continuing negotiations with France. However, he would use all of his persuasion, and "if the French court were as candid as is Vienna's," he could see "the most pleasant vistas for both."[5] In a less cryptic vein the chancellor added: "I have been highly flattered by the missive of the marquise. Please assure her of this sentiment, as of my devotion and respect. . . . I would be very grateful indeed, if, recalling her promise, she could send me a likeness of the most lovable woman. I have been waiting impatiently for it these three years."[6] It was not unknown in Vienna that Frederick's envoy at Versailles was trying to make himself agreeable to the marquise.*

While Kaunitz thus added deliberately to the confusion in the "secret committee" of Louis XV, a quixotic event was shaking his own court, and he may have welcomed its preoccupation with that scandal. The wife of the Spanish ambassador had refused to kiss the hands of Their Majesties, and the court of Madrid—"whose amity we can ill afford to lose, considering the present crisis in Europe"[7]—supported the proud lady. Her attitude, if condoned, would be "an enormous blow to the praeminentia Caesaris,"[8] Khevenhüller noted, and Rudolph Colloredo was appalled. Kaunitz, having taken his time, worked out a solution—no foreign dignitary would henceforth be allowed to kiss hands—and Ulfeld drafted a "special protocol" embodying the change in protocol.

Maria Theresa bore him no ill will for having extorted a fortune from her. After the Spanish affair was resolved the imperial couple dined at Ulfeld's new townhouse, which he had built and was still decorating out of those moneys. In the same January week they had dinner in the "palace of the Directorium," where Haugwitz showed them the spacious offices and his own apartments, "which are magnifiques." They also saw "the new chapel, which is panelled all over with marble and gold. . . . There was a game of faro after the meal [and then] the eleven-year-old daughter of the host and some other young ladies and gentlemen performed a little comedy. . . . It lasted over an hour."[9]

Back in March, 1755, Maria Theresa had been most impatient when some of the younger courtiers had mentioned a new plan for theatricals in Schönbrunn. "Everybody thinks of nothing but amusements and dances," the Prussian ambassador, Von Klinggräff, reported her as bursting out, "while my own head is crowded by so many different problems, and all of them are far from amusing!"[10] Thoughts of the new sultan in Constantinople and of rebellious Croatia had preoccupied her at that time. The crisis of spring, 1756, does not seem to have soured her taste for social pastimes.

As early as January 8 Starhemberg had related rumors of an Anglo-Prussian understanding. Maria Theresa was not in need of rumors to divine the British intention to force her into a great anti-French coalition, and doom the New System. Kaunitz, self-assured and composed,

---

* So was Newcastle. In June he had sent her—not the first of presents—"two barrels of beer." (Letter of the French ambassador to Mme. de Pompadour. In Richard Waddington, Louis XV et le renversement des alliances, 99.)

kept her au courant, down to trivia, with his efforts to stiffen the back-bone of the court of Versailles, which had dispatched an envoy extraor-dinary to Berlin. On March 13 Kaunitz had double-edged news to report from France.

Starhemberg had received Louis XV's pledge of neutrality for the time of negotiations. But he had been refused a neutrality treaty. The ambassador saw quite well why the French did not wish to "acquiesce in *l'entière destruction du roi de* Prusse." They feared, "not altogether without reason, that we would always keep a *porte de derrière* open and return to the Old System with the Maritime Powers . . . after the Prussian thorn has been pulled out of our flesh." They were waiting, Starhemberg pointed out, for "definitive commitments on our part."[11]

Kaunitz' offers however, remained couched in ambivalent language. Its artful bypaths may have been past the ken of Maria Theresa. They did not shatter her trust in the Almighty, Who would "take mercy on my House and help it regain, for His own glory, that which . . . was lost to Prussia."[12] For years she had now gratified, now vexed, her ad-visers by marginalia scrawled on their drafts of communications with ambassadors or foreign courts. Now there were no such marginalia.* She had nothing to contribute toward the "political algebra" of Kaunitz. Was she not also loath to be sullied by the dissimulation it compelled him to practice? Divorcing herself from it, she could look forward to his success without a shadow of scheming upon her. Social diversions were not necessarily out of tune with this frame of mind.

But it was above all for her children's enjoyment that she did not forego this carnival's fêtes, in fact could not get enough of them. Or was it? "The usual Thursday dance for the little Royalties on February 5. . . . The tenth, ball with the young Royalties masked and disguised as flowers, Archduchess Marianne *en tulipe,* Archduchess Maria [Mimi] as sun flower. . . . A special surprise for the emperor was devised for the twelfth by the empress herself, the anniversary of their nuptials. She had all the twelve children, even the small [Maria] Antonia, don fancy costumes, and thus the charming group made their appearance."[13]

Maria Theresa was in her fortieth year. She showed it. People had begun to call her "the fat one," and she knew it. Well might she dis-play the children on the flower-strewn stage of the Hofburg, or its par-quet, to keep her Francis aware of the blessings bestowed on their union. For, as it happened, he was enjoying himself hugely this winter.

The astounding change in his mood was due, originally, to the great good luck of John Adam Auersperg, the Empire's master of the horse.

---

* "Not a single of Kaunitz' drafts from April, 1755, to September, 1756 . . . bears a minuting remark from the hand of the empress, and only one of them her *placet.*" (E. Guglia, *op. cit.,* II, 133.)

Thirteen years Francis' junior, and carrying a count's title as the younger son of a princely family, this genial shooting and gambling companion had been created a prince in his own right upon the coronation at Frankfurt. He became a widower in 1753—and, not so long after, the favored suitor of Neipperg's daughter, a girl of sixteen the perfection of whose physical charms was matched by the size of her dowry. As it turned out soon, all of that money and Auersperg's own could not sustain the extravagance of the young lady, who during her father's Luxembourg governorship had been exposed to the sight of high living in Brussels and Spa. In those surroundings she had also acquired a premature ease of manner and a taste for drawing-room fun such as was not to be found in the nobility's unmarried young women in Vienna. She "neither possessed any uncommon endowment of mind nor . . . a very cultivated understanding."[14] But this did not stand in the way of her instantaneous success. It surely did not make her any less attractive to the emperor.

She had been married for only a short while when Francis, "accompanied by a number of gentlemen," extricated himself from his wife's devotional rounds in Prague to "call on the princess at Rotenhaus, where she took the waters."[15] In May, 1756, the lord marshal confided to his journal: "In the morning the empress rode [from Laxenburg] to the town to celebrate the Holy-Cross Day at St. Joseph's. She returned at noon. . . . In the meantime the emperor had left on a *parti de plaisir* with a small group. . . . Such little outings and amusements have become more and more frequent this year, their prime mover being the young princess Auersperg. As early as this year's carnival, the emperor began to show a special liking for her, in fact, as some people say, *une inclination marquée.*"[16] The time was not too remote when the diarist would mention the "well-known close friendship"[17] or record another telltale episode and the "special remarks and comments"[18] in its wake.

"I have been assured unanimously by all who knew the princess," an English traveler wrote twenty years after that spring of 1756 (and four years after the premature death of the princess), "that no description can convey an adequate picture of her attractions. She was of the middle size, her complexion a clear brown, her eyes [were] grey, her hair [was] chestnut, luxuriant, and glossy. But her face and cast of countenance were of that kind to which no painter could ever do justice; because, when she conversed, a thousand graces lighted up in it, and gave her an animation beyond the power of art to imitate. . . . She never laboured to please. Nature had done all. . . . She excited love without awakening envy or rivalry in her own sex; and she made no enemies, because she never attempted raillery or ridicule."[19] High society called her, simply, *la belle princesse.*

No *billets doux* from the hand of Francis, this most remiss of letter writers, have come to light. The assumption that Mme. Auersperg was his mistress rests, to this day, on the view that his contemporaries took of the attachment. Even Khevenhüller ceased beating about the bush in the end and would refer to her as "the emperor's beauty."

There was no tradition of *maîtresse en titre in* the Vienna court. The routine wantonness of Versailles, the Hanoverian concubinages, or the byblows of Dresden, had no counterpart in Vienna. Some of its monarchs (surely Joseph I and Charles VI) had not been faithful husbands. But the lady loves of them all had been kept in their place and bastards, whenever such existed, had remained unrecorded.* Popular gossip had little to go by and never rose over prudent whispers; and society folk, hypocritical themselves about their amours, willingly played the hypocritical game of their master. This aura of quasi-secrecy suited the pious monarch. Religious scruples aside, it spared him embarrassment in his inner circle and preserved the modicum of coziness it afforded the ruler. Count Althan remained the bosom friend of Charles VI even though the countess was, rightly or wrongly, considered his mistress; similarly, Francis saw no reason why he should deprive himself of Auersperg's pleasant company because of the involvement with the princess.

There was some comedy, along with some pathos, in the imbroglio. Did the two men share the favors of *la belle princesse?* And what about Prince Charles de Ligne? This very young and very handsome Belgian had met her before her marriage and continued to pay attentions to her.

De Ligne was destined to become a soldier of mark, a diplomatist whose charm was legendary, and no mean man of letters. The authenticity of his posthumously published memoirs has been questioned. Still, the passage dealing with Mme. Auersperg offers a glimpse of Francis, the aging lover, which is not inconsistent with the picture to be culled from more reliable sources. "This good sovereign loved informal parties, women, and young people [reads that passage]. One day he had me dress up as a lady, and tried to convince a gentleman who was on the look-out for a wife that I was the girl destined for him. . . . At that time I shared the favors of Vienna's most attractive woman with the emperor, the good, the excellent, the loyal, the amiable, sincere, jolly, and even handsome Francis I. Whenever the empress came to the theater, he did not dare leave their box. But one night, her attention being occupied, he slipped away and into the box where I used to go regularly. His lady friend and I were not a little alarmed by his sudden appearance [although] we knew that he loved us both. He asked me what

* The last Habsburg bastard to gain distinction was Juan d'Austria, a son of Charles V.

play was being performed. It happened to be *Crispin rival de son maître*, and I could not bring myself to pronounce the words. He insisted. So, half-embarrassed, half convulsed with laughter, I finally told him . . . and withdrew in haste, leaving it to the beautiful charming woman to find in her brilliant imagination a story that would account for both our embarrassment and my precipitous withdrawal."*20

"Her inconsistency excluded [the emperor] from the sole possession of her heart; he was not less permanently attached to her."21 Nor did her frivolity in money matters ever chill his ardor. Parsimonious as he was, he again and again paid the debts she had run up. He loved watching her at the gaming table, a picture of reckless youth, and yet "so gentle of manner."22 He was forty-eight in 1756; she was eighteen.

We can of course no more than guess at the feelings of earlier Habsburg princesses betrayed by their consorts (although we know of the revenge that the widow of Joseph I took on his last paramour while Charles was on his way to Vienna from Barcelona). But Maria Theresa could claim a distinction unique in the Habsburg annals—she had married for love. She frowned at Francis' neglect of secrecy and decorum; and the thoughtlessness with which he was lacerating her pride surprised her. It was, however, her apparent loss of attraction for the "adorable husband" that hurt her truly.

Her jealousy became patent when Francis in the spring of 1756 suggested that the court go to Laxenburg more often than routine demanded. She knew, as did scores of people, that the emperor had invited the princess and her complaisant husband to stay at the lodge whenever the imperial family was in residence. The more eloquent Francis became in explaining his wish for more frequent Laxenburg sojourns, the more doggedly did his wife plead the pressure of her work and Kaunitz' poor health, which would prevent him from making regular trips to the lodge. So Francis acquired a villa for the Auerspergs in the vicinity of Laxenburg and had it furnished. He would drop in there very often on his return from shooting. "In the [princess'] society, and that of a select group of both sexes, he spent many of his evenings. A supper of ten or twelve courses was provided, where [she] presided, and at which all form of etiquette was banned."23

In later years Francis also forced *la belle princesse* on his family. "At dinner I am seated between Marianne and Amalia," the empress wrote to her Mimi, probably in 1761, "and the emperor sits between Elizabeth and *la* Auersperg."24 "You have married for love . . ." she re-

* Cf. Wraxall II, 182: "When [the empress] was not present at the performance [he] always repaired to the Princess' box. . . . [He] usually stood behind her, concealed from view; and the box was locked in order to prevent intrusion. Notwithstanding these precautions, a cough he suffered from generally betrayed his retreat, and divulged the secret to the world."

minded the newly-wed Mimi five years later. "Try to amuse your husband . . . lest he feel more at his ease elsewhere. . . . Happiness in marriage consists of mutual trust. Mad love vanishes soon. A married couple must respect and be useful to each other. They must be sincere friends. . . . I have seen you jealous of your friends. Be careful not to be jealous of your husband. This would be a straight way of estranging him. You must not even joke about that point. Banter leads to reproaches, bitter words creep in . . . and dislike ensues. The more confidence you show your husband, the less you attempt to interfere, the closer will he remain to you."[25]

But these words came from a remorse-ridden Maria Theresa widowed for less than a year. She was more down-to-earth when as an old woman she said to one of her *Kammerfräuleins*: "Let me warn you. Don't marry a man who has nothing to do."[26]

XVI

"Political Algebra" Triumphant?

SOME TWENTY years after these days in which war and peace hung in the balance, Maria Theresa wrote to a confidante of her declining years: "It often comforts me to know that the years . . . that are gone will not return, and that every moment brings me closer to death. However, I tremble at the thought of the horrible account I will have to render."[1] In another such hour of morbid contrition she drew for her own use a list of "all my frailties and the sins I committed from ignorance and then put out of my mind. . . ." and she opened that register by accusing herself "before God" of having waged "war out of pride."[2]

By the mid-fifties pride in achievement had begun to mingle with the pride in the blood of the Habsburgs. She did not claim as her own the accomplishments of her reformers. But had it not been her determination to pull affairs out of their rut that had made possible the reform work? And had it not been sustained, throughout countless conflicts, by her preparedness to risk the love of her subjects, as indeed the support of the families close to her throne?

King Frederick tended to disparage the new wind blowing in the Hofburg. He chuckled over its zeal in adopting his methods. One may surmise that he was taken aback when one of his own high officials, late in 1755, returned from Vienna filled with admiration for the changes that had taken place there. Carl Joseph Fürst had been dispatched to settle the complex problem of the Silesian debt and thus was in a position to observe at first hand the financial management at Vienna. "What other sovereign," he wrote, "could in seven years of peace have lifted affairs to the level on which they are now? Even in the distant future, posterity will acknowledge that Maria Theresa was one of the great women rulers of history. Surely the House of Habsburg has never had her like."[3] Fürst had come to Vienna with all the ingrained prejudices of the Prussian civil servant. He marveled at a Count So-and-so, who "wants to see everything with his own eyes . . . [and] is not to be seen at court, or the *soirées* and shooting parties."[4]

This paragon of application was not unique. A novel attitude toward public service was apparent, and Haugwitz' "Silesian" methods were scoffed at less and less as their results were emerging. In 1745 the Venetian ambassador had estimated the revenue at twenty million florins; it had doubled by 1754, with the Hereditary Lands contributing no less than seventeen million. Interest payments to debtors were no longer the exception, and some loans were actually repaid in 1755.

How justified the empress was in hoping for relief from the fiscal woes that had bedeviled the wars of her house—this was a question even Haugwitz was hesitant to answer. The mounting danger of losing the British banker did not alarm Kaunitz. He counted on drawing on the resources of France, a country still rich despite ill luck at sea and mismanagement at home. His plan for using French money was to be ready at the propitious turn in Starhemberg's negotiations.

That turn was far out of reach in April, 1756. Louis XV seemed still to be unreceptive to the idea of an alliance such as would serve Kaunitz' purpose. "Everything proves that the reluctance to abandon the king of Prussia is very great here, or that one pretends that it is," Starhemberg related. The French "wish to leave him powerful enough to use him against us at their pleasure. Whatever I may say, they do not believe that he ever could become a real menace."[5]

It may well have been true that Bernis and the septuagenarian Rouillé did not "gauge the advantages Britain could possibly derive from her agreement with Prussia"[6] and were taking it lightly. But the diplomatic success of the "pirates" in London angered the king only a little less than did the disloyalty of Frederick, who had given him no advance notice of the understanding with Britain. Soon ominous rumors of secret clauses in the Westminster convention—it was Kaunitz who spread them—reached the court of Versailles. Its special envoy to Berlin met with equivocations as he began to negotiate the renewal of the treaty.

Frederick did not itch to get involved in Britain's conflict with the French; to spare their sensibilities, he had excluded Belgium from the guarantees laid down in the Westminster convention. By keeping the French emissary wondering about Prussia's intentions, he presumably wished to warn Versailles of further flirtations with Vienna. As for the czarina, he relied on London's diplomats to prevent her from breaking out. In fine, he felt fairly secure in April, 1756.

There can be no doubt that the acquisition of Silesia had not sated Frederick's long-range aspirations. His dominions were still disjointed and indefensible as a unit. In 1752 he had deposited a sealed memorandum for Prussian kings to come which recommended acquisitive policies. He himself, for all we know, did not plan to pursue them. He certainly did not in the mid-fifties. Defending his ill-gotten gains was a different matter, however; and the thought of a preventive war presented itself to his mind even while his belief in the pacific effect of the Westminster convention was still unshaken. Every day furnished him new proofs of Maria Theresa's desire to despoil him of the fruit of his victories. He knew how busy Starhemberg was.

As it was, the ambassador, now trying to pin down Bernis, now Rouillé, appeared to make no progress. In these weeks Louis XV's interest was focused on the seizure of Minorca, Britain's island stronghold in the Mediterranean. A new squadron had been constructed and was being fitted at Toulon. It set sail in the first days of April.*

A wave of optimism swept the court at Compiègne. It furthered Starhemberg's ends. On May 1 Bernis and Rioullé signed an agreement with him and Louis XV approved it within twenty-four hours. It went a long way toward satisfying Kaunitz and alienated Frederick still more from his French alliance. This First Treaty of Versailles, as it later was called, spelled out Maria Theresa's neutrality in the Anglo-French war but did not demand—such was Kaunitz' dexterity—the dissolution of her ties with the Maritime Powers. Either signatory was guaranteed armed assistance by the other if attacked on the Continent. There was no mention of the Belgium-Parma deal, or of Silesia, for that matter.

"I see with pleasure," Newcastle wrote to one of his diplomats, "that it is the work only of one man, Count Kaunitz, of whom you know I have long been doubtful. . . . I wish and shall endeavor by the courts of Spain and Sardinia to bring the court of Vienna back."[7] Evidently Keith had not strongly enough impressed on the duke that this "one man," politically speaking, was in these weeks the court of Vienna. The great willpower of the Queen of Hungary had been a byword among her fellow princes throughout the eight years of war. What they had heard about her reforms in the following years had lent even stronger colors to that image. Her allies had not yet measured the full extent of her dependence on Kaunitz, whose tactical vacillations had blinded them to his firmness.

It would seem that the British cabinet, rent by personal jealousies and their efficiency impaired by a succession of changes, did not realize in

* The commander of the expeditionary force was Richelieu, who had become a soldier of merit since his ambassadorial days in Vienna. He had distinguished himself at Fontenoy, and before Genoa had frustrated the final Austro-Sardinian efforts.

time that the Westminster convention might play into Kaunitz' hands. At all events, they let three months pass before delivering a copy of it to Vienna. Keith, talking to Kaunitz, justified it as "perfectly inoffensive, calculated to maintain the peace of the Empire, and to relieve the empress-queen from her apprehensions of the king of Prussia." He concluded by demanding an explanation "on the subject of the supposed negotiation with the court of Versailles."[8] These negotiations were as good as deadlocked at that time, and Kaunitz gave no pertinent answer. When reply he now did after a delay of a month, he "peremptorily refused to give an explanation."[9] Starhemberg's good news was in his hands.

It took Keith another week to get an audience of Maria Theresa. She had not transferred her detestation of Robinson to his successor. As he entered her apartments at Schönbrunn on that spring day, he found himself received with "affability and condescension."

Newcastle had recommended plain language to him. Wasting no time on amenities, he submitted that Kaunitz' note "contained an absolute renunciation of the ancient and true system of Europe."[10]

"The empress answered . . . that it was not she that had abandoned the Old System [Keith wrote] but that it was my court that abandoned her, and that system together, in making the treaty with the king of Prussia." She did not deign even to consider what to Newcastle had been the heart of his design all along—a good understanding between the courts of Vienna and Berlin. She "would own freely," Keith went on in his account, "that she and the king of Prussia were incompatible together, and that no consideration upon earth should ever make her enter into an alliance where he was a party."[11]

Keith must have been a very unhappy man at this hour. His country's humiliation on the Minorcan shores had followed a series of reversals overseas. Proceeding to discharge his duty, he touched on Her Majesty's "supposed negotiations with the French court."

"Why should you be surprised," Maria Theresa asked, "if, following your example in concluding the treaty with Prussia, I should enter an engagement with France?"

Nothing could convince him, the ambassador said, that "she would connect herself with the inveterate enemy of her person and family." Unless he saw with his own eyes her sign manual "at the bottom of a treaty with that crown," he would disbelieve that the alliance had come into existence.

"I am far from being French in my disposition," she rejoined, "and do not deny that the court of Versailles has been my bitterest enemy. But I cannot conceal that the cessions which Great Britain extorted from me at the peace of Dresden, and at Aix-la-Chapelle, have totally disabled me. I have little to fear from France. I am unable to act with vigor, and have no other resources than to form such arrangements as will secure what remains."

"Will you, the Empress and Archduchess," Keith exclaimed, "so far humble yourself as to throw yourself into the arms of France?"

"Not into the arms, but on the side of France," she said in a spirited repartee reminiscent of her earlier days. No doubt she enjoyed this moment, which repaid her for uncounted blows inflicted on her pride by the demanding ally. Yet she went on to say: "I have hitherto signed nothing with France. I know not what may happen. But whatever happens, I promise you on my word of honor not to sign anything contrary to the interests of your royal master."[12]

The original document of the Versailles treaty had been in her possession for four days, and she was to ratify it a mere six days after Keith's audience, observing that "this was the first treaty she ever had signed with joy and de *bonne coeur*."[13] Maria Theresa did not like talking untruth; and knowing she would sign the treaty, she must have realized that she was being less than candid. This perhaps was the reason why she continued to listen to Keith with a patience the more remarkable for this being her birthday, with a long program of celebrations in the offing.

When the ambassador enlarged on the issue of Belgium—the discord over whose trade and defense had done so much to wreck the alliance— she did not remind him of the Barrier Tractate. She did however, hint at an accommodation of France in Belgium—and where, Keith must have wondered, would then be her consideration for the "interests of his royal master."

Finally she said, in a stance of resignation: "I no longer have it in my power to take an active part in distant transactions. I am therefore little concerned for the remote parts of my dominions. . . . I have truly but two enemies whom I dread, the king of Prussia and the Turks; and as long as I and the Empress of Russia continue on the same good terms as now subsist between us, we shall I trust be able to convince Europe that we are in a condition to defend ourselves, against those adversaries, however formidable."[14]*

Keith's government had not informed the czarina beforehand of their negotiations with Prussia. News of the Westminster convention threw her into a towering rage. Esterhazy, making the most of the incompatibility of the convention with her own treaty with Britain, stoked the flames

---

* "Their Majesties have not talked to me," the French ambassador wrote to Rouillé on May 19, "but on the thirteenth [the day of Keith's audience] the empress, leaving her apartment on the way to dinner, gave me a little wink as she walked past me . . ." (R. Waddington, *op. cit.*, 340.)

of her fury; and Bestuzhev, bribed by Williams, could barely prevent an open breach between St. Petersburg and London. Elizabeth notified Williams that his government's subsidies would not be accepted unless she was satisfied that the eighty thousand troops she had pledged were to be used against King Frederick only. By the time Maria Theresa saw Keith she also had it in black and white that she could count on massive Russian assistance even if war started with an Austrian attack on Prussia. Indeed, the czarina would "not rest until . . . Silesia was again in the hands of the empress-queen."[15] Such was Elizabeth's mood that she seemed ready to take the offensive at once and alone; and Kaunitz, who was painfully conscious of the inability of his court to provide her with campaign funds, had not an easy time bridling her ardor.

For reasons best known to himself, Bestuzhev kept his envoy in Vienna in the dark about the change in his court's relations with Britain. In an audience that the Russian asked of both the empress and her husband, he besought them not to break with the Maritime Powers. So did his colleagues from Holland and Sardinia; and Augustus of Saxony sent an emissary to Vienna to deflect his venturesome cousin by marriage from her new path.

On the *publicum* the breach with the old allies made a deep impression. Word of "this great and well-nigh unimaginable *événément*"[16] had transpired from Paris, as "French *vivacité*"[17] made a mockery of the secret so carefully guarded in Vienna. Taking up the hoary tale of Maria Theresa's ingratitude, common people, as well as the still disgruntled critics of her reforms among noblemen, pointed out how easily she had forgotten the flow of English gold. Anti-French bias had for decades been a concomitant of Austrian loyalty. It could not be undone overnight. Keith contended that "some of the . . . ministers displayed their discontent in a sullen acquiescence."[18] He also repeated a story to the effect that the fifteen-year-old Archduke Joseph, egged on by his *ayo*, had inquired of his mother "if she deemed herself safe in trusting France who had so often deceived her. Though frequently repulsed, he . . . importunately urged her not to separate from England, from whom she and her family had derived such effectual assistance."[19] There was, then and later, no end to accounts of last-minute objections on the emperor's part to the treaty. No doubt he disliked it fiercely. But these were the very days the "*supçons d'une parfaite intelligence*" between him and Mme. Auersperg were "growing apace,"[20] and he surely was not eager to antagonize his wife by dissuading her from the consummation of her grand project. Twice during this month, as lots were drawn for a driving party, he "happened" to get *la belle princesse* as his carriage companion.

Still, Francis attended conference meetings. In one of them—precisely a month after Keith's audience—it was decided that "precautionary military dispositions" were called for. But "needless ostentation" must be avoided in drawing "troops, especially cavalry, closer *ad centrum*, so as not to give any pretext for premature actions and hostilities."[21] The meeting arrived at a consensus "only *finaliter.*" The lord marshal was not present.

One of his daughters, a young widow, was getting married to Count Bethlen, a Hungarian whose suit the empresss had furthered after his conversion to the Roman faith. From a subordinate post in the Transylvanian chancellery she had raised him to its top and turned over to him "the sum of fl. 20,000 which the estates had voted, the money to go to meritorious men in the administration of the province."[22] The wedding was celebrated with much to-do. "On the morrow of the nuptials [Khevenhüller wrote] we were returning from late Mass when we saw a *voiture à quatre* approach at breakneck speed. Anticipating a pleasant surprise . . . we all of us made haste to meet the carriage, from which His Majesty alighted with Princess Auersperg, Countess Losy, and Count St. Julien. The emperor insisted on being taken to the dressing room of my daughter, where in his habitual manner he engaged in some *polissonneries*. After the midday meal, he decided to watch the peasants' dance for which my wife had made the arrangements. He admired the nimbleness of these good people and the accuracy of their steps . . . [and] could scarcely tear himself away. He thanked my wife most affably for the amusement, and on his return [to Schönbrunn] gave the empress a glowing account."[23]

How patiently did she listen to his chatter? Did she not interrupt him to mention Koch's memorial? She had ordered the secretary—who was no stranger to war, having served in Prince Eugene's quartermaster's corps—to survey the state of her armed forces. Koch's conclusions were nothing if not outspoken. An attack on King Frederick could not be thought of for the time being. Even with auxiliary armies, such as might arrive, the risks it would court must be considered forbidding.

Kaunitz decided to postpone the war until the spring of the following year.

Along with the czarina's rebuff to Britain, her clamorous lust for Prussia's destruction had eroded the trust of its king in the deterrent effect of the Westminster convention. Signs of the belligerence of the empress-queen were multiplying. The chief clerk of the Saxon chancellery, one Menzel, had been in Frederick's pay since 1752; and as Bestuzhev kept Augustus' premier au courant with his own talks with Esterhazy, there was precious little Frederick did not know about them. Even though a leakage in Dresden was suspected in the Vienna chancellery as early as 1754, the identity of the spy had not been detected. It was different with Weingarten, a brother of the secretary of the empress' embassy in Berlin. In the spring of 1756 he himself revealed his treachery in a lachrymose confession. Kaunitz, who had recruited many agents abroad—sometimes he was their dupe—painted the incident, a muddled affair, as an unheard-of crime to the empress. When Frederick offered to comply with her demand for Weingarten's extradition if only he, the king, "were told where the man could be found,"[24] Maria Theresa decided to drop the matter, disgusted by the cynicism of the *méchant homme*.

By that time Frederick appears to have made up his mind. Voices from London which reverberated in all the chancelleries of Europe, calling the empress "ungrateful" and "ill-advised," and condemning her "scandalous proceedings with the court of France,"[25] could not gloss over Frederick's realization that he had made a blunder: the Westminster convention would not shield him against the coalition that Kaunitz was building. Meanwhile the Franco-Prussian treaty had lapsed.

France's old alliance with Sweden was intact. Her emissaries had bribed many of the Empire's princes. And Rouillé kept assuring his king that war was not imminent; what Frederick should have called his encirclement, had the word then existed, would prevent him from breaking out. Starhemberg, on the other hand, could be put off for a long time.

Louis XV, in his hope for Continental peace, did not reckon with his military nobility. They had never got over the disappointment of Aix-la-Chapelle, where their crown seemed to have been tricked out of the spoils gathered by its great marshal, while the Prussian conquests had been explicitly sanctioned. Now those men, who looked upon themselves as De Saxe's worthy successors, were smelling powder. Envious of the ascendancy of the navy, they started drawing D'Argenson into the pro-Austrian camp; and its least likely partisan was rising in Belle-Isle, Maria Theresa's quondam archfoe.

Frederick had no high opinion of the French army. About Maria Theresa's he was of two minds and at all events could not afford to leave the initiative to Browne, whom he respected. In the first days of July he ordered Von Klinggräff to seek an audience of the empress-queen. She asked him to come to Schönbrunn on the twenty-sixth. "Following his instructions . . . the ambassador inquired after our present military preparations, and said that his king could not bring himself to believe that the empress-queen intended to make war on him. Although our chancellor had briefed Her Majesty . . . she was loath to rely on her memory in so important a matter. She read her reply from a small sheet of paper, and on the ambassador's request read it to him two or three times more. The empress was gracious enough [Khevenhüller's entry closes] to tell me about everything that had happened, and to describe Klinggräff's embarrassed *contenance* over and over again."[26]

Both her excellent memory and her gift for spontaneous speech were proverbial. Well might her conduct in this "very strange audience"[27] astound the staid Prussian. Kaunitz, evidently wary lest her impetuousness carry her past the confines of his "algebra," had convinced her that it would be "as superfluous as improper" to let Von Klinggräff repeat to her face—"shamelessly and despite facts which speak for themselves"— that his king, so far from mobilizing an army, was "only transferring certain units from some garrisons to some others."[28] The chancellor's own brief text, as read to Von Klinggräff by Maria Theresa, avoided provocative language. "The generally critical situation [it read] caused me to deem necessary the measures I am taking for my security and the defense of my allies. These measures are not intended to menace anybody."[29]

A short month before, Browne had written to the Hofkriegsrat: "It goes without saying that for our part we have no alternative but to place ourselves as soon as we can in a position to resist this invasion, if not immediately by a counter-offensive, at least in the beginning by an adequate defensive." At the same time, he pointed out that his troops in Bohemia were "scattered far and wide," and everywhere lacked pontoons. And casting the first somber light on the reformed army, he also owned that "our regular officers do not have the habit of getting to know the neighborhood of their stations, so as to be able to orientate themselves, if the need arises."[30] However, Browne had always been full of gripes, and the Hofkriegsrat took his words with more than a grain of salt. The decision not to strike in 1756 made speed unnecessary.

It was not only Koch's sobering memorial that had changed the timetable. Kaunitz also wished to put some teeth in the treaty with France. True, it freed the empress' army from the task of defending Belgium and the Italian dominions while at the same time facing the Prussian, and lifted from her the fear of machinations on the part of Turkey. But the twenty-four thousand troops Louis XV had pledged—pledged only for the case of attack on Austria!—were not likely to be of help in the great labor of "knocking down the king of Prussia." "Now is the moment we need Mme. de Pompadour more than ever. . . ." wrote Starhemberg. "She wishes to be held in esteem, and in fact deserves it."[31]

There is evidence that the celebrated courtesan was a frigid woman and that it was not only the king's promiscuous appetites that had estranged him from her bed.[32] At the same time, she was "the only person possessed of the secret of . . . dispelling his boredom."[33] Behind the vanity that Kaunitz took for granted in her sex, he also espied the altogether masculine lust for power that pushed her on. The puerile rivalries at Versailles, topping the mediocrity of the king's advisers and their frivolity, had begun to smooth her climb to the place of the supreme wire-puller of the destinies of the kingdom.

Bernis was on the verge of attaining cabinet rank. Kaunitz, no doubt tongue in cheek, had called this creature of hers a "great man" such as "France and her allies stand in need of."[34] Starhemberg, as we can gather safely, lost no time passing the word on to the protectress of the abbé. Now the chancellor wrote her: "It is beyond question that everything agreed to thus far between the two courts is owed to your zeal and sagacity. I cannot deprive myself of the pleasure of telling you so, and thanking you for the willingness to be my guide up to this hour. Nor do I conceal from you that Their Imperial Majesties give you all the credit due, and in regard to you entertain all the feelings you can possibly wish for. What has been done seems to me to merit the approval of an unbiased public, as well as of posterity. But what remains to be done is too great, and too much worthy of yourself, to allow you to stand aloof, instead of trying to contribute toward completing a work that cannot but make your name forever dear to your country. Hence I am convinced that you will continue to devote your labors to so important a task. If you will do so, success is certain. . . ."[35] Whether or not Maria Theresa saw this letter is outside our knowledge. She was to see others, however, written to that oddest of all of the supporters of the Habsburgs' struggle for power.

Kaunitz had set his sights on French subsidies to Russia and French participation in the fight against Prussia. He was not prepared to yield anything in return. Within twenty-four hours of posting his epistle to the marquise he informed Starhemberg that the empress would not cede even the smallest part of Belgium before having returned to Silesia with French assistance. The ambassador implored her to be more generous. She answered him with her own hand (and in her own grammar and spelling) directly Von Klinggräff had bowed out of her presence on July 26: "However stubbornly the French court may be trying to hold fast to the decision to take no active part in the war . . . you will nevertheless not let them confuse you, and will stick to [this] point, as to all others, as *conditiones sine qua non*."[36] She was well aware that Starhemberg now was dealing with a court that had lost its only powerful ally. And George II had declared war on Louis XV.

Some years before, Francis, in one of his spurts of activity, had asked for a critique of the generals' corps. In that study—its author was either Prince Charles or Neipperg—Browne had been described as an "excellent general filled with valor and ambition . . . courageous and inventive, if somewhat rash in putting forward projects he does not have to execute himself." Also, he tended to "keep his own person in mind a good deal and, when occasion arises, to topple his superiors. . . ." Whatever the impression of this double-edged judgment on Maria Theresa's mind may have been, by 1756 Browne's choice for the Bohemian command was a foregone conclusion. He also was given authority over the corps stationed in Moravia under Prince Piccolomini, a "modest person . . . and incapable of self-interest."[37]

At the Hofkriegsrat Neipperg substituted for the senescent Joseph Harrach as chairman. He did not undervalue Browne, whose criticism of Vienna's delaying methods he ascribed at first to the field marshal's failure to realize that a full-scale mobilization would brand his empress the aggressor. In August his complaints grew increasingly pressing. Time and again he spoke of the equipment that was missing and pointed out that the number of mounted troops was sorely inadequate.* And, as Browne, having not been a member of the Military Commission, remarked with some acerbity, the new staff system had not, in reality, been put into practice. And where were the Croats? Where, above all, the Hungarians, who should have joined him long before?

Their gentry had not forgotten the slights suffered in the Diet of 1751. According to the Venetian ambassador, writing in 1754, discontent was ripe in some of the counties, where there also was fear lest the queen's "German conflicts . . . should expose the kingdom itself to invasion."[38] The year after, the appointment of Lorraine-born court generals as commanders of certain fortified places had elicited protests from the magnates. Knowing her Hungarians, Maria Theresa did not expect them to come forward with advance payments on future contributions, as had some of the Austro-Bohemian estates in the spring. But the Hungarians' flat refusal to deliver provisions to Browne's army galled her. She summoned the Palatine, Lewis Batthyány, to Vienna. He submitted that his nation must not neglect its own security, as it would if it diminished its resources and the supply of labor. Why did not the Bohemians provision the troops on their own soil with greater zeal than they apparently were doing? (Why not indeed? Fear stalked the country, as Browne informed Kaunitz, "and the behavior of the aristocracy is scandalous."[39]) The Palatine, bent on striking a bargain, did not find it hard to extract from the queen the tariff amendments she had denied the Diet five years before. As some of the landowners began to equip bands of mounted irregulars upon Batthyány's return to Pressburg, Maria Theresa praised these efforts to the skies. There was no need to tell her that light troops were invaluable in the mountainous border regions of northern Bohemia. Reports on their tactics, if not always reading for delicate ears, had fascinated Maria Theresa throughout the wars of the 1740's and often sustained her hopes when accounts of the strategy of her commanders and their actions made for the worst reading of all.

* One general in Vienna suggested that the veterans' hospitals should be combed for "seasoned cavalry men . . . who regret their retirement, into which only their inability to carry out the movements of the new drill methods forced them." (Khevenhüller, Vol. 1756–57, Anmerkungen und Anhang, 181.)

On August 17 the imperial couple reviewed one of the crack regiments passing through Vienna. Earlier in the month the emperor had slipped away twice from Vienna to visit his new property of Schlosshof. But what he wanted more than anything else was to go to Hollitsch, as was his wont at this time of the year.

On the eighteenth Von Klinggräff handed the chancellor another note. Using blunt language, and curt, it accused the empress-queen of scheming aggression in concert with Russia and demanded her solemn pledge that she would not attack the king either this year or the next.

Cristiani had arrived in Vienna some days earlier and pleaded for prudence. So did Colloredo. The Hofkriegsrat maintained that King Frederick was only saber-rattling. Kaunitz, taking advantage of the emperor's impatience to be off to Hollitsch, had his view prevail in the meeting of August 20 held in the Hofburg: to write out the requested pledge—write it out under duress—was bound to destroy the prestige of the Arch House forever.

Von Klinggräff was kept waiting in the antechamber while the meeting was in progress. As soon as it had adjourned Maria Theresa gave him audience. Few words were exchanged. Accepting the memorial he had brought, she promised an answer in writing. Francis, accompanied only by Quinquin Esterhazy, had boarded his traveling coach directly after the meeting.

The empress followed the next morning, taking only one of her ladies along. The full vacation company, including Mme. Auersperg (without her husband), did not leave Vienna until forty-eight hours later.

By then Von Klinggräff had Kaunitz' reply note. It advised the ambassador that there was no such thing as an Austro-Russian plan for attack, that the treaty of 1746 was a purely defensive agreement, and that the movements of Browne's troops were merely a consequence of His Prussian Majesty's own dispositions close to the borders of the Bohemian kingdom.

In Hollitsch, on August 24, "a German comedy was performed, with the chief stoker of the empress, Stöckel, taking the part of Pickle-Herring. . . . This had been arranged as a surprise for Her Majesty, who is greatly devoted to that man; and to make sure the secret would not leak out, the emperor himself had been directing all rehearsals."[40] On the same night, Frederick quitted Berlin. He was not to see it again for seven years.

XVII

Third War Over Silesia

THE WORST THAT CAN HAPPEN," Maria Theresa wrote to Starhemberg from Hollitsch on August 22, "is a lost battle and the occupation of a large part of the Bohemian kingdom. This would of course entail financial sacrifices well-nigh past our resources, and also bring grievous harm to my faithful subjects." But why dwell on the risk of a "temporary disadvantage"? For temporary it would be. Surely defeat would not result in any new territorial cessions being extorted from her at the subsequent settlement. Victory, on the other hand, besides restoring Silesia to her, would weaken her most formidable adversary and most likely create conditions for permanent peace. Therefore, she summed up in a spirit not altogether unworthy of her addiction to games of chance, the possibility of "a temporary disadvantage has to be weighed against [that of] a lasting and invaluable profit."[1] Kaunitz, who was in Vienna, knew nothing of this missive. It opens a window on Maria Theresa's inmost thoughts at a time his dazzling ideas virtually restricted her to the role of their executor.

The imminence of hostilities gave her a different role. As she thrust herself into matters military she once again became the directing, controlling, prodding agent of the paramount task of the hour. It was she who kept the Hofkriegsrat on their toes, requesting daily reports. It was she who in August expedited the marching orders for regiments stationed in the Tyrol, Lombardy and Croatia. It was she, too, who convinced the Hofkriegsrat, or at any rate told them, that the frontiersmen, cleansed of the last vestige of mutinous thoughts, would be on the march in no time.

They assembled but slowly; and Browne, still sorely deficient in light

(274)

troops, such as were indispensable in northern Bohemia through whose defiles Frederick was expected to penetrate the kingdom, was, in addition, covered insufficiently at his right flank in Moravia, where Piccolomini commanded a force of less than fifteen thousand. What, on the other hand, were the numbers at Frederick's disposal? One hundred thousand? One hundred and twenty thousand? Or one hundred and fifty thousand? Nobody seemed to know. A stream of suggestions on recruitment issued from the desk of Maria Theresa. Not all of them were feasible and many duplicated earlier directives.

If intelligence on the king's effectives, as his dispositions, was missing, Browne needed none to be awake to the superiority of the Prussian gunnery. As for his own, "little more than two thirds of the artillery could be brought up . . . and cannon balls . . . were found to be of the wrong caliber. . . ." Horses were lacking in the rear; "a train of forty or fifty metal pontoons had to be left behind in Vienna." The magazines were "practically emptied of flints and cartridges for carbines and pistols. . . ."[2] The empress did not ascribe the complaints of the field marshal to the well-known critical bent of his mind or the sufferings some lingering disease had for some time been imposing on him. She for one recalled well how events had vindicated his gloomy reports from Silesia in 1740—a fact played down by Neipperg when all had been lost.

One circumstance she thought Browne was not doing justice to. Who could compare her new army with the outnumbered raw recruits or worn-out veterans who had found themselves under attack in the first Silesian campaign? Or with the ragged, half-starved troops Browne had had to make do with in the later Italian campaigns, his dispositions more often than not jeopardized by conflicts with Pallavicini in Milan or the little king in Turin? No, no. Koch in his pessimistic memorial had not, after all, contended that Daun's methods were ineffectual or that the ranks were not well drilled and well trained. Had she not with her own eyes seen the modern battalions on uncounted visits to camps? Had she not time and again admired their discipline in formation and their firing skill? And had not the ovations greeting her proved the fine morale of the soldiers? And how many subalterns had Koch met himself—those junior officers whose spirit she had raised by admitting them to her court, irrespective of extraction?

There was comfort from a different quarter also. Out of a total of six million florins requested from the lands as a special *contributale*, close to two million had been delivered by August 17; and Chotek, who now managed treasury business under the *Directorium*, was almost certain that sixteen million, or even eighteen, would be available in due course. Such affluence in the war chest had been unheard of for two generations. The *mater castrorum* put it to use forthwith. All officers of the army in

Bohemia were given three months' pay as a bonus, and provisions were made for their families, whose distress during the campaigns of the forties had consistently lowered the morale of junior officers in the field. "I expect to receive a plan for the hospitals," the empress also ordered, "as I have been always served ill in this respect, and am concerned greatly about the *conservation* of the enlisted men."[3]

Apparently such fresh troops as were on the march to Bohemia by the end of August made it their business to pass through Hollitsch. On the thirtieth "the empress reviewed the Purpatori Dragoons. . . . Today, review of the Saxe-Gotha Dragoons."[4] The emperor on his part "rode to hounds, and was more fortunate than the other day, inasmuch as the scent was not lost, and the stag given the *coup de grâce*." He "went a-coursing with the archduke [Joseph] and some of us, and several rangers" the following day. "After a collation we dropped in at the stud-farm, where we had a game of *faro*. At night a group of our ladies and gentlemen acted a new pantomime."[5] Francis nevertheless was up very early next morning. He presently summoned the lord marshal and Batthyány to his rooms.

A report from Dresden had arrived before dawn. It contained "long-winded stories of certain movements of Prussian troops"—"just *terreurs paniques*,"[6] as Francis observed. Even when one of Browne's generals rode up to the lodge in the afternoon and confirmed the news from the embassy at Dresden, the emperor refused to take the tale seriously. On a drive through the woods he "bantered about it all."[7]

Returning to the lodge, he found a relay courier from Vienna waiting for him. "The Prussian van crossed the Saxon border on August 27 [actually, 29] and the king himself is following with the *gros de l'armée*." Augustus was "said to have concentrated his 17,000-man army at Pirna" on the reputedly inaccessible plateau overlooking the Elbe a few miles upstream from Dresden. "He seems to be determined to go there himself with his princes, Xavier and Charles." And so he did, as Kheven-hüller was to learn some hours later. He also learned that Augustus' wife, who had remained in Dresden with the rest of the royal family, was "being treated with great scorn and *indignement*" by the Prussians who had reached the capital. And the "countryside is being dealt with most harshly, notwithstanding initial assurances to the contrary."[8]

The week was not over when, at Versailles, Augustus' young daughter, the dauphine, stormed into the presence of her father-in-law brandishing a report from Dresden. Louis XV detested emotional scenes. But he had grown fond of the little Saxon princess. Her tears, had Kaunitz known about them, would have given him no mean pleasure. Tears had also "stood in the eyes of the empress" as she related the news

Maria Theresa in her early forties

The Empress toward the end of the Seven Years' War

to Khevenhüller, Batthyány, and some others in Hollitsch, "so deeply did events in Saxony affect her."[9]

"September 3 [reads Khevenhüller's next entry] we watched the Birckenfeld and Lucchesi Cuirassiers march by in the morning, rode to hounds after the midday meal, and at night there was a repeat performance of the pantomime."[10] One may doubt whether the empress was present, for she was to leave Hollitsch at five A.M. the following day. "The emperor, who had planned to stay there until the seventeenth, likewise decided to cut short his sojourn."[11] He was to return to Vienna around the tenth with his entourage.

The first thing Kaunitz said to the empress was that "no one could have foreseen that the Prussian king, without the slightest provocation, would use such strongarm methods against Saxony." (Browne had, if only on August 25, and in tentative words.) As Kaunitz went on to say, the king's sole intention was to "push things to extremes in order to extract from Your Majesty the declaration he asked for." But even if given it, he still "would not evacuate Saxony before Your Majesty's army in Bohemia and Moravia had been disbanded, and transferred to distant billets."[12]

As early as mid-August Frederick's new friends in London had foreseen that he would strike. They were awake to what another century was to call war guilt. So, for instance, they asked the court of Madrid to decide for itself "whether in such circumstances the king of Prussia [could] be looked upon as the aggressor, even should he be forced to start hostilities."[13] Once he had started them Newcastle's envoys everywhere pointed, as the true origin of what had happened, at Maria Theresa's resolution to destroy Prussia. In actual fact her warlike preparations—and, even more so, the czarina's—might have justified Prussian action against either or both, even in the eyes of men free from the *partipris* of the British statesmen. Augustus of Saxony, however, had not been preparing for war. His alliances with Maria Theresa and Elizabeth were purely defensive. Thus Frederick's invasion of the electorate branded him the breaker of peace.* Kaunitz could not expect him, if he were appeased now, to repeat that performance the next year. Having invaded Lutheran Saxony, the king had given the lie to his repute as a new Gustavus Adolphus, as disseminated in London. But more important still for Kaunitz was the task of keeping alive Maria Theresa's conviction that she was the aggrieved party once again. Although his great hour had

---

* This odium did not leave him indifferent. No sooner had he occupied Dresden than he seized the archives. Within a few weeks he published, to prove the existence of an Austro-Saxon conspiracy, some documents allegedly found there. It did not need Vienna's subsequent refutation, in print, to raise everywhere in Europe grave doubts about the authenticity of those "finds."

come too soon for the Hofkriegsrat's comfort, he had no intention to let it slip by.

Moreover, a jubilant note from Starhemberg, written on August 20, had come to Kaunitz' desk during the absence of the empress. "At long last [it opened] I have arrived at the point toward which we had striven to steer this court all along."[14] Louis XV's tacit consent to the dismemberment of Prussia was as good as certain. The Belgian cessions—partly to Don Philip, partly to France directly—were to be effected only after the recovery of Silesia. And the king now was ready to use the twenty-four thousand troops he had pledged for defensive purposes, if not for offensive operations against Prussia, at least for a demonstration on her borders. At the same time, the ambassador had talked the French out of insisting on the immediate delivery of the two Belgian ports or the Vienna court's formal break with Britain.

Kaunitz knew that he still had a long road to travel at Versailles. But looking back at the road he had covered—covered while retaining his hold over Maria Theresa—would have gratified also a man of far less self-esteem than was his. He had sized up the weakness of French policy makers even in Aix-la-Chapelle; while apparently making a fool of himself in Paris, he had taken the measure of the men, sincere or selfish, who took it upon themselves to pose as the king's advisers; and in the very months that Mme. de Pompadour was losing her grip on Louis XV as a woman, he, Wenceslas Kaunitz, had begun banking on her power. He had set his trap with subtlety and perseverance. He relied on his firm hand to spring it. Whether his monumental vanity allowed him to give credit to his mistress for following his lead with a docility entirely alien to her nature—this will never be known. A lady's man, if a slightly comical one, he may well have ascribed his dominance over her to the power he thought he had over women; and no one will ever know how far off the mark was that conceit.

The involuntary Saxon co-belligerent was considered of little worth in Vienna. Within a week he had become an encumbrance for Browne, who, to provision the Pirna encampment, had to send comparatively large detachments through the tightening Prussian cordon. Browne's pleas, supported by letters from the empress, to march the beleaguered men into Bohemia while the going was good, found no hearing with the elector, who may have hoped to work out some arrangement of his own with the invader. The new problem only fired the endeavors of the empress to furnish Browne with more manpower and more of the needed equipment.

The incompleteness of the reform work was obvious. One innovation that had remained on paper was the army-staff system. The Hofkriegsrat acted as though it had never been introduced. With Joseph Harrach unable by now to leave his house, his replacement no longer could be postponed, and as the proceedings were still directed by Neipperg, Leopold Daun, his competitor for the office, out of fairness or prudence, kept his counsel.

Whatever the opinions emanating from the Hofkriegsrat may have been, Maria Theresa trusted Browne as fully as she had none of the generals in the forties save Lewis Khevenhüller. Back in those days Browne's obstinacy had sometimes clashed with her own and made her angry. That memory did not lessen her confidence. Nor, on the other hand, did it stifle the freedom with which she was giving advice. Her mind, as it always had, veered from essentials to details, from grand strategy to trivia. "Should not Prussian deserters who arrive with their muskets be paid at least three florins each?" she inquired one day. "The fatigue hats of the cavalry are still here," reads one of the scraps of paper she would bring to the meetings. "They must be shipped off at once. Should the men be fitted out with blankets against the cold or some sort of *capot?*"[15] Horses recently purchased outside Habsburg territory "must not be transported through Prussian territory. Too dangerous. A detour is preferable. . . . I have sent Neipperg a new declaration by the Jew [?] about horses; should he be turned down altogether, and, if not, what answer is suggested? . . . The pontoons could have been shipped already. . . . Officers must at once be given baggage instructions, so they will know what stuff to buy, and avoid unnecessary expenses. . . . If there is not enough money on hand [in Vienna] for the officers' three-month bonus, these sums could be advanced by the regiments. . . ."[16]

On September 5 the conference sat in her absence. She was five months with child, and an unseasonable heat wave made her fear Kaunitz' insistence on shut casements in his anxiety to evade the perils of draft. Khevenhüller, who had left Hollitsch two days after the empress, and of course had been in the emperor's company all the time, did not disguise his growing misgivings. Yes, yes, he had voted for turning down Von Klinggräff's demand two weeks before. But he had done so in the belief that Browne's and Piccolomini's forces were capable of resisting an invasion. Now he was suddenly told that they were not. And to make things worse, the *"publicum* are just as faint-hearted as they were in 1744. . . ." The most reasonable course to take under these circumstances was "to stay out of harm's way, face the world as it is, and give the king in Prussia a reply that would pacify him."[17] Kaunitz had no mind to stand for such nonsense. Conciliation could only postpone the inevitable! Of course the decision was for Her Majesty alone to make, he wrote her upon adjournment. If she wished to follow his—and Batthyány's and Ulfeld's—advice, he would go ahead and hand the note, as prepared, to Von Klinggräff; if not, he would compose a different text and submit it to her shortly. "Am totally in favor of the former," she replied forthwith, "and the note to Von Klinggräff must be consonant with all our *resolutiones*."[18]

Frederick did not wait for that note. To close the ring around Pirna, he sent one of his corps into the Bohemian borderland. The detachment Browne sent out to blunt that thrust was compelled to withdraw after meeting the Prussians with spirited action. "No proper declaration of war," recorded Khevenhüller on the nineteenth, "and yet hostilities against us have commenced in full earnest. . . . The emperor returned from an outing to Schlosshof earlier than expected on account of inclement weather, as well as happenings in the field."[19] Colloredo had two documents ready for the signature of the monarch—a *dehortatorium* enjoining the Margrave of Brandenburg from disturbing the Empire's peace, and an edict that released his officers and soldiers from their oath. On September 25 Von Klinggräff departed from Vienna without observing the customary formalities. On Maria Theresa's orders, his passports had been withheld until her own ambassador had left Berlin.

Three days later Piccolomini—who, to Browne's dismay, had followed a conceit of his own, taking up positions to face Schwerin's army—related strange news. The aged Prussian field marshal had extended an invitation to him (and repeated it) "in order to bring about, perhaps, a good and genuine understanding between our sovereigns. . . . Honorable conditions might well be worked out."[20] Evidently the last-minute offer tempted Francis, for it was to him that Kaunitz addressed his opinion. "If Your Majesty will deign to recall the past," he wrote in a slightly patronizing tone, "you will find, in the *démarche* of the King of Prussia, the ruse most characteristic of him at the start of any war in which he is the aggressor. Did he not employ [that same ruse] as he began making war on us as soon as Emperor Charles, of glorious memory, had breathed his last. . . . He only wants to amuse himself, and sow suspicion."[21] Piccolomini was ordered to ignore the questionable overtures. By that time sizable reinforcements, some of them even from distant Transylvania, had reached him, as well as Browne. A French officer in the latter's camp wrote to D'Argenson: "All the cavalry and infantry are in an extremely good state despite the long marches made by most of the regiments. The officers and soldiers are filled with the best will in the world, and place the deepest confidence in their chief."[22]

The Hofkriegsrat had formed their own idea of what Frederick was up to. He would try to occupy northern Bohemia, thereby depriving the empress of the revenue of that, of late, quite prosperous region. Wintering there, he would prepare for a thrust at Vienna. That enterprise had failed before, as Neipperg did not tire of pointing out; it was certain to fail again. In Vienna's three parish churches the monstrance was kept exposed for three days. Although people, high and lowly, flocked to the solemnly lit churches, that act betokening war—and which had not in living memory ever gained efficacious support for the army—did not lay the general apprehension. Kaunitz, who had little patience with the *publicum's* moods, nevertheless took pains preparing his version of the new conflict with King Frederick, and why it had come to a head. The *Diarium* published the proclamation three days ahead of the Prussian declaration of war.

October 4 was Francis' name day. "Shortly after 8 A.M. a courier arrived from Browne's headquarters. He took his pouch immediately to the emperor who in wartime . . . wishes to receive news first, so as to inform the empress according to [the nature of] events. But letters reaching other persons at the same time reported on an engagement said to have been fought near Lobosits; and as the emperor did not care to reveal the contents of his communication, everybody was bewildered and nervous, not least because we remembered only too well the courier who, on St. Francis's Day, had brought the story of the defeat of Soor to Frankfurt."[23] Kaunitz summoned the foreign ambassadors to the chancellery late in the afternoon and informed them of an indecisive engagement that had taken place in northern Bohemia about halfway between Prague and the Saxon border.

Actually the ailing field marshal had executed a successful holding action. His inventiveness surprised the king more than did the fighting spirit of the Austrian troops or the composure most of them had shown under his cannonades. In the end Browne, mindful of the Saxons' relief, which a deeper involvement might jeopardize, had retreated in exemplary order after having frustrated pursuit.

As if to rid himself of the sobering experience, Frederick disseminated, at home and abroad, fantastic stories about the great victory he had gained. In a letter to Starhemberg Kaunitz laid down a proud maxim: never would the empress-queen engage in similar rodomontades, as she had no desire to resemble the king in any way or manner.

Looked at as a trial run, Lobosits should have given greater satisfaction to Maria Theresa than it did at first blush. Except for the plundering Croats, the reformed army had done its duty. True, the generals came in for faint praise in Browne's account. But he could truthfully say, as he did, that he had been the master of his decisions. The saga of the invincible king had never affected Browne, who had watched him but once—at Mollwitz.

Only too pleased to adopt his self-confidence, the men in Vienna did little to meet Browne's renewed demands and even began to pay less and less heed to the empress' own urgings which descended on them in a never-subsiding flow. Nor did the conference act, when they did, with dispatch. There was one man who continued to warn against Frederick— and Maria Theresa knew only too well that that man, Colloredo, parroted Francis.

There were people who said that the war was just a nuisance for him. The proliferation of meetings, the long talks in which his old friend Neipperg involved him, and the letters to be signed in the correspondence with Browne and Piccolomini interfered with the peak of the hunting season, with his trips to Schlosshof, and with Mme. Auersperg's little parties. As if to restrict his pastimes still more, the Hofkriegsrat were talking about an army to be raised in the *Reich*, and new notes had to be perused and signed by its anointed head.

He was aware that the new friendship with France was bound to clip the wings of the selfish princes. He did not like the New System any better for it. It had wiped out his lingering hope for getting back his Lorraine. French lust of dominance had been a byword of Francis' kin for three generations. He could not help mistrusting French intentions, whatever his wife might say. The self-importance of her Kaunitz had grown to be a thorn in the emperor's flesh. His resentment of the ubiquitous man erupted in the conference meeting of October 10, a Sunday. The immediate cause for the painful scene was Francis' eating habits.

Stout though he was by now, he had never been a trencherman. (Nor was he partial to wine or cordials, and diluted the former with plenty of water). While Theresa polished off a slice of cake or a croissant with each of the many cups of café au lait she took in the course of the forenoon, Francis, going without breakfast, yet did not touch any food before midday dinner. As the Sunday meeting dragged on past that hour, the empress at three P.M. "suggested a recess, or else the emperor should have a bowl of soup brought in for himself." No, said he, he would sit through the meeting with his stomach empty. But, "unable to dissimulate his impatience, he turned to Count Kaunitz with an expression of fury, and remarked that one ought to meet earlier whenever the *materiae deliberandae* were so voluminous."[24] This was an ungracious thing to say to a notoriously late riser; and Francis, as we may safely conclude from a similar incident some time later, felt regret as soon as he had had his belated repast.

It was altogether too much for him. No matter how much distraction his personal life may have offered him in these months, the mounting crisis drove his undignified situation home to him with greater poignancy than ever before. Unsure of himself though he had become, he knew that he had a head for financial management. But while he was kept abreast of treasury business *"d'une certaine façon,"*[25] his views were hardly paid any attention to even as the proud campaign funds were dwindling. Such measures as were belatedly taken to meet Browne's requests had excluded thrift and played havoc with the budget. By mid-October the need for cash was so great that the empress, who by the French treaty had the choice between the twenty-four-thousand-man force and a certain sum of money, had to opt for the latter.

October 15, St. Theresa's feast, turned out to be a saddening day. A "limping messenger" (to use the day's term for the bearer of evil tidings) brought word of Browne's failure to relieve the Pirna encampment. The Saxon generals not only had interfered with his dispositions but also had refused to obey their own sovereign's orders and extorted his permission to surrender. But that crowning scandal became known to the empress only after Browne had led his corps back to safety in what even his enviers admitted was a brilliant maneuver and Augustus was on his way to refuge in his Warsaw.

The elector's ill luck was not, to Kaunitz' mind, an unmitigated disaster even after Frederick, in one fell swoop, pressed the absentee's troops into his service. (Officers were released against the pledge not to take up arms again.) That breach of the code of warfare gave Frederick a very bad name throughout the *Reich*. It also fortified Maria Theresa's conviction that she was, besides a thief's victim fighting for what was hers, the protectress of morality, as crowned heads must practice it. At the same time, the kind of European renown that for a lifetime had been denied the Habsburg army appeared to accrue to it. On November 2 Starhemberg wrote: "The military, the statesmen, the courtiers, and even the women talk only about Browne. They admire what he accomplished, and only fear lest he expose himself too much to danger. Everybody here hopes for his safe return to his camp. In fine, I am certain that the French were not more concerned about their own army when it was in Bohemia than they are at present about ours."[26] Of the sudden popularity of the "enlightened" King of Prussia among the *philosophes* of Paris and similar fry, Starhemberg had nothing to say.

On November 3, St. Hubertus's Day, the emperor was his old jolly self at the fete following the traditional chase. "To be sure, all of Vienna's attractive ladies were present, including the one who still has the *préférence*. . . ."[27] His wife was trying company in these weeks, even though Kaunitz' prediction had come true and Frederick was withdrawing his troops from Bohemia. She was brought to bed with a son—her fourth—on December 8. (It was to be the last child she gave birth to.) The postnatal depression of the following weeks was a novel experience for Maria Theresa. She needed all of her strength to keep au courant with the negotiations that Nicholas Esterhazy was carrying on in Russia. To engage her interest whenever it seemed to be flagging, Kaunitz would often remind her of the "many hounds" he would "sick on the king to make him succumb." She was not to be seen in any of the churches on Christmas Day. A week later she was in the midst of an ordeal which could not but dwarf her physical discomforts.

On January 5 Louis XV was boarding his carriage in the great courtyard of Versailles when a man detached himself from the crowd in the dusk and struck the hallowed person of the monarch. Wielding a penknife, the feebleminded wretch inflicted barely more than a scratch on the king. But Louis did not doubt but that he was at death's door and for a fortnight persisted in that belief. It was shared everywhere in Europe. Subversive forces were said to have guided the hand of the assassin. Imposing new taxes to finance the war, Louis XV had become involved in a conflict with the *parlement* of Paris (one of several juridical bodies that also claimed a share in the domestic policies of the kingdom), and popular criticism had been far more outspoken than on earlier, not dissimilar occasions. Knowing, as we do, of what kidney were the councilors of the king and his mammoth household, we do not wonder at their indifference toward that restlessness outside their own little grand world. But their blindness to the true condition of the king beggars belief. They had one thought only—how to secure their offices, sinecures, and pensions past his demise—and their ruthless pursuit of that goal gave no room to ordinary reasoning. All government business had ground to a halt. As Starhemberg related, nearly everybody was giving a wide berth to Mme. de Pompadour with unabashed rudeness; only Bernis, Belle-Isle, and the Prince of Soubise, her nominee for the command of an army, were still keeping faith with her. And as the priests hovering over the king day and night kept urging her instantaneous removal, her ruin was not at all unlikely even if he should recover.

Vis-à-vis the empress, Kaunitz had always minimized the great role that the marquise held in his game at Versailles. But Maria Theresa had divined enough about it by then to plumb the depths of his alarm. Her instinct had long before led her to gauge the lust for power spurring the woman behind the throne of the Most Christian King. Far better than Kaunitz, the lukewarm Christian, did she appreciate the power, at the king's sickbed, of priests who had been withholding the sacraments from him for years. Whether Louis XV should die or survive, the assassin might turn out to have cut short the life of the French alliance.

In the very days when Maria Theresa was in the throes of that measureless fear, her eldest son came down with the smallpox. His three brothers of course guaranteed the succession. However, a recent protest on Prussia's part against Joseph's candidacy as Roman king—the project

she herself had spurned throughout her tug of war with the British—
still exercised her as an impudent reminder of the "mock emperorship"
of Charles VII. It turned the boy, for whose life she was trembling, into
a symbol of the indisputable claim of Habsburg blood to the Empire's
crown. And no sooner had the archduke recovered, with tormenting
slowness—as, amid a steady flow of tormenting rumors, had her "dear
brother" at Versailles—than her Mimi, the apple of her eye, contracted
the dread disease.

At this juncture Browne returned to Vienna, his health improved.
To his surprise, not only did Neipperg and Daun (now president of the
Hofkriegsrat) each present a campaign plan different from his own, but
also the emperor came forth with strategic ideas. A portent more disconcerting still was Prince Charles's presence in Vienna.

His proclamation as commander-in-chief had been debated at least
since the turn of the year. After the Empire declared war on King
Frederick in January, one of its sovereign bishops had warned Maria
Theresa in the most forceful language against the appointment. The
prime advocate of Charles's commandership was Neipperg. Francis
adopted the plan, his enthusiasm growing in step with Khevenhüller's
eloquent support. The thought of letting Browne, that grandson of an
Irish squire, win fame at the helm of the Habsburg army seemed in-
sufferable to the lord marshal. Apart from his unbending notion about
keeping men in the place ordained by their extraction, he pressed
Charles's return to supreme command with a mind enthralled by the
idea that the house of Lorraine had been absorbed by the house of
Habsburg.* He may not have called Charles a prince of the blood in
so many words. But Charles belonged to the manhood of the Arch
House—did he not?—and thus "knocking down" the Prussian was his
business, above anybody else's!

Once the project was under consideration, Maria Theresa could not
reject it out of hand without arousing suspicions that Francis' infidelity
was turning her careless of his love of his brother and their common
pride. As it was, she herself was still very fond of Charles. The aura of
manliness about him had retained some of its attraction for her. But
there were, so to speak, rational reasons also for giving the command to

---

* Khevenhüller would not dream of referring to Maria Theresa's offspring as
Habsburg-Lorrainers. He objected violently, if in the end in vain, to having the
style of Royal Highness bestowed on the archdukes and archduchesses in deference
to the royal rank the Lorraine family boasted in its own right.

Maria Theresa herself, to use a modern term, evidently repressed the thought
of having given birth to Lorraine progeny. When Prince Charles lay dying in the
summer of 1880 she wrote to her daughter Marie Antoinette: "You put it very
well as you observed how sad it was to watch the extinction of the House of
Lorraine." (*Correspondance secrète de Maria-Thérèse et le Cte. de Mercy-Argenteau.*
. . . III, 444.)

the prince. While he had failed many times, he had not done so always. His Bavarian victory on the eve of the Prague coronation occupied a special niche in the memory of the empress. The Rhine passage and his advance on Strasbourg had been creditable achievements. His sanguine criticism of Traun in 1744 had come close to persuading Maria Theresa that he himself, rather than the old cunctator, had squeezed the Prussians out of Bohemia. Seen in the light of the long labors of the reformers as they were creating a new kind of army, Charles's intemperate carpings about the morale of his soldiers whenever he lost a battle did not seem unfounded in retrospect. Fairness demanded to let him make war with disciplined troops for a change.

It was Neipperg who broke the news of Charles's appointment to Browne, who, such was the offer of the empress, should share the command with the prince. Browne—who had been made a knight of the Golden Fleece the day before—declared that two men on top were bound to harm the unity of command, and volunteered on the spot to serve under His Royal Highness. On March 14 he set out on the return trip to Bohemia, "much pleased by the tokens of good graces garnered in Vienna"[28] (as Kaunitz, no doubt with an eye on Browne's fame in France, let Starhemberg know). The "enormous, magnificent baggage"[29] of Charles was shipped to Prague. He himself, having sprained an ankle as one night he alighted from his carriage, stayed behind in Vienna. On April 11 Browne wrote him: "Flattering myself that Your Royal Highness will be so good as to agree to my arrangements, I make bold to beg you to rely on my vigilance and attention: these I will never cease to employ, as my feeble talents direct, toward the good and essential advantage of the service."[30] On the same day, the convalescent prince joined one of "those *parties fines*" of his brother "which have become routine ever since the latter grew so gallant."[31]

His consort closed her eyes to those merry goings-on. Or else she had not the time to pay them attention. She was enjoying the pressure of work. Its mere multifariousness had restored to Maria Theresa the sense of activity and command which was as indispensable to her well-being as were fresh air and brisk walks. She was in good spirits. Her Mimi had overcome the smallpox without any blemish to her white face. And the empress was certain at last of massive Russian assistance. In fact, it might well deter Frederick from attacking, and the initiative would be hers. She could not marvel enough at the finesse of Kaunitz.

The jealousy of Russian expansion, going back to her father's day, had never abated in Vienna. Yet Maria Theresa had thought it wise to agree at least to a part of the czarina's program of conquest shortly before the Versailles treaty was concluded. As soon as it was, she had second thoughts about her generosity; and Esterhazy was instructed to enlighten Bestuzhev on the distinction that must be drawn, after all, between taking back a robber's loot—as the empress-queen would be in Silesia—and grabbing, as the czarina was proposing to do, all of Courland and what not. And as long as the ambassador would be at it, he might as well divulge the empress' own, far more sensible plan concerning those territories, to wit, the establishment of her second son as Duke of Prussia.

Esterhazy had not an easy time drawing Elizabeth's mind away from her dreams of aggrandizement even without dwelling on the idea of such a Habsburg dukedom. Neither was it a small job to follow Kaunitz' directive to the effect that the subsidies pledged the czarina must be talked about only in very vague language. And, to compound the ambassador's troubles, a new threat had risen at the very heart of Kaunitz' design.

Frederick had come to contemplate a reconciliation with Maria Theresa through the good services of the Russian court. Bestuzhev (who in the course of his career had accepted bribes from Vienna as well as London) now was the recipient of money gifts from Berlin. Afterward Esterhazy was to pride himself on having undermined the czarina's trust in the "rogue." In truth, her determination to give no hearing to "Chevalier" Williams, who was under orders to press Frederick's proposition, was not in need of any support. Her hostility toward Frederick had grown nothing short of savage as, rapidly aging, she had had to watch her nephew and heir develop an idolatrous admiration for the Prussian. Having declared herself a party to Maria Theresa's defensive alliance with the Most Christian King in January, she signed, on February 2, a war convention with the empress. Apraxin, the czarina's marshal, had been mobilizing for many months. At the time of Prince Charles's appointment the Hofkriegsrat estimated the Russian army poised on Frederick's border at sixty thousand troops.

XVIII

The Battle of Prague

IN AFTER DAYS certain unhappy Frenchmen spoke of spurious proofs of Anglo-Prussian campaign plans that Starhemberg had presented in order to lure the king still farther along the road of Kaunitz' construction. The actual story is less sinister. What Maria Theresa did was to pass on to Louis XV a letter from the hand of George II which informed her that the "unjust and vindictive intention of France" left him no choice but to "discharge his obligations toward Prussia." This, the empress wrote to Starhemberg, justified her "before God and in the eyes of the world" in accepting the French proposals with a clear conscience.[1]

These proposals, incorporated in a new treaty (signed a year to the day of the first) included an annual one-million subsidy to the empress and the pledge of an army of 105,000 troops; the Belgian cessions were to be effected only after Silesia's conquest, and the two ports handed over only after receipt of the first subsidy payment. It is true that Louis XV, committing himself fully to the empress' war with nary an advantage for himself, was swayed by Mme. de Pompadour, who had emerged from her ordeal, her willpower steeled. Yet he could flatter himself to be moved by reason. He was certain of throwing in his lot with tomorrow's victors. Britain's efforts to keep Russia out of the confederacy had been futile; and playing on Sweden's wish to recover Pomerania, Kaunitz' wiles had carried the day at Stockholm in spite of the queen, Frederick's sister. The army clique at Versailles merely scoffed at Cumberland's zeal to avenge Fontenoy with the Hanoverian, Brunswickian, and Hessian mercenaries he was raising.

When Kaunitz dispatched the ratification instrument of the new treaty to Starhemberg, he asked him to advise Belle-Isle and Bernis of both Their Majesties' special appreciations, tokens of which would be forthcoming. "Furthermore, Their Majesties have decided to present Mme. Pompadour with a keepsake. If only we knew what. Her Majesty therefore wants you to give her word as to whether that gift should consist of money, a little box bearing a likeness of her, some lacquered Indian object, such as we have a nice supply of here, or a piece of jewelry."[2] It was to take another eventful year and a half before the marquise received the *vieux-lacque* secretary she had let it be known would afford her pleasure. The empress herself had chosen, from her collection, the "most beautiful and exquisite pieces"[3] of lacquered wood-work, which were shipped to Paris. The finished escritoire was then brought to Vienna for Maria Theresa's inspection, along with the minia-ture portrait of her that, set in a frame of precious stones, was to adorn the dainty desk. Obviously the empress was not free from feminine vanity in dealing with a woman to whom beauty had opened the gates to power.

An endlessly repeated story (which may have originated with, and certainly became popular through, a Prussian publication of 1758, *Lettre de la Marquise de P. à la Reine d'Hongrie*) has Maria Theresa herself write a billet to go with the present. The letter that the gift's recipient wrote to the empress after asking for Starhemberg's permission does not mention any such direct communication from her. Maria Theresa was to become very touchy about the persistent gossip. "You are mistaken," she wrote in 1763 to Charles VII's daughter (who had married Saxony's heir), "if you believe that I ever had personal dealings with *la* Pompa-dour. There never was a letter! Not that my ministers did not use her as an intermediary. Like everybody else, they had to make up to her. But never any intimacy! Such a road would not have been to my taste."[4]

On the morrow of the battle of Lobositz Browne had written to Francis: "I must admit that I find the King of Prussia's conduct quite incomprehensible; in the course of the late campaign it seemed to be in no way that of a great captain. . . . This is the usual danger with people who act by caprice, without system, and independently of the rules of war."[5] Whether or not this view swayed the counsels in Vienna, it cer-tainly played into the hands of the men who, from Kaunitz down, did not wish to take the offensive in the spring of 1757. They began to per-suade themselves that the danger was not imminent and buried what offensive plans were being concocted in a welter of minor concerns. Shortly before Browne's trip to Vienna the Hofkriegsrat had impressed on him the necessity of conserving "the advanced magazines as long as we possibly can,"[6] in other words, of keeping the bulk of his army in winter quarters.

Rumors of ominous preparations in the Prussian camp were not missing after Browne's return to Prague. They did not shatter his "unfortunate sense of security," although Maria Theresa herself instructed him as early as April 1 to "take all troops, wherever possible, out of their positions."[7] That directive was still a far cry from a call to attack; and Kaunitz, advising Browne "to risk nothing drastic,"[8] actually weakened the orders of the empress, who, besides Daun, seems to have been the only person in Vienna alert to the magnitude of the peril. However, a feverish condition from which her eldest daughter, poor misshapen Marianne, was suffering in these weeks appears to have drawn the mind of the empress away from affairs in the field for many hours. Her insistence on having the patient given the last sacraments was encountering objections, and such lack of religious scruples in her own entourage bewildered her no end. Browne kept dismissing what he now considered alarmist stories which reached him from occupied Saxony. There was a morsel of truth in Khevenhüller's remark that "nothing could ever deflect [Browne] from his opinion once he had formed it."[9] On the very day that Frederick broke into the kingdom, Browne wrote to the absentee commander-in-chief: "It is unbelievable how the King of Prussia is wearing out his troops by marches and countermarches, which have served no purpose thus far."[10]

If the intelligence apparatus of the Hofkriegsrat was practically nonexistent, Browne's own was of the most rudimentary. He was griping about the "materialistic . . . outlook" of the population (who indeed did not fancy the thought of having their region turned into the scene of pitched battles again). "Even the news and reports you receive from the nobility are worth little more than those from the rest. . . . I can say without boasting that wherever I have been I have spared nothing in order to obtain good spies, but I must confess that nowhere have I been worse served than here."[11] He did not yet realize how ill he was being served by his subcommanders, including Count Serbelloni, who, having replaced Piccolomini, was thought of highly in Vienna as a cavalryman and tactician. .

On April 20 four enemy armies invaded Bohemia. Old Schwerin entered it from Silesia without being interfered with in the least by Serbelloni. Young Königsegg made some attempts to stop Prince Bevern-Brunswick's column advancing from Eastern Saxony but soon began to retreat toward Prague. North of the town Browne was in haste assembling his forces, to meet the threat from Frederick's own battalions, who marched up the Elbe valley and were about to be reinforced by the corps of Maurice Anhalt-Dessau.

The Prussian strength amounted to 113,000 troops, Browne's to 114,000. But his miscalculations deprived him of the support of nearly half his forces—to say nothing of the ineptness or faintheartedness of his subcommanders. They may have been both. The increasing ratio of desertion throughout March and April had sapped their spirit. And the sudden change in the supreme command bemused them and turned them mindful of their future standing at court and unwilling to risk their reputation for the sake of Browne's glory. Serbelloni, who consistently stayed out of Schwerin's way and finally pitched tents some eighty miles to the east of Prague, let the cat out of the bag as he said that he "had no intention of cooking the soup just for someone else to drink."[12]

In the meeting of April 29 the generals at Browne's headquarters voted down his suggestion to launch an attack despite the king's superior numbers. The day after, Frederick bivouacked within sight of the towers of Prague. The same night Prince Charles, having journeyed in easy stages, entered Browne's camp. The Hofkriegsrat's instructions he carried bore a postscript from the hand of his sister-in-law, who had received the news of the Prussian advance with all of her old *fumo*: "I demand that not only [young] Königsegg . . . but all other generals, too, turn in a precise account of how the rank and file acquitted themselves. I want to know whether they behaved cowardly, or committed excesses on the withdrawal. Punishment will follow."[13] She did not inquire whether the soldiers had been led to the attack or shown how to stand fast. The generals' reports were to be of small consequence by the time they reached Maria Theresa. What her brother-in-law put down somewhat later no doubt was exaggerated. Yet the account of his coming into Browne's presence at headquarters offers a glimpse of the sense of catastrophe that was permeating it. Browne, the prince recalled, was "in a very sorry condition, and not a little distraught. The first thing he said to me was that he was in a state of utter misery, and wished he were dead. He thereupon burst into tears. . . . I was shocked to see the army in complete confusion; nobody had any orders or knew what he was supposed to do. A frightful consternation, the like of which I have never seen in our armies before, affected everyone from general to private, and I would say that the field marshal hardly knew what he was about."[14]

Actually Browne was soon to press the idea of an attack. When Charles brushed it aside, the field marshal asked—indeed begged—for a mere four thousand men to recapture the initiative, or at least save the town. The prince, talking to the assembled generals, declared that Prague, after all, had been lost three times and recaptured thrice. Money could buy fresh provisions should Prague's magazines fall into enemy hands; it could not overnight replace an army decimated in battle. The generals sided with the commander-in-chief. On May 1 they took the bulk of their forces across the River Moldau to makeshift encampments south of the town.

But no sooner had this been accomplished than the generals' council reversed their decision, persuaded by Browne's view that not all was lost and moved by his exhortations to help him prevent Schwerin's junction with Frederick. Defying Prince Charles's ill grace, they prevailed on him to order Serbelloni to "come as close to the main army as you possibly can, so you might join it, if necessary."[15] This wording was scarcely conducive to speed the march of the prudent general.

By May 5 nothing could thwart the union of the two enemy armies. It took place before daybreak of the sixth. Charles's conflict of opinion with Browne did not blind him to the imminence of action—or, for that matter, alter his resolve not to fight it in a reckless spirit. He had the army take up positions at three A.M. Little seemed to be happening for three hours. To be sure, two Prussian columns were advancing, but changed direction when some cannonballs, fired at random, fell into their ranks. At this juncture the *de facto* command of Austrian operations began sliding into Browne's hands.

Count Lucchesi, a "man of too much enterprise rather than too little,"[16] was given permission to attack from the right flank, even though the rolling country was time and again hiding the enemy from his sight. Only around ten o'clock did he see the foe—his entire army, in fact—with Schwerin's troops, horse and all, picking their way through the marshy meadows which were in full view. No preparations had been made for dealing with this advantageous contingency; and the inexorable progress of the Prussians, although scarcely in battle order, began to unnerve Lucchesi's men. Suddenly Browne turned up in their midst and tried to restore their morale. At the same time, the artillery—its amazing mobility was the fruit of Liechtenstein's training over the past years— sent a hail of destruction into the Prussian foot, who were poised to follow the charge that Schwerin had launched upon reaching firmer terrain. Browne lost no time. He led massed infantry down the incline to meet the line of Frederick's fusiliers, who, spoiling for the kill, were withholding their fire. It was when a ball felled the commander that their sangfroid broke. As they turned tail before the Austrian bayonets, Schwerin galloped back, grasped one of their colors, and succeeded in stopping the incipient rout. He had covered but little ground, a band of reanimated men behind him, when a volley of grapeshot killed him.

Browne did not tarry on the scene of what looked like certain success. Riding over to the left, he put himself at the head of the attack its commander had opened and which was losing momentum under the murderous fire of Frederick's second line. As, sword in hand, he was penetrating its ranks, his hussars saw him being thrown by his mount. A cannonball had shattered his left leg. "Why not here?" he exclaimed, pointing at his head. So at least the story was to be told in Vienna.[17]

Unlike Frederick's soldiers, Maria Theresa's were not panicked by the fall of their leader. Inflamed by thirst for revenge, they swept on, driving the bluecoats before them. But their valor alone could not stem a sudden assault by reinforcements brought up by the Prussians.

The king, having espied a gap opening between the Austrians' right and left, was throwing in a massive body of fresh troops. Browne, barely extricated from under his mount, ordered the second line of the left to rush a specified number of battalions to the scene of the breakthrough. The commander, enjoined by Charles not to budge under any circumstances, did not obey Browne's order; and by the time His Royal Highness confirmed it, Frederick had split the Austrian army in two. A certain senior officer, riding up to the prince "to ask a question, could elicit no answer from [him] and watched him ride off without saying a word. [He] was eventually brought to Nusle to be bled, but as he still had no idea where he was, he had to be carried to Prague."[18]

Lucchesi's troops, by now at the mercy of wild rumors—about Browne's fate, about the regiments north of the town—did not lose heart until a flanking maneuver doomed their valor. Still, they withstood two successive attacks of Prussian hussars. Only the third onslaught, which coincided with the arrival of news to the effect that the northern regiments had in fact given up fighting and were streaming toward Prague's gates, precipitated the headlong flight toward safety.

Some forty-five thousand men reached it. Fifteen thousand, their retreat in jeopardy, were fleeing southward. Browne, in danger of capture, had been rescued by a small command, put on a caisson, and transported to his mansion in Prague. It was to him—not to the commander-in-chief—that the victor's emissary was taken as he came at nightfall to demand surrender. Several versions of Browne's reply—none of them polite in language—have survived in the chronicles of that bloody day.

XIX

A Sublime Moment

O N MAY 2 MARIA THERESA had ordered Daun to join the prince in the field. His departure caused no sensation in Vienna, even though the first trickle of refugees from Bohemia and their tales of woe gave the *publicum* more than an inkling of the Prussian advance. Three days later—on the very eve of the battle, as it turned out—Wenceslas Kaunitz was dispatched to Bohemia. Reminiscent of Frederic Harrach's journey to Dresden in December, 1745, the chancellor's mission gave rise to hopes for, or fears of, an impending peace settlement.

Misled by stories of a great victory that Kaunitz picked up on the highway, he was crushed by the account he was given upon meeting Daun. Much as he detested to forsake a night's rest, he put pen to paper at three A.M.—as he made a point of noting—to write to the emperor: "The mere thought of the perils to which I might expose the health of Your Imperial Majesties by the disastrous news I have to relate would make me shudder, if the awareness of what I have reason to expect from Your Majesties' strength of spirit did not re-assure me. . . . I spent part of the night with the field-marshal to see what can be done. I have to praise his zeal and sagacity."[1]

"The sadness that has taken hold of the court and its ministers, and the man in the street as well, is indescribable,"[2] the Venetian ambassador notified his Senate. Still, not even the young general, John O'Donnel, Maria Theresa received on May 11 could convince her that the army reform had been a total failure. This emotional Irishman, "a brave officer and a veteran of Lobositz, could not hold back his tears . . . [before] he told what had happened . . . and said that the cavalry could not possibly have behaved worse."[3] Even while O'Donnel, in her antechamber, described to a group of horrified courtiers the last phase of the battle, she sat down to warn her brother-in-law against giving up Prague.

The prince, who a week before had entertained that very idea, promptly declared that *"l'honneur germanique"*[4] forbade him to yield where Belle-Isle had withstood all pressure in 1742 with a far smaller garrison. To be sure, it was Browne who, from his bed, organized the manning of the ramparts and virtually forced the commander-in-chief to order sorties.

Nor for long was the field marshal capable of impressing his counsel on Charles. After the surgeons had amputated his leg the old ailment returned to plague the veteran of so many campaigns—and so many interarmy conflicts—with excruciating pains. His powers were sinking. The wish of the moribund man to be transported to Vienna in order to "consult a physician . . . as there is none of competence in Prague"[5] was not acted upon.

After his death the empress gave Browne's regimental proprietorship to his young son, sending Khevenhüller in his closet into a paroxysm of rage. Winding up, in his journal, a character sketch of Browne, as intemperate as it was biting, he noted with regard to the honor bestowed on his son: "Men *de fermeté et d'une vertue austère* cannot but disapprove of such misplaced generosity. In view of the events . . . they not only think [that act] improper and injudicious, but also totally out of line and fraught with peril. . . . For no regime can prevail unless its head knows how to mete out reward and punishment according to the necessity of the case."[6]

Even before the catastrophe the Hofkriegsrat had directed Daun to organize a new army with Serbelloni's regiments—should they not reach Prince Charles in time—as its nucleus. Kaunitz, returning to Vienna on May 11, could report that Serbelloni's corps was reassembling in Daun's encampment some twenty miles to the southeast of Prague, as were the fugitives from the carnage under its ramparts, who had arrived in ragged formations. This account, if still spotty, made for a ray of light piercing the gloom at Vienna.

"The evil is great indeed," Kaunitz declared in a note to the embassies in St. Petersburg, Paris, and Stockholm. "We have to deal with a swift-moving dangerous enemy, who is intent upon knocking us down, and perhaps even on marching on Vienna. The greatest evil of all, to be sure, would come to pass if we and our allies lost heart, instead of meeting greater danger with greater efforts."[7] Apraxin, suddenly conscious of the politics the heir to the throne might pursue should the ailing czarina die, had confined his activities to laying siege to an East

Prussian border fortress. And the great French army, having crossed the Rhine with much panoply, was not advancing. Experience had taught Maria Theresa not to bank on loyalty in misfortune. Her thoughts, both at her writing desk and her *prie-dieu*, were with Daun and Daun only. Toward the end of the month he was in command of thirty thousand troops. But what was the morale of these men? Had Serbelloni maintained the discipline of his soldiers while he had kept them inactive?

The empress, enlisting as her spokesman the most uncompromising of her advisers, Haugwitz, authorized Daun to use generals as he would see fit and relieve from command any he considered inept or lacking in spirit. "What grieves me most," she wrote in a letter to Daun himself, "is the fact that . . . my hussars did not fight one single action of consequence or *éclat* this year. Thus, I cannot give them any credit either at home or abroad."[8] Some hours later she was told what was wrong with her cavalrymen.

The Hofkriegsrat meetings now tended to include the conference ministers, along with certain *ad hoc* advisers and Haugwitz, who would come with two or three of his subordinates. On May 28 Liechtenstein joined that group. This wealthiest and most independent of magnates had not always been happy with the army-reform work. In fact, he had resigned from his military post in Hungary the year before. Now, in that meeting, he burst out. "Using imprudent and downright indecent language, he directed his reproaches straight at the empress. The bad state of affairs in the mounted regiments must be laid primarily on the doorstep of those economy-minded new measures that had been introduced. The officer tried to keep himself and his horses in fine shape at the expense of the common soldier, who in turn did likewise at the expense of the populace."[9] That striking disclosure cowed Maria Theresa into restraining her temper. She said "over and over again that she was always willing to learn. However, she could not but judge by what she had been told by everybody—to wit, that both officers and enlisted men did not fare badly in her service, comparatively speaking."[10]

Liechtenstein "did not, from that day on, come to these meetings."[11] His revelations preyed on the mind of the empress. Had the reorganizers neglected to pay proper attention to ordinance? Or had the transition from the estates' supply system—contracting with civilian entrepreneurs—to the army's own administration opened a wedge to indifference? Or had selfish class-consciousness in the officers' corps eroded their initial sense of cooperation? Or had the Hungarian horsemen been infected by lingering discontent in their counties?

It was to the Hungarian, Nadasdy, the ranking hussar general in Daun's army, that Maria Theresa gave instructions more drastic than even those she sent the commander himself. Nadasdy must day and night keep the light troops mindful of their honor as well as their duty.

Merit would not have to go begging for reward. One hundred ducats would be given to any hussar capturing an enemy standard, and three hundred to any who, sword in hand, hacked a path into the enemy's ranks. On the other hand, the articles of war must be applied with all of their rigor to any soldier who had endangered an action's success through premature pillage. This much for the troops. As for the officers, Nadasdy had authority to assess, singlehanded, their conduct. Merciless chastisement would descend on those he found wanting. Upon him, above all men, depended the outcome of new operations! As the Hof-kriegsrat—and whoever else felt called upon to tender advice in Vienna—were contemplating only small-scale enterprises, Daun had been advised to keep his main force out of the way of the corps that the king had detached, under Bevern's command, to thwart any Austrian approach to Prague.

Meanwhile hopes for effective support from France had sustained a sudden blow. Starhemberg reported on ominous developments in the kingdom. Its manpower had been strained by shipments of troops to America and Minorca; trouble was brewing among the Protestants in the south; and in Paris itself nearly everybody looked with disfavor on further commitments across the Rhine. Even before this communication came to Vienna, the immobility of the French army, as it continued to watch Cumberland, had caused disappointment.

A letter from Louis XV to the empress seemed to give the lie to Star-hemberg's pessimism. It announced the formation of a fresh corps which would pitch tent near Strasbourg. Presently inquiries went out whether that force would be marched to Bohemia. No answer was forthcoming. But a French general, on his way to Augustus in Warsaw, stopped over in Vienna. Invited by Maria Theresa to sit in at one of the meetings, he volunteered advice—the French army was, after all, familiar with the battlegrounds of Bohemia—and then, being asked to do so, dispatched one of the officers of his suite to Daun.

The incompleteness of the reform, now in the open, had not de-stroyed Maria Theresa's confidence in Daun's organizational talent. To be sure, his reliance on manuals had been looked upon with reserve by some of his fellow generals (and some had also resented his elevation to a field marshal's rank in peacetime). But these petty memories did not disquiet the empress. Of account to her was Daun's apparent deference to the lassitude of the Hofkriegsrat during the past winter. Was he not too soft-hearted altogether to weld his motley army into an integrated body ready to strike? And, then, he had never held independent command.

His numbers had risen to fifty-six thousand troops by the end of May. He was not deficient in guns. Retreating northeastward in very slow marches, he was lengthening the lines between Bevern and the king, whose army, harassed by the sorties from Prague, had not yet succeeded in closing the ring around its eight-mile wall. At the same time, he held regular meetings with his improvised staff, had his colonels drill their soldiers, and managed to recruit local scouts wherever he moved. For all that, he shied away from overruling the instructions, brought by the French colonel, to avoid a large-scale engagement. Directed what not to do, he asked what to do, in fact, asked, much in the style of a Lobkowitz, for definite orders. A letter from Maria Theresa's hand empowered him to engage Bevern should conditions be propitious.

But barely had her courier ridden out of the precincts of Schönbrunn than a messenger from Prague entered them carrying grave news. Frederick's heavy batteries were bombarding the town; its magazines, supposed to be bursting with provisions, had turned out to be half empty; and the population, saddled with a garrison its own size, was growing restless. What fate demanded of Maria Theresa, then, was to risk either Prince Charles's army in Prague's surrender or Daun's in a great battle for the relief of the town. Indeed, his defeat might deprive her of both armies at one fell swoop and render her defenseless. No third army was anywhere near Bohemia. Rushing from one meeting to the next, or walking in the Corpus Christi procession by the side of Francis, or saying her prayers in church or chapel, she was aware that the decision could not be postponed much longer.

The meeting of June 7 came to the conclusion that Prague would be at the mercy of a famine within two weeks. The same night, the empress gave carte blanche to Daun, pledging that she would never, never blame him for failure, whatever his decision. Still, she added in an anguished postscript, "it would be immeasurably better, if Prague could be liberated without fighting a pitched battle."[12]

In these very hours Frederick readied a corps to lead it himself to a conjunction with Bevern. Leaving his best guns behind for the siege operations, he was certain that the combined force of forty thousand troops could foil Daun's intentions. He did not despise the talents of Daun. Recalling his own swift invasion, the king could have no respect whatever for the Austrian subcommanders. His enormous losses in the battle of Prague had confirmed his old admiration for the individual courage of the empress' common soldiers; but the collapse of their morale under his final thrust could not but add to his self-assurance.

We know nothing about the trust that Daun may have felt in the enlisted men brought with such suddenness under his command. He had long taken the full measure of Frederick's generalship. He had been present at Chotusitz, Hohenfriedberg, and Soor and had been the only man in Vienna to put the king's tactics at Lobositz over Browne's.

He proceeded with a caution that might have done honor to his late master, Traun. Informed of Frederick's union with Bevern, Daun spent three days searching for defensive positions from which he might conceivably launch a counterattack. A chain of hills to the west of the town of Kolin, overlooking the highway to Prague from the south, was his final choice.

It was from the ridge of one of these elevations that Daun, in the small hours of June 18, caught sight of the first clouds of dust on the highway. Stretching farther and farther west to his view as the sun was rising, these dust clouds enveloping the Prussian battalions did not allow him to appreciate their strength. At about five o'clock a rustic came to tell that the king had assembled his commanders in a tavern known as the Golden Sun, a mere mile to the west on the farther side of the highway.

As the situation of the Austrian entrenchments gave them protection from an immediate flanking maneuver, Daun assumed that the enemy would attempt a frontal attack across the sparsely wooded slopes. He did not discount the danger of the king's hussars overriding his own cavalrymen in the clash. His plan to break the élan of the assault by fire counted on stout hearts in the ranks.

Von Ziethen, the hero of Hohenfriedberg, opened the battle, as Daun had foreseen, with a charge against his left wing, which occupied the lowest of the hills. The melee was brief. His dragoons turned tail; and the king's grenadiers, who followed his hussars, were gaining ground despite the cannonballs hurled into their serried ranks. Daun, relying on the strong second line he had formed, did not throw infantry into the fray—a move that would have compelled him to silence his guns. He kept the men back until they could aim at the miter-capped grenadiers who were inching up past the dead and the wounded. Only as his regular musketry appeared to unnerve the survivors did he order his first line down the incline, bayonets fixed.

The hand-to-hand fighting on the slope and in its underbrush had lasted an hour already when Frederick decided to turn on Daun's center. The king sent wave after wave of his best battalions to the attack through the barrage of Daun's bombardiers; wave after wave were halted by the white-coated Austrians, whose steadfastness was growing with each repulse. Daun, who had been under fire nearly all the time and sustained two light wounds, was giving "his orders with clarity," and answering "questions in the midst of any incident in an orderly manner."[13]

Around noon he saw Prussian cavalry being brought in again—and then it dawned upon him that the king had spent his infantry. It was then too that Daun realized his superiority in numbers. He must have marveled at the gambler in Frederick the Great.

The battle of Kolin was, in its closing and most bloody phase, decided by the empress' mounted troops of recent ill fame. To compound the irony, three regiments of Saxon dragoons who had been stationed in Poland played no mean part in the push toward the highway. In vain did Von Seydlitz lead his regiments to the charge. The dismounted cuirassiers of Daun's right wing, firing their carbines from behind trees and boulders, outflanked the king's last reserve of foot and all but annihilated its bewildered men.

The sun still stood high when Frederick, much as he had as the tyro of Mollwitz, galloped off the battlefield. A courier sent from his flight to his generals ordered them to call an end to the carnage and withdraw the mauled army. Only in his tent before Prague did the king learn that he had sacrificed a good third of his troops at Kolin and that forty-five pieces had been captured by the enemy. Nadasdy was harrying the retreating battalions with his irregulars. One of their detachments, venturing farther afield, seized a courier who carried a letter from Frederick's brother Prince Henry to their sister Amalia. "Phaeton has crashed to the ground at length [this curious family billet read] and we do not know what is to become of us. The eighteenth of June will forever remain a baleful day for Brandenburg. Phaeton took care of his own person, getting away before the loss of the battle was really certain."[14]

In Schönbrunn word of an action against Bevern had been expected since June 17. Once it was known that his army had united with the king's, the "impatience, suspense, and anxiety became indescribable."[15] They spread from the imperial apartment to the government offices, and from their anterooms to the *publicum* and even the lecture halls of the university. Only Kaunitz kept his self-possession: early on the morning of June 18 he discussed with the hardly attentive empress her ambassador's recall from the court of St. James's "which would lead automatically to Keith's . . . recall from Vienna."[16] Forty-eight hours later the miraculous story of Kolin was brought to Schönbrunn by a simple courier.

It was a sublime moment. For almost sixteen years Maria Theresa had been yearning for it. The more hardened Europe had grown to the memory of Silesia's rape, the more deeply had she felt that the wound was not healing—that in fact she did not want it to heal. Although she had submitted to God's will, she had, in her core, never doubted that He, "to spread His own glory, would take mercy on my House. . . ."[17] As Charles VI had defied countless disillusions, confident that the Almighty would give him a son, so his daughter had not allowed disaster upon disaster to destroy her hope that He would bless her just fight. When Daun's official messenger arrived at noon to the sound of twenty-four trumpets and delivered an account of the battle, Khevenhüller "made bold to say to the empress that the great victory was due, next to the discipline the commander sustained, to her religious fervor."[18]

The elder archdukes and archduchesses were present at the *Te Deum* sung in the palace chapel. In the afternoon their parents called on Mme. Daun, the *Feldmarschallin*, to share in her pride and afford her a share in their elation. Tears stood in the eyes of Maria Theresa as, over a cup of café au lait, she opened her grateful heart to the victor's wife and daughter of the unforgotten *ayah*.

After Daun's younger brother, two days later, had ridden through the jubilant town and laid the captured enemy colors at her feet, the empress made another impromptu visit. It surprised the court. Joseph Harrach had never been one of her favorites. As long as he had clung to the presidency of the Hofkriegsrat, he had strained her patience almost beyond endurance. Besides, she could scarcely expect the senile man to grasp the momentous nature of these days' events. But Harrach had been her father's last appointee to high office. Did Maria Theresa, having carried to new glory the Habsburg colors, so often disgraced under Charles VI, think about *him* in this hour at Harrach's mansion?

Upon their return to Schönbrunn the imperial couple found more good news waiting for them. Daun had joined up with Prince Charles, whose first sizable detachment had ventured out of Prague, and the Prussians appeared to start breaking tent. "*Par un effect de sa vivacité naturelle*, the empress did not take the time to read the report through . . . [and] represented the move as the consequence of a full-scale engagement, remarking in an aside that now the prince, too, would be given due credit despite all the ill luck that had previously dogged him." Familiar as everybody was with her seemingly inexplicable devotion to her brother-in-law, "many people took offense at that ill-placed observation of hers."[19]

They overrated her capacity for self-deception. On this very day she established the Military Order of Maria Theresa, which was to honor exploits different in kind from Charles's indeed. The Maria Theresa knighthood was made contingent upon the aspirant's having performed an act of consequence in combat without, or in defiance of, orders received. Whether or not this singular proviso sprang from the head of the empress, it was in accord with the view she had formed of her officers' corps: it was not lacking in physical bravery and fortitude; initiative and firmness of purpose were at a premium.

On June 23 Daun—he had been given the grand cross of the new order—wrote to Koch: "To my great dismay, I see that many misunderstandings divide the generals of [Prince Charles's] army. Its discipline leaves much to be desired. Here I am, then, under the command of His Royal Highness. I rejoice in it without any petty reservations. Her Majesty can rest assured that I will serve His Royal Highness to the best of my abilities, provided she deigns to hearken to me, graces me with her trust, and does not lend her ear to all sorts of people."[20]

Alas for Her Majesty, the prince, now in command of numbers far superior to Frederick's, did not have heart to join battle with him. Even Francis grew impatient with the pusillanimous behavior of his brother and told him so in a succession of reproachful messages, as Prince Charles, instead of trying to obliterate the enemy on his retreat, appeared bent only on securing territory in isolated enterprises. One of these, to be sure, destroyed the king's hope of taking a stand in Bohemia and rubbing out the memory of the first defeat of his life. If we wish to take at their face value the letters he wrote to his kin, he was contemplating suicide.

His situation was hopeless indeed. The defeat at Kolin, compounded by the failure to capture Prague and its garrison, had raised the allies' spirits. The Russians broke into East Prussia, the Swedes into Pomerania, and two French armies advanced upon his kingdom. In September Cumberland, his small army of German mercenaries trounced by Richelieu in July, capitulated in an armistice which left Hanover defenseless. In October one of the empress' hussar generals took a raiding party into Brandenburg and humiliated Berlin itself. Thirty-odd princes had delivered contingents to the army of the Empire; and its commander, Saxe-Hildburghausen, joined forces with Soubise to march toward Prussian-held Saxony.

An erroneous report of the czarina's death had caused Apraxin to withdraw his victorious troops from East Prussia. But Charles and Daun had entered Silesia. Frederick nevertheless turned westward to meet Soubise and the imperialists. Vastly outnumbered, he outwitted that group on Saxon territory on November 5 and cut it to pieces "in one of the most singular maneuvers . . . of military history."[21] A mere four weeks later he turned up in Silesia to avenge Kolin in a bloody battle and drive the Austrians from the duchy, which a jubilant Maria Theresa had assumed to be in her grip after the surrender of Breslau.

When the news of Soubise's debacle reached London, a delirium of joy seized public opinion. The great outsider, William Pitt, who for so many years had been opposing involvements in the German quarrels, reversed his policies. Appalled by disasters overseas, he rallied Parliament by whatever means were at hand, compelled his old king to repudiate Cumberland's "convention" with Richelieu, and wrested from crown and cabinet the power of directing the war. To put it in the famous boast of his hindsight, Pitt had decided to "conquer America in Germany" by exhausting, on the Continent, France's resources and sapping her fighting spirit. Nine months after Kolin, subsidies in amounts such as the Queen of Hungary would not have dared dream of in the days of the Old System started to flow into Frederick's war chest.

The years of warfare ahead were to lift him to the pinnacle of world fame. Still, he was to experience grievous setbacks, as well, both on the battlefields and in the councils in London. Prussia was on the very brink of ruination when a freakish event turned the king's fortunes. Having prevailed, he could deny Silesia to Maria Theresa's house forever. If compared to the empires lost and gained overseas, it was but a speck of land. Posterity would not measure the resulting power shift in Europe by the size of the duchy.

In the course of that third, and longest, war over it, the Austrian armies, partly under new leadership, proved their mettle on some celebrated occasions. But none of those victories, and none of the blows the empress had to sustain in the field, or through the policies of her allies, would ever dim her sunny memory of Kolin. Writing to Daun on one of its latter-day anniversaries, she evidently thought it superfluous to properly date her letter. She headed it, simply:

The Eighteenth.
The Birthday of the Monarchy.[22]

As little averse to a rhetorical flourish as had been the young queen, she was exaggerating. Indubitably, it was above all the memory of the pristine happiness of June, 1757, that guided her pen. Yet the phrase, proud and grateful at once, contained a kernel of truth. Humbled in the Empire, weakened in defense, unsure of her alliances, and overwhelmed with debts, she nevertheless could watch her lands enter a period of transformation—a rebirth, in a manner of speaking. Frederick's struggle for survival kindled a Prussian, as indeed German, patriotism his father would have gaped at. The sense of cohesion that commenced to pervade the Habsburg dominions and turn them into the *"totum"* of Prince Eugene's dreams had less spectacular and more complex reasons.

———————•⌁⌁•———————

The future held untold trials in store for Maria Theresa. The sudden death of her Francis, while making him hers alone once again, all but broke her heart. The smallpox thinned her flock of children. Joseph's apparent contentment in marriage was cut short by the demise of his enigmatic young wife. Maria Theresa's own smoldering disagreement with the doctrinaire heir, again and again erupting in open conflict, made her tremble with indignation and with fear for the future. The irresponsibility of two if not three of her daughters—whose happiness she had traded for dynastic gains as a royal matter of course—filled her with dark forebodings.

In step with the growth of her moderation, she won Europe's respect. But, as one of Poland's partitioners, she lived to be made sport of abroad as a lachrymose hypocrite. With a single-mindedness equal in passion to her search for *dédommagement* in the mid-forties or her will to war in the mid-fifties, she frustrated Joseph's plan for another great passage at arms with Frederick in the late 1770's. Yet she did not become the idol of her subjects. The expanding middle classes at best took her rule for granted. The peasantry tended to blame her rather than local authorities for the hardships still besetting their lives. The waxing dreariness of her court estranged the new generation of wellborn.

To those of us who try not to judge Maria Theresa by the standards of another day or the thought of her own in other parts of the world, it should be rewarding to reflect that the lonely old woman in Schönbrunn had one great consolation. She could recall her courage in laying the foundations of the unitary monarchy, whose blessings for the dynasty were becoming apparent. For no matter how honestly she may have thought of herself as the mother of her subjects, she could not help being aware first and foremost—and even when she spoke of the State (which, after all, was something different in kind from her entailed patrimony)—that she was a daughter of the Arch House.

As, by its nature, common sense excludes its possessor from being conscious of it in his own makeup, she could not perceive what, for the Arch House's subjects, would give meaning to her daring as a reformer. It was common sense pure and simple, and an instinct for practicality. The long-range effects of the Theresian reforms were to give strength to the monarchy in the changing world of the two following generations and to lend it resilience even past the time that its *raison d'être*, for good or for ill, had begun being debated.

Notes and References

With very few exceptions, sources have been cited only for direct quotation. Writers of letters and/or their recipients have been noted only if not given in the body of the work.

Abbreviations

Arneth	Alfred Ritter von Arneth. *Geschichte Maria Theresias.*
Briefe	*Briefe der Kaiserin Maria Theresia an ihre Kinder und Freunde.*
Coxe	William Coxe. *History of the House of Austria.*
Guglia	Eugen Guglia. *Maria Theresia.*
Kh	*Tagebuch des Fürsten Khevenhüller-Metsch.*
Pod	Otto Christoph Graf v. Podewils. *Diplomatische Berichte.*
Test	*"Kaiserin Maria Theresias politisches Testament."*

1: In the Aftermath of a World War

1. Emanuel Sylva-Tarouca to Frederic Harrach, May 13, 1741. Harrach Archives. In Egbert Silva-Tarouca. *Der Mentor der Kaiserin,* 42.
2. Winston S. Churchill. *Marlborough, His Life and Times.* Two-volume edition, London, 1947, I, 472. In Nicholas Henderson, *Prince Eugen of Savoy,* 61.
3. To Guido Starhemberg, February 7 and May 30, 1703. *Feldzüge des Prinzen Eugen von Savoyen, herausgegeben von der Abteilung für Kriegsgeschichte des k. k. Kriegsarchivs,* Vienna, 1876–92. I Ser., V, Suppl. 21, pp. 6 and 72. In Henderson, *op. cit.,* 77.
4. Coxe, IV, 124.
5. *Ibid.,* 126.
6. *Ibid.,* 127.
7. *Ibid.,* 128.
8. Arneth, IV, 267.
9. Pod, 66.

10. Silva-Tarouca, *op. cit.*, 282.
11. Kurt Pfister, *Maria Theresia. Mensch, Staat und Kultur der spätbarocken Welt*, 31.
12. Pod, 66.
13. Lady Mary Wortley Montagu. *The Letters and Works*, I, 212.
14. Hans Pirchegger (Franz Martin Mayer). *Geschichte und Kulturleben Deutschösterreichs von 1526 bis 1792*, 257.
15. John Stoye. *The Siege of Vienna*, 75.
16. Hans Tietze. *Wien. Kultur, Kunst, Geschichte*, 210.
17. *Ibid.*
18. Dr. E. Vehse. *Memoirs of the Court, Aristocracy and Diplomacy of Austria*, II, 151.
19. Test, 47.
20. Silva-Tarouca, *op. cit.*, 144.
21. Ameth, IV, 547.

II: "Sweet Little Cavalier"

1. Nationalbibliothek, Vienna. In Guglia, I, 21.
2. Briefe, IV, 6.
3. Coxe, IV, 482.
4. Tagebücher Kaiser Karl VI. 1723–1734. In Fred Hennings. *Und sitzet ihr zur linken Hand. Franz Stephan von Lothringen*, 61 ff.
5. Arneth, I, 354.
6. *Ibid.*
7. Guglia, I, 32.
8. Hennings, *op. cit.*, 127.
9. *Ibid., passim.*
10. *Ibid.*, 132.
11. *Ibid.*, 136.
12. Coxe, IV, 124.
13. Hennings, *op. cit.*, 138.
14. Coxe, IV, 239.
15. Hennings, *op. cit.*, 142
16. *Ibid.*, 143.
17. *Ibid.*, 147.
18. Arneth, I, 355.
19. Hennings, *op. cit.*, 162.
20. *Ibid.*, 166 ff.
21. *Ibid.*, 169 ff.
22. *Ibid.*, 171

III: A Pot of Mushrooms

1. Harold Acton. *The Bourbons of Naples*, 17.
2. Coxe, IV, 307 ff.
3. *Ibid.*, 310 ff.
4. *Ibid.*, 316.
5. Keith to Newcastle, Coxe, IV, 317, note.
6. Robinson to Harrison, December 31, 1735. *Ibid.*, 317: "*Monseigneur, point de cession, point d'Archiduchesse.*"
7. Test, 31.

8. Ameth, I, 356.
9. Guglia, I, 23.
10. Pfister, *op. cit.*, 17.
11. Hennings, *op. cit.*, 178.
12. Ameth, I, 356–58 (entire correspondence).
13. *Ibid.*, 357.
14. *Ibid.*, 359.
15. *Ibid.*, 360.
16. Henderson, *op. cit.*, 289.
17. Coxe, IV, 323.
18. Ameth, I, 44.
19. Canalis to Ulfeld, September 4, 1738. In Arneth, I, 362.
20. Hennings, *op. cit.*, 201.
21. *Ibid.*
22. Ameth, I, 363.
23. Hennings, *op. cit.*, 196, 197.
24. Briefe, II, 383.
25. Hennings, *op. cit.*, 199.
26. Test, 49.
27. To Maria Christina, 1766. In Adam Wolf. *Marie Christine, Erzherzogin von Österreich*, II, 216.
28. Hennings, *op. cit.*, 201.
29. Briefe, II, 383.
30. W. H. Lewis. *The Scandalous Regent*, 208.
31. Coxe, IV, 349.
32. *Ibid.*, 350.
33. Molitoris to Richecourt, January 6, 1740. In Arneth, I, 51.
34. Oswald Redlich. *Das Werden einer Grossmacht*, 317.
35. Coxe, IV, 355.
36. Robinson to Harrington. In Coxe, IV, 358.
37. Hennings, *op. cit.*, 201.
38. Robinson to Walpole. In Coxe, IV, 364.
39. Test, 26.
40. Briefe, IV, 517.
41. To Ulfeld, March 31, 1762. In Briefe, IV, 199.
42. A. R. von Arneth. *Prinz Eugen von Savoyen*, III, 483.
43. Coxe, IV, 332, note.
44. Henderson, *op. cit.*, 282.
45. *The Present State of Germany* (anonymous). In Manfred Schlenke. *England und das fridrizianische Preussen*, 93.
46. Schlenke, *op. cit.*, 100.
47. Arneth, I, 53.
48. Coxe, IV, 387.
49. Guglia, I, 46.
50. Pfister, *op. cit.*, 16.
51. Ameth, I, 54.
52. Porter to Walpole, March 29, 1741. In Coxe, IV, 387, note.

iv: Enters Frederick

1. Constantin von Wurzbach. *Biographisches Lexikon des Kaisertums Österreich*, Vol. 37, 179.

2. Coxe, IV, 190 ff.
3. Guglia, I, 47.
4. Test, 26 ff.
5. Coxe, IV, 190.
6. *Allgemeine Deutsche Biographie*, Vol. 35, 480.
7. Coxe, IV, 190.
8. *Ibid.*
9. Test, 41.
10. Guglia, I, 55.
11. Silva-Tarouca, *op. cit.*, 275.
12. Arneth, I, 366.
13. Zeno to Senate, March 8, 1738. *Ibid.*
14. Test, 72.
15. *Ibid.*, 41.
16. *Ibid.*, 26.
17. Pod, 40, note.
18. Test, 36.
19. Guglia, I, 58.
20. Test, 75.
21. Kh, May 5, 1747.
22. Olenschläger. *Geschichte des Interregni nach dem Ableben Kaiser Karoli VI.* (1742), I, 37 ff. In Guglia, I, 52.
23. *Ibid.*
24. *Parliamentary History of England*, Vol. XI, 611. In Schlenke, *op. cit.*, 108.
25. Schlenke, *op. cit.*, 108 ff.
26. Coxe, IV, 399.
27. Hennings, *op. cit.*, 213.
28. Von Borcke to Berlin. In Guglia, I, 61.
29. Test, 30.
30. Guglia, I, 61 ff.
31. Test, 30.
32. Ameth, I, 374.
33. Coxe, IV, 402 ff. "The account of this audience is taken from Mr. Robinson's dispatches to Lord Harrington, Dec. 21, 1740." It is not too far-fetched to assume that the garrulous grand duke gave a blow-by-blow account to Robinson right after the audience. Archdeacon Coxe, in quoting ambassadorial reports, sometimes abridged them and often changed indirect into direct discourse.
34. Coxe, IV, 403.
35. To Francis, December 11, 1740. In Christopher Duffy. *The Wild Goose and the Eagle. A Life of Marshal von Browne*, 39.
36. Coxe, IV, 403.
37. Guglia, I, 68.
38. Report of Hanoverian ambassador. In Guglia, I, 70.
39. Test, 30.
40. *Ibid.*, 31. For "clean" ["*regulier*"] see *ibid.*, 111.
41. Test, 27.
42. Arneth, I, 224.
43. Test, 30.
44. *Ibid.*, 27.
45. *Ibid.*, 36.

46. *Ibid.*, 32.
47. *Ibid.*
48. *Ibid.*, 33.
49. Henderson, *op. cit.*, 281.
50. Guglia, I, 73.
51. Ameth, IV, 519.
52. Test, 26.
53. Madame du Noyer, *Lettres historiques et galantes* . . . (1715). In Silva-Tarouca, *op. cit.*, 18.
54. Draft, Silva-Tarouca Archives. Silva-Tarouca, *op. cit.*, 188.
55. Th. G. von Karajan. *Maria Theresia und Graf Sylva-Tarouca. Anhang,* 23 ff.
56. *Ibid.*, 4–9.
57. Robinson to Harrington, April 22, 1741. In Coxe, IV, 411, note.
58. Guglia, I, 75.

v: Queen of Hungary

1. Arneth, I, 205.
2. *Ibid.*, 392.
3. *Ibid.*, 390.
4. Guglia, I, 80 ff.
5. Saint-Severin to Puysieux, August 28, 1748. In Arneth, III, 486.
6. *Directory of National Biography*, Vol. 49, 47 ff.
7. Guglia, I, 77.
8. *Ibid.*, 81.
9. *Ibid.*
10. Hyndford to Harrington, June 12, 1741. In Coxe, IV, 416–17.
11. *Ibid.*, 418.
12. *The Affecting Case of the Queen of Hungary in Relation Both to Friends and Foes* . . . , 26 ff.
13. Guglia, I, 100.
14. Test, 65.
15. Coxe, IV, 429, note.
16. Guglia, I, 105.
17. Capello to Senate, June 30, 1741. In Arneth, I, 402.
18. *Ibid.*, 277.
19. *Ibid.*, 278.
20. Coxe, IV, 439.
21. *Ibid.*
22. *Ibid.*, 438.
23. State Papers, Domestic, Various, 3, January 16, 1741. In Schlenke, *op. cit.*, 117.
24. Robinson to Harrington, July 2, 1741. In Coxe, IV, 419.
25. *Ibid.*
26. Guglia, I, 108.
27. Coxe, IV, 421.
28. *Ibid.*
29. *Ibid.*, note.
30. Guglia, I, 90 ff.
31. *Ibid.*, 86.
32. *Ibid.*

33. *Ibid.*, 91.
34. Robinson to Harrington, August 9, 1741, and Frederick's *Oeuvres Posthumes*, I, 180. In Coxe, IV, 422 ff., 424.
35. Guglia, I, 92.
36. *Ibid.*, 95.
37. Pfister, *op. cit.*, 54.
38. Frederick to Hyndford, September 24, 1741, Walpole Papers. In Coxe, IV, 428.
39. Guglia, I, 96.
40. *Ibid.*
41. *Ibid.*, 110.
42. *Ibid.*, 96.
43. Coxe, IV, 440.
44. Guglia, I, 110.
45. Coxe, IV, 440 ff.
46. *Ibid.*, 441.
47. Kolinovics, *Nova Ungariae Periodus*, 492. In Arneth, I, 299 ff.
48. Coxe, IV, 441.
49. Arneth, I, 300.
50. *Ibid.*
51. Kolinovics, *op. cit.*, 530. In Arneth, I, 305.
52. Briefe, III, 126.

vi: The "Mock Emperor"

1. Guglia, I, 118.
2. Briefe, IV, 140.
3. *Ibid.*, 141.
4. Arneth, I, 340.
5. *Ibid.*, 414.
6. Test, 79.
7. Arneth, II, 460.
8. *Ibid.*, 461.
9. *Ibid.*
10. *Ibid.*
11. Guglia, I, 130.
12. Briefe, IV, 214.
13. Test, 27 ff.
14. Kh, May 27, 1772.
15. Guglia, I, 132.
16. Pod, 72.
17. Arneth, II, 9 ff.
18. Moriz Bermann, *Maria Theresia und Kaiser Joseph II. in ihrem Leben und Wirken*, 485.
19. *The Affecting Case of the Queen of Hungary . . .* , 18.
20. Guglia, I, 147.
21. *Ibid.*, 146.
22. Arneth, II, 468.
23. Guglia, I, 149.
24. Ameth, II, 475.
25. Coxe, IV, 450.
26. Test, 28.

27. Wolf and Zwiedeneck-Südenhorst, *Österreich unter Maria Theresia, Josef II. und Leopold II.,* 15.
28. Ameth, II, 13.
29. Guglia, I, 154.
30. Duffy, *op. cit.,* 68.
31. *Gentleman's Magazine,* December, 1742, 656. In Schlenke, *op. cit.,* 130.
32. Capello. In Arneth, II, 61.
33. Wasner to Maria Theresa, May 5, 1742. W. Michael, *Englische Geschichte im achtzehnten Jahrhundert* (1896–1955). Vol. V, 28, 154. In Schlenke, *op. cit.,* 184.
34. Guglia, I, 158.
35. *Ibid.,* 160.
36. *Ibid.,* 161.
37. *Ibid.,* 173.
38. Test, 102.
39. Guglia, I, 163.

VII: Carrousel in Vienna

1. Draft. In Guglia, I, 165.
2. Coxe, IV, 461.
3. Guglia, I, 180.
4. *Ibid.,* 179 ff.
5. Coxe, IV, 464.
6. *Ibid.*
7. Ameth, II, 490.
8. *Ibid.,* IV, 147.
9. Coxe, IV, 457.
10. *Ibid.,* 465.
11. *Ibid.,* 460.
12. *Ibid.*
13. *Ibid.,* 467.
14. *Ibid.,* note.
15. Guglia, I, 364.
16. *Ibid.*
17. *Ibid.*
18. Karajan, *op. cit., Anhang,* 10.
19. Pod, 53, note.
20. Ameth, II, 527.
21. *Miscellaneous Thoughts on the Present Posture Both of our Foreign and Domestic Affairs* (London, 1742), 77 ff. In Schlenke, *op. cit.,* 211.
22. Arneth, II, 508.
23. *Ibid.,* 246.
24. *Ibid.,* 514.
25. Test, 44.
26. Arneth, II, 227.
27. *Ibid.,* 230.
28. *Ibid.*
29. *Ibid.,* 480.
30. Guglia, I, 329.
31. Ameth, II, 111.

32. Wolf. *Die Vertreibung der Juden aus Böhmen 1744 und deren Rück-kehr 1748* (1869). In Guglia, I, 331.
33. Capello to Senate. In Arneth, II, 247.
34. Bermann, *op. cit.*, 517.
35. Guglia, I, 192.
36. *Ibid.*, note 3.
37. *Ibid.*, 315.
38. *Ibid.*
39. Kh, June 25, 1743.
40. Guglia, I, 190.
41. *Ibid.*
42. *Ibid.*, 191.
43. Coxe, IV, 476.
44. Robinson to Carteret, July 3 and 6, 1743. *Ibid.*
45. To Ulfeld, August 25, 1743. In Briefe, IV, 185.
46. Duffy, *op. cit.*, 83.
47. Coxe, IV, 478 ff.
48. Briefe, IV, 184.
49. *Ibid.*, 185.
50. Ameth,, X, 751.
51. N. W. Wraxall. *Memoirs of the Courts of Berlin, Dresden, Warsaw, and Vienna*, II, 157 ff.

VIII: *"Le Monstre!"*

1. Coxe, V, 39.
2. Silva-Tarouca, *op. cit.*, 103.
3. Coxe, V, 39 ff.
4. Pod, 82.
5. Coxe, V, 40.
6. Pod, 85.
7. *Maria Theresia und Joseph II. Ihre Correspondenz . . .*, I, 203.
8. Kh, June 28, 1744.
9. *Ibid.*
10. Silva-Tarouca, *op. cit.*, 100.
11. Test, 31.
12. Briefe, IV, 186.
13. Kh, March 3, 1745.
14. Pod, 98.
15. *Ibid.*
16. Test, 51.
17. Pod, 98.
18. Test, 51.
19. To Kaunitz, December 23, 1744. In Silva-Tarouca, *op. cit.*, 276.
20. Arneth, II, 286.
21. Guglia, I, 200.
22. Thun to Maria Theresa, January 7, 1741. In Guglia, I, 206.
23. Arneth, II, 503.
24. Guglia, I, 207.
25. *Ibid.*, 367.
26. Ameth, III, 451.
27. Guglia, I, 214.

28. Arneth, II, 549.
29. *Ibid.*
30. Guglia, I, 209.
31. Duffy, *op. cit.*, 86.
32. Guglia, I, 217.
33. *Ibid.*, 219.
34. *Ibid.*, 226, note.
35. *Ibid.*, 219.
36. Arneth, II, 547.
37. Guglia, I, 230.
38. Arneth, II, 563 ff.
39. Pod, 63.
40. Kh, October 12–16, 1744.
41. Kh, Vol. 1742–1744, *passim.*
42. Arneth, II, 454 ff.
43. Pfister, *op. cit.*, 99.

ix: The Highest-Placed Couple in Christendom

1. Arneth, III, 399.
2. Erizzo to Senate. In Arneth, III, 432.
3. Pfister, *op. cit.*, 83.
4. Coxe, IV, 498.
5. Ameth, III, 399.
6. *Ibid.*, 411.
7. Acton, *op. cit.*, 64.
8. Ameth, III, 411.
9. *Ibid.*, 419.
10. *Ibid.*, 426.
11. *Ibid.*
12. *Ibid.*, 82.
13. Guglia, I, 254.
14. Ameth, III, 425.
15. Guglia, I, 255.
16. *Ibid.*, 259.
17. *Ibid.*, 264.
18. Ameth, III, 427.
19. Erizzo, June 30, 1745. *Ibid.*
20. To Harrington, August 3, 1745. In Coxe, IV, 510 ff.
21. Guglia, I, 263.
22. *Ibid.*, 265.
23. Arneth, III, 429.
24. Briefe, IV, 168.
25. August 22, 1745. In Arneth, III, 429.
26. *Ibid.*, 107.
27. *Ibid.*
28. Guglia, I, 267.
29. Pierre Lafue, *Marie-Thérèse, Imperatrice et Reine*, 85.
30. Ameth, III, 431.
31. Kh, April 16, 1745.
32. Guglia, I, 268.
33. Ameth, III, 434.

34. *Ibid.,* 120.
35. Guglia, I, 272.
36. Arneth, III, 118.
37. Coxe, IV, 516.
38. Guglia, I, 270 ff.
39. Arneth, III, 435.
40. *Ibid.,* 152.
41. *Ibid.,* 447.
42. Rosenberg, October 16, 1745. In Arneth, III, 439.
43. *Ibid.,* 441.
44. *Ibid.*
45. *Ibid.*
46. *Ibid.,* 442.
47. *Ibid.*
48. *Ibid.,* 443 ff.
49. *Ibid.,* 443.
50. *Ibid.,* 444.
51. Guglia, I, 279.
52. Ameth, III, 161.
53. *Ibid.,* 444.
54. *Ibid.,* 445.
55. *Ibid.*
56. Guglian, I, 284.

x: Ruler and Ruled

1. Pod, *Zur Einführung,* 15.
2. Pod, 38.
3. Pod, *Zur Einführung,* 20.
4. Pod, 39 ff.
5. Kh, March 10, 1743.
6. Pod, 44 ff.
7. *Ibid.,* 43.
8. *Ibid.,* 44.
9. *Ibid.,* 117 ff.
10. *Ibid.,* 110.
11. Ameth, IV, 106.
12. *Ibid.,* 104.
13. Hans Prichegger, *op. cit.,* 332.
14. *Ibid.,* 257.
15. Pod, 122.
16. *Ibid.,* 118.
17. *Ibid.,* 122.
18. Adam Wolf. *Aus dem Hofleben Maria Theresia's,* 273.
19. Pod, 114–15, note.
20. Kh, July 1, 1748.
21. Lady Mary Wortley Montagu, *op. cit.,* I, 215.
22. *Ibid.,* 218.
23. Pod, 113.
24. Kh. March 10, 1743.
25. [Count Nils Bark] *Das Urtheil eines schwedischen Diplomaten über den Wiener Hof im Jahre 1756,* 290.
26. Pod, 113.

27. *Maria Theresia und Joseph II. Ihre Correspondenz*, II, 146.
28. Pod, 109.
29. *Ibid.*, 58 ff.
30. *Ibid.*, 115.
31. *Ibid.*, 114.
32. Bermann, *op. cit.*, 786.
33. Pod, 114, note.
34. Kh, January 5, 1748.
35. Karajan, *op. cit.*, *Anhang*, 13–24.
36. *Ibid.*, 23 ff.
37. *Ibid.*, 15 ff.
38. Test, 101.

xi: A Royal Revolutionary

1. Briefe, IV, 166 ff.
2. *Ibid.*, 169.
3. *Ibid.*, 170.
4. *Ibid.*, 171.
5. *Ibid.*, 173.
6. *Ibid.*, 175.
7. *Ibid.*, 176.
8. *Ibid.*, 174.
9. *Ibid.*, 166.
10. Guglia, I, 322.
11. *Ibid.*
12. *Ibid.*, 323.
13. *Ibid.*, 321.
14. Ameth, IV, 11.
15. Leopold von Ranke. *Maria Theresia, ihr Staat und ihr Hof im Jahre 1755* (Aus den Papieren des Grosskanzlers Fürst), 22.
16. Test, 53 ff.
17. Ameth, IV, 11.
18. Test, 50 ff.
19. *Ibid.*, 50.
20. *Ibid.*, 51.
21. Duffy, *op. cit.*, 113.
22. Arneth, III, 449.
23. Guglia, I, 222, note.
24. Arneth, II, 535.
25. Ameth, III, 407.
26. *Ibid.*
27. Coxe, V, 4.
28. Kh, Vol. 1745–1749, *Anmerkungen und Anhang*, 416.
29. Guglia, I, 287.
30. *Ibid.*
31. Sir Arthur Vilettes. In Duffy, *op. cit.*, 145.
32. Arneth, III, 459.
33. *Ibid.*, 249.
34. Robinson quoting Maria Theresa. In Coxe, V, 10 ff.
35. Duffy, *op. cit.*, 149.
36. Pod, 53.
37. Ameth, III, 467.

38. Guglia, I, 293.
39. Arneth, III, 469.
40. Diedo to Senate. In Arneth, III, 289.
41. Arneth, III, 294.
42. *Ibid.*, 478.
43. Jon Manchip White. *Marshal of France, The Life and Times of Maurice de Saxe*, 222.
44. Kh, August 7, 1747.
45. Guglia, I, 299.
46. Ameth, III, 474.
47. Robinson to Chesterfield. In Coxe, V, 21 ff.
48. Kh, September 20, 1747.
49. *Ibid.*, November 29, 1747.
50. Kh, Vol. 1745–1749, *Anmerkungen und Anhang*, 417.
51. Arneth, III, 482.
52. *Ibid.*, 483.
53. Robinson to Newcastle, May 1, 1748. In Coxe, V, 27 ff.
54. To Kaunitz, Ameth, III, 486.
55. Coxe, V, 29.
56. Ameth, III, 486.
57. Test, 53.
58. *Ibid.*, 86.
59. *Ibid.*, 42 ff.
60. Kh, May 2, 1749.
61. Test, 101.
62. *Ibid.*, 88.
63. Kh, May 2, 1749.
64. Arneth, IV, 22.
65. Test, 63.
66. Pod, 124.
67. Ameth, IV, 508.
68. Pod, 120.
69. Arneth, IV, 22 ff.
70. Coxe, V, 24.
71. Arneth, III, 488.
72. *Ibid.*
73. Guglia, I, 313.
74. To Ulfeld, August 1, 1748. In Arneth, III, 489.
75. Keith to Newcastle, November 6, 1748. In Coxe, V, 34.
76. Test, 86.
77. Pod, 131.
78. Guglia, II, 28.
79. Arneth, IV, 509.
80. Silva-Tarouca, *op. cit.*, 149.
81. *Aufzeichnungen des Grafen William Bentinck über Maria Theresia*, 81.
82. *Ibid.*, 89.

XII: The New System

1. Kh, Pod, 67 note.
2. Karajan, *op. cit.*, Anhang, 14.
3. Pod, 67.

4. Arneth, II, 347 ff.
5. Pod, 66.
6. Briefe, IV, 304.
7. Adam Wolf. *Aus dem Hofleben Maria Theresia's*, 169.
8. *Ibid.*, 170.
9. Bentinck, *op. cit.*, 25.
10. Guglia, I, 306.
11. Bentinck, *op. cit.*, 66 ff.
12. White, *op. cit.*, 173.
13. To Ulfeld. In Ameth, III, 456.
14. Ameth, III, 264.
15. Ranke (Fürst), *op. cit.*, 12 ff.
16. Pod, 49 ff.
17. *Maria Theresia und Marie Antoinette. Ihr geheimer Briefwechsel*, e.g., 222.
18. Arneth, IV, 267 ff.
19. *Ibid.*, 534.
20. *Ibid.*, 273 ff.
21. *Ibid.*, 275 ff.
22. To Newcastle, April 10, 1749. In Coxe, V, 41 ff.
23. Guglia, II, 96.
24. Arneth, IV, 283.
25. Bentinck, *op. cit.*, *Einleitung*, xxxiv.
26. Pod, 53.
27. Guglia, II, 109.
28. Arneth, IV, 325.
29. *Ibid.*, 323.
30. *Ibid.*, 332.
31. *Ibid.*, 544.
32. *Correspondance secrète entre le Comte A. W. Kaunitz-Rietberg et le Baron Ignaz de Koch*, 147.
33. *Ibid.*, 113 ff.
34. Arneth, IV, 546.
35. *Ibid.*, 531.
36. *Ibid.*, 237.
37. Kh, July 2, 1758.
38. Arneth, IV, 82.
39. *Ibid.*, 73. Obviously quoted from C. F. Nicolai, *Briefe* ... (anon.), 1755.
40. Tron to Senate. In Arneth IV, 524.
41. *Ibid.*, 201.
42. *Ibid.*, 212 ff.
43. Wolf, *op. cit.*, 240 ff.
44. Arneth, IV, 214.
45. *Ibid.*, 220.
46. *Ibid.*

XIII: A Teeming Nursery

1. Briefe, IV, 452.
2. Pod, 68 ff.
3. Ranke (Fürst), *op. cit.*, 8.
4. Pod, 70.

5. *Briefe,* IV, 5 ff.
6. Arneth, IV, 168.
7. *Ibid.,* 162.
8. *Ibid.,* 165 ff.
9. *Ibid.,* 522.
10. *Ibid.*
11. Memoir of the Duke of Saxe-Teschen. In Arneth, VII, 503.
12. Adam Wolf. *Marie Christine, Erzherzogin von Österreich,* I, 5.
13. Arneth, VII, 430.
14. *Briefe,* IV, 104.
15. *Ibid.,* 103.
16. Kh, October 2, 1752.
17. Adam Wolf. *Aus dem Hofleben Maria Theresia's,* 139.
18. *Correspondance secrète entre le Comte A. W. Kaunitz-Rietberg et le Baron Ignaz de Koch,* 85, 65.
19. Williams to Newcastle, July 15, 1753. In Coxe, V, 44.
20. Kh, October 31, 1752.
21. *Correspondance secrète . . . ,* 280.
22. Christoph Heinrich von Ammon (date "September 17, 1756" obviously erroneous). In Pod, 142 ff.
23. Test, 31.
24. *Correspondance secrète . . . ,* 159.
25. Guglia, II, 110.
26. Arneth, IV, 347.
27. *Briefe,* IV, 228.
28. Karajan, *op. cit., Anhang,* 26 ff.
29. *Ibid.,* 28 ff.
30. Bentinck, *op. cit.,* 99.
31. E.g., Wolf, *op. cit.,* 179.
32. Arneth, IV, 518.
33. Guglia, I, 361.
34. *Maria Theresia und Joseph II. Ihre Correspondenz,* I, 147–48, note.
35. Wolf, *op. cit.,* 337.
36. Silva-Tarouca, *op. cit.,* 281.
37. Arneth, IV, 510.
38. Schlenke, *op. cit.,* 193.
39. Arneth, IV, 257 ff.
40. *Ibid.,* 533.
41. Coxe, V, 44, note.
42. *Ibid.,* 45, note.
43. Arneth, IV, 511.
44. Guglia, II, 72.
45. Arneth, IV, 53.
46. *Ibid.,* 49.
47. *Ibid.*
48. Kh, March 10, 1757.
49. Arneth, IV, 512.
50. Test, 38.
51. Ranke (Fürst), *op. cit.,* 10.
52. Guglia, II, 71.
53. *Ibid.,* 69.
54. *Ibid.,* 76.

55. *Ibid.*, 77.
56. *Ibid.*
57. Arneth, IV, 116.
58. Guglia, II, 81.
59. *Ibid.*, 85.
60. *Ibid.*, 80.
61. Arneth, IV, 123.
62. Ignaz Beidtel. *Geschichte der österreichischen Staatsverwaltung*, I, 39.
63. Arneth, IX, 164 ff.

xiv: Ascendancy of Wenceslas Kaunitz

1. Guglia, II, 16.
2. Arneth, IV, 24 ff.
3. *Ibid.*, 515.
4. *Ibid.*, 94.
5. *Ibid.*, 104.
6. Guglia, II, 21 ff.
7. Arneth, IV, 357.
8. *Ibid.*, 354.
9. *Ibid.*, 351.
10. *Ibid.*, 385.
11. *Ibid.*, 361.
12. *Ibid.*, 363.
13. *Ibid.*, 368 ff.
14. Wolf, *op. cit.*, 218.
15. *Ibid.*
16. *Ibid.*, 221.
17. Arneth, IV, 177, 523.
18. *Ibid.*, 175.
19. François Fetjö. *Un Habsbourg révolutionaire. Joseph II*, 37.
20. Wolf, *op. cit.*, 223.
21. *Ibid.*, 197 ff.
22. *Ibid.*, 199 ff.
23. *Ibid.*, 200.
24. Ranke (Fürst), *op. cit.*, 11.
25. Arneth, IV, 355.
26. Schlenke, *op. cit.*, 192.
27. Coxe, V, 50.
28. Kh, March 31, 1755.
29. Arneth, IV, 376.
30. *Ibid.*, 549.
31. *Ibid.*
32. Guglia, II, 130.
33. Arneth, IV, 550.
34. *Ibid.*
35. *Ibid.*, 551.

xv: "Try to Amuse Your Husband . . ."

1. To Hardwicke, September 21, 1753. William Coxe, *Memoirs of the Administration of the Right Honourable Henry Pelham*, II, 493. In Schlenke, *op. cit.*, 194.

2. Arneth, IV, 404.
3. Kh, January 25, 1756.
4. Arneth, IV, 414.
5. *Ibid.*, 415.
6. *Ibid.*
7. Kh, January 27, 1756.
8. *Ibid.*
9. Kh, January 28, 1756.
10. Guglia, II, 125.
11. Kh, Vol. 1756–1757, *Anmerkungen und Anhang*, 149.
12. Test, 82.
13. Kh, February 5–12, 1756.
14. Wraxall, *op. cit.*, II, 181.
15. Wolf, *op. cit.*, 220.
16. Kh, May 3, 1756.
17. *Ibid.*, June 1, 1759.
18. *Ibid.*, June 25, 1759.
19. Wraxall, *op. cit.*, II, 180 ff.
20. De Ligne, *Mémoires*, 27 ff.
21. Wraxall, *op. cit.*, II, 182.
22. *Ibid.*, 180.
23. *Ibid.*, 182.
24. Briefe, II, 356.
25. Wolf, *Marie Christine, Erzherzogin von Österreich*, II, 216 ff.
26. Karoline Pichler. *Denkwürdigkeiten aus meinem Leben*, I, 28.

xvi: "Political Algebra" Triumphant?

1. Briefe, IV, 510.
2. Guglia, II, 236.
3. Ranke (Fürst), *op. cit.*, 10.
4. Arneth, IV, 69.
5. *Ibid.*, 426.
6. *Ibid.*
7. To Mitchell, May 28, 1756. In Schlenke, *op. cit.*, 195.
8. Coxe, V, 68.
9. *Ibid.*, 69.
10. *Ibid.*
11. To Holderness, May 16, 1756. State Papers Foreign. In Schlenke, *op. cit.*, 227.
12. Coxe, V, 69 ff.
13. Kh, May 19, 1756.
14. Coxe, V, 70.
15. Arneth, IV, 435.
16. Kh, May 19, 1756.
17. *Ibid.*
18. To Holderness, May 15, 1756. In Coxe, V, 73.
19. Coxe, *ibid.*
20. Kh, May 8, 1756.
21. *Ibid.*, June 9, 1756.
22. Kh, June 13, 1756. Added by Khevenhüller's son.
23. Kh, June 14, 1756.

24. Arneth, IV, 479.
25. Schlenke, *op. cit.*, 227.
26. Kh, July 26, 1756.
27. *Ibid.*
28. Arneth, IV, 480.
29. *Ibid.*
30. Duffy, *op. cit.*, 198, 199.
31. Arneth, IV, 556.
32. Jacques Levron, *Secrète Madame de Pompadour*, 123 ff.
33. *Ibid.*, 127.
34. Arneth, IV, 557.
35. *Ibid.*, 556 ff.
36. *Ibid.*, 557.
37. Arneth, V, 468.
38. Corer to Senate. *Ibid.*, 470.
39. Arneth, V, 471.
40. Kh, August 24, 1756.

xvii: Third War Over Silesia

1. Guglia, II, 146.
2. Duffy, *op. cit.*, 201.
3. Arneth, V, 469.
4. Kh, August 30–31, 1756.
5. *Ibid.*, September 1, 1756.
6. *Ibid.*, September 2, 1756.
7. *Ibid.*
8. *Ibid.*
9. *Ibid.*
10. *Ibid.*, September 3, 1756.
11. *Ibid.*, September 4, 1756.
12. Kh, Vol. 1756–1757, *Anmerkungen und Anhang*, 206.
13. Holderness to Keene, August 24, 1756. In Schlenke, *op. cit.*, 228.
14. Guglia, II, 139.
15. Kh, Vol. 1756–1757, *Anmerkungen und Anhang*, 227.
16. Arneth, V, 467.
17. Kh, Vol. 1756–1757, *Anmerkungen und Anhang*, 214.
18. Arneth, V, 13.
19. Kh, September 19, 1756.
20. Arneth, V, 472 ff.
21. Kh, Vol. 1756–1757, *Anmerkungen und Anhang*, 228.
22. De Lameth to D'Argenson, September 21, 1756. In Duffy, *op. cit.*, 210.
23. Kh, October 4, 1756.
24. Kh, October 10, 1756.
25. Kh, December 31, 1757.
26. Arneth, V, 111.
27. Kh, November 3, 1756.
28. Arneth, V, 497.
29. Corer, April 16, 1757. In *ibid.*
30. Duffy, *op. cit.*, 236.
31. Kh, April 11, 1757.

XVIII: The Battle of Prague

1. February 17, 1757. In Arneth, V, 143.
2. *Ibid.*, 493.
3. Kaunitz to Starhemberg. *Ibid.*, 494.
4. *Kaiserin Maria Theresia und Kurfürstin Maria Antonia von Sachsen, Briefwechsel 1747–1772*, 185.
5. Duffy, *op. cit.*, 233.
6. February 2, 1757. *Ibid.*, 234.
7. Kh, June 26, 1757.
8. Kh, Vol. 1756–1757, *Anmerkungen und Anhang*, 329.
9. Kh, June 25, 1757.
10. Arneth, V, 497.
11. December 22, 1756. In Duffy, *op. cit.*, 239 ff.
12. Cognazzo. *Geständnisse eines österr. Veterans in Hinsicht auf die Verhältnisse zwischen Österreich und Preussen* (1778–89), II, 282. In Duffy, *op. cit.*, 244.
13. Arneth, V, 497 ff.
14. *Relations de ma Campagne de 1757*. In Duffy, *op. cit.*, 245.
15. Arneth, V, 165 ff.
16. *Ibid.*, 9.
17. Kh, June 26, 1757.
18. Duffy, *op. cit.*, 254 ff. Cf. *Österreichische Militärische Zeiteschrift*, 1822, I, 149–169. In Arneth, V, 179.

XIX: A Sublime Moment

1. Arneth, V, 499.
2. *Ibid.*
3. Kh, May 11, 1757.
4. Duffy, *op. cit.*, 257.
5. Arneth, V, 503.
6. Kh, June 28, 1757.
7. Arneth, V, 185.
8. *Ibid.*, 190 ff.
9. Kh, May 28, 1757.
10. *Ibid.*
11. *Ibid.*
12. Arneth, V, 195.
13. Kh, June 22, 1757.
14. G. A. Ruzzini in a copy (in French) attached to his (Italian) report to Venice of July 9, 1757. In Arneth, V, 502. The nickname "Phaeton" had been coined by Frederick's mother.
15. Ruzzini, June 18, 1757. In Arneth, V, 503.
16. Kh, Vol. 1756–1757, *Anmerkungen und Anhang*, 367.
17. Test, 82.
18. Kh, June 20, 1757.
19. Kh, June 22, 1757.
20. Arneth, V, 503.
21. Coxe, V, 98.
22. *Österreichische Militärische Zeitschrift*, 1824, I, 194. In Ameth, V, 200.

Bibliography

This is in no sense a complete bibliography of the subject. Only a limited number of general works has been included.

I

The Affecting Case of the Queen of Hungary in Relation Both to Friends and Foes: Being a Fair Specimen of Modern History. (Ascribed variously to George Lyttelton or David Mallet.) London, 1742.

[Count Nils Bark.] "Das Urtheil eines schwedischen Diplomaten über den Wiener Hof im Jahre 1756," ed. Fritz Arnheim, in *Mitteilungen des Instituts für österreichische Geschichtsforschung.* Vienna, 1889, pp. 287–94.

Aufzeichnungen des Grafen William Bentinck über Maria Theresia, ed. Adolf Beer. Vienna, 1871.

Th. G. von Karajan. *Anhang* to "*Maria Theresia und Graf Sylva-Tarouca.*" Vienna, 1859.

Correspondance secrète entre le Comte A. W. Kaunitz-Rietberg et le Baron Ignaz de Koch, 1750–1752, ed. Hanns Schlitter. Paris, 1899.

Fürst Johann Josef Khevenhüller-Metsch. *Tagebuch 1742–1773,* ed. (as "Aus der Zeit Maria Theresias") Rudolf Graf Khevenhüller-Metsch and Dr. Hanns Schlitter, 7 vols. Vienna and Leipzig, 1907–25. [Vols. not numbered. Diaries 1750–51, 1760–63, 1768–69 lost in MS.]

Maria Theresia und Joseph II. Ihre Correspondenz, sammt Briefen Josephs an seinen Bruder Leopold, ed. Alfred Ritter von Arneth, 3 vols. Vienna, 1867.

Briefe der Kaiserin Maria Theresia an ihre Kinder und Freunde, ed. Alfred Ritter von Arneth. 4 vols. Vienna, 1881.

Kaiserin Maria Theresia und Kurfürstin Maria Antonia von Sachsen. Briefwechsel 1747–1772, ed. Waldemar Lippert. Leipzig, 1908.

Maria Theresia und Marie Antoinette. Ihr geheimer Briefwechsel, ed. Paul Christoph. Vienna, 1952.

Correspondance secrète entre Marie-Thérèse et le Cte. de Mercy-Argenteau avec les lettres de Marie-Thérèse et de Marie-Antoinette, ed. (as

"Marie-Antoinette") M. le Chevalier Alfred d'Arneth and M. A. Geffroy. 3 vols. Paris, 1874.

"*Kaiserin Maria Theresias politisches Testament*" (two memoirs originally published by Alfred Ritter von Arneth in *Archiv für österreichische Geschichte*, Vol. 47, Vienna, 1871), ed. Josef Kallbrunner. Munich, 1952.

Lady Mary Wortley Montagu. *The Letters and Works*, ed. Lord Wharncliffe. 2 vols. Philadelphia, 1837.

Otto Christoph Graf v. Podewils. *Diplomatische Berichte*. Translated from the French [into German] by Gertrud Gräfin v. Podewils-Dürniz, ed. (as "Friedrich der Grosse und Maria Theresia") Dr. Carl Hinrichs. Berlin, 1937.

II

Acton, Harold. *The Bourbons of Naples*. London, 1959.

――――. *The Last Medici*. London, 1932.

Acton, Lord. "Frederick the Great," in *Lectures on Modern History*, pp. 274–86. New York, 1961.

Anderson, M. S. *Europe in the Eighteenth Century*. London, 1961.

Arneth, Alfred Ritter von. *Geschichte Maria Theresias*. 10 vols. Vienna, 1863–79.

――――. *Prinz Eugen von Savoyen*. 3 vols. Vienna, 1858.

Beidtel, Ignaz. *Geschichte der österreichischen Staatsverwaltung, 3740–1848*. 2 vols. Innsbruck, 1896.

Bermann, Moriz. *Maria Theresia und Kaiser Joseph II. in ihrem Leben und Wirken*. Vienna, 1881.

Cheke, Marcus. *The Cardinal de Bernis*. New York, 1959.

Corti, Cesar Egon Conte. *Die Kaiserin. Anekdoten um Maria Theresia*. Vienna, 1953.

Coxe, William. *History of the House of Austria*. 2nd edition, corrected. Vols. IV, V. London, 1820.

Doran, John L. "*Mann*" *and Manners at the Court of Florence*. Founded on the Letters of Horace Mann to Horace Walpole. London, 1876.

Dorn, Walter L. *Competition for Empire 1740–1763*. New York and London, 1940.

Duffy, Christopher. *The Wild Goose and the Eagle. A Life of Marshal von Browne*. London, 1964.

Fetjö, François. *Un Habsbourg revolutionnaire. Joseph II*. Paris, 1953.

Gooch, E. P. *Maria Theresa and other Studies*. London, 1957.

Guglia, Eugen. *Maria Theresia. Ihr Leben und ihre Regierung*. 2 vols. Munich, 1917.

Henderson, Nicholas. *Prince Eugen of Savoy*. London, 1964.

Hennings, Fred. *Und sitzet ihr zur linken Hand. Franz Stephan von Lothringen*. Vienna, 1961.

Hentsch, Hugo. *Die Geschichte Österreichs*. Vol. II, 3rd revised edition. Graz, 1962.

Hermann, August. *Maria Theresia als Gesetzgeberin*. Vienna, 1888.

Holborn, Hajo. *A History of Modern Germany*. Vols. 1, 2. New York, 1959, 1963.

Kann, Robert A. *A Study in Austrian Intellectual History. From Late Baroque to Romanticism*. New York, 1960.

Koser, Reinhold. *Geschichte Friedrich des Grossen*. Stuttgart, 1921.

Kretschmayr, Heinrich. *Maria Theresia*. Gotha, 1925.

Lafue, Pierre. *Louis XV*. Paris, 1952.

———. *Marie-Thérése, Imperatrice et Reine* (1717–1780). Paris, 1957.

Leitich, Ann Tizia. *Augustissima*. Zurich, 1954.

Levron, Jacques. *Secrète Madame de Pompadour*. Paris, 1961.

Lewis, W. H. *The Scandalous Regent*. New York, 1961.

Ligne, Prince de. *Mémoires*, ed. Eugene Gilbert. Paris, 1914.

McNeill, William H. *Europe's Steppe Frontier, 1500–1800*. Chicago, 1964.

Marczali, Henrik. *Hungary in the Eighteenth Century*. Cambridge, 1910.

Mitranov, Paul von. *Joseph II. Seine politische und kulturelle Tätigkeit*. Translated from the Russian [into German] by V. von Demelic. 2 vols. Vienna, 1910.

Pfister, Kurt. *Maria Theresia. Mensch, Staat und Kultur der spätbarocken Welt*. Munich, 1949.

Pichler, Karoline. *Denkwürdigkeiten aus meinem Leben*, ed. Emil Karl Blümml. 2 vols. Munich, 1914.

Pirchegger, Hans (Franz Martin Mayer). *Geschichte und Kulturleben Deutschösterreichs von 1526 bis 1792*. Vienna, 1931.

Plumb, J. H. *Sir Robert Walpole. The King's Minister*. Boston, 1961.

Pöllnitz, Ch. L. von. *Mémoires pour servir à l'histoire des quatres derniers souverains de la maison de Brandebourg*. 2 vols. Berlin, 1792.

Ranke, Leopold von. *Zur Geschichte von Österreich und Preussen Zwischen den Friedensschlüssen zu Aachen und Hubertusburg*. Containing "Maria Theresia, ihr Staat und ihr Hof im Jahre 1755. Aus den Papieren des Grosskanzlers Fürst." Vol. 30 of *Sämmtliche Werke*. Leipzig, 1875.

Redlich, Oswald. *Das Werden einer Grossmacht*. Brünn, 1942.

———. "Die Tagebücher Kaiser Karl VI." in *Gesamtdeutsche Vergangenheit*. Festgabe für Heinrich Ritter von Srbik zum 60. Geburtstag. Munich, 1938.

Schlenke, Manfred. *England und das friderizianische Preussen 1740–1763*. Freiburg/Munich, 1963.

Silva-Tarouca, Egbert. *Der Mentor der Kaiserin*. Vienna, 1960.

Simon, Edith. *The Making of Frederick the Great*. London, 1963.

Stoye, John. *The Siege of Vienna*. London, 1964.

Tietze, Hans. *Wien. Kultur, Kunst, Geschichte*. Vienna, 1931.

Valjavec, Fritz. *Der Josephinismus. Zur geistigen Entwicklung Österreichs im achtzehnten und neunzehnten Jahrhundert*, 2nd ed. Munich, 1945.

Vehse, Dr. E. *Memoirs of the Court, Aristocracy, and Diplomacy of Austria*. Translated from the German by Fritz Demmler. Vol. II. London, 1856.

Waddington, Richard. *Louis XV et le renversement des alliances*. Paris, 1896.

Wagner, Fritz. *Europa im Zeitalter des Absolutismus 1648–1789*. Munich, 1948.

Wandruska, Adam. *Das Haus Habsburg*. Stuttgart, 1956.

Wedgwood, C. V. *The Thirty Years War*. London, 1938.

Weiss, J. B. *Maria Theresia und der österreichische Erbfolgekrieg*. Vienna, 1863.

White, Jon Manchip. *Marshal of France. The Life and Times of Maurice de Saxe*. London, 1962.

Wolf, Adam. *Aus dem Hofleben Maria Theresia's. Nach den Memoiren des Fürsten Joseph Khevenhüller*. Vienna, 1859.

————. *Maria Christine, Erzherzogin von Osterreich.* 2 vols. Vienna, 1863.

Wolf, Adam, and Hans Zwiedeneck-Südenhorst. *Maria Theresia, Josef II. und Leopold II.,* 1740–1792. (Wilhelm Oncken, Allgemeine Geschichte in Einzeldarstellungen, III, Vol. 9.) Berlin, 1855.

Wraxall, N. W. *Memoirs of the Courts of Berlin, Dresden, Warsaw and Vienna.* 2 vols. Dublin, 1799.

Index

About the Author

ROBERT PICK, born and educated in Vienna, became known in this country as a novelist and essayist in the 1940's. He was awarded a Guggenheim Fellowship in 1946. Having held a variety of jobs since making the United States his home, he worked for a number of years as an editor for a New York publishing house. An American citizen, Robert Pick lives with his wife in Manhattan and spends the summer months in Woodstock, New York.

Format by Sidney Feinberg
Set in Linotype Electra
Composed, printed and bound by The Haddon Craftsmen, Inc.
HARPER & ROW, PUBLISHERS, INCORPORATED